D1605505

CLAUDIUS PTOLEMY
THE GEOGRAPHY

TRANSLATED AND EDITED BY

EDWARD LUTHER STEVENSON

WITH AN INTRODUCTION BY

PROF. JOSEPH FISCHER, S.J.

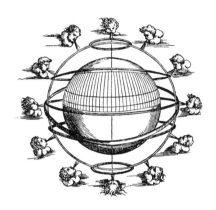

DOVER PUBLICATIONS, INC.

NEW YORK

Published in Canada by General Publishing Company, Ltd.,
30 Lesmill Road, Don Mills, Toronto, Ontario.
Published in the United Kingdom by Constable and Company, Ltd.,
3 The Lanchesters, 162–164 Fulham Palace Road, London W6 9ER.

This Dover edition, first published in 1991,
is an unabridged republication of the work originally
published by The New York Public Library, N.Y., 1932,
in an edition limited to 250 copies and with the title
Geography of Claudius Ptolemy.

Manufactured in the United States of America
Dover Publications, Inc., 31 East 2nd Street,
Mineola, N.Y. 11501

Library of Congress Cataloging-in-Publication Data

Ptolemy, 2nd cent.
The Geography / Claudius Ptolemy ;
translated and edited by Edward Luther Stevenson ;
with an introduction by Joseph Fischer.
p.   cm.
Reprint. Previously published: Geography of Claudius Ptolemy.
New York : New York Public Library, 1932.
ISBN 0-486-26896-9 (pbk.)
1. Geography, Ancient—Maps.   2. Geography, Ancient.   3. Maps,
Early—Facsimiles.   I. Stevenson, Edward Luther, 1860–1944.
II. Ptolemy, 2nd cent. Geography of Claudius Ptolemy.   III. New
York Public Library.   IV. Title.
G1005 15—.S7   1991 <G&M : Vault : fol.>
912.3—dc20   91-4188
CIP
MAP

TABLE OF CONTENTS

č

BOOKS AND CHAPTERS

TABLE OF CONTENTS

TABLE OF CONTENTS

TABLE OF CONTENTS

Preface

PREFACE

CLAUDIUS PTOLEMY (ca. 90–168 A.D.) holds a place among the foremost of those who have made contributions to the science of geography. It is not a little surprising that there has never appeared a complete English, German, or French translation of his work in this field, often as his name is to be met with in the literature which treats of the expansion of geographical knowledge and the cartographical records of the same.

In his *Introduction* Professor Fischer has called attention to the lack of a thoroughly satisfactory edition of Ptolemy's Geography, and in the preparation of this translation based upon the generally recognized best Latin and Greek texts, and, it may be further noted, upon the critical texts and studies of Wilberg and Müller, this puzzling fact stands in the forefront of the difficulties with which it has been necessary to contend. No one edition is alone a safe guide.

There are doubtless imperfections in the translation; it, however, has been done with great care and labor. That there is a lack of exact agreement with this or that text will be noted by those who critically examine the translation. With very few exceptions geographical names have been given as in the original Greek or Latin texts. Occasionally the modern English word has been preferred. The intention has been to give that reading which, in the translator's best judgment, is a faithful presentation of what Ptolemy intended to set down in his great work. As close an adherence to the original as possible has been the aim, never overlooking the fact that not a few of his sentences, particularly in Book I and also in Book VII, are considerably involved. It has been stated that this fact may have contributed much to deter readers from a critical study of his Geography, particularly of his Book I, but which, of course, must be read to be able to understand the remaining seven.

It is in the field of mathematical geography that Ptolemy's fame as a geographer especially rests, into which field he was led through his interest in mathematical and astronomical studies. Herein, it may be stated, his was the most considerable attempt to place the study of geography on a scientific basis, giving to him, therefore, first place among the ancient writers on the subject. Perhaps it is the completeness of his system, as has been noted, that especially contributed to that end. There is in it the appearance of a finality, a complete summing up of what had been contributed by those who had preceded him — by Hipparchus, by Eratosthenes, and especially by Marinus. His work is indeed the main foundation of our geographical knowledge of the classical day. "The whole of modern cartography has developed from his Atlas."

He made but little contribution to descriptive geography, noting, as he does, the imperfect character of his own information concerning many parts of the earth, chiefly because of their size and their remoteness, and the difficulty with which one is confronted in an effort to discriminate between statements made by

geographers who had preceded him, and between statements also to be found in itinerary records, in the records of travelers and explorers.

Marinus (ca. 70–130 A.D.) appears to have been regarded his most reliable source and inspiration, whom he praises for his diligence and sound judgment, and whom he seems to have followed closely; yet he points out his many defects.

In chapters six to twenty of Book I we find his principal references to this noted Tyrian, his close contemporary, and it is from Ptolemy alone we have practically our only information concerning that great geographer.

Ptolemy considered it as his chief task *to reform the map* of the inhabited earth; perhaps we may well say *the maps*, considering, as he did, that the only trustworthy method in map-making had its basis in the determination of the latitude and longitude of places.

Professor Fischer, as will be noted, has presented a most admirable summary of Ptolemy's assumed task as a geographer, his methods and achievements, his relation to Marinus and to certain others who were his predecessors in this particular field, to the relation of text and maps in his Geography, to the renaissance of Ptolemy's Geography more than a millennium after his day, in which revival Donnus Nicolaus Germanus was a great leader.

In his Books II–VII he lists more than eight thousand localities, giving what he thought to be the correct latitude and longitude of each, in which, of course there are numerous errors, as we know to-day. The remarkable fact, however, is that he was so nearly accurate in his records; that Ptolemy purposely falsified his records is hardly to be entertained for a moment.

It would be a task of years to carry through to completion a comparative study of the geographical information which we find set down in the various manuscript and printed editions of his work.

Since the issue of the first printed edition of Ptolemy's Geography more than fifty editions have appeared, varying greatly in contents and in value; in some of these the text is incomplete, and in many the maps do not appear.

Good editions of Ptolemy are regarded as items of great interest by those libraries and private collectors so fortunate as to possess copies.

More than forty manuscript copies of the geography are known, and here again there is great variation in the status. The number of those copies which can be considered fairly complete is not large; many are but fragments. The fine existing manuscript copies are in both Latin and Greek, the former dating from the Renaissance period or from the early fifteenth century, the latter as early as the eleventh century, and are the oldest ones known. Of his Geography in Arabic there is a fine copy in Constantinople dating from about the middle of the fifteenth century, and there are a few fragmentary copies extant.

In Europe during recent years a very considerable amount of scholarly research activity has been turned to an investigation of the character and influence of Ptolemy's Geography. Prominent among those who have labored diligently within this field may be named my very good friend Professor Fischer, Paul Dinse,

Gudmund Schütte, Otto Cuntz, Carl Müller, Curtius Fischer, Lauri O. Th. Tudeer, and there are yet others.

It perhaps first would be observed by one who critically examines his maps, that in what were remote regions his most striking errors are to be noted. Important and lengthy lists of errors have been well referred to by certain Ptolemy students; that is, to certain coasts, for example, set down as rivers, to the names of certain mountains given as those of tribes, to a number of actually mistaken names, to certain names doubled or trebled, to the addition of an initial letter to certain names. One can easily become confused in an attempt to search out what we may call the correct spelling of very many of the names as set down in the various editions of his Geography. No special attempt, in this translation, has been made to pass upon the relative merit of the variations; it indeed will be found that many of the names recorded in the text do not exactly agree with the Ebner manuscript map records. That has been selected which, as before noted, has seemed to the translator to be the preferable one. Here again the reader may be referred to such critical studies as those of Wilberg and Müller and to the studies of a number of modern investigators of high rank.

A reference may well be made to his recorded length and breadth of the inhabited earth. He seems to have been the first to give to the terms *length* and *breadth* the designation *longitude* and *latitude*. He greatly exaggerated the total longitude of the inhabited earth, and yet he reduced this from that given by Marinus and by others who had preceded him. He increased by almost one third the length of the Mediterranean; he makes the Indian Ocean an enclosed sea by joining the southeastern region of Asia to southern Africa, and by those who accepted his geography this might well have been the reason for less vigorous and less early effort to reach the Indies of the East by an attempt to circumnavigate Africa; he increased very greatly the size of the island Ceylon (Taprobana). Yet who is there who will not be remarkably impressed with the near approach to accuracy of his records, in the main, not forgetting the time in which he lived? Let the concluding paragraph of Professor Fischer's *Introduction* here be read.

To this translation there has been added, in full size reproduction, the twenty-seven maps of the *Codex Ebnerianus* now belonging to The New York Public Library, to the very remarkable importance of which manuscript attention has been called. Two other maps have been added: the Ruysch Map in the 1508 printed edition of Ptolemy's Geography, and the New World Map in the 1522 printed edition, having the name "America" conspicuously appearing across what we now call South America, where Waldseemüller, in his great World Map of 1507, had placed it.

The *Codex Ebnerianus* is a copy of the Geography prepared by Donnus Nicolaus Germanus, great indeed as a geographical editor and copyist, the maps in this manuscript being largely taken as a basis for the earliest printed editions. (Mention may be made here of the study of "Donnus Nicolaus Germanus, sein Kartennetz, seine Ptolemäus-Rezensionen und -Ausgaben . . . zur Erinnerung an die 450.

Wiederkehr des Ausgabejahres 1482 der Ulmer Ausgabe," by Wilhelm Bonacker and Dr. Ernst Anliker, in *Schweizerisches Gutenbergmuseum Zeitschrift für Buchdruck-, Bibliophilie- und Pressegeschichte*, Bern, 1932, Jahrg. 18, nos. 1–2.) Excepting the published reproduction of the *Codex Athous graecus* in 1867, but not of great value, the reproduction in connection with this English translation is the latest complete modern reproduction of Ptolemy's maps from a manuscript copy. (To the forthcoming issue of the *Codex Urbinas graecus 82*, Professor Fischer has called attention.)

It perhaps will not be without interest here to note that it has been my very great pleasure, but recently, to have issued, in a limited number of copies, a complete facsimile edition, photographed and hand colored, of one of the finest Donnus Nicolaus Germanus manuscripts of Ptolemy's Geography known. A typical renaissance dedication of a great scholar, that of Donnus Nicolaus [Nicholaus] to Duke Borso of Modena, his illustrious patron, as found in this edition, and written at a time when Ptolemy's Geography was approaching the period of its greatest influence, is presented with this translation as a second *Introduction* immediately preceding Book I.

It is the sincere hope that this first English translation of Claudius Ptolemy's Geography may find favor particularly with Ptolemy students, and lend some inspiration to those who seek pleasure and profit through a wider acquaintance with the great geographers of antiquity.

EDWARD LUTHER STEVENSON

Yonkers, N. Y., 1932

Introduction

INTRODUCTION

O N the occasion of his visit in Feldkirch I first heard from Dr. Edward Luther Stevenson that he purposed translating the text of Ptolemy's Geography into English. Since such a translation does not exist, either in English or in German, the information pleased me very much.

Of course I did not conceal from myself and my courageous and enterprising friend the difficulty of the task. A critical edition of the Greek text which would meet all justifiable demands has never yet appeared, nor is there any Latin, Italian or French translation extant that reproduces adequately the previously published Greek text. Dr. Stevenson knew all this; nevertheless he has taken upon himself the exceedingly meritorious labor of translating the eight books of Ptolemy's Geography into English. After much painstaking toil the work is at last successfully completed.

Since in the course of these years I have always testified to a lively interest in the translation, it did not come to me as something unexpected when Dr. Stevenson asked me several months ago to write an introduction to his successfully completed translation of the Geography.

The wish of a scholar so illustrious for his investigations in the field of historical geography and cartography, that I would write an introduction to his translation, I could all the more readily comply with, since my own comprehensive introduction to the great Vatican publication of Ptolemy: *Claudii Ptolemaei Geographiae Urbinas Codex graecus 82 phototypice depictus*, has at length appeared in fair proof. The title of this introduction reads: *Josephi Fischer S. J., Commentatio de Cl. Ptolemaei vita, operibus, influxu saeculari.* References to this Commentary are indicated in the following pages by the word *Commentatio.*

In a manner deserving gratitude Stevenson offers, in addition to the text, a reproduction of the Ptolemy maps, from the valuable *Codex Ebnerianus* of the Lenox Library collection in The New York Public Library. The choice of the *Codex Ebnerianus* is a very fortunate one, since this Codex furnishes the original copy for the maps in the important Roman editions of Ptolemy of the years 1478, 1490, 1507, and 1508, in which the Ptolemaic maps are reproduced more accurately than in most other editions: see *Jos. Fischer S. J., An important Ptolemy manuscript with maps, in The New York Public Library (United States Catholic Historical Society, Historical records and studies, New York, 1913, v. 6, part 2, p. 216–234),* also *Commentatio, p. 340–343.*

That the maps essentially belong to the Geography of Ptolemy, and offer with essential accuracy the original Ptolemy maps, I have shown in the two treatises: *Ptolemäus und Agathodämon (Kaiserl. Akademie der Wissenschaften in Wien, Denkschriften, philos.-hist. Klasse, Wien, 1916, Bd. 59, Abhandl. 4, p. 71–93);*

also *Ptolemäus als Kartograph* (*Geographische Bausteine, herausgegeben von Prof. Dr. Herm. Haack, Gotha, 1923, Heft 10, p. 113–129*), as also in the *Commentatio, p. 104–171*.

Since the *Commentatio* is not yet published, and since the most important question for the right understanding and the accurate translation of the text is the question of the maps, we will first try to determine from Ptolemy's own words whether he intended to add maps to the γεωγραφικὴ ὑφήγησις.

That Ptolemy himself wished to add maps to his "Guide to the drawing of the world map" is clear and evident from the often overlooked second sentence of the second chapter of Book I: Προκειμένου δ' ἐν τῷ παρόντι καταγράψαι τὴν καθ' ἡμᾶς οἰκουμένην σύμμετρον ὡς ἔνι μάλιστα τῇ κατ' ἀλήθειαν (But now as we propose to describe our habitable earth, and in order that the description may correspond as far as possible with the earth itself).

The choice of the word καταγράφειν, which Ptolemy always applied in the sense of representing graphically, or of drawing, as well as the exact designation of that which is to be represented (τὴν καθ' ἡμᾶς οἰκουμένην, "our inhabited earth"), and also the statement about the manner of the representation (σύμμετρον ὡς ἔνι μάλιστα τῇ κατ' ἀλήθειαν) with the utmost possible faithfulness of the real earth, prove incontestably that he regarded as his proper task the representation of our oekumene cartographically with the utmost possible accuracy.

How Ptolemy, toward the end of his life (about 150 A.D.), after the completion of his chief astronomical work, the *Almagest*, and of his great astrological work, the *Tetrabiblos*, in which he also treats important geographical questions (*Commentatio, p. 33–56*), came to devote himself to the cartographical representation of the habitable earth, this he himself tells us with all desired clearness in the sixth chapter of Book I.

After praising highly his contemporary Marinus (ca. 70–130 A.D.) who had devoted himself all his life with great zeal and good judgment to the revision of his world map (τῆς τοῦ γεωγραφικοῦ πίνακος διορθώσεως,) and after he had made in several editions (ἐκδόσεις πλείονες) the results of his comprehensive preliminary labors accessible to the contemporary world, Ptolemy continues as follows: "If the latest edition of the 'Emendation of the world map' of Marinus left nothing further to wish for, except that the map was missing, then we would be content to draw the map of the oekumene in accordance with the Commentaries of Marinus (ποιεῖσθαι τὴν τῆς οἰκουμένης καταγραφὴν) without adding anything else (μηδέν τι περιεργαζομένοις)." Since, however, Marinus (1) has assumed some things without sufficient reason, and (2) has not with sufficient care seen to it that the drawing of the world map is (a) made easier, and (b) that it should be as nearly accurate as possible, then apart from the main task, namely, the drawing of the map, two subordinate problems are to be solved in order to make the work of Marinus more nearly perfect (εὐλογώτερον) and more useful (εὐχρηστότερον).

The positive reference to the words of Ptolemy just cited, which in my study, *Ptolemäus und Agathodämon, p. 71–93; Separatabzug, p. 1–25*, I established still

more decisively, has found approval among those of my professional colleagues, who earlier had publicly espoused the opposite view. Thus Professor Theodore Schöne, whose excellent study: *Gradnetze des Ptolemäus*, in the first book of his Geography (*Chemnitzer Gymnasialprogram, 1909*) is often quoted, wrote me, February 10, 1917, "that Ptolemy proposed drawing a map of the oekumene is so evidently stated in I, 6, 2, that I do not quite understand how, under Berger's influence, I was able to doubt it. The map, of course, was not to serve merely for his private use, but was to be a contribution to the work as had been the case with Marinus. The study of your work will, I think, induce other doubters also to consult I, 6, and this passage joined with your other reasons, surely will produce universal conviction." (*Commentatio, p. 119, note 1.*)

The fact that *Hugo Berger, Geschichte der wissenschaftlichen Erdkunde der Griechen, 2. Auflage, Leipzig, 1903,* and some of his pupils believed that they must contest the Ptolemaic authorship of the maps transmitted with the text, has its chief support in the Agathodämon legend. Literally this runs: ἐκ τῶν κλαυδίου πτολεμαίου γεωγραφικῶν βιβλίων ὀκτὼ τὴν οἰκουμένην πᾶσαν ἀγαθὸς δαίμων ἀλεξανδρεὺς μηχανικὸς ὑπετύπωσα (*Urb. graec. 82, p. 110, v. 2, 47–52*); in other manuscripts, as for example in the Greek Codex 1401 in the Bibliothèque Nationale, Paris, we find ὑπετύπωσε instead of ὑπετύπωσα. This legend is found both in the A- and the B-redaction, that is, both in the Ptolemy manuscripts which, besides the map of the world, exhibit twenty-six provincial maps, and in those which besides the map of the world, present sixty-four small provincial maps and sometimes in addition four general maps. As to the various Ptolemy redactions, see: *Joseph Fischer, Die handschriftliche Ueberlieferung der Ptolemäus-Karten (Verhandlungen des achtzehnten Deutschen Geographentages zu Innsbruck, Berlin, 1912, p. 224–230*) of which a condensed summary is given in *Petermanns geographische Mitteilungen, August, 1912, p. 61–63;* also *Ptolemäus und Agathodämon, p. 81–89; Commentatio, p. 105, and p. 209–213; Der Codex Burneyanus graecus 111* in the *Festschrift: 75 Jahre Stella Matutina, Feldkirch, 1931, v. 1, p. 151–159,* and in the same work the further bibliographical references on p. 152, notes 1–4. The legend is found, as said, in *Codex Urbinas graecus 82,* at the end of Supplements, which refers to a world map that differs in many respects from the world map of Ptolemy. Since these Supplements have been accredited by certain students to Ptolemy himself (see Nobbe, in his critical edition of the text of Ptolemy: *Claudii Ptolemaei Geographia, Lipsiae, 1913, v. 2, p. 176–190, 255–264*), it is not to be wondered at that they did not recognize, without looking into the manuscript copies of the tradition, that they had ascribed to Ptolemy what did not belong to him (the Supplements), and had denied to him what is incontestably to be acknowledged as his, i. e. the maps, except the map of the world.

It is a strange caprice of fate that just that map of the world which one so often sees copied as Ptolemy's map of the world does not go back to Ptolemy. That it does not show the modified spherical projection which, according to Ptolemy's plain words (at the end of the last chapter of Book I), was certainly to

be expected, but the simple conical projection, Schöne has already correctly noted and for this reason has justly denied that Ptolemy could be regarded as the originator of the world map.

In the meantime Professor Dr. Adolf Deissmann has succeeded in finding in the Serail Library of Constantinople, a Ptolemaic manuscript in Greek which gives the world map in the modified spherical projection as used by Ptolemy. Professor Deissmann kindly placed at my disposal text and maps of this manuscript in photographic reproduction. It was my first impression that I had before me the genuine world map of Ptolemy, but I was soon convinced that although the projection is that of Ptolemy the contents of the map do not correspond at all to Ptolemy's data as they are found in the last three chapters of Book VII, but have been greatly modified by the additions of Agathodämon (*Commentatio, p. 515–521*). In the final results of my earlier investigations nothing therefore is changed by the new discovery; the twenty-six provincial maps of the A-redaction, and the sixty-four small provincial maps of the B-redaction go back to Ptolemy, but the world map, essentially the same in both the A-redaction and the B-redaction, is to be accredited to the Alexandrian geographer Agathodämon.

When Professor Dr. Albert Herrmann, in his treatise: *Marinus, Ptolemäus und ihre Karten* (*Zeitschrift der Gesellschaft für Erdkunde, Berlin, 1914, p. 780–787; Sonderabdruck, p. 1–7*), and *Die Seidenstrassen von China nach dem Römischen Reich* (*Mitteilungen der Geographischen Gesellschaft, Wien, 1915, p. 472–500*), tried to furnish evidence that Ptolemy did not need to draw any maps since Marinus added to his first edition maps which would have essentially met the demands even of his latest edition of the text, he doubtless recognized that Marinus added maps to his first editions of the *Emendation of the world map*. That this, however, would have met the demands of his latest text edition, or even the text of Marinus as revised by Ptolemy, seems to me as absolutely untenable. So far, primarily, as the projection is concerned, it plainly appears from the twentieth chapter of Book I, that the distorting projection of Marinus does not satisfy Ptolemy at all. Furthermore, while Marinus assigned, though only rarely, an exact position to the individual cities, mountains, and other topographical objects, Ptolemy demanded that in all cases a determination as nearly exact as possible of the latitude and longitude be added.

As a matter of fact, Ptolemy, in Books II–VII, has listed some 8,000 locations determined with apparent accuracy down to five minutes. That these were copied from an extant map is obvious to anyone who takes the pains to compare the text and maps in the English edition by Stevenson. It is clear that the version based on the earlier Marinus maps and the latest Marinus text, in which the world map, outlined in uniform scale of measurement, was lacking, provides no compensation for the loss of the map; and this in fact is expressly emphasized by Ptolemy. Only in the case of the seaports, and in the case of a few inland cities, did Marinus, in the latest edition of his *Emendation of the world map*, furnish, in fairly practical details of position, a statement either of longitude or latitude. In most cases, how-

ever, he gave information about neither longitude nor latitude. It is self-evident that if the maps of Marinus had sufficed for the text of the latest edition, then not so many scholars would have endeavored, but in vain, to make amends for the missing map by supplying an adequate new one. Even Ptolemy himself could not in that case have said, as he did say, that he would complete the latest edition of Marinus by the restoration of the missing map; rather he would have been compelled to say that Marinus had undervalued his own life work since he expressed regret that it had not been possible for him to add such a map also to his latest edition; the earlier map was entirely sufficient. *That* Ptolemy neither thought nor said. For him the restoration of the missing world map was considered the main task. That the maps added to the earlier Marinus editions, however, rendered him (Ptolemy) essential service is obvious, and, as it seems to me, can still be proved.

Ptolemy wanted to restore completely, not only a map which would correspond, as far as possible, to the existing text of the latest edition of Marinus, but he wanted also to furnish an improved Marinus map altogether according to the ideas of Marinus himself. In order to attain this end and secure it for the future, he had to solve, in addition to his main problem, two secondary problems. He had (1) to submit the collected material to a reëxamination, and (2) to perfect the map-drawing (a) by an exact and tabular presentation on one plane, not on eight or more, and together the positions in longitude and latitude of that which was to be entered, and (b) by determining a proper kind of projection. How Ptolemy solved these secondary problems we learn from chapters six to twenty-four of Book I, and in detail in Books II–VII.

Since the Greek text, in many passages, is very difficult to understand, and since the Latin and Italian translations, as already remarked, frequently do not agree, and this statement also applies to the unfinished French translation of Halma, we welcome the fact that the English translation of Dr. Stevenson makes it easy for us to follow the arguments of Ptolemy.

In the first place, Ptolemy, in conformity with his plan, deals with the mistakes of which Marinus was guilty in collecting the material. These relate:

(1) to the exaggerated extension of the inhabited earth in longitude and latitude. Instead of eighty-seven degrees of latitude of Marinus, Ptolemy gets by computation eighty degrees, and instead of the two hundred and twenty-five degrees of longitude there are only one hundred and eighty degrees (*I, 6–15; Commentatio, p. 65–79*).

(2) to the definite location of cities especially, concerning which Marinus in his numerous commentaries made adjustment according to the most divergent points of view, and frequently has made either no statement at all or only contradictory ones (I, 18, 5). In my *Commentatio* I have attempted to fix the subdivisions of Marinus' latest work according to the statements of Ptolemy. In doing this it appeared that, in order to find as nearly exact as possible the definite location of a place, at least eight different sections of Marinus would have to be consulted (*Commentatio, p. 80–85*).

(3) to the determination of the several territorial boundaries (I, 16).

Before Ptolemy passes to his second task, or problem, he calls attention to a few more recent discoveries of which Marinus was ignorant. Chapter seventeen is devoted to these discoveries (*Commentatio, p. 85–89*). The rectification of many erroneous positions of Marinus, Ptolemy undertook in Books II–VII without mentioning Marinus. The second subordinate task, which concerns itself with the most faithful possible drawing of the world map, is introduced by a repetition of the words of his plan: Λοιπὸν δ' ἂν εἴη τὰ κατὰ τὴν ἔφοδον τῆς καταγραφῆς ἐπισκέ-ψασθαι (Reliquum autem erit, ut qua ratione delineanda tabula sit consideremus, I, 18, 1).

Since the inhabited earth can be represented on a globe or on a plane surface we have to consider two points in the guide to the drawing and in the drawing itself, one general and the other special. Whether the representation of the earth is to be made on a globe or on a plane, there must be in either case earnest endeavor to present in understandable form the cartographical material that is to be inserted.

The absolute necessity of a handy form of presentation of the material Ptolemy justifies under a twofold presupposition; maps either are found with the text or without. If maps are offered they have to be copied and in that process mistakes creep in unobserved, and these mistakes increase to such an extent in additional copyings that the original is scarcely to be recognized. What is to be done in such a case? Well, we go back to the original map or to a carefully made copy. But what if such can not be found? Then surely there is nothing that can be done if the material has not been offered in usable form. Most of those who have undertaken to draft the missing map of Marinus have tried to solve the problem out of Marinus' text. In most instances, in this attempt, they have failed to get the correct determination of position because Marinus did not present the data in a practical form; in one passage the longitude of a place is given, in another the latitude, and in very many instances both of these details are lacking or are contradictory (I, 18, 4).

That under such circumstances the drafting or revision of a map is impossible is self-evident. The material must be so offered that it can be practically treated and for each entry an exactly determined position must be given. When that is the case we can surely draft a map anew, and correct it where it is at fault. This secondary task Ptolemy has performed in Books II–VII. How one could conclude, however, from the performance of this task that Ptolemy repudiated his main task and added no maps to his work, is to me incomprehensible. The most convenient and most reliable means of emending a map perhaps corrupted by copying, he would thereby have sacrificed at the outset. Neither is such a change of his main purpose made more probable by saying that Ptolemy as an astronomer was accustomed to mere tabular lists, since, as we know, the astronomers of antiquity, just as do the astronomers of our day, made use of celestial globes and stellar maps. Reference to mere astronomical tables is, in our present case, all the more futile, inasmuch as Ptolemy himself made use on the one hand of the

celestial globe of Hipparchus (*Ptolemaeus, Syntaxis Mathematica, Book VII, chapter 1, ed. Heiberg, Lipsiae, 1898, v. 1, part 2, p. 11 seq.; Ptolemaeus, Handbuch der Astronomie, tr. Manitius, Leipzig, 1912, v. 2, p. 11 seq.*), and on the other hand assumed that the geographer had a celestial globe accessible. Concerning the globe question consult: *Dr. Alois Schlachter und Dr. Friedrich Gisinger, Der Globus in der Antike (Stoicheia, Berlin, 1927, Heft 8, p. 7–39, 48–58).* For the sake of certainty Ptolemy demands both, namely maps and convenient text (*Commentatio, p. 130–158; Fischer, Ptolemäus und Agathodämon, p. 78–84*).

In what manner the systematic Ptolemy would offer the improved and additional material of which use can be made he tells us in chapter nineteen of Book I: "In the case of all the provinces we have given their boundaries according to longitude and latitude; for the more important nations their positions relative to each other, in the case of the most important cities, rivers, bays, mountains and similar objects the exact positions." To these details concerning provinces, be it said by the way, the sixty-four small provincial maps of the B-redaction correspond (*Jos. Fischer, Der Codex Burneyanus 111, p. 151–157*), and they have been added in immediate connection with the text in Books II–VII.

By means of the word ἰδιάζον (special) put conspicuously at the top, Ptolemy calls attention to the contrast with the word formerly used by him: κοινόν (general). In general the requirement is that, for the drafting either on a globe or on a plane, the cartographical material must be presented in a handy way. Drawing upon a globe has its peculiar difficulties as has also drawing in a plane its special problems. Since the drawing upon a globe offers in itself a similarity with the shape of the earth, no device of art is necessary for that. The drawing upon a globe has, however, its disadvantages. One can not insert everything which a world map ought to present and can not see at one glance the entire map. These difficulties do not obtain in drawing upon a flat surface, but others in turn appear which must be overcome. Angles and surfaces must be indicated as faithfully as possible. The projection selected by Marinus in which only the parallel of Rhodes is divided in a right relation to the meridian-circle is in no respect suitable; probably the genuine spherical projection invented by Ptolemy is the most usable, and particularly the special modified spherical projection recommended by him, in which the curved parallel, and, except the middle one, the likewise curved meridians display the system of degrees on the globe. In this projection also the faithfulness of representation is best secured. Characteristic of Ptolemy's way of working, is the concluding sentence of the last chapter of Book I, in which he selects for himself the better, even if more difficult, modified spherical projection.

How Ptolemy proceeded in his labors, he himself has told us in the nineteenth chapter of Book I, by designating his chief problem as "a twofold task." He does this with perfect justice, since he wants to furnish a revised collection of material for a Marinus map that has to be outlined, and also himself to insert into the map the corrected material. The restoration of the missing Marinus map Ptolemy tried to accomplish, (1) by making a critical comparison of the materials

offered in various places by Marinus, and then, (2) by checking up the reports of those who had visited the localities in question, and the details inserted in accurately drawn maps. Notice by the way, that we learn from this last assertion how high Ptolemy rated the maps. That among the maps he used, first of all those of Marinus are to be understood, which is assuredly a reasonable hypothesis and, as we shall see later, can be proved even to-day. If according to the data just quoted, we observed the systematizer and cartographer Ptolemy at his work, we see that he had maps before him, especially the world map of Marinus in its several sections, and how he compared them with statements in the latest text of Marinus, and corrected the points of disagreement in accordance with Marinus' latest statements.

But Ptolemy was not satisfied even with that. What had been gathered from Marinus was now compared with the latest reports of investigators and with other exact maps and then corrected and inserted in the world map. Restoration of the text and of the map went hand in hand. That here a mistake might occasionally creep in, is easily seen and is shown by myself in the *Commentatio* in many concrete instances (*p. 136–163*). Here let me call attention only to one example. In the eleventh map of Asia five cities are entered which are not mentioned at all in the corresponding text. On the other hand in the description in the text of the tenth map of Asia these five cities are mentioned in three different places, but in the corresponding tenth map not a single one is entered, although there is no lack of space (*Commentatio, p. 135, 156*). It is very remarkable that the consistency is found in the A-redaction but not in the B-redaction of the Geography of Ptolemy. As it seems to me, this circumstance bears witness that in the twenty-six provincial maps of the A-redaction we have before us the first revision of the general map or, let me say, of sections of the unified map of Marinus; but in the B-redaction we have a series of maps adjusted to a text intended for convenient use, and arranged, not according to countries, but according to provinces. In the *Codex Ebnerianus*, Donnus Nicolaus Germanus, who used the A- and B-redactions for his edition, noticed the error, and corrected it according to the B-redaction.

As in this point so also in a much more important respect Donnus Nicolaus has revised the maps of Ptolemy in the spirit of Ptolemy. Instead of the modified projection of Marinus, selected by Ptolemy for his territorial and provincial maps, in which only the middle parallel of the special map was divided in right proportions, Donnus Nicolaus (who is erroneously called Donis Nicolaus in the Ulm edition of Ptolemy of 1482) has on each map divided at least two parallels in right proportion. Thereby he has attained effectively the greater similarity striven after by Ptolemy, with a drawing upon the globe. The maps of the reproduced *Codex Ebnerianus* plainly show this. Since the "Donis Projection" introduced by Donnus Nicolaus Germanus became generally known (*Fischer, Die Entdeckungen der Normannen in Amerika, Freiburg, 1902, p. 82, Beilage 6; English edition, London, 1903, p. 79*) in the Rome editions of 1478, 1490, 1507, and 1508, the Ulm of 1482 and of 1486, the Strassburg of 1513, 1520, 1522, and 1525, it has long been considered as the actual Ptolemaic one, and later on, just

this very projection has had to serve as proof that the maps of Ptolemy could not have originated with Ptolemy, since he assuredly would not have applied the "Donis Projection," but the modified Marinus projection.

We see by this example to what conclusions one is led, unless one goes back to the original source. If one had given but a casual glance at the Greek or the oldest Latin manuscripts, one would soon have been convinced that all the provincial maps of those manuscripts are actually drawn on the modified Marinus projection. In very recent times two works have appeared to which we must here allude, at least briefly. Professor Dr. Albert Herrmann, whom I have already mentioned, has tried to establish, in his study: *Marinus von Tyrus (Petermanns geographische Mitteilungen, Gotha, 1930, Ergänzungsheft 209, p. 45–54)*, in an extended and somewhat altered form, his view that the maps of Marinus would have sufficed. That Marinus, in spite of the explicit statement of Ptolemy to the contrary, added maps to his latest edition, and this, too, in the modified Marinus projection introduced by Ptolemy, is, I am convinced, untenable. To confirm this more exactly would lead us too far. Herrmann is very deserving of gratitude, however, for the two maps which he has appended to his investigations. The first might harmonize well with the conception of Marinus, as exemplified in his latest edition, but instead of the relatively few insertions (about 200) 7,000 of them or more were to be expected. How significant for the discovery of America was Marinus' idea that the earth extended beyond two hundred and twenty-five degrees of longitude is shown on the second map. This exhibits the network of Marinus. The middle parallel is that of Rhodes. As actual author of the map the learned Florentine, Paolo Toscanelli, is designated as "Marinus redivivus" with an appeal to the profound study of *Hermann Wagner, Die Reconstruktion der Toscanelli-Karte vom Jahre 1474 (Nachrichten der Gesellschaft der Wissenschaften, phil.-hist. Klasse, Göttingen, 1894, Nr. 3, p. 236)*.

The second very recent work to appear has as its author Professor Dr. Ernst Honigmann, the title of whose work reads: *Marinus von Tyros, Geograph und Kartograph (Paulys Real-Encyclopädie, Neue Bearbeitung, Bd. 14, columns 1767–1795)*. Honigmann, too, has appended to his study (col. 1785) a reconstructed Marinus map. It is indeed interesting to note how different are the two reconstructed maps. That Honigmann gives all of the names and legends in the Greek language, while Herrmann renders them in Latin, is of less consequence. Incomparably more important is the difference in the contents offered. Thus in Honigmann no mountains are found, whereas the map of Herrmann exhibits an abundance of mountain ranges. But it is not our task here to explain in detail the two very different reconstructions. Much more important is the well established conclusion that Honigmann, relying upon the clear evidence of Ptolemy, emphasizes decidedly that Marinus added no maps to his latest edition of the *Emendation of the world map.*

But Honigmann, in spite of the purpose, expressed again and again clearly and distinctly by Ptolemy, of furnishing the missing Marinus map, and especially of

thus completing the unfinished work of Marinus, writes: "The numerous passages from which Fischer in his studies *Ptolemäus und Agathodämon*, as also in his *Ptolemäus als Kartograph* tries to prove that Ptolemy had added maps to his work, are evidence, after all, only of this, that he wished to furnish a guide to map-drawing, a fact which has never been questioned." (col. 1771, note.) In saying this he says what to me is incomprehensible. Involuntarily one asks one's self: was Ptolemy really so unintelligent as to write in Book I, 2, 2: "Since it is at present our task to draw our Oekumene with the utmost possible faithfulness of representation with the actual world," and then, instead of this, offered *only tables* according to which a map of the earth might be drawn? When, then, Honigmann continues: "To be sure he (Ptolemy) has also drawn maps, the only question concerning which is, whether he also published them with the Guide," then one can scarcely withhold the query: ought Ptolemy to have renounced the easiest and safest guide to the drawing of maps, and not also have given, at the same time, the maps already prepared? It would simply appear inexplicable that Ptolemy should again and again represent the drafting of maps as his main task, while the practical furnishing of the material and the invention of a suitable projection were but subordinate tasks, and yet in spite of that could cling so obstinately to the solution of the subordinate problems, that he quite forgot the completion of his main task (*Commentatio, Supplements*).

Ptolemy completed text and maps, and text and maps he published together. That any doubt whatever could arise over this is caused on the one hand by a wrong interpretation of the already mentioned Agathodämon legend (*Commentatio, p. 109–120*) and on the other hand, by ignorance of the textual tradition of Ptolemy's Geography. In all of the oldest and most authoritative Ptolemy manuscripts of the A-redaction and of the B-redaction, maps are still found or else reference is especially made in these manuscripts to the fact that maps had been found in the original copy. This last statement holds true especially of the *Codex Vaticanus graecus 191*, which Mommsen and Müller consider so important that its testimony outweighs for them that of all the other Codices (*Commentatio, p. 166–171, and Supplements*).

As proof that both text and maps were transmitted in the same way, we may here first of all name the important Greek manuscripts of the A-redaction: the *Codex Urbinas graecus 82*, the above-mentioned, but hitherto unknown *Codex Constantinopolitanus Seragliensis graecus 57*, the *Codex Athous graecus*, the *Codex Venetus Marcianus graecus 516*, as well as the *Fragmentum Fabricianum graecum*. Also the most important manuscripts of the B-redaction show maps; unfortunately they have not yet been published. The manuscripts of the B-redaction are divided into two groups. At the head of the older group, with sixty-five maps, stands the *Codex Florentinus Laurentianus graecus Plut. XXVIII, 49*; at the head of the later with sixty-nine maps (the four outline maps of Europe, Africa, North Asia, and South Asia are later additions), stands the *Codex Mediolanensis Ambrosianus, D 567 inf.* What was said of the Greek manuscripts holds

also of the Latin manuscripts, especially of the two Florentines, Francesco di Lapaccino and Dominico di Boninsegni, and also of those of the Florentine Pietro del Massaio and Francesco Berlinghieri, and, further, of those of Donnus Nicolaus Germanus in his first redaction, to which belongs our *Codex Ebnerianus*. Concerning the question of manuscripts, see *Commentatio, p. 208–415, and Supplements.*

He who assumes that the text of Ptolemy goes back to Ptolemy himself must assume also, in accordance with the principles of a sound criticism, that the maps similarly transmitted also go back to Ptolemy. If we inquire more carefully about the relation between maps and text three interpretations are possible: (1) the maps might have been drawn according to Ptolemy's text; (2) the text might have been derived from the maps; (3) or both text and maps may show an independent transmission, so that the maps may represent the remodeled and completed Marinus maps, and the text the remodeled Marinus text. All three possibilities I have investigated thoroughly. In this investigation I came to the conclusion that the third possibility conforms to the truth (*Commentatio, p. 136–158*).

Still another legitimate objection is, however, to be met: if Ptolemy had actually added to his Geography the maps transmitted to us, then traces of them would necessarily be found in the literature of the ancient people. In my *Commentatio* I have treated in detail the question whether or not from the traditions of the subsequent time the existence of Ptolemy's maps can also be proved. The investigation revealed that the maps of Ptolemy exercised, for a long time, influence among the Greeks and Byzantines (*Agathodämon, Pappus, Marcian of Heraclea*); among the Syrians, Arabians and Armenians (*Jacobus of Edessa, al-Kindi, Muhammad ibn Musa al-Hwarizmi, Pseudo-Moses of Chorene*); among the Romans and the Germans (*Julius Africanus, Ammianus Marcellinus, Jacobus Angelus, Francesco di Lapacino, Domenico Buoninsegni, Donnus Nicolaus Germanus, Henricus Martellus Germanus, Martin Waldseemüller*); *Commentatio, p. 417–490.*

In conclusion a few more brief statements concerning the present condition of Ptolemaic investigations may perphaps be desired. Properly speaking, a biography of Ptolemy does not exist, and even the necessary preliminary labors for one are lacking. Neither is there as yet any complete critical edition of his works, such for example, as his Geography. The life-time of Ptolemy can be pretty accurately determined as extending from about 90 to 168 A.D. (*Commentatio, p. 11–20.*) The place of his scientific activity was certainly in Alexandria, but the place of his birth remains uncertain, even though weighty considerations speak for Ptolemais Hermeiu. The most usual assertion, making Pelusium his birthplace, rests upon a misunderstanding, for in Arabic the first name of Ptolemy, Claudius, is interpreted with "el Qeludī," but this can easily be read as "el Feludi." As a matter of fact Feludi or Pheludi was read and interpreted later as Pelusium (*Commentatio, p. 20–25*). If in the Middle Ages Ptolemy was often referred to as belonging to the royal family of the Ptolemies, and in the Ptolemy manuscripts

he is represented in royal costume with a crown and royal mantle, this is an error easily explained from the name Ptolemy. On the other hand our confidence is invited at the first glance by the portraiture of Ptolemy's personal appearance, which the Emir Abu'lwafā gives, and which has been preserved for us in the Latin translation of Gerhard of Cremona in the foreword to the *Almagest* edition of 1515. We get there detailed information about the figure, the color of Ptolemy's skin (albus), the red spot on his right cheek (in maxilla dextra signum habens rubrum), his mouth (os parvum), his beard (spissa et nigra), and his teeth, as also about his habits (multum equitabat et parum comedebat) and personal characteristics (fortis irae, tarde sedebatur). Boll rightly remarks, in his studies upon Claudius Ptolemy (*Jahrbücher für classische Philologie, Leipzig, 1894, Supplementband 21, p. 58*), with reference to this description, that while it was not at first evident it was "a groundless invention of our Arabians," after an exact estimate of all the circumstances he is obliged to pronounce the description altogether unreliable (*Commentatio, p. 25–28*).

Of the outward appearance of Ptolemy, then, we know nothing, but of his spiritual nature, of his intellectual aspirations, and his self-chosen life task we obtain from himself much desirable information. He has declared his intentions in these matters in the foreword to his mathematical-astronomical work, the *Almagest*. There, along with other things, he says: "We have come to believe that it is our duty, on the one hand, to regulate our actions harmoniously in order that we ourselves, in the contingencies of daily life may never forget to pay regard to noble demeanor and tactful bearing; on the other hand to devote our entire strength to intellectual activity, for the purpose of imparting instruction in theoretical knowledge, whose branches are numerous and glorious; preëminently, however, to give instruction in that realm which is specifically comprehended under the name of Mathematics." (*Ptolemaeus, Syntaxis Mathematica, Book I, ed. Heiberg, Lipsiae, 1898, v. 1, p. 4 seq.; Ptolemaeus, Handbuch der Astronomie, tr. Manitius, Leipzig, 1912, v. 1, p. 1.*) As in the *Almagest*, so in a series of lesser astronomical writings, Ptolemy realized his goal in life (*Commentatio, p. 28–31*). Ptolemy, however, also applied his extraordinary systematizing talent to labor not strictly mathematical, such as astrology, optics, harmonics. Into these works one can not, of course, enter here.

Of all the works of Ptolemy, however, that holds true, *mutatis mutandis*, what P. Leander Schönberger O.S.B. says of his Harmonic: "There speaks out of his works a magnificent universal conception. . . In Ptolemy again is condensed as in a focal point the entire musical knowledge of Antiquity; and again from this point irradiates and illumines the musical lore of the Middle Ages." (*Schönberger, Studien zum ersten Buch der Harmonik des Cl. Ptolemäus, Beilage zum Mettener Jahresbericht, 1913–14, Augsburg, 1914, p. 111.*) In none of his works did Ptolemy content himself with a mere compilation, even if never so excellent. According to the best of his knowledge and ability he tried to promote further the solution of the scientific problem at hand. "To the sober thoughtfulness of

his vision corresponds throughout his calm and serene language." (*Boll, Studien*, *p. 110.*) The fundamental principles according to which he hopes he could effect some real progress he has constantly and exactly specified, and it is a task no less profitable than stimulating to search the individual works of Ptolemy, for answer to the following questions: What did Ptolemy find at hand? What did he change, omit, or add? For what reason did he do this? How have his changes been received and how are they to be estimated according to their true significance? (*Commentatio, p. 31–32.*)

By utilizing the accessible material I have tried to answer these questions in my *Commentatio* for the geographical (*p. 56–90*) and cartographical (*p. 104–171*, and *p. 417–490*) works of Ptolemy. The reëxamination, emendation and completion of these and similar researches has been extraordinarily facilitated especially for English scholars by Dr. Edward L. Stevenson's very welcome translation of the text of the Geography, and by his publication of a cartographical supplement, which has wielded so great an influence, as the *Codex Ebnerianus*.

If this favorable opportunity is zealously utilized, surely again and again will be confirmed what I have said in my *Commentatio, p. 496*, at the end of the section, on the long-continued influence of Ptolemy with the Germans: "If we wish to-day in retrospect to establish the history of a country or the destinies of a people of the ancient world, we shall always turn with very great profit to the maps and the text of Ptolemy. The location of places, the designation of the mountains and the rivers, the disposition of the tribes may propound to us many geographical and cartographical riddles, but there will be no lack of stimulus, and many a fortunate discovery will always reward serious occupation with the text, and especially, with the maps of Ptolemy."

Jos. Fischer S. J. (*Feldkirch*)

SPHAERA IN PLANO

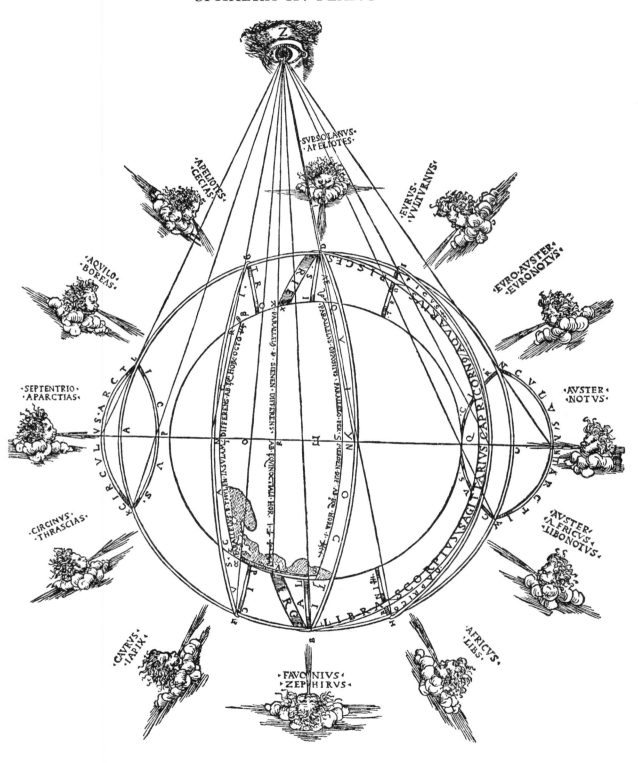

Dedication of Donnus Nicholaus Germanus

THE DEDICATION OF
DONNUS NICHOLAUS GERMANUS

To the Most Illustrious Prince and Lord
LORD BORSO, *Duke of Modena*

I AM not unaware, Most Illustrious Prince, that Ptolemy the Geographer depicted the earth with the greatest skill and the most thorough information, and that were we to attempt anything new in these studies, our work would incur the censure of many; for all those who examine this delineation of ours, contained in these maps, which we now send to You, especially if they are those who are ignorant of the art of geometry, and observe that it differs from that which Ptolemy set forth, will convict us forthwith either of ignorance or of rashness. They will affirm that we did not know our limitations, or that we were indiscreet in falsifying so great a work, as soon as they observe that we have altered it in the least particular. They will never be persuaded, nor will they think it other than impossible, if any one else should have a better method of depicting the earth, that that method had escaped the notice of such a great man as in truth was Ptolemy, for he alone, even including the many excellent geographers who flourished before him, first discerned a method by which he could represent the several localities of the entire earth in picture.

It would be much the same thing as to assert that neither the work of Homer, the prince of poets could be set in order by Pisistratus, or the divine work of Lucretius be emended by Cicero, or the paintings of Tolletana be corrected by Sepponius. Such persons are like those who will praise nothing that they do not think they can understand, since any method that they hope to understand and comprehend themselves they judge to be the best for representing the world.

If confused by the frequency of the lines of longitude, not equally distant one from the other, they might say they would the rather have that rare and vast picture of Ptolemy's set out in straight lines, than this our multiplex and elaborate picture with its inclined and curved lines.

And we do not now claim that there is anything to be found in the picture of Ptolemy that should be corrected or emended, or reduced to order, since all things were by him so skilfully and wisely represented, that nothing relating to the position of countries seems to be wanting in his maps; but we say this much that we may convict those men of their ignorance who, with or without knowledge of

such matters, are moved by a kind of envy and hatred on seeing anything set down that is beyond their comprehension, and immediately turn and abuse the author.

If those who are not altogether ignorant of geography or cosmography, and are in the habit of reading Ptolemy, will compare, with a calm mind, our picture with his, they will certainly think our picture worthy of some praise, instead of blaming it, for they will see that we undertook a hard and difficult task, and brought it to such an excellent conclusion, that they will be compelled to wonder at it, especially when they discover that we have in no particular departed from the intention of Ptolemy, although we have deviated a little from his picture.

Since Thou canst plainly see, O Most Illustrious Prince, how things are, I beseech Thee to give heed for a while to what Ptolemy says and to what we have done.

Ptolemy, as I soon learned from his writings, tells us that there is a twofold system of depicting the terrestrial sphere. The first, he asserts, is that in which instead of circles (I quote his words which are in the eighth book) we represent the meridians neither inclined nor curved but as straight perpendicular lines. The second, he says, is that in which we use everywhere curved and inclining lines, as the scheme of the places on the earth itself demands, and not straight lines.

Of the two methods he approves the second as somewhat more artistic and subtle, but in his picture he has followed the first method, if that picture be his which is to be found in old copies, and in which, it appears that anyone depicting the earth and making use of straight lines for circles, is not far from the truth. But we for our part, Most Illustrious Prince, when we were reading at our leisure his writings, which were not altogether foreign to our profession, and came upon the description somewhere in the first book near the end, wherein he says that we should regard what is done with care and with seriousness in a map rather than what is done too easily and too thoughtlessly; having read this, I say, we suddenly began to reflect by what means we ourselves might obtain some glory.

Believing that an opportunity was offered us whereby our powers might come to light by raising some monument to our industry, we immediately undertook the task of making a picture in the proper way, which would receive more general approval than previous pictures, even were he himself to be the judge.

Instead of circles we have made use of sloping lines, where they would seem to be required, that are not all equidistant (as he himself advises we should do) and the location of places falling between two parallels we have given in a reckoning from both. In order that one might make the more easily and accurately an estimate of the location of any place, which could not be clearly expressed by straight equidistant lines, we have not hesitated to express by means of parallels, in each of our pictures, the extent in miles of every degree whatsoever in longitude.

What shall I say further when in no copy of Greek or Latin text can be found a picture which tells us the size and shape of any island, or gives it proper description, or tells, in any region or province, how many and what kinds of peoples may be found, what towns, cities, rivers, harbors, lakes, and mountains, or under what place in the heavens they lie, or in what direction they face.

We have inserted certain of these things, but not all, yet all are given by Ptolemy himself in his writings; and we have distinguished boundaries by dotted lines, so that even an unpracticed eye can see them easily.

The size of the picture itself, which heretofore was too large and exceeded the common size of books, we have reduced, while carefully keeping the dimensions of all localities to a size that will make it more acceptable to those wishing to study it. The remaining work of that illustrious man we have left untouched, and it remains as it was at first.

When, therefore, I had almost finished this work, and was thinking of some distinguished person to whom to dedicate it, no one truly seemed to us to be more worthy of this dedication than Yourself, for Thou art the only one, to speak the truth, of all the rulers of Italy, who is greatly delighted by such writings and pictures, and who has around him other learned men excelling in this art, and in many other arts; who can readily correct any mistake on our part, and at the same time can give commendation to what is rightly done.

Omitting other learned men dwelling in Thy city in these times, who is more skilled in mathematics than Johannes Blanchinus, or in physics than Peter the Good? Who is more learned in medicine than Sonzinus? Who is more subtle in dialectics and in philosophy than Brother Francis? Who is more skilled in civil and canon law than Franciscus Porcellinus? Who is more advanced in theology than Johannes Gattus, and at the same time more expert in Greek and Latin? Who, in fine, is more excellent in every kind of teaching than Hieronimus Castellanus? Time would fail me, O Illustrious Prince, to enumerate the famous men who serve in Thy city, and fain would I follow their virtues! Truly they would not dwell in Thy city if they did not witness Thee (because Thou knowest that virtue is the guide of the life of men) giving Thy support to men who are eminent as teachers, and leading them from taking the ease they deserve to the active business of reading and writing. And so Thy integrity and Thy virtue can never be praised as they deserve. As in Thy past life Thy virtue has devoted itself to learning, may it still show favor to the learned, and by its munificence draw the rest of mankind to the same zeal for virtue.

Accept then, O Most Beneficent Prince, Who art the Ornament of our Italian nobility, this work, which we have dedicated to Thee, and which we now send Thee, not so much that Thou shouldst read it as that Thou shouldst correct it. If in it Thou shouldst find anything blameworthy, I beg that Thou mayest ascribe it not so much to weakness of my mind as to the greatness and difficulty of the task.

But shouldst Thou find that in this work we have labored for the common good not in vain, then we earnestly beseech Thee that in many other different arts, which hitherto have remained untouched, it may be permitted to us by Thy kindness and liberality to give free exercise to our talents.

FAREWELL

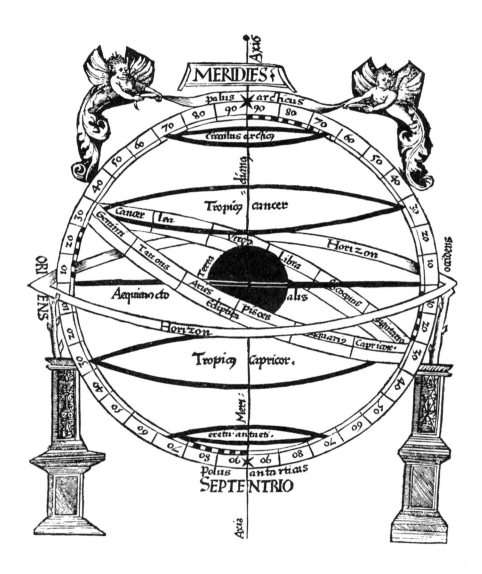

PTOLEMY'S ARMILLARY SPHERE

Geography of Claudius Ptolemy

BOOK ONE

CHAPTER I

In what Geography differs from Chorography

GEOGRAPHY is a representation in picture of the whole known world together with the phenomena which are contained therein.

It differs from Chorography in that Chorography, selecting certain places from the whole, treats more fully the particulars of each by themselves—even dealing with the smallest conceivable localities, such as harbors, farms, villages, river courses, and such like.

It is the prerogative of Geography to show the known habitable earth as a unit in itself, how it is situated and what is its nature; and it deals with those features likely to be mentioned in a general description of the earth, such as the larger towns and the great cities, the mountain ranges and the principal rivers. Besides these it treats only of features worthy of special note on account of their beauty.

The end of Chorography is to deal separately with a part of the whole, as if one were to paint only the eye or the ear by itself. The task of Geography is to survey the whole in its just proportions, as one would the entire head. For as in an entire painting we must first put in the larger features, and afterward those detailed features

which portraits and pictures may require, giving them proportion in relation to one another so that their correct measure apart can be seen by examining them, to note whether they form the whole or a part of the picture. Accordingly therefore it is not unworthy of Chorography, or out of its province, to describe the smallest details of places, while Geography deals only with regions and their general features.

The habitable parts of the earth should be noted rather than the parts which are merely of equal size, especially the provinces or regions and their divisions, the differences between these being rather the more important. Chorography is most concerned with what kind of places those are which it describes, not how large they are in extent. Its concern is to paint a true likeness, and not merely to give exact position and size. Geography looks at the position rather than the quality, noting the relation of distances everywhere, and emulating the art of painting only in some of its major descriptions. Chorography needs an artist, and no one presents it rightly unless he is an artist. Geography does not call for the same requirements, as any one, by means of lines and plain notations can fix positions and draw general outlines. Moreover Chorography does not have need of mathematics, which is an important part of Geography. In Geography one must contemplate the extent of the entire earth, as well as its shape, and its position under the heavens, in order that one may rightly state what are the peculiarities and proportions of the part with which one is dealing, and under what parallel of the celestial sphere it is located, for so one will be able to discuss the length of its days and nights, the stars which are fixed overhead, the stars which move above the horizon, and the stars which never rise above the horizon at all; in short all things having regard to our earthly habitation.

It is the great and the exquisite accomplishment of mathematics to show all these things to the human intelligence so that the sky, too, having a representation of its own character, which, although it can not be seen as moving around us, yet we can look upon it by means of an image as we look upon the earth itself, for the earth being real and very large, and neither wholly nor in part moving around us, yet it can be mapped by the same means as is the sky.

CHAPTER II

What presuppositions are to be made use of in Geography

WHAT Geography aims at, and wherein it differs from Chorography, we have definitely shown in our preceding chapter. But now as we propose to describe our habitable earth, and in order that the description may correspond as far as possible with the earth itself, we consider it fitting at the outset to put forth that which is the first essential, namely, a reference to the history of travel, and to the great store of knowledge obtained from the reports of those who have diligently explored certain regions; whatever concerns either the measurement of the earth geometrically or the observation of the phenomena of fixed localities; whatever relates to the measurement of the earth that can be tested by pure distance calculations to determine how far apart places are situated; and whatever relations to fixed positions can be tested by meteorological instruments for recording shadows. This last is a certain method, and is in no respect doubtful. The other method is less perfect and needs other support, since first of all it is necessary to know in determining the distance between two places, in what direction each place lies from the other; to know how far this place is distant from that, we must also know under what part of the sky each is located, that is, whether each extends toward the north, or, so to speak, toward the rising of the sun (the east), or in some other particular direction. And these facts it is impossible to ascertain without the use of the instruments to which we refer. By the use of these instruments, anywhere and at any time, the position of the meridian line can easily be found, and from this we can ascertain the distances that have been traveled. But when this has been done, the measurement of the number of stadia does not give us sure information, because journeys very rarely are made in a straight line. There being many deviations from a straight course both in land and in sea journeys, it is necessary to conjecture, in the case of a land

journey, the nature and the extent of the deviation, and how far it departs from a straight course, and to subtract something from the number of stadia to make the journey a straight one.

Even in sailing the sea the same thing happens, as the wind is never constant throughout the whole voyage. Thus although the distance of the places noted is carefully counted, it does not give us a basis for the determination of the circumference of the whole earth; nor do we ascertain an exact position for the equatorial circle or for the location of the poles.

Distance which is ascertained from an observation of the stars shows accurately all these things, and in addition shows how much of the circumference is intercepted in turn by the parallel circles, and by the meridian circles which are drawn through the places themselves; that is to say, what part of the circumference of parallel circles and of the equatorial circle is intercepted by the meridians, or what part of the meridian circles are intercepted by the parallels and equatorial circle.

After this it will readily be seen how much space lies between the two places themselves on the circumference of the large circle which is drawn through them around the earth. This measurement of stadia obtained from careful calculations does not require a consideration of the parts of the earth traversed in a described journey; for it is enough to suppose that the circuit of the earth itself is divided into as many parts as one desires, and that some of these parts are contained within distances noted on the great circles that gird the earth itself. Dividing the whole circuit of the earth or any part of it noted by our measurements which are known as stadia measurements, is a method not equally convincing. Therefore because of this fact alone it has been found necessary to take a certain part of the circumference of a very large celestial circle, and by determining the ratio of this part to the whole of the circle, and by counting the number of stadia contained in the given distance on the earth, one can measure the stadia circumference of the globe.

When we grant that it has been demonstrated by mathematics that the surface of the land and water is in its entirety a sphere,

and has the same center as the celestial globe, and that any plane which passes through the center makes at its surface, that is, at the surface of the earth and of the sky, great circles, and that the angles of the planes, which angles are at the center, cut the circumferences of the circles which they intercept proportionately, it follows that in any of the distances which we measure on the earth the number of the stadia, if our measurements are correct, can be determined, but the proportion of this distance to the whole circumference of the earth can not be found, because no proportion to the whole earth can thus be derived, but from the similar circumference of the celestial globe that proportion can be derived, and the ratio of any similar part on the earth's surface to the great circle of the earth is the same.

CHAPTER III

How, from measuring the stadia of any given distance, although not on the same meridian, we may determine the number of stadia in the circumference of the earth, and vice versa

THOSE geographers who lived before us sought to fix correct distance on the earth, not only that they might determine the length of the greatest circle, but also that they might determine the extent which a region occupied in one plane on one and the same meridian. After observing therefore, by means of the instruments of which I have spoken, the points which were directly over each terminus of the given distance, they calculated from the intercepted part of the circumference of the meridian, distances on the earth.

As we have said, they assume the location of the points to be in one plane, and the lines passing through the terminals of the distance, to the points which are directly overhead, must necessarily meet, and the points where they meet would be the common center of the circles. Therefore if the circle drawn through the poles were intercepted by lines drawn from the two points that were marked overhead, it would be understood that it formed the total extent of the intercepted circumference compared with the whole circuit of the earth.

If a distance of this kind is not on the circle drawn through the poles, but on another of the great circles, the same thing can be shown by observing in like manner the elevation of the pole from the extremities of the distance, and noting simultaneously the position which the same distance has on the other meridian. This we have clearly shown by an instrument which we ourselves have constructed for measuring shadows, by which instrument we can easily ascertain a great many other useful things. For on any day or night we have the elevation of the north pole, and at any hour we have the meridian position of the given distance by performing a single measurement, that is, by measuring the angle that the greatest circle drawn through the line of the distance makes with the meridian circle at the vertical point: in this way we can show the required circumference by means of this instrument, and the circumference of the equatorial circle which is intercepted between the two meridians, these meridians being parallel and circles like the equator. According to this demonstration, if we measure only one straight distance on the surface of the earth, then the number of stadia of the whole circuit of the earth can be ascertained. And as a result of this we can obtain the measurements of all distances, even when they are not exactly on the same meridian or parallel, by observing carefully the elevation of the pole, and the inclination of the distance to the meridian, and vice versa. From the ratio of the given part of the circumference to the great circle, the number of the stadia can be calculated from the known number of stadia in the circuit of the whole earth.

CHAPTER IV

Carefully observed phenomena should be preferred to those derived from the accounts of travelers

SINCE this is so, travelers who have journeyed over the regions of the earth one by one, had they made use of observations of a similar kind, would have been able to give us a wholly correct description of our habitable earth. But when no one except Hipparchus has given us the elevation of the north pole, and even he, of only a few places out of the great number known to geographers, and since he has marked but a small number of the sites that are on the same meridian; and when others coming after him have noted the position of the places opposite each other, not giving us those of equal distance from the equator, but only those lying on the same meridian, taking this from successful voyages made to the north and to the south; and calculating most of their distances, especially those which extended to east or west, from a certain general tradition, not because of any lack of skill or because of indolence, on the part of the writers, but because in their time, the use of exact mathematics had not yet been established; and when in addition to this not many eclipses of the moon have been observed at the same time in different localities as was that eclipse at Arbela which was noted as occurring there at the fifth hour, from which observation it was ascertained by how many equinoctial hours, or by what space of time, two places were distant from each other east or west; it is just and right that a geographer about to write a geography should lay as the foundation of his work the phenomena known to him that have been obtained by a more careful observation, and should make the traditions subordinate to these, so that the relative positions of localities may be determined with greater certainty and be more nearly accurate than is possible by relying on primitive traditions.

CHAPTER V

Attention must be paid to the latest researches because the earth, in the course of time, undergoes change

AFTER these preliminary remarks we are able to make a beginning of our work. Since, however, all regions cannot be known fully on account of their great size, or because they are not always of the same shape or because not yet satisfactorily explored, and a greater length of time makes our knowledge of them more certain, we think we should say something to the readers of our geography on the subject of varying traditions at various times, viz., of some portions of our continents, on account of their great

size, we have as yet no knowledge; with regard to other parts we do not know what is their real nature, because of the negligence of those who have explored them in failing to give us carefully prepared reports; other parts of the earth are different to-day from what they were, either on account of revolution or from transformation, in which processes they are known to have partially passed into ruin.

We consider it necessary therefore for us to pay more attention to the newer records of our own time, weighing, however, in our description these new records and those of former times and deciding what is credible and what is incredible.

CHAPTER VI

Concerning the geographical narrations of Marinus

MARINUS the Tyrian, the latest of the geographers of our time, seems to us to have thrown himself with the utmost zeal into this matter.

He is known to have found out many things that were not known before. He has searched most diligently the works of almost all the historians who preceded him. He has not only corrected their errors, but the reader can clearly see that he has undertaken to correct those parts of the work which he himself had done badly in the earlier editions of his geographical maps. If we examine closely his last work we find few defects. It would seem to be enough for us to describe the earth on which we dwell from his commentaries alone, without other investigations.

When, however, he appears to agree with certain others in a conclusion that is unworthy of belief, most often in questions concerning the method of drawing, or when he refuses to give the attention he should to an opportune invention, we have been moved by no unworthy motive to think, as regards part of his reasoning and method, that we could bring forward something more in keeping with the rest of the work and its author. And this without wasting words we will endeavor to do to the best of our ability, dwelling briefly on each kind of error as reason dictates.

First of all let us deal with that which pertains to history. He considers that our earth extends a greater distance in longitude eastward, and to a greater distance in latitude southward than is right and true. For not unreasonably we call the distance extending from the setting to the rising sun the longitude, and the distance from the north to the south pole the latitude, when we mark the parallels in the vault of the heavens. Moreover the greater distance we call longitude, which is accepted by all, for the extent of our habitable earth from east to west all concede is much greater than its extent from the north pole to the south.

CHAPTER VII

The opinions of Marinus relating to the earth's latitude are corrected by observed phenomena

FIRST of all, Marinus places Thule as the terminus of latitude on the parallel that cuts the most northern part of the known world. And this parallel, he shows as clearly as is possible, at a distance of sixty-three degrees from the equator, of which degrees a meridian circle contains three hundred and sixty. Now the latitude he notes as measuring 31,500 stadia, since every degree, it is accepted, has 500 stadia. Next, he places the country of the *Ethiopians*, Agisymba by name, and the promontory of Prasum on the same parallel which terminates the most southerly land known to us, and this parallel he places below the winter solstice.

Between Thule and the southern terminus he inserts altogether about eighty-seven degrees which is 43,500 stadia, and he tries to prove the correctness of this southern termination of his by certain observations (which he thinks to be accurate) of the fixed stars and by certain journeys made both on land and on sea. Concerning this we will make a few observations.

In his observation concerning the fixed stars, in the third volume of his work, he uses these words: "The Zodiac is considered to lie entirely above the torrid zone and therefore in that zone the shadows change, and all the fixed stars rise and set. Ursa Minor begins to be entirely above the hori-

zon from the north shore of Ocele which is 5,500 stadia distant. The parallel through Ocele is elevated eleven and two-fifths degrees.

"We learn from Hipparchus that the star in Ursa Minor which is the most southerly or which marks the end of the tail, is distant from the pole twelve and two-fifths degrees, and that in the course of the sun from the equinoctial to the summer solstice, the north pole continually rises above the horizon while the south pole is correspondingly depressed, and that on the contrary in the course of the sun from the equator to the winter solstice the south pole rises above the horizon while the north pole is depressed."

In these statements Marinus narrates only what is observed (on) the equator, or between the tropics. But what, after being learned from the records or from accurate observations of the fixed stars, are the happenings in places south of the equator, he in no wise informs us, as if one should place southern stars rather than equatorial directly overhead, or assert that mid-day shadows over the equator incline south, or show all the stars of Ursa Minor risen or set, or some of them visible at the time when the south pole is raised above the horizon.

In what he adds later he tells us of certain observations, of which, nevertheless, he is not entirely certain in his own mind.

He says that those who sail from India to Limyrica, as did Diodorus the Samian, which is related in his third book, tell us that Taurus is in a higher position in the mid-heavens than in reality it is and that the Pleiades are seen in the middle of the masts, and he continues, "those who sail from Arabis to Azania sail straight to the south, and toward the star Canopus, which there is called Hippos, that is the Horse, and which is far south. Stars are seen there which are not known to us by name, and the Dog Star rises before Procyon and Orion, and before the time when the sun turns back toward the summer solstice."

For these observations concerning the stars Marinus clearly states that some places are located more northerly than the equator, as when he says that Taurus and the Pleiades are directly over the heads of the sailors. As a matter of fact these stars are near the equator. He indeed shows some stars to be

no further south than north, for Canopus can be seen by those who dwell a long distance north of the summer solstice; and several of the fixed stars, never seen by us, can be seen above the horizon in places south of us, and in places more toward the equatorial region than those in the north, as around Meroe. They can be seen as is Canopus itself, which, when appearing above the horizon is never visible to those who dwell north of us. Those who dwell toward the south call this star Hippos, that is the Horse, nor is any other star of those known to us called by that name.

Marinus infers that he himself determined by mathematical proofs that Orion is entirely visible, before the summer solstice, to those who dwell below the equatorial circle; also that with them the Dog Star rises before Procyon, which he says is observed as far south even as Syene. In these conclusions of Marinus there is nothing appropriate or of value to us because he extends the position of his inhabited countries too far south of the equator.

CHAPTER VIII

They are also corrected by measuring journeys on land

IN computing the days one by one, occupied in journeying from Leptis Magna to Agisymba, Marinus shows that the latter locality is 24,680 stadia south of the equator. By adding together the days occupied in sailing from Ptolemais Trogloditica to Prasum he concluded that Prasum is 27,800 stadia south of the equator, and from these data he infers that the promontory of Prasum and the land of Agisymba, which, as he himself expresses it, belongs to Ethiopia (and is not the end of Ethiopia), lies on the south coast in the frigid zone opposite to ours. In a southerly direction 27,800 stadia make up fifty-five and three-fourths degrees, and this number of degrees in an opposite direction (i. e. north) marks a like temperate climate, and the region of the swamp Meotis, which the *Scythians* and *Sarmatians* inhabit.

Marinus then reduces the stated number of his stadia by half or less than half, that is to 12,000 which is about the distance of

the winter solstice from the equatorial circle. The only reason for this reduction that he gives us is the deviation from a straight line of the journeys and their daily variations in length. After he has stated these reasons, it seemed to us necessary not only to show that he was mistaken, but also to reduce his figures by the required one-half.

At the outset, when writing of the journey from Garama to Ethiopia he says that Septimius Flaccus, having set out from Libya with his army, came to the land of the *Ethiopians* from the land of the *Garamantes* in the space of three months by journeying continuously southward. He says furthermore that Julius Meternus, setting out from Leptis Magna and Garama with the king of the *Garamantes*, who was beginning an expedition against the *Ethiopians*, by bearing continuously southward came within four months to Agisymba, the country of the *Ethiopians* where the rhinoceros is to be found.

Each of these statements, on the face of it, is incredible, first, because the *Ethiopians* are not so far distant from the *Garamantes* as to require a three months' journey, seeing that the *Garamantes* are themselves for the most part *Ethiopians*, and have the same king; secondly, because it is ridiculous to think that a king should march through regions subject to him only in a southerly direction when the inhabitants of those regions are scattered widely east and west, and ridiculous also that he should never have made a single halt that would alter the reckoning. Wherefore we conclude that it is not unreasonable to suppose that those men either spoke in hyperbole, or else, as rustics say, "To the south," or "Toward Africa" to those who prefer to be deceived by them, rather than take the pains to ascertain the truth.

CHAPTER IX

They are also corrected by measuring journeys by water

CONCERNING the voyage from Aromata to Rhapta, Marinus tells us that a certain Diogenes, one of those who were accustomed to sail to India, having been driven out of his course, and being off the coast of Aramata, was caught by the north wind and, after having sailed with Trogloditica on his right, came in twenty-five days to the lake from which the Nile flows, to the south of which lies the promontory of Rhaptum. He tells us also that a certain Theophilus, one of those who were accustomed to sail to Azania, driven from Rhapta by the south wind came to Aromata on the twentieth day. In neither of these cases does he tell us how many days were occupied in actual sailing, but merely states that Theophilus took twenty days, and Diogenes, who sailed along the coast of Trogloditica, took twenty-five days.

He only tells us how many days they were on the voyage, and not the exact sailing time, nor the changes of the wind in strength and direction, which must have taken place during a voyage of such long duration. Moreover he does not say that the sailing was continuously south or north, but merely says that Diogenes was carried along by the north wind while Theophilus sailed with the south wind. That the wind kept the same strength and direction during the whole voyage is related in neither case, and it is incredible that for the space of so many days in succession, it should have done so. Therefore although Diogenes sailed from Aromata to the swamps, to the south of which lies the promontory of Rhaptum, in twenty-five days, and Theophilus from Rhapta to Aromata, a greater distance, in twenty days, and although Theophilus tells us that a single day's sailing under favorable circumstances is calculated at 1,000 stadia (and this computation Marinus himself approves) Disocorus nevertheless says that the voyage from Rhapta to the promontory of Prasum, which takes many days, as computed by Diogenes is only 5,000 stadia. The wind, he says, varies very suddenly at the equator, and squalls around the equator on either side of the line are more dangerous.

From these considerations we thought we ought not to assent to the numbering of the days, because it is plain to all that on the reckoning made by Marinus, the *Ethiopians* and the haunts of the rhinoceros should be moved to the cold zone of the earth, that is, opposite to ours. Reason herself asserts that all animals, and all plants

likewise, have a similarity under the same kind of climate or under similar weather conditions, that is, when under the same parallels, or when situated at the same distance from either pole.

Marinus has shortened the measures of latitude around the winter solstice, but has given no sufficient reason for his contraction. Even should we admit the number of days occupied in the series of voyages that he relates, he has shortened the number of daily stadia and has reasoned contrary to his customary measure in order to reach the desired and correct parallel. He should have done exactly the opposite, for it is easy to believe the same daily distance traveled as possible, but in the even course of the journeys, or voyages or that they were wholly made in a straight line, he ought not to have believed. From them it was not possible to ascertain the distance but it was correct to assert that in latitude the places in question extended beyond the equator. Even this could be known with greater certainty from astronomical observations. Any one could have ascertained exactly the required distances if he had, with more skill in mathematics, considered what takes place in those localities. Since this observation was not made, it remains that we follow what reason dictates, that is, we must ascertain how far the distance extends beyond the equator. We can also ascertain what we require to know through information concerning the kinds, the forms, and the colors of the animals living there, from which we draw the conclusion that the parallel of the region of Agisymba is the same as that of the *Ethiopians* and extends from the winter solstice to the equator; although with us in places opposite to that region, that is, in the summer solstice, they do not have the color of the *Ethiopians*, nor is the rhinoceros and elephant to be found, yet in places not far south of us the inhabitants are moderately black such as from the same cause are the *Garamantes*, whom Marinus himself describes, and whom he places neither under the summer solstice nor north of it, but much too far to the south. In the regions around Meroe the inhabitants are very black, and closely resemble the *Ethiopians*, and there we find that elephants and other kinds of monstrous animals are bred.

CHAPTER X

Ethiopia should not be placed more to the south than the parallel which is opposite the parallel passing through Meroe

IN agreement therefore with this information, viz., that the inhabitants are *Ethiopians*, as those who have sailed there have told us, Marinus describes the region of Agisymba and the promontory of Prasum, and the other places lying on the same parallel, as situated all on one parallel, which is opposite the parallel passing through Meroe. That would place them on a parallel distant from the equator in a southerly direction 16° 25′ or about 8,200 stadia, and by the same reckoning the whole width of the habitable world amounts to 79° 25′ or altogether 40,000 stadia.

Now the distance between Leptis Magna and Garama, according to Flaccus and Maternus, is placed at 5,400 stadia. The time of their second journey was twenty days, a more nearly correct time than the first because it was directly north, while the first journey of thirty days had many deviations. The travelers who several times made the voyage kept the reckoning of each day's distance, and this was not only properly done, but done of necessity on account of the changes of the water and the weather. Just as we should have doubts with regard to distances that are great in extent, and rarely traveled, and not fully explored, so in regard to those that are not great and not rarely but frequently gone over, it seems right to give credit to the reports of the voyagers.

CHAPTER XI

The errors of Marinus in calculating the longitude of the habitable earth

HOW far the latitude of the habitable earth extends is clear to us from what we have just stated. Marinus gives us the longitude, between two meridians, enclosing a total space of fifteen hours. It seems to us that the distance eastward is shown to be greater than it should be, and that if it be reduced, as it ought to be, it will be seen to include not quite the space of twelve hours, that is, by locating the Fortunate Islands at the extreme west and placing

at the extreme east the *Seres*, Sina and Cattigara.

The distance from the Fortunate Islands to the Euphrates at Hieropolis, which we place with Marinus on the parallel passing through Rhodes, must be reckoned according to the number of stadia, determined by Marinus, both because of the continual measuring of this distance by voyagers, and because Marinus has corrected the reports of the distance by ascertaining the allowance to be made for deviation and the variations of the rate of travel. Marinus also makes one degree of the three hundred and sixty which the largest circle contains, measure 500 stadia on the surface of the earth, a measurement which is proved by distances that are known and certain. Likewise the circle which passes through Rhodes, Marinus shows to be 36° distant from the equator, and each degree to measure approximately four hundred stadia, and the excess of that number (according to an exact reckoning of the location of the parallels), in some measure counterbalances the defect in the others, and is negligible in the whole computation.

The distance from the Euphrates at Hieropolis to the Stone Tower, Marinus gives as eight hundred and seventy-six schena, or 26,280 stadia. The distance from the Stone Tower to Sera, the capital of the *Seres*, which is a journey of seven months, he computes at 36,200 stadia. Since these two distances are measured on the same parallel, we shall shorten both by making a necessary correction, as it is clear that Marinus made no reduction for deviations in either journey, and in computing the second journey fell into the same mistakes as those he made when measuring the distance between the *Garamantes* and Agisymba, for in that measurement he reckoned the number of stadia traversed in four months, and was compelled to make a reduction. It is quite possible that the rate of travel was not uniform over so long a space of time, and that this was the case in the seven months' journey it is not unreasonable to suppose, and it is more likely to have been the case, than in the journey from the *Garamantes* to Agisymba. This last journey was made by the king of the country, as was becoming with no small preparation, and was made

wholly in fine weather. The journey from the Stone Tower to Sera was exposed to winter tempests, for it lies, according to Marinus himself, on the parallel that passes through Byzantium and the Hellespont. Wherefore there must have been many deviations in that journey, especially since it was undertaken for the purpose of carrying merchandise. Marinus tells us that a certain Macedonian named Maen, who was also called Titian, son of a merchant father, and a merchant himself, noted the length of this journey, although he did not come to Sera in person but sent others there.

Marinus does not seem to agree with the findings of these merchants, and he especially disagrees with the statements of the merchant Philemon whose reckonings make the length of the island of Hibernia from east to west a twenty days' journey. Marinus would not believe this, although Philemon told him that he himself had heard it from the merchants themselves.

Marinus says of the merchant class generally that they are only intent on their business, and have little interest in exploration, and that often through their love of boasting they magnify distances. In their journey that occupied seven months they brought no information worth remembering, and what they related on their return about the time they had consumed in travel was nothing but an extravagant statement.

CHAPTER XII

The calculation of longitude corrected by land journeys

FOR these reasons therefore, and because the journey is not on one and the same parallel, for the Stone Tower is on the parallel that passes through Byzantium, and Sera is more to the south and on the parallel that passes through the Hellespont, it seems to us proper that the number of the stadia, viz., 36,200, which was computed from a journey of seven months, should be cut down to not less than one-half; and for an easier understanding only to one-half; so that the distance in stadia may be computed as 18,100, or forty-five and one-fourth degrees.

It would be inept and absurd should any one follow on both journeys, that is, on this

journey and on the journey from the Garamantes, reasoning which led to this conclusion, for the reason was based upon the difference noted in the animals which inhabit the region of Agisymba, animals which can not be transferred to localities outside the limits of those assigned to them by nature. This reason does not hold likewise in reckoning the distance of the Stone Tower from Sera, for throughout the whole distance, be the intervals great or small, there is the same temperate climate. It is much the same as though a man, who could not be convicted by law as a thief, could be convicted nevertheless, according to the rightful precepts of philosophy.

Wherefore the former distance which Marinus gave from the Euphrates to the Stone Tower, viz., 876 schena must be reduced because of deviations on the journey, to only 800 schena or 24,000 stadia; and this is verified by the particular measurements taken on that journey, and by the frequent visits made to those places on that journey. That the journey had deviations is clear from statements made by Marinus himself, for in making the journey from the ford over the Euphrates at Hieropolis through Mesopotamia to the Tigris, and through the *Garamantes* of Assyria and Media to Ecbatana and the Caspian Gates, and from there through Parthia to Hechatompilum, the right course is to follow the parallel of Rhodes, as this parallel passes through those regions. To procede from Hechatompilum to the city of Hyrcania it is necessary to deviate to the north. The city Hyrcania lies about midway between the Smyrna and the Hellespont parallels, the parallel of Smyrna is also called the parallel of Hyrcania, but the parallel of the Hellespont passes through the southern shores of the Hyrcanian sea, which are situated somewhat to the north of the city of Hyrcania which takes its name from that sea. The journey thence to Antioch Margiana through Asia, first turns to the south (since Asia is on the same parallel as the Caspian Gates), and then turns to the north, since Antioch is close to the Hellespont parallel.

From Antioch to Bactria the journey deviates to the east, and after ascending the Comedon mountains it bends to the north. From the mountains, where it comes to the plain at their base, it inclines to the south, for the mountains extend north and east. The ascent is placed by Marinus on the Byzantium parallel, and the southern and eastern ranges are located on the Hellespont parallel. The mountains themselves he places to the east, but plainly extends them so as partially to decline to the south. Likewise he says that the journey for fifty schena before coming to the Stone Tower, deviates to the north. When you have traversed the plain, at the base of the mountains you arrive at the Stone Tower, and from there you come to the mountains which run in an easterly direction, ending at Imao which is north of Palimbothris.

Adding the degrees which have been noted, they amount to sixty or 24,000 stadia. When we have added the forty-five and one-fourth degrees from the Stone Tower to Sera, the total distance from the Euphrates to Sera on the parallel of Rhodes will amount to 105° 15'. We will now add, from the distances which Marinus gives, the other degrees on the same parallel, and first of all from the meridian passing through the Fortunate Islands, as far as the Sacred promontory of Spain 2° 30', thence to the mouth of the river Baetis, and from the Baetis to the Strait and to Calpe is likewise 2° 30', being one and the same distance; from the Strait to Caralis, a city in Sardinia, is 25°; from Caralis to the promontory of Lilybaeum in Sicily 4° 30'; from Lilybaeum to Pachynus is 3°; from Pachynus to Taenarus in Laconica is 10°; thence to Rhodes is 8° 15'; from Rhodes to Issus is 11° 15'; from Issus to the Euphrates is 2° 30'; the sum of all these degrees is 72°. Hence, the length of the known earth, that is, from the meridian drawn through or terminated by the Fortunate Islands in the extreme west, to Sera in the extreme east is 177° 15'.

CHAPTER XIII

The same calculation of longitude corrected by sea journeys

ONE might then conjecture that the entire distance was only a certain total, by summing up the separate distances given by Marinus in sailing from India to the region of Sinarus and Cattigara, after taking account of deviations from a direct

course, the variations in the rate of sailing, and the position of the regions themselves.

After the promontory called Cory, which closes the bay of Colchis, he says that the bay of Argaricus is next, and that it extends to the city of Curula, a distance of 3,400 stadia.

He adds that the city is situated north of the promontory of Cory, hence we gather that the voyage, if we subtract one-third for the circuit of the bay of Argaricus, may be reckoned as 2,030 stadia, not allowing for any variation in the wind. If however we subtract one-third for the variation from a direct course owing to the winds, there remains a distance of about 1,350 stadia in a direct northerly course. When this distance is transferred to a distance measured on the equatorial parallel, and is diminished by one-half in proportion to the intercepted angle, we have the distance between the two meridians passing through the promontory of Cory and the city Curula as 675 stadia or about 1° 20′, because the parallel drawn through these points differs from the greatest circle in nothing worthy of note.

From the city of Curula the course of navigation is, so he tells us, toward the winter rising of the sun as far as Palura and measures 9,450 stadia. Subtracting one-third for changes in the direction of wind we have a distance in one direction of 6,300 stadia. Taking from this distance one-sixth we may then reduce it to the equatorial parallel and we shall then find the distance between these meridians to be 5,250 stadia or 10° 30′. The shore of the Gangetic bay he places at a further distance of 19,000 stadia.

From Palura to the city of Sada is 13,000 stadia by navigating the aforesaid bay toward the equatorial rising of the sun, and since the course is directed toward the equatorial rising we must allow for the deviation and deduct one-third. When we have done this we are left with a distance of about 8,670 stadia or 17° 20′.

Thence he makes the voyage from Sada to the city of Tamala to measure 3,500 stadia in a direction toward the winter rising of the sun. Deducting one-third for variable winds we have a distance in a straight line of 2,330 stadia, and deducting

a further one-sixth for deviation toward Velturnus we find that the distance between the meridians is 1,940 stadia or about 3° 30′ plus 20′, that is 3° 50′.

The next distance from Tamala to the Golden Chersonesus he gives as 1,600 stadia toward the winter rising of the sun, so that a like fraction being deducted there is a distance left between the meridians of 900 stadia or 1° 48′.

CHAPTER XIV
Concerning the voyage from the Golden Chersonesus to Cattigara

MARINUS does not tell the number of stadia from the Golden Chersonesus to Cattigara, but he says Alexander wrote that the shore line extends toward the south, and that those sailing along the shore came, after twenty days, to Zaba. From Zaba carried southward and toward the left, they came after some days to Cattigara. He lengthens the distance, interpreting some days to mean many days, and believing (ridiculously it seems to me) that the expression "some days" was used because the days were too many to be counted. Who is there who could not count the number of days even if they expressed the circuit of the entire earth, or what induced Alexander, when he meant many days, to say some days?

He indeed says concerning Dioscorus that he occupied many days sailing from Rhapta to Prasum. One very naturally would understand by *some days* a *few days*, for that is how we are accustomed to speak. Lest, however, we seem, like our friends, to accommodate our conjectures to the number we have laid down, let us compare the voyage from the Golden Chersonesus to Cattigara, a voyage consisting of two voyages — one voyage of twenty days to Zaba, the other of some days to Cattigara — let us compare, I say, this twofold voyage with the sailing from Aromata to the promontory of Prasum, which took the same number of days as far as Rhapta (as Theophilus relates), and many more to Prasum (as Dioscorus tells us).

Now let us, as Marinus did, agree that *some days* and *many days* correspond in meaning, when from conclusions which are in keeping with reason we have shown by

celestial phenomena that Prasum is situated on the parallel which lies 16° 25′ south of the equator, and when the parallel drawn through Aromata to Prasum is counted as 20° 40′.

Hence it is not incongruous to assign the same number of degrees to the distance between the Golden Chersonesus and Cattigara by way of Zaba. The part of this distance which lies between the Golden Chersonesus and Zaba need not be lessened, because it extends in a straight line, following the course of the equator, but the part of the distance lying between Zaba and Cattigara, because its navigation deviates to the south on its eastern shore, must be lessened, that we may bring it to the norm of the equator. If then we attribute half of the degrees to both distances on account of our knowing no difference between them, and then subtract because of known deviations a third part of the degrees measured between Zaba and Cattigara, which were at first set down as 10° 20′, we shall have a distance from the Golden Chersonesus to Cattigara equated to the position of the equator, or about 17° 10′.

We have already shown that the distance from the promontory of Cory to the Golden Chersonesus is 34° 48′. Wherefore the whole distance from Cory to Cattigara amounts to about 52°. The meridian, which is drawn through the source of the Indus river, Marinus places just west of the most northerly promontory of the island of Taprobana, which is opposite Cory. From Taprobana the meridian which runs through the mouth of the Baetis river is distant a space of eight hours, or 120°, and furthermore the meridian passing through the Baetis is 5° from the meridian drawn through the Fortunate Islands. Whence we gather that the meridian drawn through Cory is distant from the meridian drawn through the Fortunate Islands by a little more than 125°. The meridian drawn through Cattigara is distant from the meridian through the Fortunate Islands a little more than 177°, which very nearly agrees with the distance we found elsewhere by measuring the parallel passing through Rhodes.

If we grant that the entire longitude as far as the metropolis of the *Sines* is 180°, or twelve hours' interval, observing that all agree that Cattigara lies a little toward the east, then we can determine the length of the parallel, passing through the island of Rhodes as measuring about 270,000 stadia.

CHAPTER XV

Concerning discrepancies in some of the explanations of Marinus

THE general distances of Marinus, both of longitude eastward and latitude northward, we have shortened for the reasons we have already given. Besides doing this we have altered the positions of cities in several places where Marinus has given contradictory and false traditions which he took from various faulty editions with incorrect notes concerning places which were wrongly said to be opposite each other or on the same meridian. For example, he says that Tarragona is opposite Caesarea, which he calls Iol, and he says that one meridian is drawn through Tarragona and through the Pyrenees mountains, which mountains in reality are not a little to the east of Tarragona.

He also places Pachynus opposite Leptis Magna, and Himera opposite Thenis. He gives the distance from Pachynus to Himera as about 400 stadia, and from Leptis to Thenis as more than 1,500 stadia, following the writings of Timosthenes, and in another place says that Tergestum is opposite Ravenna, and from the bay in the Adriatic sea into which flows the river Tilamentus, he says that Tergestum is distant toward the summer rising of the sun 480 stadia, and that Ravenna is distant toward the winter rising 1,000 stadia. He likewise says that Chelidonia is opposite Canopus, and Achamanta to Paphos, and Paphos to Sebennitum. He places Achamanta 1,000 stadia distant from Chelidones. Now the distance from Canopus to Sebennitum, according to Timosthenes, is 290 stadia. But if this last distance is measured on the same meridians, then without doubt it should be greater as lying on the circumference of a greater parallel.

After this he says that Pisa is distant in a southerly direction from Ravenna 700 stadia, but in the division of climas and hours he puts Pisa in the third hour inter-

val and Ravenna in the fourth. From London in Britain he puts Niomagus fifty-nine miles south, in a somewhat westerly direction.

He places Mount Athos on the same parallel as the Hellespont, and yet notwithstanding this, Amphipolis, and the neighboring places on the Hellespont parallel, and adjoining one another, and those that are situated on Athos, and at the mouth of the river Strimon, he places in the fourth clima, that is, next below the Hellespont parallel. In the same way he places almost the whole of Thrace below the Byzantine parallel, and yet all its interior cities he places in the clima that is above the parallel.

He also says he will locate Trapezos on the Byzantine parallel, after showing that Satala in Armenia is sixty miles toward the south, when he draws the parallels he draws the Byzantine parallel through Satala, and not through Trapezos.

He promises that he will truthfully describe the Nile, so that one can trace its course from its source northward as far as Meroe. Likewise he says that navigation with a north wind can be made from Aromata all the way to the lakes from which the Nile takes its beginning, although Aromata is actually far east of the Nile. For Ptolemais Theron lies east of Meroe and east of the Nile a journey of ten or twelve days, and Angustiora, which is between Ocelim peninsula and Diren, is 3,500 stadia east of Ptolemais and the Adulicus gulf, and from this strait to the promontory of Great Aromata toward the east still, 5,000 stadia more.

CHAPTER XVI

In fixing the boundaries of provinces Marinus has made some mistakes

MARINUS makes some mistakes with reference to the boundaries of certain regions. For example, he makes the Pontic sea the eastern boundary of the whole of Moesia. He makes Thrace to be bounded on the west by Upper Moesia, and he makes Italy to be bounded on the north not by Rhetia and Noricum only, but also by Pannonia, and Pannonia on the south he bounds by Dalmatia only and omits Italy. He says that the *Sogdiani*, and their neighbors the *Saci*, who inhabit the middle of the habitable earth, adjoin India, but the parallels through the territory of these peoples do not closely follow those two which are drawn north of the Imaus, the most northerly mountains of India; I refer to the Hellespontine and the Byzantine parallels, but they follow the parallel which is drawn through the middle of the Pontus.

CHAPTER XVII

Wherein Marinus dissents from the findings made in our time

THESE and similar mistakes have been made by Marinus, either on account of the multitude of volumes, all disagreeing, of which he made use, or because, as he himself says, he has not yet come to the last delineation of his maps in which, so he tells us, he would make some necessary corrections in the climas and the hour indications.

In addition to these mistakes he gives us some further assignments of localities with which the knowledge of our times does not agree. For example he places the bay of Sachalita on the western shore of the promontory of Syagros, but all who navigate these parts unanimously agree with us that it is toward the east from Syagros, and that Sachalita is a region of Arabia, and from it the bay of Sachalita takes its name.

Again Simylla, an emporium of India, is not only placed by Marinus west of the Comarris promontory, but west of the river Indus, whereas in fact it is as far to the south as the mouths of the river, according to the testimony of those who have navigated those waters and have thoroughly explored those parts, and have come directly from there to us. It is called by the aborigines "Timula," and from those who have come to us we have learned many more details concerning India, especially of its divisions into provinces, and we have also learned much concerning its interior as far as the Golden Chersonesus, and from there to Cattigara. We have also learned that those who sail there sail to eastward, and those returning sail to westward.

The navigators say that the time of the passage is uncertain, and that beyond Sina is the region of the *Seres* and the city Sera. What regions lie east of this they say are

unknown, for they have stagnant marshes, in which grow reeds so thick and so large, that catching hold of them, and upborne by them, men can walk across these marshes. They say further that not only is there a way from there to Bactriana through the Stone Tower, but also a way to India through Palimbothra.

The journey from the capital Sina to the gate of Cattigara runs to the southwest, and therefore does not coincide with the meridian drawn through Sera and Cattigara, as Marinus reports, but with one drawn more to the east.

We have learned also from the merchants that from Arabia Felix they sail to Aromata, to Azania, to Rhapta, and to the regions called Barbary. This sailing is not exactly south, but southwest. The voyage from Rhapta to Prasum is also southwest.

The lakes from which the Nile takes its beginning are not near the sea, but are very far inland. The shore line from the Aromata promontory to Rhapta is otherwise than Marinus has shown it to be; nor can an ordinary day - and - night voyage be counted in stadia because of the changeableness of the winds at the equator, but is limited to about 400 or 500 stadia at the most.

There is, first of all, a continuous bay in which, after sailing for one day from Aromata we come to Panocone and to Opone, an emporium, distant one day's sail from Panocone. Sailing from the emporium, they say that we enter another bay which marks the beginning of Azame, at the entrance to which appears the Zingis promontory, and Mount Phalangis, remarkable for its three peaks. The name of this bay is Apocopa, and it takes two days and nights to cross it. After this is Parvum Litus (Little Shore), at the distance of two days' voyage, then Magnum Litus (Great Shore). Of the five distances, the last two are said to occupy the same time in sailing.

A further four days' sailing, they say, brings us to another bay, in which there is the emporium of Essina. It requires two days and nights to cross this bay; then after a day and night sail one comes to the seaport of Serapionis; thence begins the bay which leads to Rhapta, a voyage of three days and nights. At the head of this bay they say there is an emporium called Toni-

cus. From this emporium toward the Rhaptum promontory there is, they inform us, a river called Rhaptus and also a city of the same name, not far from the sea.

The bay extending from Rhaptum to the Prasum promontory, although great in size, is not of great depth. The barbarians who dwell on its shores are cannibals.

CHAPTER XVIII

The inconvenience of the method of Marinus for delineating the habitable earth

WHAT is worth remembering in tradition and story, we have thus far set down, lest we should seem to have raised doubts and to have left them unsolved, for we believe that all things will be known to us when we have settled all the particulars.

It remains for us to turn our attention to the method of making maps. There are two ways in which this matter may be treated; one is to represent the habitable earth as spherical; the other is to represent it as a plane surface. Both have this common purpose, that is, they are constructed for use, to show (in the absence of any picture) how from commentaries alone the student may be able, with the utmost facility, to construct a new map.

Recently the making of new copies from earlier copies has had the result of increasing some of the faults that were originally small into great discrepancies. If then there are not enough data for the method of constructing maps from commentaries (without any traditional pictures), it will be impossible for us to reach our desired end. That has happened in the work of Marinus several times, for copyists do not follow his last edition of a world map, but attempt to construct a map merely from commentaries. Thus they are misleading in many particulars on account of their unbecoming shape and general confusion which any one expert in geography, can easily detect. Although it is necessary to know the longitude as well as the latitude of any place that we may be able to fix its right position, nevertheless in the edition of Marinus this cannot be immediately found. For in one place he gives only the location in latitude, as in his explanation of the parallels, but in another

place he gives only the longitude; hence in his drawing of meridians we find, as a rule, no note of both longitude and latitude, but in one instance we find reference to parallels, in other instances we find meridians so noted that when we have one position we lack the other.

When we are working with commentaries, it is requisite to have a knowledge of both latitude and longitude at the same time, since in all commentaries something is always said concerning both positions. If we were not to search out, one by one, through the whole volume, the data concerning any given place, we should miss particulars which are worthy of note.

Moreover in giving the positions of cities, maritime cities are the more easily described, and he keeps generally a certain order in naming them, but in treating of cities that are inland, the same method has not been employed; for the distances between them are not noted, except in a few instances where it happens that the longitude in the one case and the latitude in another case have been given us.

CHAPTER XIX

Of the convenience of our method of delineating the whole earth

WE therefore are undertaking a double labor, first in keeping the intention that Marinus had throughout his whole work, besides that which we have obtained by corrections; and second in adding those things, with as much accuracy as possible, which to him were not known, partly on account of history then unwritten, and partly on account of a later series of more accurate maps.

In addition we have given special attention to a better method in fixing the boundaries of each particular country; we have given their particular position both in longitude and in latitude. After that, we have recorded noteworthy information concerning the inhabitants of the various countries, and their relations one to another. We have noted the chief cities, rivers, gulfs, and mountains, and all other things which in the map itself might show distances where they are worth knowing, that is to say how many

degrees (the great circle has 360 such degrees), if it is a question of longitude, the meridian drawn through a certain place is distant from the meridian that marks the utmost boundary of the west. If it is a question of latitude, then we note how many degrees the parallel drawn through it is distant from the equator on the same meridian. We are able therefore to know at once the exact position of any particular place; and the positions of the various countries, how they are situated in regard to one another, how situated as regards the whole inhabited world.

CHAPTER XX

Of the lack of symmetry in the map that accompanies the geography of Marinus

EACH method of map making has something peculiar to itself. When the earth is delineated on a sphere, it has a shape like its own, nor is there any need of altering at all. Yet it is not easy to provide space large enough (on a globe) for all of the details that are to be inscribed thereon; nor can one fix one's eye at the same time on the whole sphere, but one or the other must be moved, that is, the eye or the sphere, if one wishes to see other places.

In the second method wherein the earth is represented as a plane surface there is not this inconvenience. But a certain adjustment is required in representing the earth as a sphere in order that the distances noted therein may be shown on the surface of the globe congruent, as far as possible, with the real distance on the earth.

Marinus gives this point his deepest consideration, criticising and rejecting all previous methods of delineating distances on the surface of a sphere, yet nevertheless he chose a method which is the least satisfactory of all for locating distances with congruency. For with regard to the lines which he inserts for the parallels and meridians he writes in at equal distance from one another, as is the general custom, in the form of straight parallel lines.

Only the parallel through Rhodes has he kept in right proportion to its meridian and the circumference of the equatorial circle. This parallel is distant 36° from the equator. In this he follows almost exactly the

method of Epitecartus. In the case of the other parallels he has paid no attention whatever either to the right proportion of their length, or to their spheric shape.

At the outset, if the eye is fixed on the middle of the fourth part of the northern hemisphere, in which part the most populated portion of the world is situated, the meridians will have the appearance of straight lines, when the sphere is turned, and that surface comes directly under the eye. But this cannot be the case if they are parallel lines on account of the elevation of the north pole; for the segments of the circles clearly show their curvature in the direction of the meridian. Now according to both truth and appearance the same meridians intercept the similar but unequal circumferences of the parallels which differ in length but are always greater the nearer they are to the equator.

Marinus notwithstanding makes all the interceptions equal. The space of the climates north of the parallel passing through Rhodes, he extends beyond the actual, and the climates in the south he makes smaller than the actual. It follows that the distances of places from one another as shown on his map cannot be the same as their measured stadia, for the distances that are on the equator lack one-fifth of their given measurement, which is the proportion the parallel passing through Rhodes is less than the equator. The distances that are on the parallel passing through Thule, Marinus increases by four-fifths, which is the proportion the parallel through Rhodes is greater than the parallel passing through Thule. It being given that there are one hundred and fifteen parts into which we divide the equator, of these parts the parallel passing through Rhodes, which is 36° distant from the equator, measures 93°, and further the parallel which is 63° distant from the equator, and passes through Thule, measures fifty-two such parts.

CHAPTER XXI

What must be done should one desire to delineate the earth on a plane surface

WHEREFORE we shall do well to keep straight lines for our meridians, but to insert our parallels as the arcs of circles, having one and the same center, which we suppose to be the north pole, and from which we draw the straight lines of our meridians, keeping above all else similarity to a sphere in the form and appearance of our plane surface.

The meridians must not bend to the parallels, and they must be drawn from the same common pole. Since it is impossible for all of the parallels to keep the proportion that there is in a sphere, it will be quite sufficient to observe this proportion in the parallel circle running through Thule and the equinoctial, in order that the sides of our map which represent latitude may be proportionate to the true and natural sides of the earth.

The parallel passing through Rhodes must be inserted because on this parallel very many proofs of distances have been registered and inserted in right relation to the circumference of the greatest circle, following in this Marinus who followed Epitecartus. By thus doing we shall insure that the longitude of our earth, which is the better known, will be in right proportion to the latitude. We will now show how this may be done, treating first, as far as is necessary, of the properties of a sphere.

CHAPTER XXII

How the habitable earth may be shown on a sphere

THE intention of the individual who wishes to make a globe, having regard to the greater or smaller number of place-names he may wish to insert, will determine the size of the globe, which, in accord with his ability and purpose will be constructed. The larger it is made, the clearer and the fuller will be the description of the various places that are indicated on its surface. Whatever size the globe to be constructed may have, the position of the poles being determined, let there be connecting them a semicircle which we will place a very little distance from the globe's surface, so that when it revolves it almost touches it. Let this semicircle be narrow that it may not cover many places by its width. Divide one side into 180 divisions, and mark on this the numbers, beginning at the middle which

cuts the equator. Repeat this process for the other side.

In like manner draw the equinoctial line; divide this second semicircle into a like number of parts, viz., 180, and begin the numbering from the limit of the most western meridian. Begin the work of inscribing by noting the degrees of longitude and latitude assigned to the various places in the known commentaries. Insert each of the places in its right position on the globe, finding the position of the intersection of the parallels of latitude with the movable meridians as we previously explained.

Next inscribe the degrees of longitude found in the commentaries, at the points where the meridians cut the parallels of latitude. Mark the degrees of latitude along a meridian line, then you can put in the localities in their ascertained positions in the manner in which it is customary to fix stars on a solid sphere. We can insert meridians of whatever number we wish, by using semicircles instead of straight lines. The position of the parallels of latitude we can indicate by placing our instrument for drawing parallel lines in its proper position, which position when found with regard to one meridian, we can then adjust to the other meridians, including both meridians that shut in the habitable world.

CHAPTER XXIII

Explanation of the meridians and parallels used in our delineation

THE meridians, according to what we have already shown, will embrace the space of twelve hours. The parallel that bounds the most southern limit of the habitable world will be distant from the equator in a southerly direction only as far as the parallel passing through Meroe is distant in a northerly direction.

It has seemed proper to us to put in the meridians at a distance from each other the third part of an equinoctial hour, that is, through five of the divisions marked on the equator. The parallels that are north of the equator we have inserted so that:

The first parallel is distant from the equator the fourth part of an hour, and is distant from it geometrically about 4° 15'.

The second parallel we make distant half an hour from the equator, and geometrically distant 8° 25'.

The third parallel we make distant from the equator three-fourths of an hour, and geometrically 12° 30'.

The fourth parallel is distant one hour and is 16° 25'. This is the parallel through Meroe.

The fifth parallel is distant one and one-fourth hours, and 20° 15'.

The sixth parallel, which is under the summer solstice is distant one and one-half hours, and 23° 50', and is drawn through Syene.

The seventh parallel is distant one and three-fourths hours, and 27° 10'.

The eighth parallel is distant two hours, and 30° 20'.

The ninth parallel is distant two and one-fourth hours, and 33° 20'.

The tenth parallel is distant two and one-half hours, and 36°, and is drawn through Rhodes.

The eleventh parallel is distant two and three-fourths hours, and 38° 35'.

The twelfth parallel is distant three hours, and 40° 55'.

The thirteenth parallel is distant three and one-fourth hours, and 43° 05'.

The fourteenth parallel is distant three and one-half hours, and 45°.

The fifteenth parallel is distant four hours, and 48° 30'.

The sixteenth parallel is distant four and one-half hours, and 51° 30'.

The seventeenth parallel is distant five hours, and 54°.

The eighteenth parallel is distant five and one-half hours, and 56° 10'.

The nineteenth parallel is distant seven hours, and 58°.

The twentieth parallel is distant seven hours, and 61°.

The twenty-first parallel is distant eight hours, and 63°, and is the parallel drawn through Thule.

Besides these, one other parallel must be drawn south of the equator with the time difference of half an hour. It should pass through Rhaptum promontory and Cattigara, and should be about the same length as the parallel in the opposite part of the earth which is distant 8° 25' north of the equator.

CHAPTER XXIV

How the habitable earth can be shown on a plane so that its measurements are in keeping with its spherical shape

IN the delineation which is made in the map, the following will be our method of showing the proportions of the special parallels. We will draw a right-angled parallelogram ABGD, the side AB of which is about twice as long as the side AG. (See Figure I.)

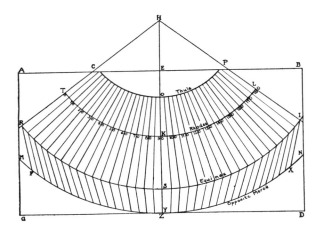

FIGURE I

Place the side AB uppermost which will represent the northern limit of the delineation. We will then divide the side AB in half by the line EZ drawn to it at right angles; and to this line we will so construct the congruent normal straight line that, midway of the length of the former line (AB), it makes one and the same straight line with EZ, that is, then, the line EH. Now let the line EH consist of thirty-four parts, then HZ will measure 131 and five-twelfths. With H as a center and at a distance of seventy-nine parts measured along the line HZ, draw the circle TKL, which will represent the parallel through Rhodes.

Then, that we may arrive at the limits of longitude which are distant at intervals of six hours measured on both sides of the point K, we will take a distance measuring four parts on the line HZ, the line of the median meridian, which is equal to five on the parallel of Rhodes, for the reason that the ratio of a great circle to that parallel is as that of a quinary number to a quaternary, as it is measured by Epitecartus. Measuring nine of these parts from the center K along

the parallel through Rhodes in both directions, we have eighteen points through which to draw meridians with H as a center. Any one of these meridians will differ in time from the next by one-third part of an hour, and also those meridians which bound the edge of the known world will be HTM and HLN.

In the same manner the parallel of Thule is drawn at an interval which is distant fifty-two parts from H in the line HZ: this is the arc COP; then we will draw the equinoctial line ISR from the center H with a radius of 115 parts, and the southernmost parallel, opposite that drawn through Meroe, MYN at an interval of 131 and five-twelfths parts distant from H.

The ratio of the arc RSI and COP will be the same as that of the numbers 115 and 52, which is the ratio of these parallels on a globe, since the line is made up of 115 parts such as the 52 of the line HO, and as the ratio of the line HS to HO so is the arc ISR to COP.

Now there remains the distance on the meridian OK or that between the parallel passing through Thule and that through Rhodes, which is found to measure twenty-seven parts, or segments, and the distance between the parallel of Rhodes and the equator which should measure thirty-six parts or segments, and finally the distance between the equator and the parallel opposite that passing through Meroe which should measure sixteen and five-twelfths like parts or segments.

Furthermore OY representing the extent in latitude of the known world is seventy-nine and five-twelfths such units, or in whole numbers eighty, the median extent in longitude represented by TKL will be 144, which agrees with those which are fixed by the authority of geographers; about the same proportion have the 40,000 stadia of latitude to the 72,000 stadia of longitude in the parallel of Rhodes. From the same center H, and at intervals distant from S the same number of parts or segments we have given above, we can draw as many of the remaining parallels as we wish.

Now indeed we are not permitted to carry the lines which are to be drawn as meridians through in one straight course to the parallel MYN but only to the equator RSI;

and with the arc MYN divided in both directions into ninety parts or segments, equal in size and number to those taken on the parallel of Meroe we can then draw to these marked points the intervening straight lines from those points marked in the equator the course of which will seem deflecting toward the south on the other side of the equator such as are the lines RF and IX.

Then, that we may the more easily mark the localities which are to be placed on the map, let us take a narrow ruler, equal in length to the line HZ or to the line HS, and so attach it at the point H that it can be moved, and when it is swung over, throughout the length of the map, one of its sides can be applied to the meridian line for its entire length, by means of a notch in the side just at the pole. This done, let us divide this side into 131 and five-twelfths parts or segments corresponding to the line HZ or at least into 115 segments on the line HS, and we then number these segments beginning at the equator. Through these numbers we shall be able to draw parallels to the southernmost parallel which we have put down on our map. If, however, we divide the meridian OY on the map into all of the segments, and put the numbers beside them, we are apt to confuse the writing in of the places situated next to them. Having divided the equator into 180° embracing a space of twelve hours, and having given them numbers beginning from the west we may always carry forward the edge of the ruler to any indicated degree of longitude. Finding then the given position in latitude by means of the division made on the ruler we can make the correct notation of every locality, just as we have demonstrated above in the case of spherical delineation.

We shall be able to make a much greater resemblance to the known world in our map if we see the meridian lines, that we have drawn, in that form in which meridian lines appear on a globe, when the axis of the eyes is imagined as directed upon a motionless globe through a point before the eyes in which occurs the intersection of that meridian and that parallel which divides respectively the longitude and the latitude of the known earth into two equal parts, and also through the center of the globe, so that the extreme parts which lie opposite each other

appear and are perceived by the eye in like condition.

First, however, in order that we may determine how great is the inclination of the parallel circles and of that plane which is passed through that point of intersection and through the center of the globe at right angles to the median meridian in longitude, the great circle limiting the hemisphere before our eyes is taken, i. e. the line ABGD (see Figure II), and the semicircle of that

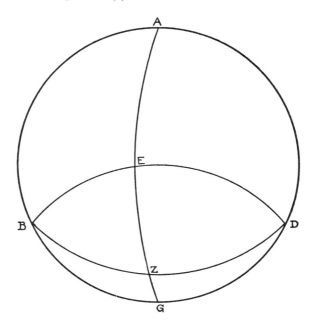

FIGURE II

meridian which divides the hemisphere in halves, is the line AEG, and the point in which, before our eyes, this semicircle intersects the parallel cutting the middle latitude, is the point E; then through the point E there is drawn the semicircle of another great circle BED so that it makes right angles with the semicircle AEG, its plane, as is apparent, falls upon the axis of the eyes; and with the arc EZ, of twenty-five and five-sixths degrees marked off (for by this many degrees, in fact, is the equator distant from the parallel passing through Syene, which is placed almost in the median latitude of the known world), there is also described, through the point Z, the semicircle BZD of the equator.

Therefore both the equatorial plane and the plane of the other parallels will appear inclined twenty-three and five-sixths degrees to the plane placed in the axis of the eyes; and of so many degrees is the arc EZ.

Now the lines AEZG and BED (see Figure III) are considered to stand in the place of the arcs, whence BE has the ratio to EZ that ninety has to twenty-three and five-sixths. And the line GA, passes through the center of the circle of which BZD is an arc, and it is proposed to find the ratio of the line HZ to the line EB. A straight line is drawn which bisects BZ at the point T, there is also then drawn TH, which plainly is the perpendicular to the line BZ. Now since the straight line BE is of ninety parts and EZ of twenty-three and five-sixths, the hypotenuse, BZ, will be ninety-three and one-tenth of the same; the angle BZE 150

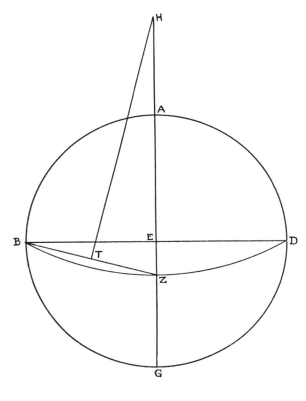

FIGURE III

and one-third (units) of the 360, which is the measure of two right angles; the other angle which is equal to THZ or twenty-nine and two-thirds of the same units. For the same reason, the ratio of the line HZ to ZT is that which 181 and five-sixths has to forty-six and eleven-twentieths. The straight line ZT has forty-six and eleven-twentieths parts as the straight line BE has ninety; therefore the straight line BE has ninety parts and ZE twenty-three and five-sixths, and we will have the straight line HZ measuring 181 and five-sixths such parts and H that point from which all parallels are drawn

when the delineation is to be made upon a plane.

Having settled these preliminaries let us draw again the map ABGD (see Figure IV), in which AB is twice the length of the line AG, and AE and EB equal. Draw EZ at right angles to AB.

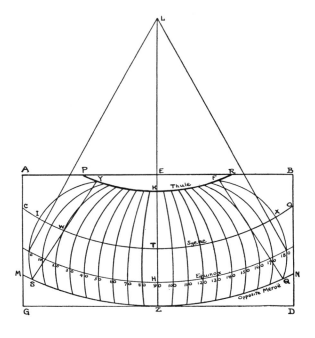

FIGURE IV

Now divide EZ into ninety parts, the number of degrees in a quadrant of a circle, then the line ZH which is marked off at sixteen and five-twelfths degrees, HT at twenty-three and five-sixths degrees, HK at sixty-three of the same; if we consider the point H as lying in the equinoctial line, then the point T will be that through which is drawn the parallel of Syene which is located almost in the middle of the habitable earth, and Z that through which will run the parallel which terminates the southern boundary of the world and is opposite the parallel of Meroe, and K is that through which is drawn the parallel which terminates the northern boundary of the known world running through the island of Thule. Now if we produce the line ZE, and in this produced line we make HL to have 181 and five-sixths of the same segments, or even 180 degrees (whether we take the one number or the other does not make much difference in our map's appearance), then let us draw the arcs PKR and CTO, and MZN, with the center L and intervals K, T, Z. In

this manner, let us keep the right ratio of the inclination of the parallels to the plane that corresponds to the line of vision when the line of vision is made to direct itself to the point T and is necessarily perpendicular to the plane of the map, so that in consequence the extreme parts of the map which are drawn opposite to one another are equally well discernible.

But, in order that longitude may agree with latitude, let it be our task to determine the eighteen meridians so that the number of semicircles may be complete, by which all longitude is embraced, since on a globe a great circle is made up of five parts such as the parallel of Thule has about two and one-fourth, that of Syene four and seven-twelfths and that of Meroe four and five-sixths, and since on either side of the meridian line ZK, at every third part of an equatorial hour, the number is completed; we take segments which on each of these three parallels are equivalent to one-third of an hour, or five degrees; that is, segments of which the line EZ contains ninety, and we make incisions on the three parallels at two and one-fourth units from K, at four and seven-twelfths from the point T, and at four and five-sixths from the point Z. Then when we have drawn the arcs through the three mutually corresponding points to represent the other meridians, as also the arcs SIY and FXQ, which are the limits of longitude, we shall also add the other arcs to represent the remaining parallels, again with the center L, and at intervals of as many segments as are to be made on the line ZK for the distance of the parallels from the equinox.

That a greater likeness to a sphere is achieved by this method than by the former will be self-evident. When the sphere stands motionless before the eyes, and is not revolved (which necessarily holds true for a plane map), and the eye rests on the middle of the object, one certain meridian which, because of the globe's position, lies at the middle of the plane passing through the axis of the eye, will exhibit the appearance of a straight line, while those on either side

appear inflexed with their concave side toward it, and the more so as they lie farther from it, which is also observed here with exact analogy, just as it is also seen that the symmetry of the parallel arcs keeps the proper ratio of one to another, not only in the equatorial line and the parallel of Thule (as was done in the former case), but in the others also, as closely as they can be made — the difficulty of doing this is evident — and that the conformity of latitude as a whole serve toward a true, general longitude ratio, not only in the parallel drawn through Rhodes, but in all of the parallels.

Now if we produce the straight line SWY, as was done in the earlier figure, the arc TW clearly makes a smaller ratio to the arcs ZS and KY than that proper one which is shown in this map and which occurs in the arc IT; and if we were to make this arc TW agree with the extension KZ of latitude, the arcs ZS and KY will be greater than those which agree with the line ZK just as arc IT itself is larger; and if we take the arcs ZS and KY to agree with the line ZK, the arc WT will be smaller than that corresponding to the line KZ, just as it is smaller than the arc IT.

Although for these reasons this method of drawing the map is the better one, yet it is less satisfactory in this respect, that it is not as simple as the other; because with that method, when the ruler is applied and carried over the map, given even one parallel drawn in and divided, individual localities can be put in place; here, however, since such a thing can no longer be done, by reason of the meridian line being inflexed at the middle, all of the other circles must be written in, and positions which lie inside those quadrate circles must be found by conjecture, after finding their relation from the given data to the whole sides which limit the areoles. Since this is so, even though for me both here and everywhere the better and more difficult scheme is preferable to the one which is poorer and easier, yet both methods are to me retained for the sake of those who, through laziness, are drawn to that certain easier method.

END OF BOOK ONE

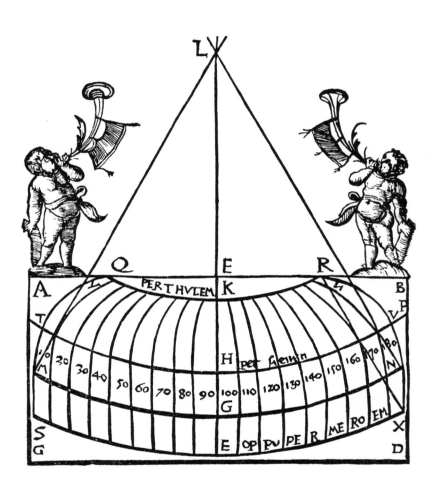

BOOK TWO

The Second Book contains the following:

A prologue of the particular descriptions, and a description of the western part of Europe including the several provinces and prefectures which are contained therein

Prologue of the particular descriptions

THAT which should be considered in general geography must here be explained, and also how the drawing of maps should be emended in keeping with the present knowledge of the known parts of our habitable earth, as far as it concerns the question of the relation of place to place, and also their likenesses, and the method of depicting them.

Beginning with the particular narration let us first make a statement respecting the degrees of longitude and latitude which have been assigned to well-known places. Approximately these are correct, since the traditions concerning them are continuously the same; that is, in the main the traditions agree. But as to the degrees ascribed to localities not as yet thoroughly explored, because of the incomplete and uncertain knowledge we have of these places, they should be computed rather from their nearness to the localities already laid down, and

the more thoroughly explored. This should be done lest any of those localities which have been inserted for completing the whole earth's picture should be without a fixed and definite place.

Therefore we have written on the margins of the pages notations respecting the different degrees of different places, and have used these as measurements, in the first place of longitude; then we have noted the degrees of latitude in such manner that if any corrections must be made, from a fuller investigation, they can be inserted in the adjoining spaces which have been left vacant between the separate pages.

Moreover we have selected the projection which we especially consider the best in the making of maps, this being the one in which we start at the right hand. The work may then proceed from places already inserted to those not yet inserted. This can best be carried out if we write in the northern latitudes before the southern ones, and the western before the eastern ones; since to the eye of the writer or reader the northern localities appear in the upper part, and the eastern appear on the right hand, on both the globe and the map of the habitable earth.

First of all, therefore, let us set down Europe which we separate from Libya by the Straits of Hercules, and from Asia, after we have put in the seas and the swamp of Myotis, by the river Tanis and by the meridian drawn through it to the unknown region; then let us put in Libya and place it likewise next to the sea which extends from the bay lying near Prasum, a promontory of Ethiopia, as far as the Gulf of Arabia. Let us separate Libya from Asia by the isthmus which extends from the interior of Heroopoliticus to our sea, and separates Egypt from Arabia and Judea. Let us do this that we may not divide Egypt, in making a division of the continent, by the Nile, because continents are bounded more properly, where it is possible, by seas than by rivers.

In the last place let us put in Asia, keeping the same plan as in the parts of each con-

tinent, of disposing of each of them according to its relation to the whole earth, and to the entire inhabited regions in the continents themselves, first writing in the coast that is most northern, then the western, and the seas and the islands that are nearest together, and those which in some particular are most worthy of mention.

After this let us distinguish, in the descriptions, the various prefectures, and provinces of the earth, treating them as we have before noted, in accord with the known positions of localities and according to what especially ought to be inserted, spurning the multitudinous traditional farrago concerning the peculiar qualities of their different inhabitants, except that, in the case of qualities renowned by general report, we make a short and suitable note on the religion and manners. In this way the opportunity will be given to any one, who desires it, for drawing the parts of the earth in maps according to the particular prefectures and provinces, one or many, and the right relation of the places of each other on the maps will be preserved, together with the right size and the right shape. Nor will it make much difference if in these maps we use parallel meridian straight lines instead of curved lines, provided we keep the proper proportion of the meridian degrees to the degrees marked on the great circle, that is the equator, which is in the middle of every map.

Having stated these things, let us begin our particular descriptions with the western part of Europe according to its provinces or prefectures.

CHAPTER I

*Location of Hibernia island of Britannia
(First map of Europe)*

A DESCRIPTION of the north coast, beyond which is located the Hyperborean ocean.

Boreum promontory	11	61	
Vennicnium promontory	12 50	61 20	
mouth of the Vidua river	13	61	
mouth of the Argita river	14 30	61 30	
Rhobogdium promontory	16 20	61 30	

The *Vennicni* inhabit the west coast; next to them and toward the east are the *Rhobogdi*.

A description of the west side, which borders on the Western ocean from the Boreum promontory which is in

promontory which is in	11	61	
mouth of the Ravius river	11 20	60 40	
Magnata city	11 15	60 15	
mouth of the Libnius river	10 30	60	
mouth of the Ausoba river	10 30	59 30	
mouth of the Senus river	9 30	59 30	
mouth of the Duris river	9 40	58 40	
mouth of the Iernus river	8	58	
Southern promontory	7 40	57 45	

The *Erdini* inhabit the coast next to the *Vennicni*, and between these are the *Magnatae;* then the *Autini;* and the *Gangani;* below whom are the *Vellabori.*

Description of the south coast, which adjoins the Vergionius ocean, from the southern promontory which is in

ern promontory which is in	7 40	57 40	
mouth of the Dabrona river	11 15	57	
mouth of the Birgus river	12 30	57 30	
Sacrum promontory	14	57 50	

The side next to the *Vellabori* the *Hiberni* inhabit, above whom are the *Usdiae* and more towards the east are the *Brigantes.*

A description of the east side touching the ocean which is called Hibernicus, beginning at the Sacrum promontory which is in

in	14	57 50	
mouth of the Modonnus river	13 40	58 40	
Manapia town	13 30	58 40	
mouth of the Oboca river	13 10	59	
Eblana town	14	59 30	
mouth of the Bubindas river	14 40	59 40	
Isamnium promontory	15	60	
mouth of the Vinderis river	15	60 15	
mouth of the Logia river	15 20	60 40	

Next to this is the Robogdium promontory.

On the side next to the *Robogdi* dwell the *Darini,* below whom are the *Volunti;* then the *Eblani;* then the *Cauci;* below whom are the *Manapi;* then the *Coriondi* who dwell above the *Brigantes.*

The following are the inland towns:

Regia	13	60 20	
Rhaeba	12	59 45	
Laberus	13 59	15	
Macolicum	11 30	58 40	
another Regia	11	59 15	
Dunum	12 30	58 45	
Hibernis	11	58 10	

Above Hibernia are the Ebuda islands five in number, the largest of which toward the west is called Ebuda 15 62

next to this toward the east likewise is Ebuda

island	15	40	62	
then Rhicina	17		62	
then Malaeus	17	30	62	30
then Epidium	18	30	62	

Toward the east of Hibernia are these islands:

Monaoeda island	17	40	61	30
Mona island	15		57	40
Adru which is barren	15		59	30
Limnu which is barren	15		59	

CHAPTER II

*Location of Albion island of Britannia
(First map of Europe)*

A DESCRIPTION of the northern coast, above which is the Duecaledonius ocean.

Novantarum peninsula, and promontory of the same name	21		61	40
Rerigonius bay	20	30	60	50
Vindogara bay	21	20	60	30
Clota estuary	22	15	59	20
Lemannonius bay	24		60	
Epidium promontory	23		60	40
mouth of the Longus river	24	30	60	40
mouth of the Itis river	27		60	40
Volas bay	29		60	30
mouth of the Navarus river	30		60	30
Tarvedum or Orcas promontory	31	20	60	15

Description of the east side which borders on the Hibernian ocean and the Vergionius ocean. From the Novantian promontory 21 61 40

mouth of the Abravannus river	19	20	61	
Iena estuary	19		60	30
mouth of the Devas river	18		60	
mouth of the Novius river	18	20	59	30
Ituna estuary	18	30	58	45
Moricambe estuary	17	30	58	20
Setantiorum harbor	17	20	57	45
Belisama estuary	17	30	57	20
Seteia estuary	17		57	
Caeanganorum promontory	15		56	

mouth of the Toesobis river	15	40	56	20
mouth of the Stuccia river	15	20	55	30
mouth of the Tuerobis river	15		55	
Octapitarum promontory	14	20	54	30
mouth of the Tobius river	15	30	54	30
mouth of the Ratostabius river	16	30	54	30
Sabrina estuary	17	20	54	30
Uxella estuary	16		53	30
Herculis promontory	14		52	45
Antivestaeum or Bolerium promontory	11	30	52	30
Damnonium or Ocrium promontory	12		51	30

Description of the south side below which is the Britannicus ocean. After the Ocrium promontory is the mouth of the Cenio river 14 51 51 45

mouth of the Tamarus river	15	40	52	10
mouth of the Iscas river	17	40	52	20
mouth of the Alaunus river	17	40	52	40
Great harbor	19		53	
mouth of the Trisantonis river	20	20	53	
New harbor	21		53	30
Cantium promontory	22		54	

A description of the eastern and the southern side next to which is the Germanicus ocean. After the Tarvedum promontory, or Orcades, by which it is known,

Virvedrum promontory	31		60	
Verubium promontory	30	30	59	40
mouth of the Ila river	30		59	40
Ripa alta (high bank)	29		59	40
Varar estuary	27		59	40
mouth of the Loxa river	27	30	59	40
Tuesis estuary	27		59	
mouth of the Caelis river	27		58	45
Taezalon promontory	27	30	58	30
mouth of the Deva river	26		58	30
mouth of the Tina river	24		58	30
Boderia estuary	22	30	59	
mouth of the Alaunus river	21	20	58	30
mouth of the Vedra river	20	10	58	30
Dunum bay	20	15	57	30
Gabrantuicorum bay with many harbors	21		57	
Ocelus promontory	21	15	56	40
mouth of the Abi river	21		56	30
Metaris estuary	20	30	55	40
mouth of the Gariennus river	20	50	55	40

Promontorium	21 15	55	5
mouth of the Sidumanis			
river	20 10	55	
Tamesa estuary	20 30	54	30
Next to this the Cantium			
promontory	22	54	

The *Novantae* dwell on the side toward the north below the peninsula of this name, among whom are the following towns:

Locopibia	19	60	20
Rerigonium	20 10	60	40

Below are the *Selgovae*, among whom are the following towns:

Carbantorigum	19	59	30
Uxellum	18 30	59	20
Corda	20	59	40
Trimontium	19	59	

From these toward the east, but more northerly, are the *Damnoni*, among whom are the following towns:

Colanica	20 45	59	10
Vindogara	21 20	60	
Coria	21 30	59	20
Alauna	22 45	59	50
Lindum	23	59	30
Victoria	23 30	59	

Further south are the *Otalini*, among whom are the following towns:

Coria	20 10	59	
Alauna	23	58	40
Bremenium	21	58	45

Next to the *Damnoni*, but more toward the east near the Epidium promontory are the *Epidi* and next to these the *Cerones*; then the *Carnonacae*, and the *Caereni* but more toward the east; and in the extreme east dwell the *Cornavi*; from the Lemannonis bay as far as the Varar estuary are the *Caledoni*, and above these is the Caledonian forest, from which toward the east are the *Decantae*, and next to these the *Lugi* extending to the Cornavi boundary, and above the *Lugi* are the *Smertae*; below Caledonia are the *Vacomagi*, among whom are the following towns:

Bannatia	24	59	30
Tamia	25	59	20
Pinnata camp	27 15	59	20
Tuesis	26 45	59	10

Below these toward the west are the *Venicones*, whose town is

Orrea	24	58	45

More toward the east are the *Taezali* and the town Devana | 26 | 59 |

Below the *Selgovae* and *Otadini* are the *Brigantes* extending to both seas, among whom are the following towns:

Epiacum	18 30	58	30
Vinovium	17 45	58	
Caturactonium	20	58	
Calatum	19	57	45
Isurium	20	57	40
Rigodunum	18	57	30
Olicana	19	57	30
Eboracum, Legio VI			
Victrix	20	57	20
Camulodunum	18	57	45

Near which on the Opportunum bay are the *Parisi* and the town

Petuaria	20 40	56	40

Below these are the *Brigantes* but some distance toward the west are the *Ordovices*, among whom are the towns

Mediolanum	16 45	56	40
Brannogenium	16 45	56	15

From these toward the east are the *Cornavi* among whom are the towns

Deva, Legio XX Victrix	17 30	56	45
Viroconium	16 45	55	45

Next to these are the *Coritani*, among whom are the towns

Lindum	18 40	56	30
Ratae	18	55	30

Next are the *Catuvellauni*, among whom are the towns

Salinae	20 45	55	50
Urolanium	19 20	55	30

Next to these are the *Iceni*, whose town is called Venta | 20 30 | 55 | 20 |

Farther eastward and near the Tamesae estuary are the *Trinovantes*, and the town

Camulodunum	21	55	

Below the peoples we have mentioned, but more toward the west are the *Demetae*, whose towns are

Luentinum	15 45	55	10
Maridunum	15 30	54	40

More toward the east are the *Silures* whose town is Bullaeum | 16 50 | 55 |

Next to these are the *Dobuni*, and their town Corinium | 18 | 54 | 10 | then the *Atrebati* and their town Caleva | 19 | 54 | 15 |

Next to these, but farther eastward, are the *Canti* among whom are the towns

Londinium	20	54	
Daruernum	21	54	
Rutupie	21 45	54	

Below the *Atrebati*, and the *Canti* are the *Regni* and the town

Noeomagus	19	45	53	5

Below the *Dobuni* are the *Belgae* and the towns

Iscalis	16		53	40
Aquae calidae (hot springs)	17	20	53	40
Venta	18	40	53	

Toward the west and south of these are the *Durotriges* whose town is

Dunium	18		52	40

Next to these, but more to the west, are the *Dumnoni* whose towns are

Voliba	14	45	52	
Uxella	15		52	45
Tamara	15		52	15
Isca, where is located				
Legio II Agusta	17	30	52	45

The islands which are near Albion island and the Orcades promontory are

Scetis island	32	40	60	45
Dumna island	30		61	20

Above these islands are the Orcades, about thirty in number, the middle of which is in

	30		61	40

Far above these is the island Thule. The part of this which extends much toward the west is in

	29		63

that which is farthest eastward is in

	31	40	63

that which is farthest northward is in

	30	20	63	15

that which is farthest southward is in

	30	20	62	40
the middle is in	30	20	63	

Eastward from the Trinovantes region there are two islands

Toliapis	23		54	20
Counus island	24		54	30

Below Magnus Portus (Great harbor) is the island Vectis, the middle of which is in

	19	20	52	20

CHAPTER III

Location of Baetica Hispania (Second map of Europe)

IN Hispania, which in Greek is called Iberia, there are three provinces, Baetica, Lusitania, and Tarraconensis.

The side of Baetica which is on the west and the north is terminated by Lusitania and a part of Tarraconensis.

The following is a description of this side: on the east

mouth of the Ana river	4	20	37	30

where the river turns from the east

	6	20	39

the locality where the river touches the border of Lusitania

	9	39

the boundary line drawn thence along Tarraconensis, which extends as far as the Balearic sea has its terminus in

	12		37	15

the sources of the river are located in

	11	40

The southern side of Baetica is terminated by the Outer sea and the Hercules strait, and by the Inner or Iberian sea. A description of this side is the following:

From the mouth of the Ana river in the Outer sea are

the *Turdetani*

Onoba estuary	4	40	37	20
Eastern mouth of the				
Baetis river	5	20	37	
sources of the river	12		38	30
Estuary near Asta	6		36	45

the *Turduli*

Menesthus harbor	6		36	20

promontory, where a bay begins, and in this is the Temple of Juno

	5	45	36	5

mouth of the Baelonis river

	6	10	36	10
Baelon town	6	15	36	5

The *Bastuli* who are also called *Phoenicians*

Menralia	6	30	36	5
Transducta	6	50	36	5
Barbesola town	7	15	36	10
Carteia	7	30	36	10

Calpe mountain (Gibraltar) and pillars of the inner sea

	7	30	36	15

In the Iberian sea mouth of the Barbesola river

	7	40	36	20
Suel	8		36	55

mouth of the Salduba river

	8	30	37	
Malaca (Malaga)	8	50	37	30
Maenoba	9	15	37	15
Sex	9	45	37	15
Selambina	10	15	37	15
Projecting land (procursus)	10	50	37	5
Abdara	10	45	37	10
Great harbor (Portus Magnus)	11	20	37	5

Charidemi promontory   11 30   36 50

The remaining part of the province, turning from the south, is terminated on the Balearic sea by the line which runs from the mentioned Charidemi promontory to the terminal position, near which is

Baria town   11 45   37 10

The *Bastuli* inhabit the sea coast from Menralia to Baria, as we have said; above whom, in the interior, which is adjacent to Tarraconensis, the *Turduli* dwell, and their interior cities are

Setia	9	10	38	50
Ilurgis	9	30	38	40
Vogia	9		38	30
Calpurniana	9	45	38	10
Caecila	9	15	38	10
Baniana	10		38	15
Corduba	9	20	38	5
Ulia	9	30	38	
Obulcum	10	10	38	
Arcilacis	8	45	37	45
Detunda	8	40	37	25
Murgis	8	15	37	20
Salduba	8	45	37	20
Tucci	8		37	10
Salar	7	30	37	
Barla	7		36	40
Ebora	6	15	36	55
Onoba	6	10	36	20
Illipula magna (greater)	9	40	38	
Selia	9	40	37	45
Vescis	9	30	37	30
Oscua	9	50	37	30
Artigis	9	40	37	25
Callicula	10	10	37	45
Lacibis	10	15	37	30
Sacilis	10	25	37	50
Lacippo	10	15	37	20
Illiberis	11		37	40

The *Turdetani* inhabit the interior region bordering on Lusitania, whose towns are

Canaca	4	40	38	
Seria	4	40	37	45
Osca	5		37	15
Caeriana	5	10	38	15
Urium	5	40	38	20
Illipula	6		38	
Segida	6	30	37	45
Ptuci	5	30	37	30
Sala	5	40	37	30
Nabrissa	5	40	37	20
Ugia	5	30	37	10
Asta	6		37	

Corticata	6	5	38	20
Laelia	6	30	38	5
Italica	7		38	
Maxilua	6	20	37	50
Ucia	7		37	40
Carissa	6	30	37	30
Calduba	6	40	37	15
Paesula	7		37	10
Saguntia	6	30	37	5
Asindum	6	30	36	50
Nertobriga	7		38	50
Contributa	7	40	38	55
Regina	7	10	38	55
Cursu	8		38	40
Mirobriga	7		38	25
Spoletinum	7	20	38	20
Illipa magna (greater)	7	40	38	10
Hispalis	7	15	37	50
Obucola	8		37	45
Oleastrum	7	10	37	30
Ursone	7	30	37	5
Baesippo	7	15	37	5
Fornacis	8	30	38	50
Arsa	8	40	38	35
Asyla	8	35	38	25
Astigis	8	15	38	20
Carmonia	8	10	38	

Celtic Baetica

Arucci	5	50	38	50
Arunda	6	30	38	50
Curgia	6	30	38	40
Acinippo	6	30	38	25
Vama	6	15	38	25

The mountains in Baetica are called the Marianus, the central part of which is in   6   37 40 and the Illipula the central part of which is located in   7 20   37 30

There is an island adjacent to Hispanic Baetica in the Outer sea, in which is the town Gadira, the location of which is in   5 10   36 10

CHAPTER IV

Location of Lusitania Hispania
(Second map of Europe)

THE south side of Lusitania, as we have indicated, is the northern boundary of Baetica; the north side borders on Tarraconensis along the western part of the Dorius river, the mouth of which opens into the Outer sea in the locality   5 20   41 50

where the river first touches the borders of
Lusitania is in 9 10 41 50
sources of the river are in 11 40 41 40

The eastern side also borders on Tarraconensis, and its termini as we have said, are
near the Anas river and the Dorius river.

The west side, which extends along the
Western ocean, is thus described:

After the mouth of the Anas river
the *Turditani*

Balsa	3	40	37	45
Ossonoba	3		37	50
Sacrum (Sacred) prom-ontory	2	30	38	15
mouth of Calipodis river	5		39	
Salacia	5	5	39	25
Caetobrix	4	55	39	30

the *Lusitani*

Barbarium promontory	4	50	39	50
Oliosipon	5	10	40	15
mouth of the Tagus river	5	30	40	30

that part of the river which touches Tarraconensis is in 9 40 30
sources of the river 11 40 40 45

Luna mountain, prom-ontory	5		40	40
mouth of the Monda river	5	10	40	50
mouth of the Vacus river	5	10	41	20

Next is the mouth of the Dorius river
in 5 20 41 50

The *Turdetani* inhabit the vicinity of the
Sacred promontory, whose interior cities in
Lusitania are

Pax Julia	5	20	39	
Julia Myrtilis	5	15	38	45

The *Celtici* inhabit that region which
from these (towns) lies toward the interior;
their cities in Lusitania are

Laccobriga	5	45	40	15
Caepiana	5	20	40	
Braetoleum	6		40	
Mirobriga	5	20	39	45
Arcobriga	5	40	39	45
Meribriga	6	10	39	40
Catraleucus	5	40	39	20
Arandis	6	10	39	5

Above these are the *Lusitani*, whose interior towns are

Lavare	5	30	41	45
Aritium	5	40	41	30
Selium	6		41	20
Elbocoris	6	30	41	15
Araducta	6	40	41	30
Verurium	7	15	41	5

Velladis	6	40	41	5
Aeminium	7	20	41	
Chretina	5	30	40	40
Arabriga	5	40	40	30
Scalabis colonia	6		40	55
Tacubis	6	20	40	45
Concordia	6	40	40	30
Talabriga	7	30	40	45
Rusticana	7	40	40	30
Mendiculeia	6	50	40	15
Caurium	6	40	40	
Turmogum	8		40	15
Burdua	7	20	40	
Colarnum	6	50	39	45
Sallaecus	6	40	39	30
Ammaea	7		39	20
Ebura	7		39	5
Norba Caesarina	7	50	39	55
Liciniana	7	20	39	40
Augusta Emerita	8		39	30
Evandria	7	20	39	15
Geraea	7	40	39	5
Caecilia Gemellina	8	40	39	30
Capasa	8	40	39	10

The *Vettones* are farthest east, whose
towns are

Lancia oppidana	8	30	41	40
Cottaeobriga	8		41	30
Salmantica	8	50	41	50
Augustobriga	8		41	15
Ocelum	8	20	41	15
Capara	8	30	41	
Manliana	8	20	41	
Laconimurgi	8	20	40	45
Diobriga	8	40	40	40
Obila	8	50	40	25
Lama	8	30	40	5

Island adjacent to Lusitania

Londobris	3		41

CHAPTER V

*Location of Tarraconensis Hispania
(Second map of Europe)*

THE western side of Tarraconensis,
which borders on the Western ocean,
is thus described: after the mouth of the
Dorius river, there follows
the *Callaici Bracares*

mouth of the Avus river	5	30	42	15
Avarus promontory	5	30	42	30
mouth of the Nebis river	5	40	42	45
mouth of the Limius river	5	30	43	15

mouth of the Minius river	5	20	43	40
sources of the rivers	11	30	44	15
the *Callaici Lucensi*				
Orvium promontory	5	30	44	
mouth of the Via river	5	40	44	20
mouth of the Tamara river	5	40	44	40
the *Artabri*				
Artabri harbor	5	20	45	
Nerium promontory	5	15	45	10

The north side, above which is the ocean called Cantabrius, is described as follows: after the Nerium promontory there is another promontory in which are the altars of the Sesti.

Promontory	5	40	45	30
mouth of the Virus river	6	15	45	30
next a promontory	6	30	45	30

In the Great harbor of the *Callaici Lucensi*

Flavius Brigantius	6	45	45	

Lapatia Coru promontory which is called

Trilecum	8	15	45	50
mouth of the Mearus river	9		45	45
mouth of the Nabius river	10	20	45	40
mouth of the Nabiala-vionis river	11	20	45	45
the *Paesici*				
Flavionavia	11	45	45	25
mouth of the Naelus river	12		45	30
the *Cantabri*				
Noega Ucesia	13		45	30
the *Autrigones*				
mouth of the Nerva river	13	10	44	40
Flaviobriga	13	30	44	15
the *Caristi*				
mouth of the Deva river	13	45	44	25
the *Varduli*				
Menosca	14	20	45	
the *Vascones*				
Oeasso town	15	10	45	5
Oeasso promontory	15	10	45	50

The side toward the south is terminated by the Pyrenees, thence extending from the mentioned promontory on the coast of our sea, where has been erected a Temple of Venus, located in

	20	20	42	20

The mountains (Pyrenees) turn slightly toward Hispania, and the middle of the bend is toward Tarraconensis

in	17		43

On the other side of Tarraconensis, that which borders on Lusitania and Baetica has been described, the remaining part which borders on the Balearic sea and looks toward the south, is described as follows: it extends to the boundary of

Baetica in	12		37	15

On the sea coast of the *Bastitani* is

Urci	12		37	25

On the sea coast of the *Contestani* are

Lucentum	12	10	37	30
Cartaga nova (new Carthage)	12	15	37	55
Scombraria promontory	12	55	38	5
mouth of the Taberis river	12	30	38	30
Alona	12	40	38	55
mouth of the Saetabis river	13		38	45
Illicitanus harbor	13	30	38	45
mouth of the Sucronis river	14		38	50

On the sea coast of the *Edetani* are

mouth of the Pallantia	14	40	38	55
mouth of the Turis river	15		39	
Dianïum	15	45	39	30

On the maritime coast of the *Ilercaones* are

Tenebrius promontory	15	55	39	40
Tenebrius harbor	15	30	40	
mouth of the Iberus river	16	40	30	
middle of this river	14		42	
sources of the river	12	30	44	

On the sea coast of the *Cosetani* are

Tarraco	16	20	40	40
Subur	16	50	40	45

On the sea coast of the *Laetani* are

Barcinon	17	15	41	
mouth of the Rubricatus river	17	30	41	
Betulon	17	50	41	20
Lunarium promontory	18	30	41	30
Diluron	18		41	45
Blanda	18	15	42	

On the sea coast of the *Indigetes*

mouth of the Sambroca river	18	30	42	10
Emporia	18	45	42	20
mouth of the Clodianus river	19		42	30
Rhode town	19	30	42	30

and then as we have said

Temple of Venus	20	20	42	20

The mountains in Tarraconensis are called the Vindius, the extremities of which

are in	9		45	
and	11	30	44	30

the Edulius, the extremities of which are

in	14	40	42	30
and	16		43	

the Idubeda, the extremities of which are

in	14	41	30
and	14 20	39	

the Ortospeda, the extremities of which are

in	12	37	40
and	14	39	40

On the Nerium promontory the *Artabri* dwell, whose towns are

Claudiomerum	5 45	45	10
Novium	6 10	44	45

Near these are the *Callaici Lucensi*, whose interior towns are

Burum	8 15	45	5
Olina	8 30	48	30
Vica	9 20	45	20
Libunca	10 10	45	20
Pintia	10 10	45	5
Caronium	7	44	45
Turuptiana	6 20	44	45
Glandomirum	7	44	30
Ocelum	8 20	44	25
Turriga	8 50	44	35
of the *Capori*			
Iria flavia	6 25	44	30
Lucus augusti	7 25	44	25
of the *Cilini*			
Aqua calida (hot spring)	6 20	44	20
of the *Lemavi*			
Dactonium	7 30	44	
of the *Baedyi*			
Flavia lambris	7 20	44	45
of the *Seurri*			
Talamina	8 30	44	30
Five Springs	8 30	45	10

Asturia joins this on the east side, and the towns in this province are

Lucus asturum	11	45	
Labernis	11	44	30
Interamnium	10 15	44	20
Argenteola	9 20	43	45
Lanciati	9 20	43	30
Maliaca	10 20	44	
Gigia	11 30	43	45
Bergidum river	8 30	44	10
Interamnium river	9	44	
Legio VII Germanica	9	43	30
of the *Brigaecini*			
Brigaecium	10	44	50
of the *Baedunenses*			
Bedunia	9 50	44	25
of the *Orniacori*			
Intercatia	11 10	44	15
of the *Lungonum*			
Paelontium	11 40	44	50

of the *Selini*

Nardinium	10 20	43	45
of the *Supertati*			
Petavonium	9 30	43	40
of the *Amacori*			
Asturica Augusta	9 30	44	
of the *Tibures*			
Nemetobriga	7 30	43	45
of the *Gigurri*			
Forum Gigurrum	8	43	45

The land between the Minius and the Dorius rivers, near the sea, the *Callaici Bracari* inhabit, whose towns are

Bracaraugusta	6	43	40
Caladunum	6 30	43	30
Pinetus	6 50	43	35
Complutica	8 20	43	25
Tuntobriga	8 30	43	25
Araducca	6	41	55
of the *Turodori*			
Aqua Flavia	6 30	43	25
of the *Nemetatari*			
Volobriga	6	42	35
of the *Calerinori*			
Celiobriga	6	42	20
of the *Bibilori*			
Forum Bibilori	7 20	43	20
of the *Limicori*			
Forum Limicori	6 50	42	45
of the *Gruiori*			
Tuda	8 20	42	45
of the *Luancori*			
Merua	7 30	42	40
of the *Quacernori*			
Aquae Quacernori	7 20	42	20
of the *Lubanori*			
Cambetum	8 10	42	20
of the *Narbasori*			
Forum Nabasori	8	42	

Around these dwell the *Vaccaei*, whose towns are

Bargiacis	9 45	43	25
Intercatia	10 15	43	25
Viminacium	11	43	30
Porta Augusta	9 40	43	20
Autraca	10	43	15
Lacobriga	10 20	43	20
Avia	10 20	43	
Segontia Paramica	9 30	43	
Gella	9 40	42	55
Albocela	9 5	42	40
Rauda	9 20	42	35
Segisama Julia	9 50	42	40
Pallantia	10 30	42	30

Eldana	9		42	20
Cougium	9	40	42	25
Cauca	10		42	20
Octodurum	9	40	42	10
Pintia	10	10	42	
Sentica	9		41	55
Sarabris	9	40	41	55

Toward the east of Asturia dwell the *Cantabri*, whose inland towns are

Concana	12	10	44	55
Ottaviolca	12	40	44	45
Argenomescum	12		44	30
Vadinia	11	50	44	25
Vellica	12	30	44	15
Camarica	11	40	44	45
Juliobriga	12	10	44	
Moroeca	11	45	43	50

Below these are the *Morbogi*, whose towns are

Bravum	12		43	40
Sisaraca	11	30	43	30
Deobrigula	11	50	43	25
Ambisna	11	10	43	5
Segisamum	12		43	10

To the east of these and of Cantabria dwell the *Autrigones*, whose inland towns are

Uxama Barca	13		44	15
Segisamonculum	13		43	55
Vircesca	12	30	43	50
Antecuia	13		43	40
Diobriga	13	15	43	30
Vindelia	12	40	43	15
Salionca	13		43	5

Beyond the *Murbogi* are the *Pelendones*, whose towns are

Visontium	11	40	42	50
Augustobriga	11	30	42	40
Savia	12	30	42	40

Below the *Autrigones* are the *Berones*, whose towns are

Tritium Metallum	13		42	50
Oliba	13		42	40
Varea	13	30	42	45

Below the *Pelendones* and the *Berones* are the *Arevacces*, whose towns are

Confluenta	11		42	35
Clunia colonia	11		42	
Termes	11	30	42	25
Uxama Argaela	11	30	42	
Segortia Lanca	12	30	41	40
Veluca	11	50	41	55
Tucris	12	40	42	30
Numantia	12	30	41	50

Seguvia	13	30	42	25
Nova Augusta	13	15	42	10

Back from the *Vaccaei* and the *Arevacces*, toward the south, dwell the *Carpetani*, among whom are the towns

Illurbida	9	40	41	40
Egelesta	10	30	41	40
Ilarcuris	11		41	35
Varada	11	30	41	30
Thermida	12		41	35
Titulcia	10	20	41	20
Mantua	11	40	41	15
Toletum	10		41	
Complutum	10	50	41	5
Caracca	11	20	40	50
Libora	9	25	40	45
Ispinum	10	15	40	45
Metercosa	10	20	40	35
Barnacis	11		40	30
Alternia	10	30	40	25
Paterniana	9	50	40	15
Rigusa	10	30	40	15
Laminium	10	50	39	55

Toward the east from these are the *Celtiberi*, whose towns are

Belsinum	13	40	41	55
Turiasso	13	30	41	50
Nertobriga	14		41	50
Bilbis	13	45	41	30
Arcobriga	13	5	41	25
Caesada	12	10	41	
Mediolum	13		41	
Attacum	13	30	41	5
Ergavica	12	20	40	45
Segobriga	13	30	40	40
Condabora	13	50	40	30
Bursada	12	45	40	35
Laxta	13	20	40	30
Valeria	12	30	40	25
Istonium	11	30	40	15
Alaba	12		40	20
Libana	12	20	40	10
Urcesa	11	40	39	45

Toward the south from these and from the *Carpetani* are the *Oretani*, and the towns

Salaria	9	20	40	
Sisapone	10		39	55
Oretum Germanorum	9	10	39	40
Aemiliana	10		39	40
Mirobriga	9	30	39	30
Salica	10	40	39	25
Libisosa	11	25	39	30
Castulo	9	30	39	

Lupparia	9 45	39	
Mentesa	10 25	39	
Cervaria	11	39	5
Biatia	10	38	45
Laccuris	10 50	38	30
Tuia	10 20	38	30

Below the eastern part of the *Celtiberi* are the *Lobetani* whose town is

Lobetum	13	40 20	

Below these and next to the *Oretani* are the *Bastitani* whose interior towns are

Pucialia	13 20	39	50
Salaria	13	39	40
Turbula	13 30	39	45
Saltiga	12	39	30
Bigerra	12 30	39	35
Abula	11 40	39	15
Asso	12	39	10
Bergula	11 20	38	55
Carca	11	38	35
Ilunum	11 30	38	40
Arcilacis	11 20	38	20
Segisa	11 30	38	30
Orcelis	11 30	38	5
Vergilia	11 30	37	35
Acci	11 45	37	35

Next to these and dwelling on the coast are the *Contestani*, and the inland towns

Menlaria	13 30	39	15
Valentia	14	39	5
Saetabis	13 10	39	
Saetabicula	13 40	38	55
Ilicis	12 20	38	30
Iaspis	12 20	38	55

Toward the east of these, of the *Bastitani*, and of the *Celtiberi*, are the *Edetani*, whose inland towns are

Caesaraugusta	14 30	41	30
Bernaba	14 10	41	15
Ebora	14 40	41	
Belia	14 10	40	45
Arsi	14 40	40	40
Damania	14 30	40	30
Leonica	14 40	40	15
Osicerda	14 15	40	10
Etobesa	14 20	39	45
Lassira	14 50	39	40
Edeta or Liria	14 25	39	25
Saguntum	14 35	39	20

Further toward the east of these are the *Ilercaones* and the inland towns

Carthago vetus (ancient)	15 20	41	20
Biscargis	14 55	41	10
Theava	15 15	40	40

Adeba	15 40	40	30
Tiariulia	15 30	40	25
Sigarra	15 5	40	15
Dertosa	15 15	40	

In the region which is included between the Iberus and the Pyrenees adjoining the *Austrigones*, through whose territory a large river flows, are located the *Caristi* toward the east, and the inland towns are

Suestasium	13 40	44	
Tullica	13 40	43	45
Velia	13 55	43	20

Below these are the *Berones* whose towns are

Trituum	13	42	50
Varra	13 30	42	40
Iliba	13	42	30

To the east of these are the *Varduli* and the inland towns are

Gebala	14	43	50
Gabalaeca	14 30	43	45
Tullonium	13 50	43	30
Alba	14 35	43	30
Seguntia Paramica	14 30	43	15
Tritium Tuboricam	13 40	43	10
Thabuca	14	42	50

Next to these are the *Vascones* whose inland towns are

Iturissa	15 25	43	55
Pompelon	15	43	45
Bituris	15 30	43	45
Andelus	15	43	30
Nemanturista	15 35	43	25
Curnonium	14 50	43	15
Iacca	15 30	43	15
Gracuris	15	43	
Calagorina	14 40	42	55
Cascantum	15	42	45
Ergavica	14 30	42	35
Tarraga	14 45	42	30
Muscaria	14 20	42	25
Setia	14 40	42	15
Alavona	14 40	41	55

And next beyond these are the *Ilergetes*, whose interior towns are

Bergusia	16 30	43	
Celsa	16	42	45
Bergidum	15 30	42	30
Eraga	16 10	42	30
Succosa	15 10	42	30
Osca	16	42	30
Burtina	15 10	41	55
Gallica Flavia	15 30	41	40

Orgia	15	41	30
Ilerda	15 35	41	25

Below these, but toward the east, are the *Ceretaii* whose town is

Julia Libica	17 20	42	45

The *Ausetani* are on the west of these, and the towns are

Aquae Calidae (hot springs)	16 40	42	30
Ausa	16 10	42	10
Baecula	17	42	15
Gerunda	17 55	42	15

And next to these are the *Castellani* whose interior towns are

Sebendunum	16 40	42	10
Bassi	17 55	42	5
Egosa	17 10	41	55
Beseda	17 30	41	50

To the west of these are the *Iaccetani* whose towns are

Lesa	16 20	42	
Udura	16 30	41	45
Ascerris	16	41	40
Setelsis	16 40	41	45
Telobis	16	41	30
Ceresus	15 40	41	20
Bacasis	16 45	41	25
Iessus	15 30	41	
Anabis	16 20	41	
Cinna	15 50	40	50

The interior towns of the *Indegetari* are

Deciana	18 40	42	35
Iuncaria	18 30	42	20

and the interior town of the *Laetanori* is

Rubricata	17 20	41	25

The islands adjacent to Tarraconensis, in the Cantabrian ocean are three peaks which are called the Trileuci, the middle of which is in

	9	46 45

In the Western ocean are the Cassiterides islands, ten in number, the middle of which is in

	4	45 30

and two islands which are called the Islands of the Gods in

	4 40	43 30

In the Balearic sea are the Pitysusa islands the lesser of which is called

Ophiusis	14 50	38	20

the greater of which is called Ebyssus, with a town of the same name

	14	38	5

And the two Balearic islands, called in Greek the Gymnesia, in the larger of which are two towns

Palma	16 10	39	15
Polentia	16 45	39	15

In the lesser of these islands are the towns

Iamna	17 10	39	30
Mago	17 30	39	30

CHAPTER VI

Location of Aquitania Gallia
(Third map of Europe)

GALLIA is divided into four provinces, Aquitania, Lugdunensis, Belgica, and Narbonensis, and the places along its coast follow in this order: after the western promontory, terminating the Pyrenees, which is located in

located in	15	45	50
mouth of the Aturis river	16 45	44	30
mouth of the Sigmatis river	17	45	20
Curianum promontory	16 30	46	
mouth of the Garumna	17 30	46	30
the middle of its course	18	45	20
source of the river	19 30	44	15
Santonum harbor	16 30	46	45
Santonum promontory	16	47	15
mouth of the Canentelus river	17 15	47	45
Pictonium promontory	17	48	
Sicor harbor	17 30	48	15
mouth of the Liger river	17 40	48	30

On the north it is bounded by that part of the Lugdunensis province which is along the river we call the Liger (Loire) as far as that locality where it turns southward in

	20	48 30

The eastern boundary is the Lugdunensis province running along the river Liger as far as its source in

	20	44 30

The south is bounded in part by the Pyrenees, and extends along Narbonensis from the source of the Liger river to that terminus in the Pyrenees to which we have referred, then along that part of the Pyrenees which extends to the Oeasso promontory.

The *Pictones* inhabit that part of Aquitania farthest north along the river and the sea, whose towns are

Ratiatum	17 50	48	20
Limonum	18	47	50

Below these are the *Santones*, and the interior town is

Mediolanium	17 40	46	45

Below these are the *Bituriges Vibisci* whose towns are

Noviomagus	17 40	46	15
Burdigala	18	45	30

Below these extending as far as the Pyrenees are the *Tarbeli* and their town

Aquae Agustae	17	44	40

Inland below the *Pictones* are the *Limovici* and the town

Augustoritum	19 40	47	45

Below these are the *Cadurci* and the town

Dueona	18	47	15

Below these are the *Petrocori* and the town

Vesuna	19 50	46	50

The *Bituriges Cubi* extend along the eastern border of those we have named and touch the region located across the Liger river whose town is

Avaricum	20 15	46	40

Below the *Petrocori* are the *Nitiobriges* and the town

Aginnum	19 30	46	20

Below these are the *Vassari* and the town

Cossium	18 30	46	

Below whom are the *Gabali* and the town

Anderedum	19 45	45	30

Below the *Gabali* are the *Dati* and the town

Tasta	19	45	15

Below these are the *Ausci* and the town

Augusta	18	45

From these toward the east are a part of the *Averni* among whom is the town

Augustonemetum	20	45

Below the *Ausci* are the *Velauni* whose town is

Ruessium	18	44	30

Below these are the *Rutani* and the town

Segodunum	17 45	44	10

Bordering on the Pyrenees are the *Convenae* and the town

Lugdunum colonia	17	44

CHAPTER VII

Location of Lugdunensis Gallia
(Third map of Europe)

THE borders of Lugdunensis which touch Aquitania have been described; and that which looks toward the ocean is described in the following order, after the mouth of the Liger river:

Brivates harbor	17 40	48	45
mouth of the Herius river	17	49	15
Vidana harbor	16 30	49	40
Gabaeum promontory	15 15	49	45

The north side which borders on the Britannic ocean is thus described: after the Gabaeum promontory

Saliocanus harbor	16 30	50	
mouth of the Titus river	17 20	50	20

the *Biducasi*

Aregenua	18	50 30

the *Venelli*

Crociatonnum	18 50	50	30
mouth of the Olina river	18 45	51	

the *Lexubi*

Noeomagus	19 30	51	10
mouth of the Sequana river	20	51	30

The eastern border is common with Belgica running along the Sequana river, the middle part of which border is located in

24	47 20

from this point it extends direct as far as the terminus in

25	45 30

The southern side is terminated by that part of Narbonensis which extends as far as the terminus in the indicated confines of Aquitania near the Cemmeni mountains, the middle part of which is in

20 20	44 30

The *Caletae* inhabit the north coast from the Sequana river, whose town is

Iuliobana	20 15	51	20

Next to these are the *Lexubi*, then the *Venelli*, after these the *Biducasi* and the *Osismi* extending as far as the Gabaeum promontory, whose town is

Vorganium	17 40	50	10

The *Veneti* occupy the western coast below the *Osismi*, whose town is

Darioritum	17 20	49	15

Below these are the *Samnites* who extend as far as the Liger river

In the interior toward the east from the *Veneti* are the *Aulircii Diablitae*, whose town is

Noeodunum	18	50

After these are the *Arvi* and the town

Vagoritum	18 40	50

After these, extending as far as the Sequana, are the *Veneliocasi*, whose town is

Ratomagus	20 10	50	20

And back from the *Samnites* toward the east are the *Andicavae*, whose town is

Iuliomagus	18 50	49	

After these toward the east are the *Aulirei Cenomani*, whose town is

Vindinum	20 45	49	20

After these are the *Namnetae*, whose town is

Condivincum	21	15	50	

Extending to the river Sequana are the *Abrincatui*, and their town is

Ingena	21	45	50	45

The *Aulirci Eburaici* extend below those we have mentioned, from the river Liger to the Sequana whose town is

Mediolanium	20	40	48

Below these on the banks of the river Liger are the *Rhedones*, whose town is

Condate	20	40	47	20

And toward the east from these are the *Senones*, whose town is

Agedicum	21	15	47	10

Near the Sequana are the *Carnutae*, and the towns

Autricum	21	40	48	15
Cenabum	22		47	50

Below these are the *Parisi*, and the town

Lucotecia	23	30	48	45

Below these are the *Tricasi* and the town

Augustobona	23	30	47	45

Below these races which we have mentioned near the Liger river, are the *Turoni*, and their town is

Caesarondunum	20	45	46	30

Below these on the border of the *Averni* who inhabit the Cemmenos mountains are the *Segusiavi* and their towns are

Rhodumna	20	15	45	50
Forum Segusianorum	20	50	45	30

Toward the east, from those we have mentioned, are the *Meldae* and the town

Latinum	23		47	30

Next to these toward Belgica are the *Vadicasi* and the town

Noeomagus	24	20	46	30

Toward the east from the *Averni* extending as far as the river which flows from the north into the Rhone river, is the race of the *Aedui*, and the towns

Augustodunum	23	40	46	30
Cabyllinum	23	50	45	20
Lugdunum metropolis	23	15	45	20

CHAPTER VIII

Location of Belgica Gallia
(Third map of Europe)

THE western border of Belgica Gallia, which is near Lugdunensis, we have described; the north which is on the Britan-

nic ocean is thus described: after the mouth of the Sequana river

mouth of the Phrudis river	21	45	52	20
Itium promontory	22	15	52	30
Gesoriacum naval station of the Morini	22	30	53	30
mouth of the Tabula river	23	30	53	30
mouth of the Mosa river (Mosel)	24	40	53	30
Lugdunum of the Batavi	26	30	53	20
Western mouth of the Rhine	26	45	53	30
Central mouth of the river	27		53	10
Eastern mouth of the river	27	20	54	

The border which looks toward the east along Germania Magna, is terminated by the Rhine river, the source of which is in

	29	20	46

that locality where the river Obrincas flows into this from the west

	29	20	46

and near the mountains which are called the Adulas, coming from the source of the river

	29	30	45	15
Jurassus mountains	26	15	46	

The south side connects with a part of Gallia Narbonensis, and extends from the common boundary of Lugdunensis and Narbonensis as far as the common terminus of the Alps and the Adulas 29 30 45 15

The *Atribati* inhabit the sea coast, near the Sequana river, whose town is

Metacum	22		51

Next toward the east are the *Bellovici*, whose town is

Caesaromagus	22	50	51	20

Next to these in that region are the *Ambiani*, and their town is

Samarobriva	22	15	52	10

Next to these are the *Morini*, whose interior town is

Tarvanna	23	20	52	50

Next beyond the Tabulam river are the *Tungri* and the town

Atuatucum	24	30	52	50

Next to the Mosa river are the *Menapi*, and their town

Castellum	25		52	15

Below these are the *Nervi* a race to which we have referred, extending northward, whose town is

Bagacum	25	15	51	40

Below these are the *Subanecti*, whose town is located on the eastern bank of the Sequana river

Ratomagus	22 30	50	

Next to these are the *Viromandues* and the town

Augusta Viromandeum	25 30	50	

Below these are the *Vessones*, whose town located toward the east of the Sequana river is

Augusta Vessonum	23 30	38 45	

Next to these near the river are the *Remi,* and their town

Durocottorum	23 45	48 30	

Toward the east from the *Remi,* and extending northward, are the *Treveri* whose town is

Augusta Treverorum	26	48 10	

Toward the south of these are the *Mediomatrices,* whose town is

Dividurum	25 30	47 20	

And below these and the *Remi* are the *Leuci,* and their towns

Tullium	26 30	47	
Nasium	24 50	46 40	

The other part of the region near the Rhine from the sea to the Obruncus river is called Lower Germania, in which on the west of the Rhine river is the town in the interior of Batavia

Batavodurum	27 15	52 30	

Below which are

Veterra	27 30	51 50	
Legio XXX Ulpia			
Agrippinensis	27 40	51 10	
Bonna (Bonn)	27 40	50 50	
Legio I Minervia			
Trajiana Legio XXII	27 30	50 35	
Mocontiacum	27 20	50 15	

Another part toward the south from the Obrincas river is called Upper Germania, in which are the towns
of the *Nemetes*

Neomagus	27 40	49 50	
Rufiniana	27 40	49 30	
of the *Vangiones*			
Borbetomagus	27 50	49 20	
Argentoratum	27 50	48 45	
Legio VIII Augusta			
of the *Tribocci*			
Breucomagus	27 50	48 20	
Helcebus	28	48	
of the *Raurici*			
Augusta Rauricorum	28	47 30	

Argentovaria	27 50	47 20	

Extending below these and the *Leuci* dwell the *Longones* whose town is

Andomatunnum	26 15	46 20	

And after the mountains which are below these, and which are called the Jurassus, are the *Helveti* near the Rhine river, whose towns are

Ganodurum	28 30	46 30	
Forum Tiberii	28	46	

The *Sequani* are below these and the towns

Dittatium	25 10	45 40	
Visentium	26	46	
Equestris	27	45 40	
Aventicum	28	45 30	

CHAPTER IX

Location of Narbonensis Gallia (Third map of Europe)

THE borders of Narbonensis are contiguous with the neighboring provincial tribes, which have been described; from the remaining (parts), those which are on the east, are terminated by the western part of the Alps from the Adulas mountains to the mouth of the Varus river, the location of which is in 27 30 43

The south is terminated by the remaining part of the Pyrenees mountains extending from the boundary of Aquitania as far as the summit of the mountains at the inner sea, where there is a Temple of Venus, and by the Gallic sea to the mouth of the Varus river. The shores of this sea are thus described:

after the Temple of Venus	20 20	42 20	
mouth of the Illeris river	21	42 40	
mouth of the Ruscionis river	21 15	42 45	
mouth of the Atagis river	21 30	42 45	
mouth of the Orobis river	21 45	42 45	
mouth of the Araurus river	22	42 50	
Agatha town	22 15	42 50	
Setius mountain	22 30	42 30	
Mariana Trenches	22 40	42 40	
mouth of the Rhodanus (Rhone) river toward the west	22 50	42 40	
eastern mouth of the Rhone river	23	42 50	

Where below Lugdunum the river turns toward the Alps 23 45 15

That part of it near the lake which is called Lemanus is in   27 15   45 15
the source of the river   28 20   44 20

Of the rivers which unite with this, in that part which is toward the north from Lugdunum are the Arar and the Dubis, the sources of the Arar flowing from the Alps are located in   28 40   44 40
the Dubis river below this is in   28 30   44 30

These rivers flow toward the north from the Alps, then turn toward the west, and the junction is in   25 20   45 30
they flow into the Rhone river in   24   45 30

In that part, which is south of the town Vienna, are the Isar river and the Druentia river, coming from the Alps; the sources of the Isar river are in   28   44
the source of the Druentia is in   28   43 45

The junction of the Isar with the Rhone is in   22 40   44
and with the Druentia is in 22 40   43 50

On the sea, next to Rhodanum are the *Avatici*

Maritime city, colonia	23	30	43	5
mouth of the Caenus river	23	45	43	

the *Comani*

Massilia city	24	30	43	5
Tauroentium	24	50	42	50
Citharistes promontory	25		42	30
Olbia town	25	10	42	45
mouth of the Argentus river	25	40	42	45
Forum Julii colonia	26	30	42	50

the *Deciati*

Antipolis	27		43
mouth of the Varus river	27	30	43

The *Volcae Tectosages* inhabit the extreme west of Narbonensis, whose island towns are

Illiberis	19	45	43	15
Ruscinon	20		43	30
Tolosa colonia	20	10	44	15
Cessero	21	15	44	
Carcaso	21		43	15
Baetirae	21	30	43	30
Narbon colonia	21	30	43	15

Next to these, extending as far as the Rhone river, are the *Volcae Arecomi*, whose inland towns are

Vindomagus	21	30	44	30
Nemausum colonia	22		44	30

To the east of the Rhone, and in the extreme north, are the *Allobroges* below the Medulli whose town is

Vienna	23	45

Below these toward the west are the Segallauni, whose town is

Velentia colonia	23	44 30

Toward the east are the *Tricastini* whose town is

Noeomagus	26 30	45

Then below the *Segallauni* are the *Cavari*, whose towns are

Acusion colonia	23	44	15
Avennion colonia	23	44	
Arausion	24	44	30
Cabellion colonia	24	44	

Below these are the *Salyes* whose towns are

Taruscon	23		43	40
Glanum	23	30	43	30
Arelatum colonia	22	45	43	20
Aqua Sextia colonia	24	30	43	20
Ernaginum	24		43	30

Below the Tricastini are the *Voconti*, whose town is

Vasion	26	44 30

Below these are the *Memini*, and their town is

Forum Neronis	25	40	44 15

Below these are the *Elycoci*, and their town is

Albaugusta	26	43 20

Toward the east of the Voconti and Memini are the *Senti*, whose town is

Dinia	27	10	44 20

Below Narbonensis are islands, the Agatha, in the region near the city of this name which is located in   22 30   42 10
and next to this Blasco in   22 30   42 20

The Stoechades, five in number, are below Citharistes the middle of which is in   25   42 15

Below the Varus river is the island Lerone   27 45   42 15

CHAPTER X

*Location of Greater Germany
(Fourth map of Europe)*

THE Rhine river terminates the west side of Germania, the Germanic ocean terminates the north side; a description of these borders is the following:

Next to the mouth of the Rhine

mouth of Vidrus river	27	30	54	45
Marnamanis harbor	28		54	15
mouth of the Amisius river	29		55	
river sources	32		53	
mouth of the Visurgis river	31		55	
river sources	34		52	30
mouth of the Albis river	31		36	15
river sources	39		50	

Cimbrian peninsula

After the Albis river a prominence

in	32		56	50
next a prominence in	35		58	20
next further north	38	40	59	30
first after the turning	39	20	59	20
part farthest east	40	15	58	30
next below this	37		57	
turning toward the east	35		56	
mouth of the Chalusus river	37		56	
mouth of the Suevus river	39	30	56	
mouth of the Viadus river	42	30	56	
mouth of the Vistula river	45		56	
source of the river	44		52	30

a river, the source of which is toward the west, flows into the Albis in 40 10 52 40

A part of the western Danube terminates the south side, of which the following locations are noted:

source of the river	30	46	20

locality where the first river which comes from Germania flows into

this	32	47	15

locality on the south side where a river flows into this which is called

Aenus	34	47	20

where a second on the north side, coming from the Gabreta forest region, flows into

this	36	46	40

where the next river flowing through the Luna forest from the north empties into

this	39	20	47	20

the bend following, whence the Danube turns toward the south 40 40 47 50 where a river from the south empties into this, which is called

Arabon	41	47	40
bend near Curtam	42	47	

bend near Carpin which of all is farthest north 42 30 48

The east side is terminated by the space which is between this bend and the Sarmatian mountains which are above it, the southern terminus of which is

located in	42	30	48	30
the northern side is in	43	30	50	30

then follows the space between these mountains and the source of the Vistula, which we have referred to above, thence following that river as far as the sea.

The most noted of the mountains which extend into Germania, are those which we have mentioned, and which properly are called the Sarmatian, and those known as the Alps above the source of the Danube, the extreme parts of which

are in	29	47
and	33	48 30

and those which are called the Abnoba, the extreme parts of which are 31 49

and	31	52

and Melibocus, the extreme parts of which

are in	33	52 30
and	57	52 30

below which is the Semanus forest; and the Asciburgius mountains, the extreme limits of which

are in	39	54
and	44	52 30

and the mountains which are called the Sudeti, the extremities of which

are	34	50
and	40	50

below which is the Gabreta forest, and between which and the Sarmatian mountains is the Orcynius forest.

Moreover, if we approach from the north, we find the lesser *Bructeri* and the *Sygambri* who inhabit Germania near the Rhine river, below whom are the *Suevi Langobardi*, then the *Tencteri* and the *Ingriones* between the Rhine and the Abnobaei mountains, and then the *Intuergi*, the *Vargiones*, and the *Caritini*, below whom are the *Vispi* and the waste land of the *Helvetians*, as far as those mountains which we call the Alps.

The *Fresians* inhabit the coast near the ocean above the *Bructeri*, as far as the river Amissis (Ems); next to these are the *Lesser Cauchi* extending as far as the river Visurgis; then the *Greater Cauchi* extending as far as the river Albis; thence the *Saxons* through the palisades of the Cimbrian peninsula; in the same peninsula above the *Saxons* on the west are the *Sigulones*, then the *Sabalingi*, then the *Cobandi*, above them

the *Chali*, and above these to the west are the *Fundusi*, and to the east the *Charudes*.

Of all these the *Cimbri* are farthest north; then next to the *Saxons*, from the Chalusus river to the Suevus river are the *Pharodini*, then the *Sidini* as far as the river Viadus, and next are the *Ruticli* extending as far as the river Vistula.

Of the races dwelling in the interior the greatest are the races of the *Suevi Angili*, who are to the east of the *Longobardi* extending toward the north as far as the middle part of the Albis river, and the *Suevi Semnonnes* whose boundaries extend beyond the Albis toward the east as far as that part, as we have said, which touches the Suevus river, and the *Buguntae*, who occupy the region as far as the Vistula.

Moreover the lesser races which are between the lesser *Cauchi* and the *Suevi* are the greater *Bructeri*, below whom are the *Chaemae*; between the greater *Cauchi* and the *Suevi* are the *Angrivari*, then the *Laccobardi*, below whom are the *Dulgumni*; between the *Saxons* and the *Suevi* are the *Teutonoari* and the *Viruni*; between the *Pharodini* and the *Suevi* are the *Teutones* and *Avarpi*; between the *Rugiclei* and the *Burguntae* are the *Aelvaeones*.

Below the *Semnones* the *Silingae* have their abodes, and below the *Burguntae* are the *Lugi Omani*; below these are the *Lugi Diduni* extending as far as the Asciburgius mountains, and below the *Silingae* are the *Calucones* on both banks of the river Albis; below whom are the *Chaerusci* and the *Camavi* extending as far as Melibocus mountain, from whom toward the east along the Albis river are the *Banochaemae*; above whom are the *Batini*, and above these, but below the Asciburgius mountains are the *Corconti* and the *Lugi Buri* extending as far as the source of the Vistula river; first below these are the *Sidones*, then the *Gotini*, then the *Visburgi* above the Orcynium forest.

Toward the east from the Abnobaeis mountains the *Casuari*, but below the *Suevi*, have their abodes, then the *Nertereanes*, then the *Danduti*, below these the *Turoni* and the *Marvingi*; below the *Camavi* are the *Chattae* and the *Tubanti*, and above the Sudeti mountains are the *Teuriochaemae*, but below the mountains are the *Varisti*;

next is the Gabreta forest; and below the *Marvingi* are the *Curiones*, then the *Chaetuori*, and then the *Parmaecampi* extending as far as the Danube; below the Gabreta forest are the *Marcomani*, below whom are the *Sudini*, then extending to the Danube river are the *Adrabaecampi*; below the Orcynium forest are the *Quadi*, and below these are the iron mines and the Luna forest, below which is the great race of the *Baemi* extending as far as the Danube, and the *Racatriae* bordering them on the river, and the *Racatae* near the bending of the river.

The towns located in Germania in the northern clima are

Phleum	28	45	54	45
Siatuanda	29	20	54	20
Tecelia	31		55	
Fabrianum	31	30	55	20
Treva	33		55	40
Leufana	34	15	54	40
Lirimiris	34	30	55	30
Marionis	34	30	54	50
another Marionis	36		55	50
Coenoenum	36	20	55	30
Cistuia	37	20	54	30
Alisus	38		55	
Laciburgium	39		56	
Bunitium	39	30	55	30
Virunum	40	30	55	
Viritium	41		54	30
Rugium	42	30	54	40
Scurgum	43		55	
Ascaucalis	44		54	15

Towns located in the clima below this are

Asciburgium	27	30	52	30
Navalia	27	20	54	
Mediolanium	28	45	53	50
Teuderium	29	30	53	20
Bogadium	30	15	52	
Stereontium	31		52	10
Amisia	31	30	51	30
Munitium	31	40	52	30
Tulifurdum	32		54	
Ascalingium	32	30	53	45
Tulisurgium	32	40	53	20
Pheugarum	32	40	52	15
Canduum	33		51	50
Tropaea Drusi	33	45	52	45
Luppia	34	30	52	45
Mersovium	35	30	53	50
Aregelia	36	30	52	20
Galaegia	37	30	52	20
Lupfurdum	38	10	51	40

Susudata	38 30	53 50	
Colancorum	39	53 30	
Lugidunum	39 30	52 30	
Stragona	39 40	52 20	
Limis lucus	41	53 30	
Budorigum	41	52 40	
Leucaristus	41 45	52 40	
Arsonium	43 30	52 20	
Calisia	43 45	52 50	
Setidava	44	53 30	

In the region below this are the following towns:

Alisum	28	51 30	
Budoris	28	51	
Mattiacum	30	50 50	
Arctaunum	30 10	50	
Novaesium	31 30	51 10	
Melocabus	31 30	50 40	
Gravionarium	31 30	50 10	
Locoritum	31 30	49 20	
Segodunum	31 30	49	
Devona	32 30	48 45	
Bergium	33	49 30	
Menosgada	34	49 30	
Bicurgium	34 30	51 15	
Marobudum	35	49	
Redintuinum	38 30	50 30	
Nomisterium	39	51	
Meliodunum	39	49	
Casurgis	39 15	50 10	
Strevinta	39 15	49 30	
Hegetmatia	39 40	51	
Budorgis	40	50 30	
Eburum	41	49 30	
Arsicua	41 40	49	
Parienna	42	49 20	
Setovia	42 30	50	
Carrodunum	42 40	51 30	
Asanca	43	50 20	

Towns in the remaining region near the Danube river are

Tarodunum	28 20	47 50	
Arae Flaviae (Flavian Altars)	30 40	48	
Riusiava	31	47 30	
Alcimoennis	32 30	47 30	
Cantioebis	32 40	48 20	
Bibacum	33	48	
Brodentia	33 45	48	
Setuacotum	34	48 20	
Usbium	35	47	
Abilunum	35 20	47 20	
Furgisatis	36	48	
Coridorgis	37 15	48 30	

Mediolanium	38	47 10	
Felicia	39	48 30	
Eburodunum	39	48	
Anduaetium	40 30	47 40	
Celamantia	41	47 40	
Singone	41 30	48 15	
Anavum	41 20	47 30	

The islands above Germania near the mouth of the Albis are called the three Saxonum islands, the middle of which is in 31 57 20

Above the Cimbrian peninsula are three other islands which are called the Alociae Islands, the middle of which is in 37 59 20

Toward the east of the Cimbrian peninsula are four islands which are called Scandia, three of which are small, the middle of which is in 41 30 58 the larger one is further east and near the mouth of the Vistula river; the extreme parts of this are,

on the west	43	58
on the east	46	58
on the north	44 30	58 30
on the south	45	57 40

This one is properly called Scandia, and the western parts of it the *Chaedini* inhabit, the eastern parts the *Favonae* and the *Firaesi* occupy, the northern parts the *Finni*, the southern parts the *Gutae* and the *Dauciones*, the central part the *Levoni*.

CHAPTER XI

Location of Raetia and Vindelicia (Fifth map of Europe)

RAETIA and Vindelicia are terminated on the west by the Adula mountains and by that tract which lies between the source of the Rhine and that of the Danube river; on the north by the part of the Danube river from its source to the place where the Aenus river empties into it 34 47 20 on the east by the same Aenus river, the extreme part of its boundary toward the south being in 34 45 15 and on the south by the Alps mountains which extend above Italy, of which those parts near Graeas have the position 30 45 20 which moreover are called the Penine Alpes near the source of the Licia river which

empties into the Danube, separating Raetia from Vindelicia in 31 30 45 30 and which is not far from the Ocra mountains in 33 30 45 30

The *Brixantae* inhabit Raetia in the north; in the south part are the *Suanetae* and the *Riguscae*, and between these regions are the *Calucones* and the *Vennontes*.

Their towns below the Danube are

Bragodurum	30	46	40
Dracuina	30 20	46	40
Viana	31	46	40
Phaeniana	31 45	46	50

Near the source of the Rhine river,

Taxgaetium	29 20	46	15
Brigantium	30	46	

Next to these,

Vicus	30 15	45	50
Ebodurum	30 40	45	50
Ectodurum	31 20	45	40
Drusomagus	31 30	46	5

Vindelicia

The northern parts of Vindelicia are inhabited by the *Runicatae;* below these are the *Leuni* and *Consuantae*, then the *Benlauni*, the *Breuni*, and the *Licati* near the Licati river.

The towns in Vindelicia near the Danube river are

Artobriga	32 15	47	10
Boiodorum	33 50	47	15

and below these

Augusta Vindelicorum	32 30	46	50
Carrodunum	33 50	46	45
Abudiacum	33 30	46	15
Cambodunum	32 50	46	
Medullum	33 50	45	40
Inutrium	32 50	45	30

CHAPTER XII

Location of Noricum
(Fifth map of Europe)

NORICUM is bounded on the west by the Aenus river, on the north by a part of the Danube river and a part of the Aenus river as far as the Cetius mountains, the location of which is in 37 30 46 50 on the east by the Cetius mountains, and on the south by that part of Upper Pannonia which is below the Cetius mountains, the extreme western part of which is terminated in 36 45 20 and by the mountains which are above Istria

and which are called Carvancas, the central part of which is in 35 45 20

The western parts of the province, beginning at the north the *Sevaces*, the *Alauni*, and the *Ambisontii* inhabit; the eastern part the *Norici*, the *Ambidravi*, and the *Ambilici*.

The towns which are in this province and which are below the Danube are

Arelate	35	47	
Claudivium Juvanum	36	46	40

and below this

Gamavodurum	34 40	46	40
Gesodunum	35 40	46	30
Bedaium	34 15	46	15
Aguntum	36 30	46	10
Vacorium	36	45	45
Poedicum	37	46	
Virunum	36 40	45	45
Teurnia	34 40	45	40
Idunum	35 10	45	30
Sianticum	36	45	30
Celeia	37	45	30

Between Italia and Noricum

Julium Carnicum	34 40	45	15

CHAPTER XIII

Location of Upper Pannonia
(Fifth map of Europe)

UPPER Pannonia is bounded on the west by the Cetius mountains and in part by the Carvancas, on the south by a part of Istria and Illyria along the parallel which extends from the terminus in the west, as we have said, through the Albanian mountains as far as the Bebios mountains, and the confines of Lower Pannonia, which is located in 41 30 45 20

It is bounded on the north by the confines of Noricum, as indicated, thence along the Cetius mountains to that part of the Danube where the Arabun river empties into it, the position of which terminus is in 41 47 40

It is bounded on the east by Lower Pannonia along the line running between the two.

The *Azali* inhabit the northern part of this province, toward the west, and the Cytni the part toward the east; to the south are the *Latobici* below Noricum, and the *Varciani* are toward the east; the central region the *Boii* occupy, and the *Colaetiani*

are in the west below them, also the *Iassi* but more toward the east, and below these are the *Oseriates*.

Below the Danube river are the towns

Vindobona	37	45	46	50
Legio X Germanica				
Carnus	39		47	
Phlexum	40		47	15
Legio XIV Germanica				
Chertobalus	40	30	47	30
Brigaetium	41		47	40
Legio I adiutrix				

Towns that are remote from the river are

Sala	38	20	46	15
Potovio	37	20	45	30
Savaria	38	20	46	40
Rispia	38	40	46	30
Vinundria	38	10	45	20
Bononia	38	40	45	40
Andautonium	38	10	45	30
Novidunum	37	50	45	20
Scarbantia	39	30	47	
Muroella	39	15	46	10
Lentudum	39	10	45	45
Carrodunum	39	40	46	
Siscia	39		45	20
Olimacum	39	20	45	30
Valina	40	30	46	45
Bolentium	40	30	46	
Siroga	40	10	46	
Sisopa	40		45	45
Visontium	40	45	45	25
Praetorium	40	45	46	15
Magniana	41		46	

Between Italia and Pannonia and below Noricum is

Emona	36	30	45	20

CHAPTER XIV

*Location of Lower Pannonia
(Fifth map of Europe)*

LOWER Pannonia is terminated on the west by Upper Pannonia from that point where the Arabus river flows into the Danube, forming those borders to which we have referred; on the south by Illyria which extends from the indicated terminus as far as the bend in the Danube near which the Save river empties into it, the location of which is in   45   44 30

It is bounded on the north by that eastern part of the Danube river which is near the mouth of the Arabus and which flows into

it, and as far as the mouth of the Save river, the description of this part of which is the following: after the Arabus river the bend near Curtain   42   47
the bend of the Danube river farthest north   42 30   48
where a river empties into it, which flowing toward the east through both Pannonias, takes its rise in two rivers coming down from the Cetius mountains which unite near Carrodunum, the more northern is the Savarias, the southern is called the
Drave   44 20   45 40
there is a bend in the Danube river near

Cornacum	44	20	45	15
a bend near Acumincum	45		45	20
a bend near Rittium	45	30	45	

where the Save river flows into the Danube, coming from the Cetius mountains running through both Pannonias first northward then eastward   45   44 30

The western parts of this province toward the north the *Amantini* inhabit, below these are the *Hercuniates*, then the *Andiantes*, then the *Breuci*; the eastern part toward the north the *Aravisci* inhabit, and toward the south are the *Scordisci*.

Below the Danube river are the towns

Curta	42		47	
Solva	42	30	47	30
Carpis	42	30	47	50
Aquincum	43		47	30
Salinum	43	30	47	
Lussonium	43	45	46	45
Lugionum	44		46	30
Teutoburgium	44	15	45	40
Cornacum	44	20	45	15
Acumineum, legio	45		45	20
Rittium	45	30	45	
Taururum	45		44	30

Remote from the river are

Berbis	42		46	
Serbinum	41	20	46	30
Jouballum	42	20	46	
Certissa	42	20	45	20
Mursella	43		46	
Cibalis	43		45	30
Marsonia	43		45	
Vacontium	43	30	46	30
Mursia colonia	43	30	45	45
Sallis	44		44	40
Bassiana	44	30	44	50
Tarsium	44	30	44	35
Sirmium	44	50	45	

CHAPTER XV

Location of Illyria or Liburnia, and of Dalmatia
(Fifth map of Europe)

ILLIRIA is terminated on the north by both Pannonias along those borders which we have referred to above; on the west by Istria along that line, one terminus of which is toward Upper Pannonia

in   36 30   45 10

the other on the Adriatic

in   36 30   44 50

It is bounded on the east by Upper Moesia along the line which leads from the indicated entrance of the Save into the Danube as far as the Scardus mountains, the terminal position of which is in   47   41 40

It is bounded on the south by the part of Macedonia along that line which runs from the indicated terminus to the Adriatic bay, the other terminus of which is

in   45   41

and then by the coast of the Adriatic to the indicated terminus near Istria. The several parts of its boundaries are in the following order: after Istria then the land of Italia in Illyria

The maritime shore of Liburnia

Alvona	36	50	45	
Flanona	37		44	50
Tarsatica	37	40	44	45
mouth of the Oeneus river	38		44	45
Volcera	38	30	44	45
Senia	39		44	40
Lopsica	39	15	44	40
mouth of the Tedanius river	39	20	44	30
Ortopla	40		44	30
Vegia	40	20	44	30
Argyruntum	40	45	44	10
Corinium	41	10	44	
Aenona	41	30	44	
Iader colonia	42		43	45
mouth of the Titus river	42	20	43	10
Scardona	42	40	43	30

Maritime shore of Dalmatia

Sicum	43		43	20
Salonae colonia	43	20	43	10
Epetium	43	40	43	
Pituntium	44		42	45
Onaeum	44		42	30
mouth of the Naronus river	44	30	42	20

Epidaurus	44	40	42	20
Rhisium	44	40	42	15
Acruvium	44	45	42	
Rhizonicus bay	45		42	
Butua	45		41	45
Ulcinium	45		41	30
mouth of the Drilo river	45		41	20
Lissus	45		41	10

The river Drilo flows from the Scardus mountains and from that other mountain which is near the middle of Upper Moesia, the location of which is in 45 40   42 40

From this another river, the Drinus, joining the Save river, empties into it on the west of the town Tauruno.

The *Ispydes*, the *Hyllaei*, and the *Bulimenses* inhabit this Istrian province bordering on the sea coast; above these in Liburnia toward the west are the *Mazaei*, then the *Derriopes* and the *Derri*, and above the *Derriopes* are the *Dindari*, above these are the *Ditiones*, and above the *Derri* are the *Cerauni*; in Dalmatia are the *Daursi*, below whom are the *Melcomenii* and the *Vardaei*, below these are the *Narensi* and the *Sardiotae* and below these are the *Siculotae*, the *Docleatae*, the *Pirustae*, and the *Scirtones* near Macedonia.

The inland towns of Liburnia are

Tediastum	39		44	50
Aruccia	39	30	44	45
Ardotium	40		44	50
Stulpi	39	30	44	40
Curcum	40	30	44	30
Ausancali	41	30	44	45
Varvaria	41	10	44	10
Salvia	41	20	44	40
Adra	42	30	44	40
Arauzona	42	30	44	20
Assesia	42	15	44	20
Burnum	42	45	44	20
Sidrona	43	30	44	30
Blanona	42	10	44	
Ouporum	43		44	
Nedinum	44	30	44	15

The inland towns of Dalmatia are

Andecrium	43	30	43	30
Aleta	44		43	10
Herona	44	20	43	45
Delminium	44	40	43	20
Aequum colonia	44	30	43	20
Saloniana	45		43	20
Narona colonia	44	20	42	45

Enderum	45	30	42	50	and Curicta, in which are two towns			
Chinna	45	40	42	30	Fulfinium	38	10	44	20
Doclea	45	20	42	15	Curicum	38	20	44	15
Rhizana	45	15	42		and the island Scardona, in which are two			
Scodra	45	30	41	30	towns			
Thermidava	46		41	45	Arba	40	40	43	40
Siparuntum	46	30	42	10	Collentum	41	40	43	30
Epicaria	45	30	41	15	Near Dalmatia are the islands			
Iminacium	46		41	20	Issa and the town	42	20	43	

The islands near Liburnia are Apsorrus, in which are two towns

					Tragurium and town	43		42	15
					Pharia and town	42		42	20
Crepsa	36	40	44	30	Corcyra Nigra	44		41	45
Apsorrus	36	50	44	30	Melita island	44	10	41	20

END OF BOOK TWO

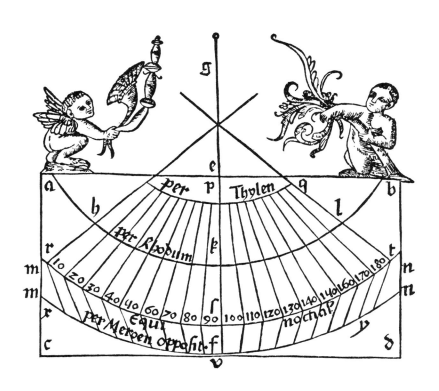

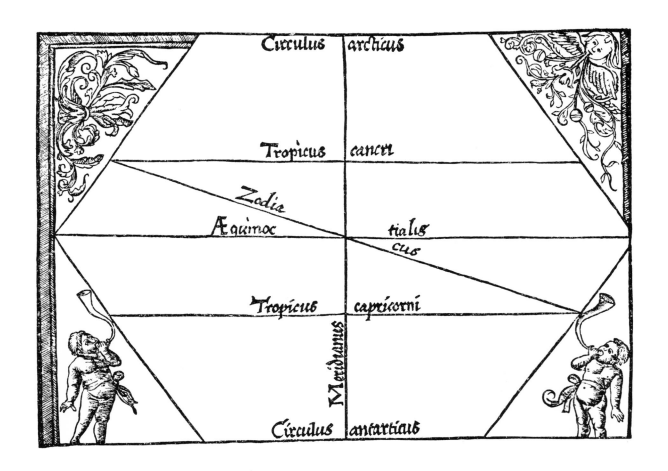

Circulus arcticus

Tropicus cancri

Zodia

Æquinoc   tialis cu6

Meridianus

Tropicus capricorni

Circulus antarticus

BOOK THREE

CHAPTER I

Location of Italy
(Sixth map of Europe)

ITALY is terminated on the west by the Alps mountains along that line, which runs, as is set down, from the Adula mountains as far as the mouth of the Varus river, the location of which is in 27 30   43 then from the shore of the Tyrrhenum sea to Naples and to the Leucopetra promontory; on the north by the Alps mountains, which are below Raetia, and by the Caravancas mountains, which are below Noricum, the location of which has been indicated above, and likewise by the shore of the Adriatic bay which extends from the Tilaventus river to the Garganus mountains; on the east by that maritime coast which extends from Garganus mountains as far as Hydruntum; on the south by the shore of the Adriatic bay (sea?) which extends from the Tilaventus river as far as the confines of Illyria, and by that coast of the Tyrrhenum

and of the Ligusticum sea, which extends from the mouth of the Varus river as far as Naples, then along the maritime coast from Leucopetra as far as Hydruntum.

The entire line of the maritime coast is thus described from the mouth of the Varus river on the Ligusticum sea:

On the coast of Massiliensium

Nicaea	28		43	5
Herculis harbor	28	15	42	45
Tropaea Augusti	28	30	42	30
Monoeci harbor	28	40	42	40

of Liguria, which in Greek is called Ligustice, near the Ligusticum sea

Albintimilium	29	10	42	45
Albingaunum	29	30	42	45
Genua	30		42	50
mouth of the Entella river	30	30	42	50
Tigullia	30	35	42	55
mouth of the Macralla	31	50	42	45
where the Boacias flows into it	31	30	43	

of the *Tusci* who in Greek are called *Tyrrhini*, near the Tyrrhenum sea are

Luna	32		42	45
Luna promontory	32		42	40
Temple of Hercules	32	40	42	45
mouth of the Arnus river	33	20	42	40
Populonium town	33	30	42	
Populonium promontory	33	30	42	
Traianus harbor	34		42	10
Telamon promontory	34	15	42	
mouth of the Osa river	34	30	42	
Cossae	35		41	55
Graviscae	35	20	41	45
Castrum Novum	35	40	41	40
Pyrgi	36		41	40
Alsium	36	15	41	40

of the *Latini* on the Tyrrhenum sea

mouth of the Tiber river	36	30	41	30
where the river turns toward the west	36	30	42	
Ostia	33	30	41	30
Antium	36	50	41	20
Clostra	37	10	41	20
Circaeum promontory	37	30	41	10
Tarracinae	37	45	41	15
Formiae	38	10	41	15

of the *Campani*, on the Tyrrhenum sea

mouth of the Liris river	38	20	41	15
Sinuessa	38	30	41	20
Volturnum	38	45	41	5
Liternum	39	10	41	10
Cumae	39	20	41	10
Misenum	39	30	41	
Puteoli	39	50	41	
Neapolis	40		40	55

of the *Picentini*, on the Tyrrhenum sea

mouth of the Sarnus river	40	5	40	55
Surentum	40		40	40
Salernum	40		40	30

of the *Lucani*, on the Tyrrhenum sea

mouth of the Silarus river	40	5	40	15
Paestum	40	10	40	
Buxentum	40		39	30

of the *Brutti*, on the Tyrrhenum sea

mouth of the Laus river	40		39	15
Tempsa town	40		39	
Taurianus cliff	40	10	48	15
Hipponiates bay	40	20	39	45
Scyllaeum promontory	39	50	38	15
Rhegium Julium	39	50	39	15
Leucopetra promontory	39	50	38	

of Magna Graecia, on the Adriatic sea

Zephyrium promontory	40	45	39	5
Locri town	40	50	38	25
mouth of the Locani river	40	55	38	35

on Scylacius bay

Scylacium town	40	45	39	40

Innermost part of Scylacium bay

	40	45	39	45
Lacinium promontory	41	30	38	45

on Tarentinus bay

Croton town	41	30	39	10
Thurium	40	55	39	30
Metapontium	40	55	39	55
Tarentum	41	30	40	

of the *Salentini*

Iapygium promontory or

Salentinum	42	20	38	45

of Calabria, on the Ionian sea

Hydruntum	43		39	5
Luspiae	42	40	39	15
Brundisium	42	30	39	40

of the *Apuli Peucenti*, on the Ionian sea

Egnatia	42	30	39	50
Barium	42	30	40	5
mouth of the Aufidus river	42	30	40	15

of the *Apuli Dauni*, on the Ionian sea

Salapia	42	20	40	20
Sipuntum	42	20	40	30

Apenestae	42	20	40	45
Garganus mountain	42	40	41	

and near the Adriatic bay

Hyrium	42	30	41	15

of the *Frentani* on this bay

mouth of the Tifernus

river	42		41	30
Buca	41	40	41	40
Istonium	41	30	41	45

of the *Paeligni* on the same (bay)

mouth of the Sarus river	41	20	42	
Ortona	40	45	42	15

of the *Maurrucini* on the same bay

mouth of the Aternus river	40	30	42	30

mouth of the Matrinus

river	39	20	42	45

of the *Piceni* on the same bay

Castrum	38	30	43	
Cupra Maritima	38		43	10

mouth of the Truentini

river	37	40	43	20
Potentia	37	15	43	30
Numana	36	50	43	40
Ancona	36	30	43	40

of the *Semnones* on the same bay

mouth of the Aesis river	36	20	43	40
Sena Gallica	36		43	40

Temple of Fortune (Fanum

Fortunae)	35	40	43	45
Pisaurum	35	20	43	45
Ariminum	35		43	50

of the *Boii Galli* on the same bay

mouth of the Rubicon river	34	55	43	55
Ravenna	34	40	44	
mouth of the Po river	34	45	44	

where a river flows from

Lario lake	29	20	44	45

where it forms one with the Dorias

river	30	40	43	45

where the Dorias river flows from the

Poenus lake	28	45	43	45

where a river flows into the Po rising in

Baenacus lake	31	45	43	30
position of this lake	30	30	45	

Above the mouth of the Po river, on the coast of Venetia

mouth of the Atrianus

river	34		44	10

of the *Carni* on the Adriatic at the innermost bend of the sea

mouth of Tilaventus river	33		44	50

mouth of the Natisonis

river	34		44	50

Istria where next to the innermost bend of the sea are

Tergestrum colonia	34	30	44	55
mouth of the Formionis river	35		44	55
Parentium	35	20	44	55
Pola	36		44	40
Nesactum	36	15	44	55

The interior towns of Istria

Pacinum	34	45	45	
Piquentum	35	30	45	5
Alvum	36		45	

Interior towns of the *Carni*

Forum Julium colonia	32	50	44	55
Concordia colonia	33	15	44	55
Aquileia colonia	34		45	

Interior towns of Venetia

Vicentia	32	10	44	30
Belunum	32	30	44	40
Acelum	32	30	44	30
Opitergium	32	40	44	45
Ateste	32	40	44	15
Patavium	32	50	44	30
Altinum	33	15	44	25
Atria	34	10	44	5

Towns of the *Cenomani* who are below Venetia

Bergomum	32		44	20
Forum Jutuntorum	31	45	44	
Brixia	32	30	44	10
Cremona colonia	32		43	40
Verona	33		44	
Mantua	32	45	43	40
Tridente	33	40	43	45
Butrium	34		43	50

Towns of the *Beluni,* who are toward the west of Venetia

Vaunia	31		44	40
Carraca	31	20	44	40
Bretina	31	40	44	45
Anaunium	31	30	44	30

Towns of the *Insubres,* who are toward the west from the *Cenomani*

Nobaria	30	30	44	30
Mediolanium	30	40	44	15
Comum	31		44	20
Ticinum	31		44	

Towns of the *Salassi,* who are below the *Insubres*

Augusta Praetoria colonia	30		44	
Eporedia	33	15	43	50

Towns of the *Taurini* who are below the *Salassi*

Augusta Taurinorum	30	30	43	40
Augusta Bagiennorum	29	30	43	20
Iria	30		43	20
Dertona	30	30	43	20

Towns of the *Libici,* who are below the *Insubres*

Vercellae	30	45	43	50
Laumellum	31	30	43	40

Towns of the *Ceutrones* in the Graian Alps

Forum Claudii	29		44	55
Axima	29	45	44	55

Town of the *Leponti,* which is in the Cottian Alps

Oscela	29		44	40

Town of the *Caturiges* in the Graian Alps

Eburodunum	29	40	44	30

Towns of the *Segusiani* in the Graian Alps

Segusium	28	30	43	55
Brigantium	29		44	5

Town of the *Nerusi* in the Maritime Alps

Vintium	28	30	43	40

Town of the *Suetri* in the Maritime Alps

Salinae	28	30	43	20

Towns of the *Vedianti* in the Maritime Alps

Cemenelum	28	30	43	5
Sanitium	28	30	42	50

The Apennine mountains are located not far above Liguria beginning at the Alps, and from Liguria extending as far as Ancona, then turning they approach the Adriatic, an extend as far as the Garganus mountains, then turning they extend toward the south to Leucopetra promontory.

Liguria, which is located below the Apennine mountains, has the following interior towns:

Sabata	29	20	43	
Pollentia	29	40	43	
Astam colonia	30	20	43	5
Albam Pompeiam	30	40	43	10
Libarnam	31		43	10

Gallia Togata is located above those mountains, extending as far as Ravenna, and it has these towns:

Placentia	31	20	43	30
Fidentiam	31	40	43	30
Brixellum	32		43	20
Parmam (colonia)	32		43	30
Rhegium Lepidum (colonia)	32	30	43	30
Nuceriam	32	30	43	20

	Long. °	Long. '	Lat. °	Lat. '
Tanetum	33	20	43	40
Mutinam	33		43	40
Bononiam	33	30	43	30
Claterna	33	50	43	30
Forum Cornelii	34	15	43	30
Caesenam	34	40	43	40
Faventiam	34	20	43	45

Towns of the *Tusci* in the interior

	Long. °	Long. '	Lat. °	Lat. '
Biracellum	31	45	43	10
Fossae Papiriane	32		42	50
Bondelia	32	30	42	50
Luca	33		43	10
Lucus Feroniae colonia	32	25	42	55
Pistoria	33	20	43	
Florentia	33	50	43	
Pisae colonia	33	30	42	45
Volaterrae	33	45	42	40
Rusellae	33	30	42	20
Faesulae	34		43	
Perusia	35	20	43	30
Arretium	34	40	42	45
Cortona	35	42	40	
Aculea	34	40	43	
Biturgia	35		42	55
Manliana	34	30	42	40
Vetulonium	34		42	30
Sena	34	20	42	30
Suana	34	50	42	25
Saturniana colonia	34		42	20
Eba	34	30	42	15
Volci	34	40	42	10
Clusium	34	40	42	20
Volsinium	35		42	20
Sudernum	35	30	42	5
Ferentia	35	30	42	20
Sutrium	36		42	10
Tarquinia	35	15	42	
Blera	35	40	41	55
Forum Clodii	35	55	41	55
Nepeta	36		41	50
Falerium	36	30	41	55
Caere	36	20	41	50

Towns of the *Semnones* in the interior

	Long. °	Long. '	Lat. °	Lat. '
Suasa	35	30	43	40
Ostra	36		43	30

Towns of the *Piceni*, in the interior

	Long. °	Long. '	Lat. °	Lat. '
Treja	36	30	42	25
Urbs Salvia	36	55	43	20
Septempeda	36	50	43	30
Cupra Montana	37	30	43	10
Firmium	37	30	42	55
Asculum	38	20	42	50
Adria	38	45	42	50

Towns of the *Umbri*, who are above the *Tusci* (Etruscans)

	Long. °	Long. '	Lat. °	Lat. '
Pitinum	34	40	43	15
Tifernum	34	40	43	25
Forum Sempronii	34	50	43	30
Iguvium	35		43	5
Aesis	35	20	43	20
Tuficum	35	30	43	5
Sentinum	36	30	42	50
Aesisium	35	20	42	45
Camerinum	36		43	
Nuceria colonia	35	50	42	40

Towns of the *Umbri* who are toward the east of the *Tusci*

	Long. °	Long. '	Lat. °	Lat. '
Arna	35	30	42	40
Hispellum	35	40	42	30
Tuder	35	50	42	20
Forum Flaminii	36		42	40
Spoletium	36	20	42	45
Mevania	36	15	42	30
Ameria	36	30	42	15
Narnia	36	30	42	30
Ocricolum	36	45	42	10

Town of the *Sabini*, who are toward the east of the *Umbri*,

	Long. °	Long. '	Lat. °	Lat. '
Nursia	36	45	42	50

Towns of the *Aequiculi*, who are east of the *Sabini*

	Long. °	Long. '	Lat. °	Lat. '
Cliternum	37	30	42	40
Carsioli	37	20	42	20

Towns of the *Marsi*, who are toward the east from *Aequiculi*

	Long. °	Long. '	Lat. °	Lat. '
Aex	37	40	42	30
Alba Fucinis	38		42	20

Towns of the *Praetuti*, who are toward the east from the *Marsi*

	Long. °	Long. '	Lat. °	Lat. '
Beregra	38	30	42	30
Interamnia	38	20	42	20

Towns of the *Vestini*, who are toward the east from the *Praetuti*

	Long. °	Long. '	Lat. °	Lat. '
Pinna	39		42	40
Avia	39		42	25
Amiternum	39		42	15
Angulus	39	30	42	30

Town of the *Marucini* in the interior

	Long. °	Long. '	Lat. °	Lat. '
Teatea	39	45	42	30

Towns of the *Latini* in the interior

	Long. °	Long. '	Lat. °	Lat. '
Rome	36	40	41	40
Tibur	36	50	42	
Praeneste	37	30	41	55
Tusculum	36	50	41	45
Aricia	37		41	40
Ardea	36	45	41	30
Nomentum	37	30	42	5

Treba	37	30	41	45
Anagnia	37	20	41	40
Velitra	37	30	41	30
Lanuvium	37	15	41	25
Atina	38	15	42	
Fidenae	38		41	55
Frusino	37	50	41	45
Ferentinum	38		41	40
Privernum	37	45	41	35
Setia	38		41	30
Aquinum	38	50	41	55
Sora	38	20	41	40
Minturna colonia	38	20	41	25
Fundi	38	10	41	30

Towns of the *Peligni* in the interior

Corfinium	40		42	20
Sulmo	40	30	42	

Towns of the *Frentani* in the interior

Anxanum	41	10	41	55
Larinum	41	30	41	30

Town of the *Caraceni*, who are below the *Frentani*

Aufidena	40	40	41	45

Towns of the *Samnites*, who are below the *Peligni* and the *Caraceni*

Bovianum	39	5	42	
Aesernia	39		41	40
Saepinum	39	40	41	50
Allifa	40		41	45
Tuticum	40	10	41	40
Telesia	40	30	41	20
Beneventum	41		41	20
Caudium	41	20	41	5

Towns of the *Campani* in the interior

Venafrum	38	40	41	40
Teanum	39		41	30
Suessa	38	40	41	25
Cales	39	20	41	30
Casilinum	39	15	41	20
Trebula	39	35	41	30
Forum Pompilii	39	45	41	15
Capua	40		41	10
Abella	40	20	41	10
Atella	40	10	41	5

Towns of the *Picentini* in the interior

Nola	40	15	40	45
Nuceria colonia	40	30	40	40

Towns of the *Lucani* in the interior

Ulci	40	40	40	30
Compsa	40	30	40	20
Potentia	40	40	40	15
Blanda	40	20	40	10
Grumentum	40	35	39	45

Towns of the *Irpini*, who are toward the east from the *Picentini* and the *Lucani*

Aquilonia	41		41	5
Abellinum	40	50	40	45
Aeculanum	41	20	40	45
Fratuolum	41		40	20

Towns of the *Apuli Dauni* in the interior

Teanum	40 41		41	25
Nuceria Apulorum (Apuli)	41	30	41	
Vibarna	42		41	
Arpi	41	40	41	15
Erdonia	41	40	40	40
Canusium	42	5	40	30

Towns of the *Apuli Peuciti* in the interior

Venusia	41	40	40	25
Celia	42	10	40	

Towns of the *Bruti* in the interior

Numistro	40	20	39	10
Consentia	40	40	39	10
Vibo Valentia	40	15	38	55

Towns of Magna Graecia in the interior

Petelia	40	45	39	
Abrystum	40	45	39	25

Towns of the *Salentini* in the interior

Rudia	41	50	39	45
Neretum	42		39	35
Aletium	42		39	20
Bausta	42	15	39	15
Exentum	42		39	10
Veretum	42	20	39	

Towns of Calabria in the interior

Sturni	42	30	39	20
Uretum	42	30	39	10

Islands which are near Italy in the Ligusticum sea

Aethale island	30	40	42	
Capraria island	32		42	
Ilva island	33		42	

These are the islands in the Tyrrhenum sea

Planasia island	34		41	
Pontia island	37	20	40	45
Pandataria island	37	50	40	45
Partenope island	38	20	40	45
Prochyte island	38	45	40	40
Pithecussa island	39	20	40	30
Caprea island	39	20	40	10
Sirenussae islands	39	30	39	55

In the Ionian sea there are five islands which are called Diomedeae located in

43	40	40	20

CHAPTER II

Location of Corsica island
(Seventh map of Europe)

CYRNUS island, which is also called Corsica, is surrounded on the west and the north by the Ligusticum sea, on the east by the Tyrrhenum sea, and on the south by that sea which lies between it and the Sardinian island.

The maritime coast of this island, if we begin in the middle on the north side, is described in this order

mouth of Volerius river	30	40	41	
Caesia coast	30	30	41	10
Tilox promontory	30		41	30
Description of the west coast				
Attii promontory	30		41	10
Casalus bay	30	15	40	25
Viriballum promontory	30	10	40	30
mouth of the Circidius river	30	10	40	25
Rhoetius mountains	30		40	20
Rhium promontory	30		40	15
Urcinium town	30	10	40	10
Arenosum coast	30	15	40	
mouth of the Locra river	30	10	39	55
Pauca town	30	15	39	45
mouth of the Ticarius river	30	15	39	40
Titianus harbor	30	10	39	35
Description of the south coast				
Ficaria town	30	30	39	30
mouth of the Pitanus river	30	45	39	20
Marianum promontory and town	31		39	10
Description of the east coast				
Palla town	31	20	39	20
Syracusanus harbor	31	20	39	25
Rubra town	31	20	39	30
Granianum promontory	31	30	39	40
Alista town	31	20	39	45
Philonii harbor	31	30	39	55
mouth of the Sacer river	31	30	40	
Aleria colonia	31	30	40	5
mouth of the Rotanus river	31	30	40	10
Diana harbor	31	20	40	20
Tutela altar	31	30	40	30
mouth of the Guola river	31	30	40	35
Mariana town	31	40	40	40
Vagum promontory	31	30	40	45
Mantinon town	31	20	41	
Clunium town	31	20	41	10
Description of the northeast coast:				
Sacrum promontory	31	30	41	35
Centurinum town	31	15	41	30
Canelata town	31		41	20

The native races inhabiting the island are the following: the *Cervini*, occupying the western part above the Aureus mountains and the location is 30 45 40 45

Below these are the *Tarabeni;* then the *Titiani;* next the *Balatini;* more to the north are the *Vanacini;* below whom are the *Celebenses;* then the *Licmini* and the *Macrini;* below whom are the *Opini;* then the *Symrbi* and the *Coymaseni;* below these but more toward the south are the *Subasani*.

The towns in the interior are

Ropicum	30	15	41	
Cersunum	30	30	41	
Palanta	30	20	40	45
Lurinum	31		40	45
Aluca	30	20	40	30
Osincum	30	30	40	30
Sermigium	30	20	40	20
Talcinum	30	45	40	30
Venicium	30	50	40	20
Cenestum	31		40	15
Opinum	31	20	40	25
Mora	30	30	40	
Matisa	30	45	39	35
Albiana	31		39	30

CHAPTER III

Location of Sardinia island
(Seventh map of Europe)

THE island of Sardinia is bordered on the east by the Tyrrhenum sea, on the south by the Africum sea, on the west by the Sardus sea, on the north by that sea which is between it and Cyrnum (Corsica) island.

The maritime coast of this island is thus described:

Description of the west coast

Gorditanum promontory	29	50	38	45
Tilium town	30		38	40
Nymphaeus harbor	30	10	38	30
Hermaeum promontory	30		38	15
mouth of the Temus river	30	15	38	
Coracodes harbor	30	20	37	35
Tarrae town	30	20	37	20
mouth of the Thyrsus river	30	30	37	10
Usellis town, colonia	30	30	36	55
mouth of the Sacer river	30	30	36	40
Osaea town	30	30	36	30
Sardopatoris temple	30	30	36	20

Neapolis	30	40	36	30
Crassum promontory	30	40	36	

Description of the southern side

Pupulum town	30	50	35	40
Solci town	31	10	35	50
Solci harbor	31	15	35	50
Chersonesus	31	30	35	45
Bioea harbor	31	40	35	50
Bioea town	31	45	35	50
Herculis harbor	32		35	50
Nora town	32		35	55
Resounding coast	32	5	35	55
Cuniocharium promontory	32	15	35	55

Description of the eastern side

Caralis town and promontory	32	30	36	
Caralitanus bay	32	10	36	20
Susaleos village	31	55	36	40
mouth of the Saeprus river	32		37	
Supicius harbor	31	50	37	30
mouth of the Caedris river	32		38	
Feronia town	31	45	38	10
Olbia town	31	40	38	30
Olbianus harbor	31	40	38	45
Columbarium promontory	31	45	39	
Ursi promontory	31	45	39	10

Description of the northeast coast

Errebantium promontory	31	30	39	20
Pluvium town	31	30	39	5
Juliola town	30	10	39	
Tibula town	30	40	38	50
Turris Libisonis, town	30	15	38	50

The *Tibulati* and the *Corsi* inhabit the parts of the island farthest north; below whom are the *Coracenses;* then the *Carenses* and the *Cunusitani;* below whom are the *Salcitani* and the *Lucuidonenses;* then the *Aesaronenses;* below whom are the *Cornenses* or *Aechilenses;* then the *Rucensi;* below whom are the *Celsitani* and the *Corpicenses;* then the *Scapitani* and the *Siculensi;* below whom are the *Neapolitani* and the *Valentini;* and farthest south are the *Solcitani* and the *Noritani.*

The towns in the interior are

Erycinum	31		38	40
Heraeum	31	30	38	40
Gurulis ancient	30	30	38	30
Bosa	30	30	38	15
Macopsisa	31	15	38	15

Below these towns are the Insani mountains

	31		38	
Gurulis nova	30	30	37	50
Saralapis	31	15	37	45

Cornus	30	30	37	45
Aqua Hypsitanae	30	40	37	15
Aquae Lesitanae	31	30	36	45
Lesa	31	30	36	35
Aquae Neapolitanae	31	45	36	10
Valentia town	31	55	36	30

The islands around Sardinia are

Phintonis island	30	40	39	15
Ilva island	30	30	39	20
Nymphaea island	29	45	38	30
Herculis island	29	20	39	
Diabate island	29	30	38	45
Accipitrum island	30		35	45
Plumbaria island	30	30	35	30
Ficaria island	33		39	
Hermaea island	33		37	20

CHAPTER IV

*Location of Sicily island
(Seventh map of Europe)*

SICILY is surrounded on the west and the north by the Tyrrhenum sea, on the south by the Africum, on the east by the Adriatic sea. The maritime shore of this island is thus described: the central part of the north side, which, terminating in a point, and more toward the north, is called

Pelorus promontory	39	40	38	35

A description of the west side on the Tyrrhenum sea

Phalacrum promontory	39	10	38	30
Mylae	39		38	30
mouth of the Helicon river	38	50	38	25
Tyndarium	38	30	38	20
mouth of the Thymethus river	39	20	38	20
Agathyrnum	38		38	15
Alontium	37	50	38	10
mouth of the Chyda river	37	45	38	5
Calacta	37	40	37	55
Alaesa	37	40	37	45
mouth of the Monalus	37	30	37	45
Cephaloedis	37	20	37	40
mouth of the Himera river	37	15	37	20
town of Therma Himera	37	5	37	15
Solus town	37		37	20
mouth of the Eleutherus	37		37	5
Panormus	37		37	
Cetaria	37		36	45
mouth of the Bathis river	37		36	40
Emporium Segestanum	37		36	30
Drepanum	36	55	36	30
Aegitharsus promontory	36	50	36	15

Description of the southern side toward the Africum sea

Lilybaeum city and promontory	37		36	
mouth of the Acithius river	37	10	36	5
mouth of the Mazaras river	37	20	36	15
mouth of the Selinuntis river	27	30	36	15
Pintia	37	40	36	20
mouth of the Sossius river	37	50	36	20
mouth of the Isburus river	38	5	36	25
Heraclea	38	20	36	25
mouth of the Hypsa river	38	30	36	25
Agrigentinum emporium	38	50	36	25
mouth of the Himera river	39		36	20
mouth of the Hipparus river	39	15	36	20
Bruca promontory	39	20	36	20
Caucana harbor	39	30	36	15
mouth of the Motycanus river	39	40	36	20
Ulixia promontory	39	50	36	15

Description of the eastern shore on the Adriatic sea

Pachynus promontory	40		36	20
Phoenicus harbor	39	45	36	30
mouth of the Erinous river	39	45	36	40
Longum promontory	39	50	36	45
Chersonesus	39	40	36	55
Syracusa colonia	36	30	37	
mouth of the Alabus river	39	25	37	20
Taurus promontory	39	30	37	30
mouth of the Pantacius river	39	25	37	35
mouth of the Symaethus river	39	35	37	40
Catana colonia	39	30	37	45
Argennum promontory	39	30	37	50
Tauromenium colonia	39	30	38	10
Messena in the strait	39	30	38	30

The mountains in this island, which are well known, are

Aetna	39		38	
Cratos	37	40	36	40

The *Messeni* occupy the northern part of this island, the *Herbitae* and *Catanei* the middle, and the southern part the *Segestani* and *Syracusi* inhabit.

The inland towns of Sicily are

Capytium	38	20	38	15
Abacaena	39		38	15
Imachara	38	30	38	
Tissa	38	50	38	

Aleta	37	50	37	50
Centuripa	38	30	37	50
Dymethus	38	50	37	50
Aetna	39	25	37	45
Agurium	38	15	37	40
Herbita	37	40	37	30
Sergentium (Ergetium)	38	30	37	30
Hydia	38	45	37	30
Leontium	39		37	30
Erbessus	37	50	37	20
Neetum	38	20	37	25
Menae	38	50	37	25
Paciorus	37	20	37	10
Assorus	37	40	37	20
Enna	38	5	37	15
Megara	39	15	37	15
Petra	38	40	37	5
Hybla	38	20	37	
Engyum	39		37	
Cotyrga	38	20	36	50
Macyrum	38	40	36	50
Acrae	39	15	36	40
Macella	37	15	36	40
Schera	37	30	36	50
Triocala	38		36	45
Agrigentum	38	30	36	40
Motyca	39	25	36	40
Segesta	37	5	36	30
Letum	37	30	36	30
Entella	37	45	36	30
Ancrina	38	10	36	35
Phthinthia	38	40	36	30
Gela	39		36	30
Camarina	39	20	36	25
Elorus	39	40	36	30
Ina	39	30	36	25
Helcethium	37	15	36	15

And the islands located around Sicily and near it are

Didyme island	39		39	
Hicesia island	39	30	39	
Ericodes island	38	20	38	45
Phoenicodes island	38	30	38	50
Vulcani island	38	50	38	35
Lipara island and town	39		38	45
Euonymos island	39	10	38	45
Strongyle island	39	30	38	45
Ustica island and town	37	30	38	45
Osteodes island	36	15	37	
Phorbantia island	36		36	20
Aegusa island	36	15	36	5
Hiera island	36		36	
Paconia island	36	30	35	50
Aeoli island	37		39	

CHAPTER V

*Location of European Sarmatia
(Eighth map of Europe)*

EUROPEAN Sarmatia is terminated on the north by the Sarmatian ocean adjoining the Venedicus bay and by a part of the unknown land, a description of which is the following:

mouth of the Chronus river 50		56
mouth of the Rubonis river 53		57
mouth of the Turuntus river	56	58 30
mouth of the Chesinus river 58 30		59 30

The terminus of its maritime coast is located on that parallel extending through Thule, which parallel is the terminus of the known sea   62   63

The terminus of Sarmatia, which extends southward through the sources of the Tanais river is   64   63

It is terminated in the west by the Vistula river and by that part of Germania lying between its source and the Sarmatian mountains but not by the mountains themselves the position of which has been indicated; on the south by Iazyges Metanastae then from the southern terminus of the Sarmatian mountains to the beginning of the Carpathian mountains which is

in   46   48 30

and by the following part of Dacia along that parallel up to the mouth of the Borysthenes river, and the shore of Pontus which is near the Carcinitus river; then along the maritime coast is

mouth of the Borysthenes river	57 30	48 30
mouth of the Hypanis river 58		48 30
Hecates forest, promontory 58 30	47 45	
Isthmus of Cursus Achilles 59		47 40

The western promontory of the Isthmus of Achilles is called

Sacred promontory	57 50	47 30

The eastern promontory is called

Mysaris promontory	59 45	47 30
Cephalonensus	59 45	47 50
Pulcher harbor	59 30	47 45
Tamyrace	59 20	48 30
mouth of the Carcinitus river	59 40	48 30

Next is the isthmus separating the Tauric peninsula, the terminus of which is on the Carcinitus bay in the

position	60 20	48 20
which is near Byce lake	60 30	48 30

On the east Sarmatia is bounded by the isthmus which is near the Carcinitus river, which is near Byce lake   60 30   48 30 Maeotis which extends as far as the Tanais river, then by the Tanais river, and by the line which extends from the sources of the Tanais river toward the unknown land as far as the indicated terminus.

This side is thus described from the isthmus which is near the Carcinitus river and along Maeotis lake:

Neontichus	60 30	48 40
mouth of the Pasiacus river 60 20		49 30
Lianum town	60	49 15
mouth of the Byce river	60 20	49 30
Acra town	60 30	49 40
mouth of the Gerrhus river 61		49 50
Cnema town	62 30	49 45
Agarum promontory	63	49 40
mouth of the Agarus river 62 30		50 30
Dark woodland, Piscatura Dei	62 40	51 15
mouth of the Lycus river	63	51 30
Hygres town	63 30	52 30
mouth of the Poritus river 64 30		53
Caroca village	65	53 30
western mouth of the Tanais river	66 20	54 20
Eastern mouth	67	54 30
Bend of the river	72 30	56
Source of the river	64	58

Above this the terminus, which I have mentioned, near the unknown land, the location of which is   64   63

Sarmatia is divided by other mountains, which are called

Peuce mountains	51	51
Amadoci mountains	55	51
Bodinus mountains	58	55
Alanus mountains	62 30	55
Carpathian mountains as we call them	46	48 30
Venedici mountains	47 30	55
Ripaei, the middle of which is in	63	57 30

The part of the Borysthenes river which is near Amodoca lake is in 53 30   50 20

The source of the Borysthenes river more toward the north is in   52   53

Of the rivers which are below the Borysthenes the Tyras separates parts of Dacia

and Sarmatia at the bend which is located in   53   48 30

The Axiaces river flows through Sarmatia not far above Dacia, and from the Carpathian mountains.

The *Greater Venedae* races inhabit Sarmatia along the entire Venedicus bay; and above Dacia are the *Peucini* and the *Basternae*; and along the entire coast of *Maeotis* are the *Iazyges* and the *Rhoxolani*; more toward the interior from these are the *Amaxobi* and the *Scythian Alani*.

Lesser races inhabit Sarmatia near the Vistula river.

Below the *Venedae* are the *Gythones*, then the *Finni*, then the *Sulones*; below whom are the *Phrungundiones*; then the *Avarini* near the source of the Vistula river; below these are the *Ombrones*, then the *Anartophracti*, then the *Burgiones*, then the *Arsietae*, then the *Saboci*, then the *Piengitae* and the *Biessi* near the Carpathian mountains.

Among those we have named to the east: below the *Venedae* are the *Galindae*, the *Sudini*, and the *Stavani*, extending as far as the *Alauni*; below these are the *Igylliones*, then the *Coestoboci* and the *Transmontani* extending as far as the Peuca mountains.

Back from the Ocean, near the Venedicus bay, the *Veltae* dwell, above whom are the *Ossi*; then more toward the north the *Carbones* and toward the east are *Careotae* and the *Sali*; below whom are the *Gelones*, the *Hippopodes* and the *Melanchlaeni*; below these are the *Agathyrsi*; then the *Aorsi* and the *Pagyritae*; then the *Savari* and the *Borusci* to the Ripaeos mountains; then the *Acibi* and the *Nasci*; below whom are the *Vibiones* and the *Idrae*; and below the *Vibiones* bordering on the *Alauni* are the *Sturni*, and between the *Alauni* and the *Amaxobios* are the *Cariones* and the *Sargati*; near the bend of the Tanis river are the *Ophlones* and then the *Tanaitae*; below whom are the *Osili* extending as far as Rhoxolanis; between the *Amaxobi* and the *Rhoxolani* are the *Rheucanali* and the *Exobygitae*; and between the *Peucini* and the *Basternae* are the *Carpiani*, above whom are the *Gevini*, then the *Bodini*; between the *Basternae* and the *Rhoxolani* are the *Chuni*, and below the mountains named from these are the *Amadoci* and the *Navari*.

Near Byce lake dwell the *Toreccadae*, and near Achilles Cursus the *Tauroscythae*; below the *Basternae* near Dacia are the *Tigri* and below these are the *Tyrangitae*.

Below the bend of the Tanais river are located:

the Alexandri Arae
(Altars)   63   57
and the Caesar Arae
(Altars)   68   56 30
and on the shore of the river is
Tanais town   67   54 40

The inland towns in the river regions around the Carcinitus river are

Carcina town	59 30	48 45	
Torocca	58 30	49	
Pasyris	58 30	49 10	
Ercabum	58 30	49 15	
Tracana	58 30	49 45	
Navarum	58 30	50	

Along the Borysthenes river are

Azagarium	56	50 40	
Amadoca	56	50 30	
Sarum	56	50 15	
Serimum	57	50	
Metropolis	56 30	49 30	
Olbia or Borysthenes	57	49	

above the Axiaces river

Ordessus	57	48 30

And near the river which flows into the Borysthenes:

Leinum town	54	50 15	
Sarbacum	55	50	
Niossum	56	49 40	

Above the Tyras river near Dacia

Carrodunum	49 30	48 40	
Maetonium	51	48 30	
Clepidava	52 30	48 40	
Vibantavarium	53 30	48 40	
Eractum	53 50	48 40	

The island located near the mouth of the Tanais river is Alopecia or Tanais island   66 30   53 30

CHAPTER VI

Location of the Tauric peninsula
(Eighth map of Europe)

THE Tauric peninsula is bounded by the isthmus which extends from the Carcenites bay to Byce lake, then by the coast of Pontus Euxinus, of the Bosphorus

Cimmerius, and of Lake Maeotus, a description of which coasts is the following:

Next, after the isthmus, which is near the Carcenites river flowing into the Pontus

Eupatoria town	60	45	47	40
Dandace	60	45	47	20
Symbolon harbor	61		47	15
Parthenium promontory	60	40	47	
Chersonesus	61		47	
Ctenus harbor	61	15	47	10
Criumetopon promontory	62		46	40
Charax	62		46	50
Lagyra	62	30	47	
Corax promontory	63		47	
mouth of the Istrianus river	63	10	47	10
Theodosia	63	20	47	20
Nymphaeum	63	45	47	30

On the Cimmerius Bosporus

Tyrictace	63	30	47	40
Panticapaea	64		47	55
Myrmecium promontory	64		48	30

On Lake Maeotis

Parthenium	63	45	48	30
Zenonis Chersonesus	63		48	45
Heracleum	62		48	30

Inland towns which are in the Tauric peninsula

Taphrus	60	40	48	15
Tarona	62	20	48	15
Postigia	63		48	15
Parosta	61	30	48	10
Cimmerium	62		48	
Portacra	61	50	47	40
Boeon	62	50	47	45
Iluratum	63	20	47	45
Satarche	61	15	47	20
Badatium	61	30	47	30
Cytaeum	62	15	47	30
Tazus	62	40	47	30
Argoda	61	45	47	15
Tabana	62	20	47	15

CHAPTER VII

Location of Iazyges Metanastae
(Ninth map of Europe)

THE region of Iazyges Metanastae is terminated on the north by the indicated boundary line of European Sarmatia beginning near the southern part of the Sarmatian mountains and extending to the Carpathian mountains; on the west by the indicated part of Germania which extends

from the Sarmatian mountains to the Danube river near the Carpis bend, thence following that river to the mouth of the Tibiscus river, which, flowing from the north, empties into it. The position of its mouth is   46   44 15

On the east it is terminated by Dacia along that river Tibiscus which rises in the Carpathian mountains. The location of these mountains is   46   48 30

The towns in this Iazyges Metanastae region are

Uscenum	43	15	48	20
Bormanum	43	40	48	15
Abieta	43	40	48	
Trissum	44	10	47	45
Parca	43	30	47	40
Candanum	44		47	20
Pessium	44	40	47	
Partiscum	45		46	40

CHAPTER VIII

Location of Dacia
(Ninth map of Europe)

DACIA is bounded on the north by that part of European Sarmatia, which extends from the Carpathian mountains to that terminus where, as we have shown, the Tyras river is deflected in its course
in   53   48 30
on the west by Iazyges Metanastae along the Tibiscus river; on the south by that part of the Danube river between the mouth of the Tibiscus river and Axiopolis, from which town as far as the Pontus and the mouth of the Danube it is called the Ister; the several sections of this southern boundary are:

After the mouth of the Tibiscus river the first turn which is west-southwest is
in   47 20   44 45
then a bend near the entrance of the Rabon river which flows from Dacia
in   49   43 30
and a bend at the entrance of the Ciabrus river which is in   49 30   43 45
a bend near the entrance of the Alutas river which comes from the north in
Dacia   50 15   44
a bend near Oescus   51   44
a bend near Axiopolim   54 20   44 45
thence the Danube river to its mouth is called the Ister as we have said.

On the east Dacia is bounded by the Ister river near the bend close to the town Dinogetia, the location of which is

in   53   46 40

then by the river Hierasus, which near Dinogetia flows into the Ister from the north, and turning eastward extends as far as the indicated bend of the Tyras river.

The *Anarti*, the *Teurisci* and the *Coestoboci* inhabit Dacia in the northern part, beginning from the west; below these are the *Praedavenses*, the *Rhatacenses*, and the *Caucoenses*; below these, in this order, are the *Biephi*, the *Burideenses*, and the *Cotenses*, and below these are the *Albocenses*, the *Potulatenses*, and the *Senses*; below these, in the southern region, are the *Saldenses*, the *Ciagisi*, and the *Piephigi*.

The most important towns of Dacia are these:

Rucconium	46	30	48	10
Docidava	47	20	48	
Porolissum	49		48	
Arcobadara	50	40	48	
Triphulum	52	15	48	15
Patridava	53		48	10
Carsidava	53	20	48	15
Petrodava	53	45	47	40
Ulpianum	47	30	47	30
Napuca	49		47	40
Patruissa	49		47	20
Salinae	49	15	47	10
Praetoria Augusta	50	30	47	
Sandava	51	30	47	30
Angustia	52	15	47	15
Utidava	53	10	47	40
Marcodava	49	30	47	
Ziridava	45	30	46	20
Singidava	48		46	20
Apulum	49	15	46	40
Zermizirga	49	30	46	15
Comidava	51	30	46	40
Ramidava	51	50	46	30
Pirum	51	15	46	
Zusidava	52	40	46	15
Polonda	53		47	
Zurobara	45	40	45	40
Lizisis	46	15	45	20
Argidava	46	30	45	15
Tibiscum	48	30	45	15
Zarmizegethusa regia	47	50	45	15
Aquae	49	30	45	20
Netindava	52	45	45	30
Tiasum	52		45	30
Zeugma	46	40	44	40
Tibiscum	46	40	44	50
Dierna	47	15	44	30
Acmonia	48		45	
Drubetis	47	45	44	30
Frateria	49	30	44	30
Arcinna	49		44	45
Pinum	50	30	44	40
Amutrium	50		44	45
Sornum	51	30	45	

CHAPTER IX

Location of Upper Moesia
(Ninth map of Europe)

UPPER Moesia is terminated on the west by Dalmatia along that line to which we have referred, leading from the mouth of the river Savus to the Scardus mountains; on the south by a part of Macedonia on a line extending along the Orbelus mountains as far as the terminus, the position of which is in   49   42 20 on the east by that part of Thrace which extends from the indicated terminus as far as the Ciabrus river the location of which is

in   50   43

and by the Ciabrus river along Lower Moesia to the junction of the Danube and the Ciabrus which is in   49 30   43 45 on the north by a part of the Danube river as far as the Savus river.

The *Tricornenses* inhabit the parts of this province near Dalmatia, the *Moesi* are along the Ciabrus river, and between them are the *Picenses*, and near Macedonia are the *Dardani*.

The towns on the Danube river are

Singidunum	45	30	44	30
Legio IV Flavia				
Tricornium	46		44	10

near which the Margus river flows into it (the Danube)

Viminacium legion	46	30	44	20
Tanatis	47		44	
Egeta	47	15	43	40
Dorticum	48		43	30
Rhatiaria Moesorum	49		43	20

Other towns remote from the Danube river are

Orrhea	46	45	43	30
Timacum	47	30	43	
Vendenis	48		42	50

Velanis	49	42	45
and the four towns of Dardania			
Naessum	47 20	42	30
Arribantium	47 30	42	
Ulpianum	48 30	42	40
Scupi	48 30	42	30

CHAPTER X

Location of Lower Moesia
(Ninth map of Europe)

LOWER Moesia is bounded on the west by that part of the Ciabrus river to which we have referred; on the south by that part of Thrace which extends from the Ciabrus river north of the Haemus mountains to the terminus on the Pontus located in 55 44 40 on the north by that part of the Danube we have before mentioned, which extends from the Ciabrus river to Axiopolis, and by the remaining part of the Danube which is called the Ister, and from the bend of this river toward the Pontus at the town Dinogetia located, as we have said in 53 46 40

The following is the order of the mouths of the Danube: the first of these mouths, which is near the town Noviodunum, has the location 54 50 46 30 then the one, farther north, surrounding the island which is called the Peuce, but on the Pontine coast is called Sacrum or Peuce, and is located in 56 46 15 the one yet further north is divided and is located in 55 46 45 the part of this section of the river which is toward the north is divided in 55 30 47 then a part of the southern section divides its course shortly before it flows into the Pontus; the part toward the north flows through a swamp which is called Thiagola located in 55 40 47 15 it flows into the Pontus from the coast which is called Thiagola or Tenue located in 56 15 47

The other part of this river section toward the south is divided in 55 20 46 45 and the part which is toward the south from this section flows into the Pontus, through that coast which is called Boreum, in the location 56 20 46 50

and this southern part is divided in 55 40 46 30

The part toward the south of this section flows into the Pontus through the coast which is called Naracium, the location of which is 56 10 46 20 the northern part is divided in the location 56 46 40 and the part from this section toward the north flows through the Pseudostomus coast, the location of which is in 56 15 46 40 the southern part flows through the coast which is called Pulcrum, the location of which is 56 15 46 30

The side of Moesia on the east is terminated by that part of the coast of the Pontus south of the mouth (of the Danube) at the indicated terminus in the confines of Thrace in 55 44 40

A description of this eastern side of Moesia after the Sacrum mouth of the Ister is the following:

Pterum promontory	56 20	46	
Istrus town	55 40	46	
Tomi	55	45	50
Callatis	54 40	45	30
Dionysopolis	54 20	45	15
Tiristis promontory	55	45	10
Odessus	54 50	45	
mouth of the Panysus river	54 45	44	50
Mesembria	55	44	40

The *Triballi* inhabit the western parts of Lower Moesia; toward the east are the *Troglodytes* who are below the Peuce mouth of the Danube; at the mouth are the *Peucini*, and the *Crobyzi* who dwell on the coast of the Pontus, and south of these are the *Oetenses* and the *Obulenses*; moreover in the section between the *Triballi* and the *Crobizi* are the *Dimenses* and the *Piarenses*.

The towns on the Danube river are the following:

Regianum	50	43	40
Oescus Triballorum	51	44	
Diacum	51 20	44	20
Novae (Legio I Italica)	52	44	40
Trimannium	52 20	44	50
Prista town	52 40	45	10
Tramarisca	53 15	45	15
Durostolum legio	53 30	45	30
Legio (XI Claudia)			
Sucidava	54	45	40
Axiopolis	54 20	45	45
Carsum	54 10	45	50

Troesmis	54	46	20
Legio V Macedonica			
Dinogetia	53 10	46	40
Noviodunum	54 40	46	30
Sitioenta	55	46	30

Between the river and the Haemus mountains are these towns:

Dausdava	53	44	40
Tibisca	55	46	20

The *Harpi* inhabit the maritime coast from that mouth of the Ister, which is farthest north, even to the mouth of the Borysthenes river, and the interior region to the Hierasus river below the Sarmatian Tyrgetas, and here also are the *Britolagae* above the *Peucini*. The following is a description of this coast:

south of the mouth of the Borysthenes river which we have mentioned as being located in	57 30	48	30
mouth of the Axiaces river	57	48	
Physca town	56 40	47	40
mouth of the Tyras river	56 20	47	40
Hermonactis village	56 15	47	30
Harpis town	56	47	15

The island towns in this region, and those near the Hierasus river are:

Zargidava	54 40	47	45
Tamasidava	54 20	47	30
Piroboridava	54	47	

between the Hierasus and the Tyras rivers

Niconium	56 20	48	10
Ophiussa	56	48	
Tyras town	56	47	40

The islands adjacent to Lower Moesia in this part which we have described are the island which is called

Borysthenes	57 15	47	40
and Achillis or Leuce island	57 30	47	40

CHAPTER XI

Location of Thrace
(Ninth map of Europe)

THRACE is bounded on the north by Lower Moesia along the line above indicated; on the west by Upper Moesia and a part of Macedonia, from the Orbelus mountains, as we have said to the terminus, the location of which is in 49   41 45 It is bounded on the south by that part of Macedonia extending from the indicated terminus to the mouth of the Nestus river, through the Pangaeus mountains, and by

the coast which runs along the Aegean sea, and by a part of the Melas bay which leads from this bay separating the peninsula from the continent; the localities along this side are

mouth of the Nestus river	51 45	41	45
Abdera	52 10	41	45
Maronea	52 40	41	40
mouth of the Hebrus river	53	41	30
Aenus town	53 10	41	30
in the Melas bay			
mouth of the Melas river	53 30	41	30
terminus of the peninsula which is in the Melas bay	53 50	41	30
the Propontis terminus of the peninsula	54 20	41	30

On the east, Thrace is terminated by the Propontis and by the Pontine coast which is called the Thracian Bosporus, thence along the coast of Pontus to the terminus on the confines of Lower Moesia, which is located in   55   44 40

The following is a description from this terminus: after the city Mesembria of Moesia

Anchialus	54 45	44	30
Apollonia	54 50	44	20
Tonzus	55	44	10
Peronticum	55 10	44	
Thynias promontory	55 40	44	
Salmydessus, shore	55 40	43	40
Philia promontory	55 30	43	30
Phinopolis	55 30	42	20
and on the Pontine coast			
Byzantium	56	43	5

Then along the Propontis

mouth of the Rathynius river	55 30	43	
mouth of the Athyra river	55 30	42	55
Selymbria	55	42	30
Perinthus	54 50	42	20
mouth of the Arzus river	54 50	42	10
Bisanthe	54 50	42	
Macron Tichos	54 50	41	50
Pactye	54 30	41	45

and next to the terminus of the peninsula to which I have referred.

Of the mountains in Thrace which are important, are the Haemus mountains which extend along the confines of Upper Moesia, and the Rhodope mountains above the Nestus and the Hebrus river, between which rivers almost in the middle near the

sea is a lake, which is called Bistonis lake, the position of which is in 52 30 41 50

The prefectures in this province bordering on both Moesias, and extending along the Haemus mountains, beginning on the west, are Dantheletica, Sardica, Usdicesica, and Selletica; those bordering on Macedonia and the Aegean sea in the following order, are Maedica, Drosica, Coeletica, Sapaica, Corpillica, and Caenica; above Maedica is Bessica; below which is Bennica, and next is Samaica; along the shore, which extends from the town Perinthus to Apollonia, is the Astica prefecture.

The inland towns of Thrace are

Praesidum	51	20	43	10
Nicopolis near Haemum	52		43	45
Ostaphus	52	30	43	30
Valla	52	40	42	43
Opisena	53	20	44	
Develtus colonia	54	20	44	15
Orcelis	54	20	43	40
Carpudaemum	54		43	5
Bizye	54	50	43	45
Sardica	50	10	43	
Terta	51	40	43	5
Philippopolis	52	30	42	45
Arzus	53	15	43	10
Tonzus	54	30	43	20
Cabyle	54	50	43	15
Bergule	54	30	43	
Pautalia	50		43	30
Nicopolis near Nestum	51	45	42	20
Topiris	51	20	42	
Pergamum	52		42	30
Traianopolis	53		42	15
Plotinopolis	53	40	42	40
Drusipara	54	30	42	40
Dyme	52	50	41	45
Cypsella	53	5	41	40
Aphrodisias	53	55	41	40
Apri colonia	54		42	
Heraclea	54	20	41	50
Lysimachia	54	10	41	30

The island which is near Thrace above the Bosporus to eastward is

Cyanea	56	20	43	20

in the Propontis is the island

Proconnesus	55	30	42	

Islands in the Aegean sea are

Thasos island and town	51	45	41	30
Samothrace island and town	52	30	41	15
Imbros island	53	20	41	15

The peninsula is bordered on the north by that line which we have said is the boundary of Thrace, by the Melas bay to the Propontis, and by that part of Propontis which is near Callipolim, the location of which is in 55 41 30 on the west by the remaining part of Melas bay, on which is

Cardia city	54	41	5

and the Mastusia promontory 54 30 40 40 on the south by the Aegean sea, on which is the town Elaeus 54 30 40 45 and which is near the promontory in 54 40 40 45 on the east by the Hellespontus, on which are these towns:

Coela	54 55	41	
Sestus	54 55	41	15

then, as we have said, the town

Callipolis	55	41	30

CHAPTER XII

Location of Macedonia
(Tenth map of Europe)

MACEDONIA is terminated on the north by the boundary line of Dalmatia, of Upper Moesia and of Thrace, the locations of which we have indicated; on the west by the Ionian sea from Dyrrachium to the river Celydnus, a description of its boundary regions is the following:

In Taulanti

Dyrrachium	45		40 55
mouth of the Panyassus river	45		40 40
mouth of the Apsi river	45	5	40 30
Apollonia	45	5	40 10
mouth of the Laus river	45		40
Aulon town and naval station	44	50	39 55

In Elimiotis

Bullis	45	39 45

In Orestis

Amantia	44 55	39 50
mouth of the Celydnus river	45	39 20

on the south it is bounded by that line which runs along Epirus to the terminus, the location of which is 47 40 38 45 along this line extends the Pindus mountain through that region, the central part of which is in 47 40 38 45

and then along Achaia to the terminus in the Maliacus bay, the location of which is 51 38 25 on this line is the Oeta mountains, the central part of which is in 50 30 28 35

In the east it is terminated by that part of Thrace to which we have referred and by the bays of the Aegean sea, which extend from the Nestos river to that which we have indicated as the terminus of the Maliacus bay, of which bay the following is a description: after the Nestos river, by which Thrace is terminated, and the mouths of which are located in 51 45 41 45

In the Strymonicus bay on the maritime shores of Edonis

Neapolis	51	15	41	45
Oesyme	50	50	41	45
mouth of the Strymon river	50	15	41	25

In Amphaxitis

Arethusa	50	10	41	20
Stagira	50	20	41	10

In Chalcidice

Panormus harbor and town	50	40	41	
Mount Athos	51		41	10
Athos promontory and town	51	15	41	15
Central part of the mountain	51	10	41	
Nymphaeum promontory	51	10	40	45

On the Singiticus bay

Stratonice	50	55	40	55
Acanthus	50	40	40	55
Singus	50	30	40	40

In Paraetia

Ampelus promontory	51	15	40	30
Derris promontory	51	15	40	20
Torone	50	45	40	25
Toronaicus bay, innermost recess	50	40	40	25
Pallenes on the narrow part of peninsula	51		40	5
Canastraeum promontory	51	15	39	55
Cassandrea	51	5	40	

On the Thermaicus bay

mouth of the Chabris river	50	40	40	5
Gigonis promontory	50	30	40	5

In Amphaxitis

Thessalonice	49	50	49	20
mouth of the Echedorus river	49	45	40	15
mouth of the Axius river	49	40	40	10

In Pieria

mouth of the Lydias river	49	30	40	
Pydna	49	40	39	45
mouth of the Haliacmon river	49	50	39	40
Dium colonia	50		39	35
mouth of the Baphyras river	50	10	39	30
mouth of the Peneus river	50	30	39	25

In Pelasgiota

Magnesium promontory	51	40	39	30
Sepias promontory	51	45	39	15
Aeanteum	51	40	39	15
Iolcus	51	30	39	15

In Phthiotis on the Pelasgian bay

Pagasae	50	50	38	55
Demetrias	50	30	38	55
Posidium promontory	51	30	38	50
Larissa	51	20	38	45
Echinus	51	10	38	45
Sperchea	51		38	40
Thebae Phthiotidis	51		38	35
mouth of the Spercheus river	51		38	35

The Strymon river rises in the mountains on the confines of Thrace and Macedonia, the sources of which are in 48 40 42 and the Axius river rises in the Scardus mountains in the location 47 41 40 and in the mountains, which are below Dalmatia, the position of which is 46 41 15 the sources of this river unite in 49 15 40 15 the river Haliacmon rises in the Candavius mountains in 46 40 40 10 the river Peneus flows from the Pindus mountains in 47 30 39 and the Spercheus river in 48 30 39 40

Among the mountains which have received a name the central position of Bertissus is in 49 10 41 15

of the Bermius mountains is	48	30	39	50
of the Cercetius mountains	46	40	39	40
of the Titarius mountains	48	40	39	30
of Mount Olympus	50		39	20
of Mount Ossa	50	40	39	20
of Mount Pelius	51	10	39	20
of the Othrys mountains	50		38	40

The inland towns of Macedonia are

In Taulanti

Arnissa	45	20	40	40

In Elimiotis

Elimia	45	40	39	40

In Orestis					Apollonia	49	30	40	30
Amantia	46		39	20	Lete	49	20	40	20
In Albani					In Chalcidice				
Albanopolis	46		41	5	Aegae	50	15	40	40
In Almopes					In Paractia				
Horma	46	45	41	30	Clitae	50	20	40	20
Europus	46	30	41	20	Moryllus	50	30	40	15
Apsalus	46	20	41	5	Antigonia or Psaphara	50	45	40	10
In Orbelia					In Emathia				
Garescus	47	50	41	40	Europus	47	20	40	20
In Eordaei					Tyrissa	47	30	39	55
Scampis	45	45	40	20	Scydra	47	40	40	20
Dibolia	45	45	40	10	Mieza	48		39	45
Daulia	45	30	40		Cyrrhus	48	10	40	40
In Aestraei					Idomene	48	30	40	50
Astraeum	46	20	40	50	Gordynia	48	40	40	15
In Paeonia					Edessa	48	45	40	20
Doberus	46	40	40	45	Beroea	48	45	39	50
Alorus	47	15	41	10	Aegaea	48	40	39	40
In Iori					Pella	49	20	40	5
Iorum	47	45	41	15	In Pieria				
In Sintica					Phylace	49	20	39	30
Tristolus	48		41	30	Vallae	49	40	39	30
Perthicopolis	48	40	41	40	In Parauaei				
Heraclea Sintica	49	10	41	40	Eriboea	46	40	39	45
					In Pelasgiota				
In Odomantica and Edonis					Doliche	47	30	39	40
Scotussa	49	30	41	50	Azorium	47	45	39	30
Berga	49	50	41	40	Pythium	47	50	39	30
Gasorus	50	15	41	55	Gonnus	48	5	39	35
Amphipolis	50		41	30	Atrax	48	30	39	25
Philippi	50	45	41	55	Iletium	49	5	39	25
In Desareti					Scotussa	49	30	39	10
Evia	46	5	40	15	Larissa	50		39	10
Lychnidus	46	50	40	20	Pherae	50	30	39	10
In Lyncestis					In Tymphaea				
Heraclea	47	40	40	40	Gyrtone	46	50	39	30
In Pelagonia					In Hestiaeota				
Audaristus	48		40	55	Phaestus	47	15	39	20
Stobi	48	50	41	20	Gomphi	47	40	39	10
In Bisaltia					Aeginium	48		39	20
Arrolus	49	10	41	20	Tricca	48	5	39	
Euporia	49	20	41	10	Ctimenae	48	45	39	10
Calliterae	49	30	41	10	Chyretiae	49		39	
Ossa	49	45	41		Metropolis	49	20	39	
In Mygdonia					In Thessali				
Antigonia	48	40	41	10	Hypata	47	50	38	50
Calindoea	48	40	40	50	Sosthenis	48	15	38	50
Baerus	48	55	40	40	Homilae	48	40	38	40
Physcae	49		41		Cypaera	49		38	40
Terpyllus	49	10	40	50	Phalanthia	49	30	38	45
Carrabia	49	5	40	30	In Phthiotis				
Xylopolis	49	20	41		Narthacium	50	10	38	45
Asserus	49	30	40	40	Coronea	50	30	38	50

Melitaea	50	40	39	
Eretria	50	15	38	50
Lamia	50	30	38	35
Heraclea	50	50	38	30

Islands adjacent to Macedonia in the Ionian sea

Saso island	41	10	39	30

in the Aegean sea

Lemnos island, in which are two towns

Myrina	52	20	40	55
and Hephaestia, inland	52	30	41	
Sciathos island and town	52	10	39	15

Peparethos islands and town

(Scopelus)	52	30	39	20
Scyros island and town	54		39	

CHAPTER XIII

Location of Epirus
(Tenth map of Europe)

THE northern side of Epirus is bounded by the part of Macedonia along the line we have before mentioned; the eastern side by that line which extends along Achaia to the mouth of the Achelous river, the location of which is in 48 25 37 50 the western side is bounded by the Ionian sea which is near the Acroceraunos mountains, a description of which coast is the following:

In Chaonia

Oricum	45		39	15

Summit of Acroceraunos

mountains	44	25	39	10
Panormus harbor	45		38	40
Onchesmus harbor	45	20	38	35
Cassiope harbor	45	30	38	25

The south side is bound by the Adriatic from the western terminus to the river Achelous; a description of this coast is the following:

In Thesprotia

Posidium promontory	45	45	38	10
Pelodes harbor	46	10	38	20
Thyamis promontory	46	10	38	
Thyamis river mouth	46	15	38	5
Sybota harbor	46	45	38	
Torone	46	50	38	

mouth of the Acherontos

river	47	10	38	
Elaeae harbor	47	15	37	55

Nicopolis near the Ampracius

bay	47	35	37	55

In Acarnanum

mouth of the Arachthus	47	50	38	15

Ampracia	48		38	20
Actium	47	40	37	45
Leucas promontory	47	50	37	20
Alyzea	48	20	37	25

mouth of the Achelous

river	48	25	37	30

Towns in the interior of Epirus
In Chaonia

Antigonia	45	15	39	10
Phoenice	45	20	38	45

Hecatompedon Dodonaeo-

rum	45	40	39	
Omphalium	45	40	38	40
Elaeus	45	40	38	30

In Cassopea, above which are the *Dolopes*

Cassopea	47		38	20

The *Amphiloci*, from whom toward the east are the *Athamanes*

Argos	48	20	38	30

the *Acarnani*

Astacus	48	15	37	45

Islands adjacent to Epirus are Corcyra, which is large, and the following is the description:

Cassiope town and promon-

tory	45	5	38	15
Ptychia	45	30	38	
Corcyra town	45	40	37	50
Leucimma promontory	46	20	37	45
Amphipyrgus promontory	45	30	37	40
Phalacrum promontory	45		38	

and Cephalenia island, in which a town of

this name is located	47	40	37	10

on the north is a promon-

tory	47	40	37	30
on the south a promontory	47	45	36	40
the island Ericusa	44	40	38	
the island Scopulus	45		37	55
the Leucas island	47	45	37	35
Echinades island	48	10	37	20

Ithaca island with town of this

name	48		37	10
Letoia island	47		36	45

Zacynthus island with town of this

name	47	30	30	30

CHAPTER XIV

Location of Achaia
(Tenth map of Europe)

THAT part of Achaia, which we have said is contiguous to the provinces in the Peloponnesus, extends to the isthmus which they call Hellas. It is terminated by

Epirus on the west, by Macedonia on the north, the border of which region we have described, and by a part of the Aegean sea; on the east by the part of the Aegean sea nearest Sunium as far as the promontory; on the south by the Adriatic sea, the coast of the Gulf of Corinth beginning at the Achelous river, then from the isthmus and the Cretian sea to the Sunium promontory. A description of the shores of this sea is the following:

After the Achelous river, which is the terminus of Epirus, on the Adriatic sea

In Aetolia

Chersonesus (promontory)	48	30	37	25
mouth of the Evenus river	49		37	30

In Locri Ozolae

Molycria	49	15	37	30
Antirrhium promontory	49	20	37	25
Naupactus	49	30	37	35
Evanthia	49	45	37	45
Chalaeum	49	55	37	50

In Phocis

Cirrha	50		37	30
Crisa	50	15	37	30
Anticyra	50	30	37	30

In Boeotia

Siphae	51	5	37	35
Creusa	51	15	37	30

In Megaris

Pegae	51	25	37	25
and Nisaea located across the isthmus	52		37	20

In Attica

Eleusis	52	20	37	15
Piraeus	52	45	37	10
mouth of the Ilissus river	52	50	37	5
Munychia harbor	53	10	37	5
Hyphormus harbor	53	30	36	50
Sunium promontory	53	35	36	45

On the eastern shore of the Aegean sea

Panormus harbor	53	40	37	
Diana temple	53	40	37	5
Cynosura promontory	53	50	37	20
mouth of Asopus river	53	30	37	25
Chersonesus promontory	53	30	37	30
Oropus	53	20	37	40

In Boeotia

Aulis	53	15	37	45
mouth of the Ismenus river	53	10	37	50
Salganeus	53		38	
Anthedon	53		38	5
Phocae	52	40	38	10

In Locri Opunti

recess of Opunti bay	52	15	38	10

Cynus	52		38	30

In Locri Epicnemidi

Cnemides	52	10	38	25
mouth of the Boagrius river	51	30	38	25
Scarphaea	51	15	38	25

The mountains in the northern part of Achaia are the Callidromus, the middle part of which is in

	49		38	15
Corax mountains	49	20	38	
Mount Parnassus	50	20	38	
Mount Helicon	51		37	45
Mount Cithaeron	51	40	37	30
Mount Hymettus	52	30	37	20

The Achelous river has its sources in the Pindus mountains, the Evenus in the Callidromus mountains, running first toward the east near the Cephisus river, which, flowing from the mountains in Boeotia unites with the Asopus river and with the Ismemo river in

	52		38

The inland towns in Hellas are

Interior of Aetolia

Chalcis	49		38	5
Arachthus	48	50	37	55
Pleuron	48	35	37	40
Olenus	49		37	50
Calydon	49		37	40

In Doris

Erineus	49		38	25
Cytinium	49	20	38	20
Boeum	49	30	38	15
Lilaea	50	5	38	15

In the interior of Locri Ozolari

Amphissa	49	30	37	50

In the interior of Locri Epicnemidii

Thronium	51	15	38	15

In the interior of Phocis

Pythia	50	10	37	45
Delphi	50		37	40
Daulis	50	20	37	50
Elatea	51		38	
Aegosthenia	50	45	37	45
Bulia	50	30	37	35

Inland town of Oputi

Opus	52		38	10

Inland towns of Boeotia

Thisbe	51		37	40
Thespiae	51	5	37	50
Orchomenus	51	20	37	55
Coronea	51	20	37	45
Hyampolis	51	30	37	55
Chaeronea	51	30	37	50
Lebadea	51	45	37	55
Copae	51	50	38	5

Haliartus	51	55	37 45
Plataea	52	15	37 40
Acraephia	52	20	38 5
Tanagra	52	30	37 55
Thebae Boeotia	52	40	37 55
Delium	53		37 45

In the interior of Megara

Megara	52		37 25

In the interior of Attica

Oenoe	52	20	37 30
Athenae	52	45	37 15
Rhamnus	53	15	37 30
Marathon	53	15	37 20
Anaphlystus	53	30	37 10

Achaean islands in the Aegean sea near the large island Euboea, of which the following is a description:

Cenaeum promontory	52	20	38 35
Atlante small island	52	30	38 30
Aedepsus	52	40	38 25
Chalcis near Euripum	53	10	38
Eretria	53	50	37 50
Amarynthus	54	5	37 45
Leo promontory	54	15	37 20
Pulchrum Littus (coast)	54	30	37 30
Carystus	54	30	37 40
Geraestus harbor	54	40	37 45
Caphereum promontory	55		37 50
Cava Euboea	54	25	37 50
Chersonesus promontory	54	30	38 10
mouth of the Budorus river	54		38 10
Cerinthus	53	50	38 10
Diana temple	53	40	38 20
Phalacria promontory	53	20	38 30
Oreus	53	10	38 25
Divum promontory	53		38 35

Near Attica and below Euboea are these islands:

Thera island, in which are two towns

Eleusin	53	50	36 25
Oea	54		36 25

Cea island, in which are three towns

Coressus	54	25	37
Iulis	54	20	37
Carthaea	54	15	36 45
town of the Ios island	54	20	36 35
Polyaegos a desert island	54	20	36 15
Therasia island town	54	45	36 20

At some distance from Cyclades are the island towns which are called

Naval station of Andros island	55		37 30
town of Andros island	54	50	37 25
town of Tenos island	55	5	37 30
town of Scyros island	54	45	37 15
town of Delos island	55	25	37 20
Oliarus	55	20	36 30
Cythnus	54	55	37
Rhene	55	5	37 10

Myconos islands

Phorbia promontory	55	45	37 10
Myconos town	55	40	37 10
town of Naxos island	55	40	37
town of Paros island	55	30	36 50
Sunium promontory	55	40	36 55
town of Siphnos island	55	15	36 45

and central parts

Seriphos	55		36 50
Pholecandros	55		36 30
Sicinos	54	50	36 35

Location of Peloponnesus

The boundaries of Peloponnesus on the north are the Corinthian gulf, the isthmus, and the Cretan sea, on the west and south the Adriatic sea, on the east the Cretan sea. The sea coast is described in this order:

Next to Pegas, a town of the Megara region, which is on the Corinthian bay of Achaia as we have stated, and

in	51	25	37 25

In Corinth

Corinthian temple of Juno	51	15	37 15
Lechaeum naval station	51	20	37
mouth of the Asopus river	51	5	37 5

In Sicyonia

mouth of Suos river	50	40	37

In Achaia

Aegira	50	15	36 55
Aegium	49	45	36 55
Erineus harbor	49	30	36 55
Rhium promontory or Drepanum	49	20	37 10
Neptune temple	49	15	37
Patrae	49		36 50
Olenus	48	50	36 45
Dyme	48	40	36 40
Araxus promontory	48	30	36 45

In Elea

Cyllene naval station	48	30	36 30
mouth of Peneus river	48	20	36 30
Chelonites promontory	48		36 20
Chelonites bay	48	20	36 15
Ichthys promontory	48	5	36
mouth of the Alpheus river	48	20	35 55
river source	49	50	36 30

In Messenia

Cyparissia city	48	35	35 45
Cyparissium promontory	48	25	35 40

mouth of the Sela river	48	30	35	35	Bucephalus harbor	51	25	36	45
Pylus	48	35	35	30	In Corinth				
Coryphasium promontory	48	30	35	25	Cenchreae naval station	51	25	36	55
Mothone	48	35	35	20	Schoenus harbor	51	40	37	
Colone	48	45	35	15	The mountains in Peloponnesus are:				
Acritas promontory	48	45	35		Pholoe mountains	49	15	36	40
On the Messenian bay					Stymphalus mountain	50	10	36	30
Asine	48	50	35		Minthe mountain	49		35	30
Corone	49		35	5	Taygetus mountain	49	40	35	15
Messene	49	15	35	15	Cronius mountain	50	30	35	45
mouth of the Pamisus river	49	20	35	15	Zarex mountain	51		35	20
its junction with the Alpheus					Towns in the interior of Achaia which				
river	49		35	55	are especially mentioned are the following:				
Phera	49	30	35	15	Pherae	49	15	36	45
Abia	49	45	35	10	Helice	49	50	36	45
In Laconia					Bura	50		36	50
Leuctra	49	55	34	40	Pellene	50	20	36	45
Taenarus promontory	50		34	20	Inland towns of Sicyonia				
On the Laconian bay					Phlius	50	50	36	40
Taenarus	50		34	45	Sicyon	51		36	50
Caene	50	5	34	50	Interior town of Corinth				
Teuthrone	50	10	34	55	Corinth	51	15	36	55
Las	50	15	35		In the interior of Elia				
Gythium	50	20	35	5	Elis	49		36	25
Trinasus naval station	50	25	35	10	Olympia Pisa	48	40	36	15
mouth of the Eurotus river	50	30	35	10	Coryne	48	30	36	10
river source	50	30	35	45	Hypanea	49	10	36	
Acria	50	35	35	10	Lepreum	48	50	35	55
Biandyna	50	45	35	10	Typanea	49	10	36	10
Asopus	50	50	35	5	In Arcadia				
Onugnathos promontory	51		35		Heraea	49	20	36	
Boeae	51	5	35	5	Phialia	49	20	36	
Malea promontory	51	20	35		Tegea	49	50	36	20
On the Argolus bay of Laconia					Psophis	49	40	36	5
Minoa harbor	51	10	35	10	Lysias	49	50	36	
Jovis Servator harbor	51	10	35	15	Antigonea or Mantinea	49	40	35	45
Epidaurus	51	5	35	30	Stymphalus	50	20	36	20
Zarex	51		35	40	Clitor	50	25	36	
Cyphanta harbor	51	10	35	45	Dipaea	50	50	36	20
Prasia	51	20	35	50	Megalopolis	50	40	36	10
In Argolis					Inland towns of Argolis				
Astrum	51	30	35	45	Nemea	51	5	36	25
mouth of the Inachus river	51	30	35	50	Cleonae	51	10	36	25
source of the river	51		36	30	Argos	51	20	36	15
Nauplia naval station	51	35	36		Mycenae	51	45	36	10
Phlius	51	45	35	55	Asine	51	35	36	15
Hermione	52		36		Inland towns of Messinia				
Scyllaeum promontory	52	30	36	5	Haliartus	48	50	35	45
On the Saronicus bay in Argolis					Ithome	48	50	35	25
Troezen	52	20	36	5	Troezen	49	10	35	25
Methone chersonesus	52	10	36	20	Inland towns of Laconia				
Epidaurus	51	50	36	25	Cardamyle	50		35	25
Spiraeum promontory	51	45	36	35	Lacedaemon	50	15	35	30
Atheniensium harbor	51	30	36	35	Cyphanta	51		35	45

Lerne	51 15	35 55	
Thurium	50 15	35 20	
Blemina	50 40	35 45	
Thalame	50 15	35 10	
Gerenia	50 10	35 20	
Oenoe	50 40	35 20	
Bityla	50	35	

Islands near Peloponnesus

Strophades, two islands	47 20	30	
Prote island	47 50	35 30	
Sphagia island	48	35	
Theganusa island	48 30	34 40	
Cythera island town	51 10	34 40	
Aegila island	51 45	34 40	
Salamis island	52	37 15	
Aegina island town	52 20	36 45	

CHAPTER XV

Location of the island Crete
(Tenth map of Europe)

THE island Crete is surrounded as follows: on the west by the Adriatic sea; on the north by the Cretan sea; on the south by the Libyan sea; on the east by the Carpathian sea. Its maritime coasts are thus described:

Description of the west coast

Corycus promontory and town	52 5	34 40	
Phalasarna	52 20	34 40	
Chersonesus	52 30	34 35	
Rhamnus harbor	52 30	34 30	
Ina chorium	52 35	34 20	
Criumetopon promontory	52 35	34 10	

Description of the south coast

Lissus	52 40	34 5	
Tarrha	52 50	34 20	
Poesilasium	53	34 30	
Hermaeum promontory	53 15	34 25	
Phoenicus harbor	53 30	34 50	
Phoenix town	53 35	34 45	
mouth of the Messalia river	53 45	34 40	
Psychium	54	34 45	
mouth of the Electra river	54 10	34 45	
Matalia	54 25	34 30	
Leo promontory	54 35	34 45	
Lebena	54 35	34 50	
mouth of the Catarrhactus river	54 45	34 50	
mouth of the Letheus river	54 50	34 55	
Inatus town	55	34 55	
Sacer mountain	55 10	35	

Hierapytna	55 15	35 5	
Erythraeum promontory	55 20	35 5	
Ampelus promontory	55 30	35 10	
Itanus town	55 40	35 15	

Description of the east side

Sammonium promontory	55 50	35 25	
Minoa harbor	55 20	35 15	
Camara town	55 10	35 20	
Olus	55	35 20	
Chersonesus	54 55	35 20	
Zephyrium promontory	54 45	35 30	

Description of north side

Heracleum	54 30	35 20	
Panormus	54 20	35 15	
Apollonia	54 10	35 15	
Cytaeum	54	35 15	
Divum promontory	53 50	35 10	
Pantomatrium	53 45	35 5	
Rithymna	53 30	35 5	
Amphimales bay	53 15	35	
Drepanum promontory	53 10	35 10	
Minoa	53	35	
mouth of the Pycnus river	52 50	35	
Cydonia	52 45	35	
Cisamum promontory	52 30	35	
Dictannum	52 25	34 55	
Psacum promontory	52 20	34 50	
Cisamus town	52 25	34 45	

The important mountains in Crete are called

Albi	52 40	34 40	
Ida mountain	54	35	
Dicte mountain	55 30	35 15	

Towns in the Cretan interior

Polyrrhenia	52 20	34 45	
Aptera	53	34 55	
Hyrtacina	53 5	34 45	
Lappa	53 15	34 55	
Subrita	53 40	34 40	
Elautherae	53 45	35	
Gortyna	54 15	34 50	
Pannona	54 40	35 10	
Cnosus	54 45	35 10	
Lyctus	55	35 10	

Islands near Crete are Claudus island, in which is a town 53 30 34

Leota island	54 30	34 10	
Dia island	54 30	35 40	

Cimolis island, in which is a town 54 20 35 30

Melus island, in which is a town 54 35 30

END OF BOOK THREE

BOOK FOUR

CHAPTER I

Location of Mauritania Tingitana
(First map of Libya)

THE western side of Mauritania Tingitana is bounded by a part of the Outer sea, which we call the Western ocean, it extends from the Hercules strait to the Greater Atlas mountains, and is thus described:

Cotes promontory	6		35	55
mouth of the Zilias river	6		35	40
mouth of the Lix river	6	20	35	15
mouth of the Subur river	6	20	34	20
Emporicus bay	6	20	34	10
mouth of the Sala river	6	10	33	50
Sala city	6	20	33	50
mouth of the Duas river	6	10	33	20
Lesser Atlas mountains	6		33	10
mouth of the Cusa river	6	40	32	45
Rusibis port	6	40	32	10
mouth of the Asana river	7		32	
mouth of the Diur river	7	20	31	20
Solis mountains	6	45	31	15
Mysocaras harbor	7	20	30	50
mouth of the Phuth river	7	30	30	30
Hercules promontory	7	30	30	
Tamusiga	8		29	55
Ussadium promontory	7	30	29	15
Suriga	8		29	

mouth of the Una river	8		28	30
mouth of the Agna river	8	30	27	50
mouth of the Sala river	8	40	27	20
Greater Atlas mountains	8		26	30

The northern side is terminated by the strait, on which, after the promontory are the following:

Tingis Caesarea	6	30	35	55
mouth of the Valon river	7		35	50
Exilissa city	7	30	35	55
Septem Fratres mountains	7	40	35	50

and by the Ibericum sea coast on which are the following:

Abila columna	7	50	35	40
Phoebi promontory	8		35	30
Iagath promontory	8	20	35	5
mouth of the Thaluda river	8	30	35	
Oleastrum promontory	8	50	35	10
Acrath	9		34	55
Taenia Longa	9	30	35	45
Sestiaria promontory	10		35	
Rissadirum	10		34	45
Metagonites promontory	10	30	34	55
mouth of the Molochath river	10	45	34	45
mouth of the Malva river	11	10	34	50

The eastern side is bordered by Mauritania Caesariensis which extends southward from the mouth of the Malva river to a terminus which is in   11 40 26
the south side moreover is terminated by the bordering races of Interior Libya along the line joining the termini, which we have mentioned.

The *Metagonitae* inhabit the parts of this province which extend along the strait; the *Socossi* the parts which extend along the Ibericum sea, and below these are the *Verves*; then below the Metagonites region are the *Mazices*; then the *Verbices*, below whom are the *Salinsae* and the *Cauni*; then the *Bacuatae*; below whom are the *Macanitae*; below the *Verves* are the *Volubiliani*; then the *Iangaucani*; below whom are the *Nectiberes*; and next is Campus Rufus, which is located in   9 30 30
below these are the *Zegrenses*; then the *Baniubae* and the *Vacuatae*. Moreover the

Maurenses and a part of the *Herpeditani* inhabit the entire east side.

The noted mountains in this land are those which are called the Diur, the central part of which is in   8 30 34
then the Phocra mountains which extend from the Lesser Atlas to the Ussadium promontory along the coast, and the western part of the Durdus located
in   10   29 30

The following towns are in the interior region of Mauritania Tingitana:

Zilia	6	10	35	30
Lix	6	45	34	55
Oppinum	7	30	35	20
Subur	6	50	34	20
Banasa	7	30	34	20
Tamusida	7		34	15
Silda (Gilda)	7	50	33	55
Gontiana	7	40	34	30
Baba	8	10	34	20
Pisciana	9		34	20
Vobrix	9	20	34	15
Volubilis	8	15	33	40
Herpis	10	20	33	45
Tocolosida	8	10	33	30
Trisidis	9		33	10
Molochath	10	10	33	5
Benta	9	30	32	50
Galapha	11		32	40
Oecath	8	30	32	30
Dorath	9		31	15
Boccana specula	9	20	29	30
Vala	8	10	28	15

The islands adjacent to this province toward the west in the Outer ocean are

Paena island	5		32
Erythia island	6		29

CHAPTER II

Location of Mauritania Caesariensis
(First map of Libya)

MAURITANIA Caesariensis is terminated on the west by the east side of Mauritania Tingitana as we have said above; on the north by the Sardoum sea from the mouth of the Malva river to the mouth of the Ampsaga river, of which the following is a description:

After the mouth of the Malva river

Magnum promontory	11	30	35	
Gypsaria harbor	11	50	34	45
Siga city, colonia	12		34	40

mouth of the Siga river	12	15	34	40
mouth of the Assarath river	12	30	34	30
Portus Magnus	12	45	34	30
mouth of the Chylimath river	13		34	
Quiza colonia	13	20	34	
Deorum harbor	13	30	33	45
Arsenaria colonia	13	50	33	50
mouth of the Cartennus river	14	15	33	40
Cartenna	14	30	33	40
Carepula	14	50	33	40
Iar vicus	15	10	33	30
Lagnouton colonia	15	30	33	30
Apollinis promontory	15	50	33	40
Castra Germanorum	15	50	33	35
Canucis	16	30	33	30
mouth of the Chinalaph river	16	40	33	20
Iol Caesarea colonia	17		33	20
Tipasa	17	30	33	20
Via	17	40	33	
Icosium	18		33	
mouth of the Savus river	18	10	33	
Rustonium	18	30	32	45
Rusicibar	18	45	32	50
Modunga	19	10	32	55
mouth of the Serbetis river	19	30	32	50
Cissa	19	45	32	50
Addyme	20		32	50
Rusuccoru	20	15	32	45
Iomnium	20	30	32	45
Rusubirsir	20	45	32	40
Rusazus	21		32	40
Vabar	21	30	32	30
Saldae colonia	22		32	30
mouth of the Nasabath river	22	10	32	30
Chobath	22	40	32	20
mouth of the Sisar river	23		32	15
Iarsath	23	20	32	5
Audum promontory	23	40	32	15

and in Numidicus bay

mouth of the Audus river	23	50	32	
Igilgili	24		32	
mouth of the Gulus river	24	40	31	50
Assarath	25	10	31	45
mouth of the Ampsagas river	26	15	31	45
river sources	26		26	

It is bounded on the east by Africa along the Ampsagas river to that point which is in   26 20 26
on the south side by the *Libyan* races along

the line, which above Gaetulia joins the southern termini.

The mountains in this province most celebrated are the Durdus mountains, the eastern parts of which are in 15 29 30 the western, as stated, in 10 29 30 the Zalacus mountains in 16 31 40 the Garaphi mountains in 16 28 40 the Madethubadus mountains the limits of which are in 13 26 40 and 17 30 26 the Cinnaba mountains 19 30 36 the Beryn mountains 20 30 31 the Phruraesus mountains, the limits of which are in 18 30 28 40 and 21 26 the Garas mountains 23 28 the Valva mountains 22 26 the western part of the Buzara located in 25 25

The *Herpeditani* inhabit the western parts of this province which are above the iron mines; below whom are the *Taladusi;* then the *Sorae*, to the south of whom are the *Masaesyli;* and below these are the *Dryitae;* then near the Durdus mountains are the *Eluli* and the *Tolotae* and also the *Nacmusi* extending to the Garaphi mountains; from the *Taladusi* toward the east extending as far as the mouth of the river Chinalaph are the *Machusi*, below whom are the Zalacus mountains and beyond this are the *Mazices;* then the *Banturari;* and beyond the Garaphi mountains are the *Aquenses*, the *Myceni*, and the *Maccurae;* and above the Cinnaba mountains are the *Enabasi;* to the east from the Zalacus mountains on the sea coast are the *Machurebi* below whom are the *Tulenses;* then the *Baniuri* below whom are the *Machures;* then the *Salassi*, the *Malchubi* and the *Montani;* then toward the east from the *Tulenses* dwell the *Mucuni* and the *Chituae* to the river Ampsagas, below these moreover are the *Coedamusi;* then the *Toducae* next to the sources of the river Ampsaga.

The inland towns in this province are

Vasbaria	12	30	34		
Celama	12	10	33	30	
Urbara	12	50	33	30	
Lanigara	12		33		
Villa vicus	12	40	32		
Atoa	12	30	31	10	
Mina	12	50	33		

Timici	13		33	10
Astacilis	13	20	33	10
Arina	13	30	30	50
Aripa	14		30	50
Victoria	14	10	33	
Giglui	14	30	32	30
Bunogora	14	30	31	30
Vagae	15	15	30	45
Manliana	15	50	28	50
Apphar	16	20	33	15
Oppidum Novum colonia (new city)	16		32	40
Burca	16	50	30	45
Tarrum	16	15	30	
Garra	16	30	32	50
Zuchabbari	16	50	32	40
Irath	17		32	
Tenissa	17	50	31	10
Lamida	18	30	32	20
Vasana	18	20	31	40
Casmara	18	10	30	50
Binsitta	18	30	30	40
Pegava	18	50	30	30
Nigilgia	18	15	30	15
Thisizima	18	30	29	30
Choezala	18	40	32	30
Aquae Calidae, colonia	18		32	10
Floria	19	20	31	40
Oppidium	19	10	31	10
Labdia	19	50	29	50
Tucca	20		31	30
Badea	20		30	45
Gasmara	18		32	40
Bida colonia	18	30	32	30
Symoetha	20	20	32	15
Thibinia	21		31	10
Izatha	21		30	20
Auximis	21		29	30

also near the sources of the Rhoemius river, which flows into the Savum river,

Suburgia	21		28	20

Then again beginning in another part, the towns are

Thudaca	19	10	32	20
Tigis	19	30	32	30
Turaphilum	21	20	31	45
Sudava	22	20	32	
Tusiatath	22	20	31	30
Ussara	22		30	40
Vazagada	22	30	30	10
Auzia	22	10	29	40
Tubusuptus	23	45	31	40
Robonda	23	20	31	20
Ausum	23		30	40

Zaratha	23 30	30 30	
Nababurum	23	30	
Vitaca	23 45	29 30	
Thubuna	23 50	28 30	
Thamaritha	23 10	27 15	
Augala	24 50	31 20	
Suptu	24 20	30 45	
Hippu	24 50	30 30	
Vamicaeda	25 10	30	
Sitiphi colonia	26	29 20	
Tumarra	26	29	
Germiana	26	28 30	
Paepia	24 50	28 15	
Vescethra	24 30	27 30	
Aegaea	26	27 10	
Taruda	25 45	26 30	

An island is near the famous town Iol Caesarea, which is called Iol Caesarea island, in which island is a town of this same name located in 17 10   33 40

CHAPTER III

Location of Africa (Second map of Libya)

THE west side of Africa is terminated by Mauritania Caesariensis on the line established by the Ampsagas river; the northern side is terminated by that part of the African sea which extends from the Ampsagas river to the Syrtis Major; of this northern side the following is a description:

After the mouth of the Ampsagas river

Numidicus harbor interior	27	31 45	
Greater Collops or Chullu	27 20	32 20	
Tretum promontory	27 40	32 45	
Rusicada	27 45	32 30	
Uzicath	28 10	32 30	
Holcochites harbor	28 40	32	
Tacatye	29	32 30	
Lesser Collops	29 20	32 35	
Siur port	29 40	32 40	
Hippo promontory	30	32 45	
Stoborrum promontory	30 10	32 40	
Aphrodisium	30	32 30	
Hippo Regius colonia	30 20	32 15	
mouth of the Rubricatus river	30 45	32 15	
Thabraca colonia	31 15	32 20	
Apollo Temple	31 40	32 50	
Neptun Altar	32	32 45	
Hippo Diarrhytus colonia	32 30	32 45	
Thinisa	33	32 30	

Apollo promontory	33 30	33 15	
Utica	33 20	32 45	
Cornelia Camp	33 40	32 30	
mouth of the Bagradas river	34	32 40	
Carthage, a large city	34 50	32 40	
mouth of the Catadas river	34 50	32 30	
Maxula colonia	35	32 40	
Carpis colonia	35	33	
Misua	35	33 15	
Clypea colonia	35	33 20	
Hermaea promontory	35	33 30	
Aspis colonia	35 15	33 20	
Curubis colonia	35 30	33 10	
Neapolis colonia	35 45	33	
Siagul	36	32 50	
Aphrodisium	36 15	32 40	
Adrumetus colonia	36 40	32 40	
Ruspina	36 50	32 40	
Leptis Minor colonia	37 10	32 30	
Thapsus	37 30	32 30	
Acholla	37 45	32 30	
Rhuspena	38	32 20	
Brachodes promontory	38 30	32 20	
Usilla	38 30	32 10	
Taphrura	38 30	32	
Syrtis Minor			
Theaenae	38 30	31 40	
Macomada	38 30	31 15	
mouth of the Triton river	38 40	30 30	
Tacape	38 50	30 30	
Gichthis	39 20	30 50	
Hedaphtha	40 10	31 15	
Zeitha promontory	40 40	31 40	
Sabathra	41	31 30	
Pisindon harbor	41 15	31 30	
Heoa	41 30	31 40	
Garapha harbor	41 45	31 40	
Neapolis or Leptis Magna	42	31 40	
mouth of the Cinyphus river	42 15	31 30	
Cisterna	42 50	31 20	
Barathra	42 20	31 30	
Triceron promontory	43 15	31 20	
Syrtis Major			
Cisternae	43 15	31	
Macomala village	43 30	30 50	
Aspis	43 40	30 20	
Sacazama village	43 50	30	
Tower of Euphranta	44 10	29 40	
Charax village	44 30	29	
Hippo promontory	46 45	29	
Oesporis village	45	29	
Philaeni village	46	29	

Below which altars of the same name terminate Africa.

The eastern side, beginning at the bend in the Syrtis, is bounded by the line which runs southward along Cyrenaica to the terminus which is in   47   25
the southern line, which extends along Gaetulia and the desert of Libya unites the two termini.

In this province are many celebrated mountains, and the eastern part of the Buzara mountains, the position of which
is   28   27
Audus mountains   28 30   29 30
Thammes mountains the extreme limits of which are in   29 30   27 30
and   32   28 30
from these mountains the Rubricatus river flows
mountains which are called
Cirna   33   30
from which run swamps connecting with the Hipponitis lake   32 40   32 30
and the Sisara lake   33   31
Mampsarus mountains, the extreme parts of which are located in   33   27 30
and   36 30   26 15
from which mountains the Bagradas river flows;
mountains which are called
Jovis   37 30   31 15
Usalaetus mountains the extreme limits of which are located in   37   38
and   39 30   26 30
from which mountains the Triton river flows, its sources are in
Tritonitis lake   38 40   29 40
Pallas lake   38 30   29 15
and that which is called the
Libyan lake   38 30   28 15
Giglius mountains   40 30   29 30
Thizibi mountains   44 15   28
Zuchabbari mountains the extreme limits of which are located in   40   26 15
and   43 30   26 40
from which mountains the Cinypus river flows from, a source, which is located in   45 15   26 10

The *Cirtesi* and the *Nabathrae* dwell in the western parts of Africa near the ocean; next, toward the east, are the *Ionti* in Numidia or the New Province extending as far as Thabraca; then the *Mideni* and the peoples dwelling in the Carthagenian region below whom are the *Libyphoenices;* then the *Machyni* to the Syrtes Minor; and below these are *Cinithi,* and the *Nigitimi* extending toward the east as far as the *Cinyphus* river and along the same river are the *Lotophagi;* then the *Samamyci* next to the Syrtes Major and near these the *Nyepi,* below whom are the *Elaeones.* Next toward the south from Cirtesiis and Numidia, below the Audus mountains are the *Musulami,* below whom are the *Nattabutes,* then the *Nisibes,* and below the *Mideni* the *Mididi,* below whom are the *Musuni;* then below the Thammes mountains are the *Saburbures,* below whom are the *Haliardi* and the *Campus Sittaphius.* From Libyphoenicia toward the south is the region of the *Bazaciti* below which the *Zutae,* then the *Cerophaei* and the *Mampsari* above the Mampsarus mountains, and below these mountains are the *Motuturi.* Below the *Machyni* are the *Machryes,* then the *Gephes,* next to these the *Mimaces,* and below the Usalaetus mountains the *Uzalae* where the Libyan desert begins. Below the *Cinithi* are the *Ogiplosi,* then the *Achaemenes,* then the *Muturgures;* below these the *Muchthusi;* below the *Nigitimi* are the *Astacures,* and below the *Lotophagi* the *Eropaei,* and next the *Dolopes,* below whom are the *Erebidae;* and below the *Samamuci* are the *Damensi* and then the *Nygbeni,* below whom are the *Nycpi;* then below the *Cinyphi* and the *Elaeones* is Macae Syrtitae and the Libyan desert.

The towns in this interior province between the Ampsagas river and the city Thabracam are

In Cirtesii

Cirta Julia colonia	26 50	31 20
Mireum	26 40	31 20
Vaga	28	31 40
Lares	27 30	30 40
Apari	27 40	29 40
Azama	27 30	27 50

In Numidia

Culcua colonia	28 30	31 15
Thunudromum colonia	28 20	30 30
Aspucca	29 30	32 20
Simisthu colonia	29	31 20
Thuburnica	30	31 40
Tucca	29 30	31 20
Thieba	29 30	30 45
Thubursica colonia	29 20	30 30

Ucibi	30		29 45
Gausaufna	29 15	31	
Lambaesa	29	30	
Legio III Augusta			
Thubutis	29 30	28 20	
Bulla Regia	30 40	31 30	
Sicca Veneria colonia	30 30	30 50	
Assurus colonia	30 50	30 30	
Naraggara	30	30 10	
Theveste	30 30	29 45	
Thunusda	31 20	32	
Madurus colonia	32	31 30	
Ammaedara	32 10	30 30	
Gazagupala	31 10	30 10	
Sedne	31 40	28 45	

Between the town Thabraca and the Bagradas river

Canopisi	32 15	32 30
Meltida	32 40	32 30
Uzan	33 15	32 20
Thisica	33 15	32
Cipipa	34	31 45
Theudali	33 20	31 40
Avitta	33 30	31 30
Tobrus	34	30 30
Iilica	34 30	30 20
Tucca	34	29 50
Dabia	33	29 45
Bendena	34 30	29 20
Vazua	33 20	29 10
Nensa	34 10	29 10
Aquae calidae	33 40	28 15
Zigira	33 10	27 50
Thasia	33	27 45
Thunuba	33 20	27 30
Musta	33 40	27 30
Themisua	34 40	28 40
Zama major	34 20	28
Timica	34 50	27 40
Tuscubis	35 30	28 10

Between the river Bagradas and the river Triton, and below Carthago are

Maxula ancient	34 10	32 30
Vol	34 45	32 30
Thimisa	35	32 10
Cuina colonia	35 30	31 30
Uthina	34 15	31 20
Abdira	34 30	30 50
Mediccara	35 30	31 10
Thuburbo	35	30 10
Tucma	35 30	30 10
Bulla Mensa	34 20	30
Cerbica	36	30
Nuroli	34 20	29 30

Ticelia	34 40	29	
Sasura	36		29 40
Cilma	35 30	29 10	
Vepillium	36 15	29	
Thabba	35 20	28 40	
Tichasa	36	28 40	
Negenta	36		27 50
Bunthum	36 15	27 20	

Below the town Adrumetum

Almaena	35 15	33
Uticna	35 40	32 45
Chrausa	36	32 40
Turza	35 40	31 50
Ulizibirra	36	31 20
Orbita	36 20	32 20
Uzita	36 50	32 20
Gisira	36 20	31 45
Zurmentum	37	31 50
Zalapa	36 45	31 45
Augustum	36 20	30 40
Leae	36 20	30 40
Avidus	36 40	30
Ubata	36 45	29 20
Tisurus	36 50	28 40
Thysdrus	37 15	32 10
Uzecia	37 45	32 10
Setiensis	37 45	31 30
Lasica	37 10	31 20
Byzacina	37 50	30 45
Targarum	37 15	30 30
Bararus	37	30 20
Capsa	37 30	29 45
Putea	37 45	29 10
Thennephis	38 20	31
Caraga	38 10	31 40
Murvis	38 10	30 45
Zugar	38	30 30

Between the two Sirtis are these towns:

Chuzis	39 30	30
Sumucis	40 20	30 30
Pisinda	41	31 10
Sabrata	41 15	30 50
Syddenis	41 40	31 10
Azuis	42 45	31 10
Gerisa	43	30 50
Iscina	43 20	30 30
Ammonis	42	30 40
Amuncla	42 40	30 10
Mousta village	42 20	28 40
Butta	42 40	28 30
Tege	42 40	27 30
Durga	43	26 30
Sycapha	43 30	30
Uddita	43 20	28 40

Galybe	43	40	29	30
Thagulis	44	10	29	

Islands along the coast of Africa, and which are near the coast

Hydras island	28		33	
Calathe island	31		33	40
Dracontia island	33	15	33	15
Aegimius island	34	15	33	30
two islands of Larunesia	37		33	30
Anemusa	39		33	20
Lopadusa island	39		33	20
Aethusa island	39	30	33	20
Cercinna island and town	39		32	15

Lotophagitis islands in which are these towns:

Girra city	39	15	31	15
Meninx city	39	30	31	20
Misynus island	44	40	30	40
Pontia island	45	20	20	15
Gaia island	46		29	40

In the high seas are the African islands:

Cossyra the island and town	37	20	34	20
Glauconis island and town	38	20	34	40
Melita island	38	45	34	40
Melita city and peninsula	38	40	34	45
Temple of Juno	39		34	40
Temple of Hercules	38	45	34	35

CHAPTER IV

The position of Cyrenaica
(Third map of Libya)

THE province of Cyrenaica is terminated on the west by the Syrtis Major and by Africa along the line running from Philaeni village toward the south to the terminus, which line extends

from	46	45	29
to	47		25

on the north by the Libyan sea along the maritime coast from the inner angle of the Syrtis to Darnis city, which is thus described:

Next after the Philaeni village

Automalax fortification	47	15	29	10
Drepanum promontory	47	15	29	20
Hyphali naval station	47	20	29	40
Diarrhoea harbor	47	15	30	
Hercules tower	47	20	30	30
Diachersis fortification	47	20	30	50
Boreum promontory, end of Syrtis	47	15	31	10
Bryon shore	47	30	31	10

In Pentapolis

Berenice or Hesperides	47	45	31	20
mouth of the Lathon river	48	15	31	20
Arsinoe or Teuchira	48	40	31	20
Ptolemais	49	5	31	10
Ausigda	49	30	31	30
Autuchi temple	49	30	31	40
Phycus promontory and Castle	50		31	50
Apollonia	50	10	31	40
Naustathmum harbor	50	20	31	40
Erythrum	50	30	31	30
Chersis village	50	45	31	20
Zephyrium promontory	51		31	20
Darnis	51	15	31	15

On the east it is bounded by a part of Marmarica along the line leading from Darnis southward to the terminus which is located in

	51	15	25

on the south by the Libyan desert along that line which joins the two mentioned termini.

Here are the provinces and the mountains which are called the Mounds of Hercules, the center of which is located in

	47	40	30	50
Velpi mountains	47	40	29	30
Baecolicus mountains	51		26	30

Maritime lake, that is the lake formed by the Lathon river, the central part of which is located in

	47	45	31	10

and the lake below Paliurus, in which there are shell fish

	52		31	10

The *Barcitae* inhabit the parts of this region below Pentapolis toward the east from the Garden of the Hesperides, from which toward the east are the *Ararauceles*; below the Garden of the Hesperides are the Mounds of Hercules, and from these toward the east the *Asbytae*; next to Africa above the Velpi mountains are the *Macatutae*, and next are the caves of the *Lasanicori*, and toward the east from these are the *Psylli*, thence a place filled with wild beasts, and then the Silphiofera region.

The inland towns of the province are the following:

Cyrene	50		31	20
Archile	50	30	31	15
Chaerecla	48	30	31	
Neapolis	49		31	
Artamis village	49	45	31	10
Zemythus	49	50	31	30
Barce	49	15	30	45
Eraga	49	40	31	

Celida	50 30	30 40
Hydrax	55 50	30 30
Alibaca	49 10	30 10
Thintis	50	30 15
Caenopolis	50 15	30 40
Phalacra	49 45	30 30
Marabina	48	30 15
Auritina	49 45	29 50
Acabis	50 30	29 40
Maranthis village	47 30	29 20
Agdan village	47 45	29
Echinus village	49 30	28 40
Philonis village	51	28 40
Arimantis village	51	28 55

The islands near this region are

Myrmex island	48 40	31 50
Laea or Venus island	50 10	31 50

CHAPTER V

Embracing all of Marmarica, Libya,
and Egypt
(Third map of Libya)

MARMARICA with Libya and Egypt is terminated on the west by Cyrenaica along that line which as is known runs from the town of Darnis southward, and by the part of Interior Libya along that meridian, to the end, the position of which is   51 15   23
on the north by the Egyptian sea. This maritime coast is thus described:

In the provinces of Marmarica are:

Azilis village	51 40	31 15
Greater Chersonesus	52	31 40
Phthia harbor	52 10	31 15
Paliurus	52 15	31 15
Batrachus harbor	52 30	31 15
Petras Minor harbor	52 45	31 15
Antipyrgos harbor	53 20	31 15
Scythranius harbor	53 30	31 10
Cathaeonium promontory	53 45	31 15
Ardanis promontory	54	31 15
Petras Major harbor	54 10	31 10

In the Libyan provinces on the sea coast:

Panormus harbor	54 20	31 10
Catabathmus Major	54 30	31 15
Aenesiphyra harbor	55	31 10
Zygris village	55 15	31 10
Chettaea village	55 30	31 10
Zagylis village	55 45	31 10
Selenis harbor	56	31 10
Trisarchi village	56 20	31 5
Apis	56 40	31 5

Paraetonium	57	31 10
Pythis promontory	57 10	31 10
Graeae Genu, harbor	57 10	31 5
Callias promontory	57 30	31 10
Zygis harbor	57 40	31 5
Leuce shore	57 50	31 10
Hermaeum promontory	58	31 15
Phoenicus harbor	58 20	31 10
Antiphra village	58 40	31 5
Derris promontory	58 50	31 10
Leucaspis harbor	59	31 5
Glaucum promontory	59 10	31 10

On the maritime coast of Mareotae province:

Chimo village	59 30	31 5
Plinthine	59 45	31
Lesser Chersonesus harbor	60	31 5
Alexandria the metropolis of all Egypt	60 30	31
Canobus the metropolis of Menelaitae	60 45	31 5

The seven mouths of the Nile:

The Heracleoticum mouth or Canobicum	60 50	31 5
the Bolbitinum mouth	61 15	31 5
the Sebennyticum mouth	61 30	31 5
the Pineptimi false mouth	61 45	31 5
Diolcus false mouth	62 10	31 10
Pathmitcum mouth	62 30	31 10
Mendesium mouth	62 45	31 10
Taniticum mouth	63	31 15
Pelusiacum mouth	63 15	31 10
Pelusium city	63 15	31 10
Gerrum terminus	63 30	31 10

Cassiotis

Casium	63 45	31 15
Outlet of Sirbonis swamps	63 50	31 10
Ostracine	64 15	31 10
Rhinocorura	64 40	31 50

It is terminated on the east by a part of Judaea which runs from the city Anthedon to the terminus which is in 64 15   30 40 and then by Arabia Petraea as far as the recess in the Arabian bay near the city Heroum which is located
in   63 30   29 50
and by a part of the Arabian bay. The coast is thus described:

Next to the turn of the bay which we have said is located in 63 30   29 50

Arsinoe	63 20	28 50
Clysina castle	63 20	28 50
Drepanum promontory	64	27 50
Philotera harbor	64 5	27 50

Myoshormus	64 15	26 45
Aeas mountains	64 20	26 10
Albus harbor	64 30	26
Acabe mountains	64 30	25 45
Nechesia	64 30	25 30
Samaragdus mountains	64 50	25
Lepte acra	64 40	(23)40
Berenice	64 5	23 50
Pentadactylus mountains	64 45	23 30
Bazium promontory	65	23

The boundary on the south extends to the indicated terminus of Interior Libya adjacent to which line is Aethiopia below Egypt.

The Bascisi mountains run through this province, the middle of which is in 52 20 30

also the Aganombri moun-

tains	54	27 30
the Asyphus mountains	55	30 30
the Aspis mountains	57 30	30 40
the Ogdamus mountains	58	29 30
the Thinodes mountains	58 30	26 40

the Azar mountains, the extreme parts of which are in 51 30 23 30
and 53 23 30

and the mountains of Libya to the west of the Nile river, the extreme parts of which are in 61 29
and 60 10 23 30

The lakes are

Cleartus lake	52	26 20
Lacci lake	55 30	26 40
Lycomedis lake	57	24
Solis spring	58 15	28
Marea lake	60 15	30 50
Moeridis lake	60 20	29 20
Sirbonis lake	64 15	31

The *Libyarchae*, the *Aniritae*, and the *Bassachitae* dwell in the north of the Marmarica province, below whom are the *Apotomitae*; and next to these, but more toward the south, are the *Augilae*, who are located in 52 30 28
after these are the *Nasamones* and the *Bacatae*; then the *Auschitae* and the *Tapanitae*, and next are the *Sentites*, the *Oebillae* and the *Aezari*.

In the Libyan province, which is near the sea, dwell the *Zygritae*, the *Chattani* and the *Zygenses*; toward the south are the *Buzenses* and the *Ogdaemi*, next to these the *Adyrmachidae* and next is the Ammoniaca region which is located in 55 30 28

next are the *Anagombri*, the *Iobacchi*, and the *Ruaditae*.

The maritime region of the Mareota province is called Taenia; in the interior dwell the *Goniatae* and the *Prosoditae*, next is the Sciathica region which is located in 60 40 30 20

The *Mastitae*, the *Nitriotae*, and the *Oasitae* occupy the parts toward the south which are located in 59 30 29 30
next to these are the *Libyaegypti*. The Arenosa and the Sitibunda regions extend along the entire south side of Marmarica and Libya. The *Arabaegypti Ichthyophagi* occupy the entire maritime coast along the Arabian bay in which are mountain ridges

Troici stone mountains	62 40	29 15
the Alabastrites mountains	63	28
the Porphyrites mountains	63	26 40
the Nigri stone mountains	63	24 40

the Basanites stone moun-

tains	64	23 30

The interior villages of Marmarica are

Leucoe	51 20	30 45
Moccheris	52 20	31
Albi Camini	53 10	30 50
Menelaus	53 40	31
Gaphara	54	30 25
Masuchis	53 30	30 40
Masadalis	51 20	30 30
Abathuba	51 30	30
Albi Clivi	52 30	30 15
Tacaphoris	53 50	30 10
Dioscurorum	52 30	28 50
Migo	53 30	28 30
Saragina	53 15	28
Alo	53 15	28 30
Mazacila	54 20	26 30
Billa	54 30	25 40

and in Augilae and Nasamones

Augila	52 30	28
Magri place	54 20	27 50

The villages of the Libyan provinces are

Tachorsa	54 30	30 50
Azicis	55	31
Nemesium	55 30	30 50
Tisarchi	55 50	30 50
Philonis	55 50	30 30
Sophanis	56 30	30 50
Bibliaphorium	56 20	30 40
Scope	56 40	30 30
Calliae	57	30 50
Leodamantium	57 30	31
Catabathmus minor	58	30 50

Pedonia	58	20	31	
Pnigeus	58	30	30	30
Glaucum	59		30	30
Tuccitora	55	10	30	15
Thanuthis	55	40	29	45
Pednopum	57	15	29	40
Climax	57	40	30	10
Siropum	56	20	28	45
Mareotis	58		28	20

and in the Ammoniaca region

Alexandri Castra	56	30	28	10
and the town Ammon	55	30	28	

The towns and villages of Mareota province are

Monocaminum	59	10	30	50
Halmyrae	59	40	30	50
Taposiris	59	50	30	50
Cobii	59	10	30	30
Antiphili	59	30	30	20
Hierax	59	40	30	40
Phamotis	60		30	40
Ancient Marea village	60		30	10

and in the Sciathica land

Sciathica	60	40	30	20

Near the Moeris lake are

Bacchis	60	30	29	40
Dionysias	60	30	29	

and in Oasitae are

Oasis Minor	60	15	28	45
Oasis Major	59	30	26	55

The provinces which are along the Nile have important towns.

That is called the Great Delta which begins where, from the Great river, the Agathodaemon is diverted and flows through the Heracleoticum mouth; that which is called Bubasticus flows through the Pelusiacum mouth, and the branching where the delta is formed is located in 62 30

It is called the Little Delta where the river Busiricus branches from the river Bubastico which flows through the Pathmiticum mouth. This Little Delta is located in 62 40 30 20

A third delta can also be mentioned located between that which we generally call the Middle Delta where a river branches from the Bubastico, which flows through the town Athribis and the Pineptimi mouth. This third delta is located in 62 15 30 5

In the Great Delta two rivers are diverted toward the north from the river Agathodaemon, one of which is called the Therenuthiacus river which flows through the Sebennyticum mouth; its branching is located in 61 30 30 15 the other which is called the Taly river flows through the Bolbitinum mouth, and the branching of this Taly river is located in 61 30 50

The Buticus river which runs along at a nearly equal (even) distance from the maritime coast joins the Therenuthiacum, the Athribiticum, the Busiricum and the Bubasticum, from which others springing from adjacent marshes and lakes flow into the sea through the remaining mouths, some of which are connected, as we have said, with the Great river.

That is commonly called a low region around these rivers, in which are provinces and important cities.

In the nome and metropolis of Alexandria

Hermopolis Parva	61		30 50

In the nome and metropolis of Andropolites

Andron city	61	20	30 20

In the nome and metropolis of Letopolites

Interior Latona city	61	30	30 5

Between the Great river and the river Taly (from the Great river toward the east)

Metelites the nome and metropolis

Metelis	61		31

Between the Great river and the Therenuthiacum river are the towns:

Phthenetu nome and metropolis

Butus	61	20	30 45

Cabasites nome and metropolis

Cabasa	61	30	30 40

Saites nome and metropolis

Sais	61	30	30 30

and on the Great river toward the east

Naucratis town	61	15	30 30

Prosopites nome and metropolis on the east bank of the Great river

Niciae	61	30	30 20

Between the Therenuthiacum and the Athribiticum rivers are

Sebennytes nome in a low region and its metropolis

Pachnamunis	61	40	31

Xoites nome and metropolis

Xois	61	40	30 35

Phthemphuthi nome and metropolis

Tava	61	40	30 25

Between the Athribiticum and the Busiriticum rivers

Onuphites nome and metropolis

Onuphis	62	5	30	40

Athribites nome and metropolis

Athribis	62	30	30

Mendesius nome and metropolis

Thumuis	62 20	30	50

Upper Sebennytes nome and metropolis

Sebennytus	62 20	30	20

Busirites nome and metropolis

Busiris	62 30	30	15

Leontopolites nome and metropolis

Leontopolis	62 15	30	35

Between the river Busiricus and the river Bubasticus is

Nesyt nome and metropolis

Panephysis	62 40	31	5

Tanites nome and metropolis

Tanis	62 45	32	50

Pharbaethites nome and metropolis

Pharbaethus	62 45	32	30

To the east of the Bubasticus river is

Sethroites nome and metropolis

Herculis lesser city	63 20	31	

Arabia nome and metropolis

Phacusa	63 10	30	50

Bubastites nome and metropolis

Bubastus	63 5	30	40

Heliapolites nome and metropolis

Oniu	62 30	30	10

and on the border of Arabia and Aphroditopolis

Babylon	62 15	30	
Heliopolis	62 30	29	50
Heroum city	63 10	30	

through which and the city Babylon flows the mountain stream Traianus

The following tribes are toward the south from the Great Delta and the Lower region and are called the Seven tribes, the first is the tribe *Memphites* and the metropolis on the east bank of the river

Memphis	61 50	29	50

And then to the east of the river in the interior, the town

Acanthon	61 40	29	40

In which part the river separates, forming an island Heracleopoliten by

name	62	29	45

and in this island

Nilopolis	62	29	30

and the metropolis to the west of the river is

Herculis city	61 50	29	10

Arsinoites nome and metropolis in the interior

Arsinoe	61 40	29	30

and the naval station

Ptolemais	61 40	29	20

To the east of this island

Aphroditopolites nome and metropolis of the name Aphroditopoles

	62 15	29	40

then also to the east of the island

Ancuron city	62 20	29	20

The rivers unite which form an island

in	62	28	45

Next, to the west of the river is the nome Oxyrynchites and the metropolis in the interior

Oxyrynchus	61 40	28	50

then the nome Cynopolites and the metropolis on the east river bank

Co	61 50	28	40

opposite which is an island

Canum city	62 10	28	40

then on the east bank of the river is

Acoris	62	28	30

in the interior

Alabastron	62 30	28	20

The nome and metropolis Hermopolites to the west of the river inland is

Hermopolis the great	61 40	28	25

and next on the west bank of the river is

Phylacae	61 50	28	15

The nome toward the east of the river Antinoites and the metropolis

Antinoi city	62 5	28	10

to which nome are to be added the two Oasitae

Those which are toward the south from the Seven Nomes are called Thebais and the Upper Region. Then toward the west of the river are the Lycopolites nome and metropolis in the interior

Lycopolis	61 45	28

Hypselites nome and metropolis

Hypsele	62	27 50

Aphroditopolites nome and metropolis in the interior are

Aphroditopoles	61 20	27	40
Crocodilorum city	61 40	27	20

Thinites nome and metropolis

Ptolemais Hermiae	61 50	27	10

then inland toward the west from the river

Abydos	61 40	26	50

Diopolites nome of the upper region and metropolis

Jovis a small town	61 50	26	40

Tentyrites nome and metropolis

Tentyra	61	50	26 10

and a village in the interior

Pampanis	61	30	25 45

Here is Memnon and in the interior the village

Pathyris	61	30	25 30

Hermonthites nome and metropolis

Hermonthis	61	50	25 20
and then Laton town	61	45	25
Apollinopolis greater city	61	50	24 40

then the inland village

Phonthis	61	40	24 20
and the island Elephantine	61	30	23 55

Toward the east of the river

Antaeopolites nome and metropolis

Antaei in the interior	62	20	27 40
and next Passalus	62	10	27 30

Panopolites nome and metropolis

Panopolis	62		27 20
next Lepidotorum town	62		26 50
then Chenoboscia	62		26 30
next Caene town	62	10	26 20

Copties nome and metropolis in the interior

Coptos town	62	30	26

next Apollinopolis lesser

city	62	30	25 55

Thebarum nome and metropolis

Jovis greater town	62		25 30
then Tuphium	62		25 20
then Chnubis	62		25
then Ilithyiae town	62	5	24 45
then Toum inland	62	15	24 20
then Ombi	62		24 5
then Syene	62		23 50

then Dodecaschoenus, from which toward the east are the *Arabes Adaei;* among whom on the east bank of the river after the Lesser Cataract

which is located in	61	50	23 45

are

Hiera Sycaminos	61	45	23 40
Philae	61	40	23 30
Metacompso	61	40	23 5

in which region on the west bank of the river is

Pselcis	61	30	23 5

The islands near Libya and Egypt in the Egyptian sea are

Aedonis island	52	40	31 50
Tyndarii three cliffs	55	50	31 30
Aenesippa island	56	30	31 40
Phocussae two islands	56	50	31 30
Pedonia island	58	30	31 30
Didymae two islands	60		31 30
Pharos island	60	20	31 5

In the Arabian bay are these islands

Sapphirine island	64	50	28
Veneris island	65	15	25
Agathonis island	65	15	23 40

CHAPTER VI

The location of Interior Libya
(Fourth map of Libya)

INTERIOR Libya is bounded on the north by Mauritania, Africa, and Cyrenaica along those lines which we have mentioned as their southern limits; on the east by a part of Marmarica along the meridian passing through the town Darnis and extending as far as the mentioned terminus of Marmarica, then by Aethiopia located below Egypt along the same meridian to the terminus which is located

in   51 15 south 3 10

It is terminated on the south by Interior Aethiopia, in which is the Agisymba region, and along that line which we have said runs in the western direction to the bay in the Outer sea which is called Hesperius or the Great bay located in   14   4

on the west by the Western ocean, from the bay which we have mentioned, to the terminus of Mauritania Tingitana, its maritime coast being thus described:

From the terminus of Mauritania Tingitana

mouth of the Subus river	9		25
mouth of the Salathus river	9 40		22
Salathus town	9 40		22
mouth of the Chusar river	10		21 40
Ganaria promontory	9 30		20 30
mouth of the Ophidis river	10		20
Bagaza town	11		19
mouth of the Nuius river	10		18 20
Soloentia promontory	9 30		17 30
Massa river mouth	10 30		16 30
Iarzitha town	10		15 30
Daras river mouth	10		15
Magnus Portus	10		14
Baba town	10 30		13
Arsinarium promontory	8		12
Rysadium promontory	8 30		11 30

then in Hesperius bay

Stachir river mouth	9 30		11
Periosius harbor	11		10 30

Catharum promontory	12 30	9 30	
Nias river mouth	13 30	9	
Hesperi Cornu promontory	13	8	
Masitholus river mouth	14	6 40	
Hypodromus Aethiopia	14	5 15	

The important mountains in this Libya are the Mandrus mountains, from which the Salathus and other rivers up to the Massa river flow; the middle of these mountains is in   14   19 the mountains which are called Sagapola from which the Subus river flows; the middle of these mountains is in 20 20   22 the Rysadius mountains, in which the Stachir river takes its rise flowing through the Caeonia lake not far from the mountains and the Nias river; the middle of the mountain range is in   17   11

Theon which are also called Ochema mountains from which flows the river Masitholus, the middle of this mountain range is in   19   5 and the Caphas mountain range from which the river Daras flows: the middle of the range is located in   17   10 and that which is called the Usargala mountain range from which the river Bagradas flows; the middle part of the range is located in   33   20 30 the river Bagradas flowing through Africa empties into the sea in   34   32 40 then the Girgiri mountains from which the river Cinyps flows, rising from two sources which are located in   40   21
     45   21
These two rivers unite in   42   25

The Thala mountain range, the middle part of which is located in 38   10 and the Garamantica defile 50   10 the Arualtes mountains   33   3 the Arancas mountains   47 30   1 30

There are two great rivers in the interior; one of these is the Gir uniting, as it were, the Garamantica defile and the Usargala mountains. There is a turning of the river in   42   16

Into the Gir a river empties flowing from the Chelonitides marshes, the middle of which is in   49   20

Moreover joining the Gir, ceasing as they say, but running under ground, is another river, the western terminus of which is in   46   16

the eastern terminus of which forms the Nuba lake the position of which is   50   15

The other large river is the Niger flowing from the Mandrus mountains and the Thala mountains which form the Nigritis lake which is in   15   18 from the north two rivers flow into the same from the Sagapola and the Usargala mountains; a deflection toward the east forms the Libyan lake the location of which is in   35   16 30 and toward the south moreover there is a turn toward the Daradus river but in two locations   21   17 and   21   13 30

Gaetulia is located below Mauritania, the Desert of Libya below Africa and Cyreniaca. The great races which inhabit Libya are the *Garamantes* extending from the sources of the Bagradas river to the Nubas lake, and the race of the *Melanogaetuli*, who occupy the land which is between the Sagapola mountains and the Usargala mountains, and the *Aethiopian* race of the *Girei* who dwell toward the south from the Gir river, and the *Aethiopian* race of the *Nigritae* who are north of the Nigir river, and the *Daradi* who dwell along the river of that name (Daradas) where it empties into the sea, and the *Perorsi* who are more to eastward and more remote from the sea as far as the mountains which are called Theon Ochema, and the land of the *Aethiopian Odrangidiae* located between the Caphas and the Thala mountains, and the *Mamaces* who are below the Thala mountains, and the *Nubae* dwelling on the western side of the Garamantica defile, and the *Derbiccae* who are toward the west from the Arancas mountains.

These are the minor races: the *Sirangae*, the *Mausoli*, the *Autolalae* occupying the region which is on the sea below Gaetulia extending as far as the Mandrus mountains; next to the same mountains are the *Babi*, the *Malcoae* and the *Mandori* extending as far as the *Daradi*; next to these are the *Sophucaei*, and below the Rysadius mountains are the *Leucaethiopes*, between whom and Perorsi stretches the Campus Rufus; then from the Sagapola mountains toward the north are the *Pharusi*; from the Usargala mountains toward the north are the *Natem-*

bes, and along the Girgiri mountains are the *Lynxamatae* and the *Samamyci*, and between the Mandrus mountains and the Sagapola mountain are the *Salathi* and the *Daphnitae*, also the *Zamazi*, the *Aroccae*, the *Cetiani* extending as far as the *Nigritas Aethiopes;* below the Usargala mountains are the *Suburpores*, and below the Girgiri mountains toward the *Geramantes* are the *Maccoi*, the *Dauchitae*, and the *Caletae* extending as far as the Nuba lake; then from the *Daradi* toward the east are the *Machurebi*, and next to the *Sophucaeis* are the *Solenti;* from these toward the east are the *Anaticoli* or *Pharausi*, the *Churitae* and the *Stachirae* extending as far as the Caphas mountains, between whom and Theon Ochema mountains are the *Orphes;* below these are the *Tarualtae*, the *Climatitae*, also the *Africerones* a great race; and back from *Odrangides Aethiopes* but toward the south are the *Achaemae*, and south of the *Mimaces* are the *Gongalae;* next to these are the *Nanosbes* then the *Nabathrae* extending as far as the Arualtes mountains; and between the Libyan lake and the Thala mountains are the *Alitambi* and the *Maurali;* between these and Nuba lake are the *Harmiae*, the *Thalae*, the *Dolopes*, also the *Astacuri* up to the Garamantica defile; and the *Aroccae* to the north from the Aranca mountains, the *Asaracae* to the east; between the *Derbiecenses* and the *Arualtes* mountains are the *Dermones;* and below the *Africerones* almost to the south wind are the *Aganginae Aethiopies;* to the east of these below the same Arualten mountains, up to the Arancas mountains are the *Xylicces Aethiopes*, and next to these the *Achalicces Aethiopes.*

The towns in this region along the coast are

Autolala	10		23	50
Thuilath	11	30	21	40
Tagana	12	30	20	15
Magura	12	30	15	
Ubrix	14	20	13	20
Iarzitha	16	20	12	15

Above the Nigir river but more remote from it are the towns

Talubath	18	40	22	40
Malachath	20	20	20	15
Tucabath	18		19	30
Byntha	24		21	

and below the river, this town:

Anygath	20	30	14	

Near this river, on its north bank

Pesside	19		18	
Thige	21		17	30
Cuphe	23	15	18	
Nigira metropolis	25	40	17	40
Vellegia	28	30	17	40
Tagama	30		17	
Panagra	31		16	40

On the south bank of the river are

Thupae	16	30	16	40
Punse	18		17	
Saluce	19	30	17	
Thamondocana	23		17	
Durdum	31		15	

Near the source of the Bagradas river

Silice	29	24	30
Buthuris	31	24	
Anygath	33	24	
Thabudis	33	22	
Siccathorium	34	23	
Capsa	34	21	30

And near the sources of the Cinyps river

Gelanus	40	24	30
Vanias	41	22	40
Sabae	43	23	
Buata	39	21	30
Bedirum	41	21	40
Garama metropolis	43	21	30
Thumelitha	41	19	

below the river Gir

Gira metropolis	36	18

And on the north bank of this river

Thycimath	38		19	40
Geva	39		19	
Badiath	40		17	
Ischeri	41	30	16	30
Turcumuda	41	30	15	
Thuspa	43		17	40
Artagara	44		18	
Rubune	46		19	
Lynxama	48	30	20	40

The islands near Libya in the Western ocean are

Cerne island	5	25	40
Junonia island or Autolala	8	23	50

and the six Beatorum islands:

Inaccessa island	0	16	
Iunonia island	1	15	15
Pluvialia island	0	14	15
Capraria island	0	12	30
Canaria island	1	11	
Ninguaria island	0	10	30

CHAPTER VII

Position of Aethiopia below Egypt
(Fourth map of Libya)

AETHIOPIA, which is below Egypt, is terminated, as we have indicated on the north, by Libya and Egypt; on the west by a part of Interior Libya along the meridian extending from Darnis to the southern terminus of Libya which is located in 51 15 south 3 10 on the south by the line leading from this terminus along the remaining part of Aethiopian Interior to the Rhaptum promontory, which is located in 73 50 south 8 25

It is terminated on the east by a part of the Bay of Arabia and the Red sea, and the Barbaricus sea to the Rhaptum promontory, the description of which is the following:

After the Bazium promontory referred to above:

Prionotus mountains	65	22	30
Chersonesus	65	22	
Mnemeum promontory	65 30	21	30
Isius mountains	65 30	21	20
Profundus harbor	65	21	10
Dioscuror harbor	65	21	
Cereris Speculae promontory	65 20	20	15
Aspis promontory	65 30	19	45
Diogenis promontory	65 40	19	40
Satyron mountains	65 40	19	
Monodactylus mountains	65 30	18	30
Taurus mountains	65 40	18	
Harbor Deorum Tutorum (protecting deities)	65 30	17	30
Evangelon harbor	65 45	17	
Ptolemais Venationum (hunting preserve)	66	16	25
Ara Eratonis promontory	66 30	16	
Sabasticum mouth	67	15	
Magnum Littus (great coast)	66	14	15
Colobon promontory	68	13	40
Sabat town	68	12	30
and in the Aduliticus bay			
Montuosa Chersonesus	68	12	10
Adulis	67	11	40
Saturni promontory	68	11	40
Antiphili harbor	72	10	15
Mandaith village	73 15	10	20
Arsinoe	73 45	10	40

After the strait in the Red sea

Dire town in the promontory	74 30	11	
Then in Avalites bay			
Avalites market place	74	8	25
Malao market place	75	6	30
Mondu market place	78	7	
Mosylum promontory and market place	79	9	
Cobe market place	80	8	
Elephas mountains	81	7	30
Acanna market place	82	7	
Aromata promontory and market place	83	6	
In the Barbaricus bay			
Pano village	82	5	
Opone market place	81	4	15
Zingis promontory	81	3	30
Phalangis mountains	80	3	30
Apocopa	70	3	
Austri Cornu promontory	79	north 1	
Parvum Littus	78	south 1	
Magnum Littus	76	south 2	
Essina	73 30	south 3	30
Sarapionis station and emporium	74	south 3	
Tonice market place	73	south 4	15
mouth of the Rhaptus river	72 30	south 7	
Rhapta metropolis of Barbaria a short distance from the sea	71	south 7	
Rhaptum promontory	73 50	south 8	25

The remaining part of the Nile, after the Great Cataract, is described as follows through the names of the villages adjacent to it:

After Pselcis and the Lesser Cataract the location of which is in 60 30 22 30 on the west bank of the river are the villages

Tasitia	60 30	22	
Boon	62	21	40
Autoba	61 30	21	30
Phthrui	61 15	21	20
Pistre	61	20	40
Ptemithis	61	20	15
Abuncis	59 30	20	
Cambysis Aerarium (granary)	59	18	
Erchoas	59 30	18	
Satachtha	60 30	18	
Moru	61 30	18	40
Nacis	62	19	30
Tathis	61	17	

On the east bank of the river are the villages

Pnups	62	22
Berethis	62	21 30
Gerbo	62	21
Pataeta	61 40	20 30
Pontyris	61	20
Primis Minor	60	19 30
Arbis	60 30	18 30
Napata	63	20 15
Sacole	63	19 30
Sandace	63	18 30
Orbadaru	62 40	18
Primis Major	62	17

Here the Nile river on the west and the Astaboras on the east form the Meroe island region, in which island are the following towns:

Meroe	61 30	16 25
Sacolche	61 40	15 15
Eser	61 40	13 30
Daron village	62	12 30

The junction of the river Nile and the river Astapus 61 12 then the junction of the river Astaboras and the Astapus 62 30 11 30 Where the Nile river becomes one through the union of rivers which flow from two lakes 60 2 Western lake 57 south 6 Eastern lake 65 south 7 Coloe lake, from which flows the Astapus river 69 equator The towns remote from the river in the interior are Axume where is the king's palace 65 11 Coloe town 69 north 4 15 Maste town 65 south 4 15

The mountains in this region toward the west of the Nile river, extending along the entire Nile which are commonly called the Aethiopian mountains are celebrated, the position of which is 55 23 and 55 8 30 the mountains to the east of the Nile are called the Garbatum the middle of which is in 69 6 and the Elephas mountains 78 5 30 and those near the lake, are called the Pylaei mountains 65 equator the Maste mountains 68 south 5 The land which is near the Arabian bay and the Aualites gulf, along the sea is called

Troglodytica as far as Elephantas mountains, in which region are the *Adulitae*, and the *Aualitae* near a bay of this name, and the *Mosyli* above the promontory with a market place of this name. The entire maritime coast to the Rhaptum promontory is called Azania; the interior region is called Barbaria, in which there are many elephants.

The *Colobi* occupy that part of the region toward the east from the river which is near the Bazium promontory; next to these toward the south are the *Tabieni*; then the *Sirtibes*; next to these are the *Attiri*; then the *Babylleni* and the *Rhizophagi*; then the *Axumitae* and the *Sobridae*; next the *Molibae*, the *Megabardi*, and the *Nubae* toward the west from the *Aualitae*; then below the *Molibae* are the *Blemyes*; below whom are the *Dedacae*, and the *Pechini* between the river Astapus and the Garbatum mountains; from whom toward the west are the *Strathophagi Aethiopes*; toward the south from the mountain are the *Catadrae* and the *Myrrhifera* the land stretching up to the Coloe lake, after which are the *Mastitae* to the lake of the Nile.

To the west, from this part of the Nile river, those occupy the land after the greater cataract, who pasture the Triacontaschaenus region between the Aethiopian mountains and the Nile river, after these toward the south are the *Euonymitae*; then Aethiopia Media and the *Sebridae*; these races also inhabit the island of Meroe, and below them are the *Gapachi*; below these the *Ptoemphanae*, and below these the *Cadupi*; next to these are the *Elephantophagi Aethiopes*; below these the *Pesendarae*, and beyond the lake the Cinnamomifera land; moreover between the Nile and the Astapus river, toward the island of Meroe, are the *Memnones* and more to the south are the *Sapaei*. In the remaining parts of the land toward the west from the Aethiopian mountains next to the sandy and dry region dwell the *Phazaniae* and the *Bacalitides* races; then the *Scenitae* and the *Tralletae*, after these the race of the *Daradi*; then the *Orypaei Venatores* next to these the *Nygbenitae Aethiopians*.

The following islands are near Aethiopia below Egypt in the Arabian bay:

Astarta island	66	22 30

Ara Minervae island	66 10	21	30
Gypsitis island	67	19	40
two islands of Gomadean	67 30	19	
Myronis island	67	18	
Catathra or Chelonitides islands, two in			
number	68	17	30
Orisitides two islands	67 30	17	
Magorum island	68	16	
Daphnine island	68 30	15	20
Acanthine island	68 30	15	
Macaria island	68 30	14	
Avium island	69	14	
Bacchi and Antibacchi	69 30	13	15
Panis island	68 40	12	
Diodori island	70	12	30
Isidis island	70	11	30

In the Bay of Avalites is the

Mondi island	77	8	30

next to Aromata are these islands

Amici island	85	4	
the two Menae islands	84	2	30
Myrice island	83 30	1	

Then to the east of these islands is the sea called Hippalum near which is the Indian sea.

CHAPTER VIII

Location of Interior Aethiopia
(Fourth map of Libya)

AETHIOPIA, which is below this land and entire Libya, is terminated toward the north by the indicated southern boundary lines of the land which we have treated, which extends from the Great bay of the Outer sea to Rhaptum promontory as we have said, and is located
in   73 50 south 8 25
then by a part of the Western ocean which is near the Great bay; by the unknown land toward the west and the south; toward the east by the Barbaricus bay, which near the shallow sea is called Breve, from the Rhaptum promontory even to the Prasum prom-

ontory and the unknown land. Prasum promontory moreover is located
in   80   south 15
    Near this is an island toward the east, the name of which is
Menuthias; it is located
in   85   south 12 30
    Around this bay the *Anthropophagi Aethiopians* dwell, and from these toward the west are the Mountains of the Moon from which the lakes of the Nile receive snow water; they are located at the extreme limits of the Mountains of the Moon.
           57   south 12 30
and   67   south 12 30
    Moreover above these are the *Rhapsi Aethiopians:* the *Ichthyophagi Aethiopians* dwell in the Great bay toward the Western ocean, and toward the south of this to the unknown land are those who are commonly called the *Hesperi Aethiopians;* toward the east are the *Athaca Aethiopians;* and more toward the east, adjoining the entire Libyan country is much Aethiopian land in which elephants are born entirely white, and rhinoceroses and tigers; next to the unknown land of Aethiopia is a region of wide expanse called Agisymba.
    This region has many and high mountains near the unknown land, the majority of which are without name, but those which bear names are:
Dauchis mountains, the middle of which
is in   15   south 13
Ion mountains, the middle of which is
in   10   south 8 25
Zipha mountains, the middle of which is
in   25   south 8 25
Mesche mountains, the middle of which is
in   25   south 13
Barditus mountains, the middle of which is
in   45   south 6
(Toward the south from the inhabited land to the south pole the degrees are not definitely known 73 35 or full 74.)

END OF BOOK FOUR

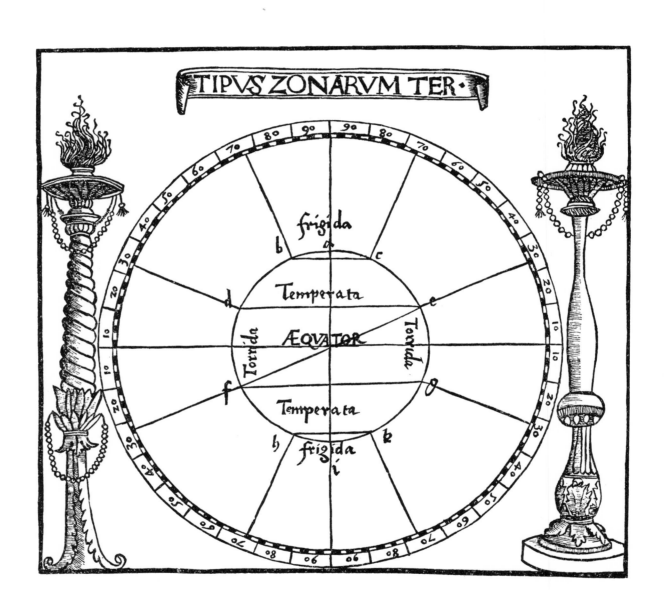

TIPVS ZONARVM TER·

BOOK FIVE

CHAPTER I

Location of Pontus and Bithynia
(First map of Asia)

THE Pontus and Bithynia province is terminated on the west by the mouth of the Pontus and by Thracia which is called the Bosphorus, and by a part of the Propontis. The maritime coast is thus described:

The promontory of Bithynia which is at the mouth of the Pontus, in which are

Temple of Diana	56	25	43 20
Chalcedon	56	5	43 5
Acritas promontory	56	30	42 55
Trarium	56	54	42 45
Nicomedia	57	30	42 30
Astacus	57	20	42 30
Olbia	57		42 30
Posidium promontory	56	10	42 25
mouth of the Acanius river	56	45	42 15
Ascania lake	56	45	42

Prusias	56	40	42 5
Apamea	56	40	41 55
Dascylium	56	35	41 55
mouth of the Rhyndacus river	56	20	41 45
river sources	57		40 30

On the north it is bounded by a part of Pontus Euxine, which is thus described: after the mouth of the Pontus and the Temple of Diana

Bythinias promontory	56	45	43 20
Artane castle	57		43 5
mouth of the Calpas river	57	40	43 5
mouth of the Sangarius river	58		42 45
first bend of the river	57	30	42
second turning	61	20	42
third turning	58	45	41
river sources	60	50	40 50
mouth of the Hyspius river	58	40	42 45
mouth of the Elata river	58	50	43
Diospolis (Iovis oppidum)	58	45	43 20
Heraclea on the Pontus	59		43 30
Psyllium	59	30	43 30
Tium	60		43 30
mouth of the Parthenius river	60	15	43 30
river sources	62	30	43 30
Cromna	60	35	43 35
Cytorum	60	45	43 35

On the south it is bounded by that which properly is called the confines of Asia, along the line leading from the Rhyndacus river to the terminus which is

in   61   41 15

On the east it is bounded by Galatia next to Paphlagonia along the line leading from the mentioned terminus near the town Cytorum on the Pontus.

The most noted mountains in this region are the Orminius the central part of which is located in   59 40   42 40 and the Mysian Olympus mountain   57   41 30

The *Chalcedoni* occupy the maritime coast from the mouth of the Pontus to the river Hyspius, the *Mariandyni* from Heraclea as far as the town Cytorum; beyond the

mountain Orminius are the *Caucones*, and the Timonitis region is below the *Chalcedoni*, and below this Bogdomanis region, from which toward the east is Zygiana.

The following are the inland towns:

Libyssa	57	15	42	45
Eriboea	57	10	42	20
Gallica	57	45	42	25
Tatavium	57	45	42	
Prusa on the Hypius river	58	30	42	35
Dedacana	59		42	25
Protomacra	58	45	42	
Claudiopolis or Bithynia	59	20	42	45
Flaviopolis or Cratea	60		43	
Timaea	59	45	42	20
Clitae	60	30	43	
Laganea	60	35	42	30
Nicaea	57		41	55
Caesarea or Myrleana	56	40	41	40
Prusa near Mount Olympus	57		41	40
Agrilium	57	30	41	40
Dables	58	40	41	40
Dadastana	59	30	41	45
Juliopolis	60	10	42	

the islands near this region are

Cyanea	56	30	43	25
Thynias and Daphnusia	57	40	43	20
Erythinus crags, islands	58	30	43	15

CHAPTER II

*Location of Asia properly so called
(First map of Asia)*

ASIA, properly so called, is bounded on the north by Bithynia along the line we have designated; on the west by the remaining part of the Propontis and the Hellespont and by the Aegean, the Icarian, and the Myrtoum seas; a description of its maritime shores is the following: on the Propontis

Mysia Minor Hellespontica

Cyzicus	56		41	30
mouth of the Aesepus river	56		41	20
mouth of the Granicus river	55	50	41	30
Parium	55	35	41	25
Lampsacus	55	20	41	25

on the Hellespont

Abydus	55	20	41	15
mouth of the Simoentus river	55	20	41	10
Dardanum	55	15	41	5

mouth of the Scamander river	55	15	41	
Sigeum promontory on the Aegean sea	55	10	41	

Phrygia Minor or Troas

Alexandria Troas	55	25	40	40
Lectum promontory	55	25	40	25
Assus	56		40	15

Mysia Major

Gargarum	56	10	40	20
Palaesepsis	56	15	40	30
Antandrus	56	30	40	20
Adramyttium	56	30	40	
Poroselene	56	30	39	45

In Aeolis

Cane promontory	56	15	39	30
Pitane	56	10	39	45
mouth of the Caicus river	56	30	39	35
river sources	58	30	40	30
Elaea	57		39	25
Myrina	57	15	39	15
Hydra promontory	57		39	5
Cyme	57	20	39	
Phocaea	57	10	38	50
mouth of the Hermus river	57	30	38	45
where the Hermus and the Pactolus rivers unite	58	10	39	20
sources of the Hermus river	60		40	
sources of the Pactolus river	59		39	

In Ionia

Smyrna	57	40	38	35
Clazomenae	57		38	35
Erythre	56	40	38	35
Argennum promontory on the Icarian sea	56	30	38	25
Teos	57	10	38	25
Lebedus	57	30	38	20
Colophon	57	40	38	
mouth of the Cayster river	57	45	37	50
river sources	60	15	39	20
Ephesus	57	40	37	40
Trogilium promontory	57	10	37	40
mouth of the Maeander river	57	40	37	30
where the Lycus river unites with this	59		38	40
sources of the Maeander river	62	30	39	30
sources of the Lycus river	60		37	45

In Caria on the Myrtoum sea

Pyrra	57	50	37	10
Heraclea	58		37	10

Miletus	58		37	
Iasus	57 50	36 50
Bargylia	57 50	36 40
Myndus	57 40	36 25

In Doris

Scopias promontory	57 20	36 25
Halicarnassus	57 50	36 10
Ceramus	57	36

Cnidus town and promontory 56 15 36

On the south it is terminated by the Rhodian sea, on which is

Onugnathos promontory	56 40	35 50
Loryma	57 20	35 35
Cressa harbor	57 40	36
Phoenix castle	58	36 10
Physca	58 15	36 10
mouth of the Calbis river	58 45	36 5
Caunus	59 10	36

On the east is the border of Lycia, from the terminus located near Cannus which is in 59 30 37 50

On the south it is terminated by the Milyade region of Lycia which is located in 61 37 50

and by Phamphylia along that line leading from the indicated terminus to that which is located in 61 20 38 35

and on the east by Galatia along the line which is the boundary of Bithynia, the middle of which turns toward the east; the location of this bend is in 62 15 39 15

Very important mountains are in Asia of which the central localities are:

Ida mountain	56	41
Cillaeus mountains	56	40 40
Temnus mountains	57 40	40 30
western part of Dindymus	61	40 40
Sipylus mountains	59	39 10
Tmolus mountains	58 30	38 30
Mimas mountains	57 10	38 30
Mesogis mountains	58 40	38 10
Mycale mountains	58	37 40
Cadmus mountains	59 20	37 40
Phoenix mountains	58	36 20

The interior towns of Mysia Minor in Hellespontica are

Scepsis	56 30	41
Sacra Germa	56 15	41 15

The inland town of Phrygia Minor or Troas is

Ilium 55 20 41

Towns in the interior of Mysia Major are

Daguta 57 30 41 20

Apollonia on the Rhyndacus river 57 41 15

Traianopolis	56 40	40 15
Alydda	57 30	40 15
Prepenissus	56 50	40 25
Pergamus	57 25	39 45

the *Olympeni* people are in the north, the *Grimenothuritae* in the west, whose town is Traianopolis; in the south are the *Pentademitae*; and the people in the middle between these are the *Mysomacedones*.

Towns in Lydia

Perpera	57 50	40
Mosteni	58	39 55
Hierocaesarea	57 15	39 30
Nacrasa	58 20	39 30
Thyatira	58	39 20
Magnesia near the Sipylus	58 40	39 10
Juliogordus	59	39 55
Aegara	57 50	38 50
Hypaepa	58	38 25
Sardes	58 20	38 45
Philadelphia	59	38 50
Dioshieron	59 40	38 55
Metropolis	58	38

In Caria

Tripolis	59 30	38 30
Laodicea on the Lycus	59 45	38 20
Antiochia on the Meander	59 10	38 30
Itoana	59 15	38 25
Trapezopolis	59 30	38 15
Nysa	59	38 15
Aphrodisia	59 20	38 10
Tralles	58 40	38 5
Magnesia on the Meander	58 30	38 5
Apollonia	59 25	37 55
Heraclea	59 30	37 55
Priene	58	37 25
Harpasa	58 25	37 35
Orthosia	59	37 35
Neapolis	59 25	37 35
Bargaza	58 20	37 25
Amyzon	58 15	37 10
Alabanda	58 40	37 20
Stratonice	59	37 10
Alinda	59 10	36 50
Badessus	58	36 15
Mylasa	58 20	36 30
Hydissa	58 30	36 30
Idymus	59	36 35
Thera	59	36 15
Pystus	59	36 25

the *Erizeni* a people near Phrygia.

In Maeonia on the confines of Mysia, of Lydia and of Phrygia

Saittae	58	10	40	15
Dadales	58		40	20
Cadi	58	30	40	25

Towns of Greater Phrygia

Synnaus	58		41	15
Dorylaeum	58	15	41	20
Midaium	59	30	41	20
Tricomia	60		41	10
Ancyra	58	20	41	10
Nacolea	59		41	
Tribanta	59	40	40	35
Dioclea	60		40	55
Amorium	60	30	41	15
Abrostola	60	30	40	50
Cotiaium	58	40	40	40
Aezani	59		40	20
Conna	59	15	40	30
Lysias	59	50	40	30
Cercopia	59	25	40	15
Eucarpia	60		40	5
Prymnesia	60	20	40	20
Docimaeum	60	15	40	30
Synnada	60	50	40	5
Gammausa	61	15	40	40
Melitara	61	30	40	20
Juliopolis	61	30	40	10
Acmonia	59	50	39	20
Eumenia	60	10	39	50
Druzon	60	20	39	55
Tiberiopolis	60	15	39	30
Bleandrus	60	30	39	10
Stectorium	61		39	15
Silbium	61	40	39	15
Philomelium	62	15	39	20
Pelta	61	20	39	10
Metropolis	61	15	39	25
Apamea Cibotos	61	10	38	55
Hierapolis	60		38	15
Cibyra	60	30	(37)	55
Diocaesarea	61		38	15
Sanis	61		38	30
Themisonium	60	10	38	10
Phylacaeum	60	20	38	20
Sala	60	15	38	20
Gazena	60	40	38	

The peoples near Lycia are the *Lycaones* and the *Themisoni*; near Bithynia are the *Moccadeni* and the *Cydisses*; below these are the *Pelteni*; then the *Moxiani*; then the *Phylacenses*, below whom are the *Hierapolitae*.

The island near Asia, and which is near the Hellespont is

Tenedos island and town	55		40	55

Island in the Aegean sea

Lesbos, an Aeolian island, around which are

Sigrium promontory	55		40	
Eressus	55	15	39	40
Pyrrha	55	25	39	30
Malia promontory	56		39	25
Mytilene	55	40	39	40
Argennum promontory	55	40	39	50
Methymna	55	25	40	25
Antissa	55	15	40	10

Islands in the Icarian sea are

Icarus island	56	45	37	20
Chios island and town	56	20	38	35
Phanaea promontory	56	20	38	15
Posidium promontory	56	25	38	25
town of Samos island	57		37	35
Ampelos promontory	56	30	37	30

Islands in the Myrtoum sea, and towns of Amorgus island are

Arcesine	56		37	
Aegialus	56	10	36	50
Minoa	55	50	36	50
town of Cos island	55	40	36	25
town of Astypalaea island	55	40	36	25

Islands in the Rhodian and Carpathian seas

Syme island	56	40	35	40
town of Casus island	56	30	35	15

Around the Carpathian island

Thoantium promontory	57		35	20
Ephialtium promontory	57	20	35	20
Posidium town	57	20	35	25

Around the Rhodian island

Panos promontory	58		35	55
Camiros	58	20	35	15
Lindos	58	40	36	
Ielyssos	58	20	36	

CHAPTER III

Location of Lycia
(First map of Asia)

LYCIA is terminated on the west and the north by Asia along the boundary which we have mentioned above; on the east by a part of Pamphylia along the line leading from the terminus on the confines of Asia through the Masicytus mountains, as far as the sea in   61 50   36 30 on the south by the Lycium sea, of the coast

of which the following is a description: after
Cannus

Calinda	59	20	35	55
Chlyda	59	40	35	55
Carya	59	50	35	55
Daedala	60		35	55
Telmissus	60	10	35	55
mouth of the Xanthus river	60	20	36	
river sources	60		37	40
Patara	60	30	36	
Antiphellus	60	30	36	20
Andriaca	61		36	20
Aperlae	61		36	25
mouth of the Limyrus river	61	10	36	25
Aperroe	61	20	36	20
Sacred promontory	61	30	36	15
Olympus town	61	40	36	20
Phaselis	61	50	36	25

Cragus mountains, the location of the middle part of which is in   60   36 40

The inland towns in Lycia near the
Cragus mountains are

Cydna	59	30	37	10
Symbra	59	40	36	50
Octapolis	59	35	36	35
Comba	59	50	36	30
Sidyma	59	50	36	40
Pinara	59	50	36	25
Araxa	59	50	36	5
Tlos	60	15	36	30
Xanthos	60	15	36	10

and near the Masicytus mountains are the
towns

Corydalla	60	15	36	50
Sagalassos	60	40	36	55
Rhodia	61		36	45
Trebenda	61	10	37	15
Phellos	60	35	36	30
Myra	61		36	40
Limyra	61	5	36	35

In Mylias

Podalia	60		37	30
Nysa	60		37	15
Choma	60	20	37	20
Candyba	60	40	37	10

In the Cabalia region

Bubon	60	20	37	40
Oenoanda	61		37	40
Balbura	60	40	37	30

Islands adjacent to Lycia are

Megiste island	60	40	35	45
Dolchiste island	61	15	35	45
Chelidonia, V cliffs	61	30	36	

CHAPTER IV

Location of Galatia
(First map of Asia)

GALATIA is terminated on the west by
Bithynia and a part of Asia along the
boundary to which we have referred above;
on the south by Pamphylia from the terminus indicated on the border of Asia to the
other bay on this same parallel located
in   64 15 38 35
on the east by the part of Cappadocia which
extends from this terminus to that on the
shore of Pontus, in   65 10 43 10
on the north by a part of Pontus, of which
the following is a description: from the maritime city Cytorum

Climax castle	61	10	43	50
Teuthrania	61	30	44	
Carambis promontory	61	20	44	25
Callistratia	61	30	44	15
Zephyrium	61	45	44	5
Abonitichos	62		44	
Cinolis	62	30	44	
Stephane village	62	55	43	55
Armene	63	20	43	55
Sinope	63	50	44	
Cyptasia	63	40	43	40
Zagorum	64		43	30
mouth of the Zalecus river	64	15	43	20
mouth of the Halys river	64	30	43	10
bend in the river	64	15	40	15
Amisus	65		43	5

The mountains in Galatia worthily celebrated are the Olgassys the middle of which
is in   63   42
and the eastern parts of the Dindymus
mountains   62   41 20
and that which is called the hill of Celenarum, the middle of which is
in   62 30 39 30

The *Paphlagonian* race occupies the
maritime coast, whose towns and villages
inland are

Zagira	61	40	43	40
Plegra	62	30	43	30
Sacora	63	20	43	40
Helvia	61	40	43	
Tobata	62	20	43	
Germanicopolis	63		43	
Gelaca	63	40	43	15
Zoaca	63	15	43	15
Dacasye	61	40	42	40
Mosium	61	5	42	20

Sacorsa	62		42	15
Pompeiopolis	62	30	42	15
Conica	62	45	42	30
Andrapa or new				
Claudiopolis	63	15	42	20
Sabanis	63	50	42	20
Titua	64	15	42	30
Eusene	60	40	42	40

In the interior of Paphlagonia toward the west are the *Tolistobogi*, whose towns are

Germa colonia	61	30	42	
Pessinus	61	10	41	30
Vindia	61	40	41	40
Andrus	61	30	41	20
Tolastachora	61	15	40	55
Vetistum	62	20	40	40

Next to these toward the east are the *Tectosagae* whose towns are

Ancyra metropolis	62	40	42	
Olenus	62	15	42	
Corbeuntos	62	40	41	40
Agrizama	62		41	30
Vinzela	62	30	41	20
Rosologia	63		41	25
Sarmalia	63	20	41	25
Dictis	62	40	40	50
Carima	63		40	40
Landosia	63	40	40	45

From these toward the east are the *Trocmi*, whose towns are

Tavium	63	55	41	40
Lascoria	63	15	42	
Androsia	64	20	42	5
Claudiopolis	63	50	42	
Carissa	64	40	41	40
Phubatina	64	10	41	30
Dudusa	63	50	41	20
Saralus	64	30	41	20
Ucaena	64	10	40	55
Rastia	64	30	41	

Below these races, as we have said, are the *Prosilemmenitae* adjoining those with whom they have relations, and below these are the *Bizeni* in part of Lycaonia, among whom are the towns

Petenessos	62	15	40	30
Ecdaumava	63	20	40	25
Sivata	64	15	40	25
Ardistama	64		40	10
Cinna	63	20	40	
Congustos	62	40	39	50
Tyriaeum	63		39	30
Laodicea combusta	63	40	39	40

Vasada	64		39	25
Perta	64	20	39	30

Then below these to the west is a part of the Pisidiae region, and the towns

Apollonia	62		39	
Antiochia Pisidiae	62	30	39	
Amblada	61	50	38	50
Neapolis	62	40	48	45

Eastward is Isauria and towns

Sabatra	64	20	39	15
Lystra	64		39	
Isaura	63	50	38	40

Among these is the race of the *Orondicori* and the towns

Misthium	63		39	15
Pappa	63	20	38	50

CHAPTER V

Location of Pamphylia
(First map of Asia)

PAMPHYLIA is terminated on the west by Lycia and a part of Asia along the boundaries to which we have referred; by Galatia on the north along the indicated border of Galatia; on the east by Cilicia and part of Cappadocia to the line leading from the terminus near Galatia to the Pamphylian sea, the terminus of this line at the sea is in 63 50 36 45 on the south by the same Pamphylian sea, a description of the shores of which is the following after Phaselis the town of Lycia:

The shore of Pamphylia

Olbia	62		36	55
Attalia	62	15	36	30
mouth of the river				
Cataractes	62	15	36	35
Magydos	62	40	36	30
mouth of Cestrus river	62	50	36	30
mouth of river Eurymedon	63		36	35
Side	63	5	36	40

Cilicia Aspera maritime towns

Melas river	63	10	36	40
Coracesium	63	35	36	40
Syedra	63	50	36	45

The towns in the interior province of Phrygia Pisidia are

Seleucia Pisidia	62		38	30
Ancient Beudos	61	30	38	10
Baris	61	50	38	25
Conane	61	50	38	5
Lysinia	61	15	38	15
Cormasa	61	10	37	55

In Cabalia

Cretopolis	61	15	37	30
Pogla	61	40	37	40
Menedemium	61	20	37	40
Uranopolis	61	40	37	20
Pisinda	61	40	37	10
Ariassus	62	5	37	10
Milyas	62	30	37	25
Termessos	62	10	37	15
Corbasa	62	20	37	5

Inland towns of Pamphylia

Perge	62	15	36	50
Sileum	62	25	36	50
Aspendus	62	15	36	45

The inland towns of Pisidia

Prostama	62	15	38	20
Adada	62	55	38	15
Olbasa	62	40	38	
Dyrzela	63	10	38	20
Orbanassa	63	20	38	
Talbonda	63	45	38	
Cremna colonia	63		37	50
Conmacum	62	50	37	40
Pednelissos	63	30	37	50
Unzela	63	15	37	30
Selge	63		37	20

Inland towns of Cilicia Aspera

Laerte	63	40	37	25
Casae	63	50	37	30
Lyrbe	63	45	37	5
Colobrassus	63	20	37	10
Cibyra	63	15	36	45

Islands adjacent to Pamphylia

Crambusa	62	30	35	50
Apelbusa	63	15	35	50

CHAPTER VI

Location of Cappadocia
(First map of Asia)

CAPPADOCIA is bordered on the west by Galatia and a part of Pamphylia along the line which we have noted leading from Pontus to the terminus, the position of which is in 64   37 40 on the south by Cilicia along the line extending through the Taurus mountains as far as the Amanus mountains to the terminus in   70   37 20 and by a part of Syria through the Amanus mountains to the Euphrates river, the location of which is in   71 20 38 on the east by the indicated section of Greater Armenia along the Euphrates river to that point where, coming from the north, it is then deflected from the east, the location of which is in   71   42 30 then along the line of the Moschicos mountains and to the terminal in 73   44 30 thence running to the indicated terminus on the coast.

On the north it is terminated by a part of Pontus Euxine from the city Amisus of Galatia to the terminus which is located in   72 20   44 45

The maritime coast of this region is described in this order:

Leucosyri

Ancon	65	40	43	20
mouth of the Iris river	66		43	
First bend of the river	67	15	41	20
Second bend of the river	66		41	20
river sources	68		41	

In the country of Pontus Galaticus which is called Phanaroea

Themiscyra	66	20	43	5
Herculis promontory	66	50	43	20

Pontus Polemoniacus

mouth of the Thermodontos

river	67		43	15
river sources	68	30	42	45
Polemonium	67	15	43	5
Iasonium promontory	67	30	43	15
Cotyora	67	35	43	15
Hermonassa	67	50	43	15

Pontus Cappadocia in the Sidene region

Ischopolis	68	20	43	20
Cerasus	68	50	43	20
Pharnacia	69	20	43	5
Hyssi harbor	70	45	43	20
Trapezus	70	50	43	5

and in Cissios

Ophius	71		43	25
Rhizus harbor	71	10	43	35
Athenarum promontory	71		43	45
Chordyle	71	20	43	45
Morthula	71	40	43	45

mouth of the Archabis

river	72		44	
Xyline	72	5	44	10
mouth of the Cissa river	72	10	44	20
Apsorrus	72	20	44	30
mouth of the Apsorrus river	72	20	44	40

where the Glaucus river and the Lycus river

flow into this	72	30	43	45
sources of the Glaucus river	72	45	43	
sources of the Lycus	71	15	43	
Sebastopolis	72	20	44	45

Noted mountains running through Cappadocia are the Argeus, the extreme parts of which are in

65	30	40	30

and

66	30	39	40

from which a river flows called Melas and empties into the river Euphrates
in

71		39	20

and the mountain Antitaurus extending from the Taurus mountains to the Euphrates river; the part along the Taurus mountains is located in

65	30	38	30

and

67	15	39	15

that which is along the Euphrates is
in

67	30	39	40

and

71	30	41	15

and the Scordiscus mountains the extreme parts of which are located
in

68		41	

and

69		42	30

The following are the interior towns and villages of Cappadocia below Leucosyros, which are on the borders of Galatia:

In the interior of Pontus Galaticus

Boenasa	65	30	42	45
Sebastopolis	66		41	20
Tebenda	66	40	42	10
Amasia	65	30	42	
Choloe	66		42	
Etonia	65		41	30
Piala	65	45	41	40
Pleuramis	65	15	41	20
Pida	66	40	41	45
Sermusa	66	20	41	25
Comana Pontica	67		41	30

In the interior of Pontus Polemoniacus

Gozalena	66	30	42	40
Eudiphus	67	20	42	10
Carvanis	67	40	42	10
Barbanissa	68		42	20
Ablata	68	20	42	
Neocaesarea	67	20	41	50
Saurania	68		42	
Megalula	67	40	41	40
Zela	67	30	41	20
Danae	68		41	
Sebastia	68		40	40
Mesoroma	68	30	41	45
Sabalia	68	20	41	40
Megalossus	68	10	41	20

In Pontus Cappadocia inland

Zephyrium	68	20	43	
Aza	69		42	30
Cocalia	69	30	42	45

Trapezusa	70	30	43	5
Asiba	71	20	43	15
Mardara	71	30	43	40
Camuresarbum	72		43	30

In the Chamanene prefecture

Zama	65	40	40	45
Andraca	65		40	20
Gadasena	65	45	40	55
Vadata	65	20	40	
Sarvena	65	40	40	30
Odoga	66		40	20

In the Sargaurasena prefecture

Phiara	67		41	
Sadagena	66	20	40	45
Gauraena	67		40	30
Sabalassus	66	30	40	25
Ariarathira	67	20	40	45
Maroga	67	30	40	30

In the Garsauritis prefecture

Phreata	65		40	
Archelais	64	45	39	40
Nanassus	65	30	39	45
Diocaesarea	65	30	39	30
Salambriae	65	15	39	20
Tetrapyrgia	60		39	20

In the Cilicia prefecture

Mustilia	66	15	40	20
Siva	66	30	40	5
Campae	66	15	39	45
Mazaca or Caesarea	66	30	39	30
Cyzistra	67		39	20
Euagina	67	10	40	15
Archalla	67	30	40	
Sobara	67	10	39	40

In Lycaonia

Adopissus	64	40	39	15
Canna	64	45	39	
Iconium	64	30	38	45
Paralais	64	45	38	45
Corna	65		38	25
Chasbia	65	10	38	45
Barattha	65	30	38	30

In the Antiochiana prefecture

Derbe	64	20	38	15
Laranda	64	45	38	5
Olbasa	65	20	38	10
Musbanda	64	50	37	50

In the Tyanitiis prefecture

Dratae	65	30	39	
Tyana	66		38	55
Bazis	66	15	38	55
Siala	66	30	38	55

The part of Armenia Minor farthest north is called Orbalisene, below this Aetu-

lane, then Haeretica and below this Orsene and further south after Orsene is Orbisene, the towns on the Euphrates are

Sinibra	71		42	30
Aziris	71		42	
Ladana	71		41	40
Sismara	71	30	41	25
Zimara	71	30	40	40
Dascusa	71		40	25

In the interior within the mountainous region are

Satala	69	30	42	10
Domana	70		42	5
Tapura	70	30	42	10
Nicopolis	69		41	40
Chorsabia	69	40	41	45
Charax	70	30	41	45
Dagona	68	40	41	20
Seleoberea	69	30	41	
Caltiorissa	69	50	41	15
Analibla	70	20	41	10
Pisingara	68	30	40	55
Godasa	69		40	45
Eudoexata	68	15	40	25
Carape	71	20	41	
Casara	70	30	40	40
Oromandus	69	40	40	30
Ispa	70	30	40	20
Phuphena	69		40	15
Arane	69	45	40	10
Phuphagena	68	30	39	50
Mardara	69	5	39	45
Varpasa	67	50	39	30
Orsa	68	30	39	30

In Melitene
on the river Euphrates

Dagusa	71		40	5
Siniscolon	71		39	45
Melitene	71		39	30

toward the interior from this

Zoparissus	70		40	
Titarissus	69	45	39	45
Cianica	69	20	39	30
Phusipara	70	30	39	40
Eusimara	70	10	39	30
Iassus	69		39	30
Ciacis	69	30	39	15
Leugaesa	70	15	39	10
Carmala	70	40	39	20
Semissus	70	30	39	20
Ladoeneris	69	30	38	50

In the Cataonia prefecture

Cabassus	67	15	38	35
Tynna	66	50	38	30

Tirallis	67		38	20
Cybistra	66		38	15
Claudiopolis	65	40	37	50
Dalisandus	66	20	37	50
Podyandus	67		38	
Comana Cappadocia	68		38	
Mopsucrene	67	20	37	30
Tanadaris	68	20	37	45
Leandis	68	40	37	40

In the Murimena prefecture

Sindita	67	30	39	10
Cotaena	68	15	39	10
Zoropassus	69	20	39	
Nyssa	68	20	38	40
Arasaxa	67	30	38	30
Carnalis	68	45	38	30
Garnaca	68	30	38	10

In the Laviansena prefecture on the Euphrates river

Corne	71		39	15
Metita	71		39	
Claudias	71		38	45

In the interior from these

Caparcelis	70	10	39	
Zizoatra	70		38	45
Pasarne	70	30	38	30
Cizara	69	20	38	30
Sabagena	68	50	38	10
Nosalene	69	50	38	20
Laugasa	69	20	37	50

In the Arauene prefecture near the Euphrates river

Juliopolis	71		38	25
Barzalo	71		38	10

Toward the interior from this

Serastere	70	40	38	15
Lacriassus	70	15	38	10
Entelea	70		37	45
Adattha	69	30	37	30

CHAPTER VII

Location of Cilicia
(First map of Asia)

CILICIA is terminated on the west by that part of Pamphylia to which we have referred above; on the east by that part of Syria extending along the Amanus mountains; from the terminus located near Cappadocia, to the Issicus bay and Amanicae port; the location of this terminus is 69 30 36 20 on the north by the part of Cappadocia which extends along the Taurus mountains;

on the south by Cilicius strait and the Issicus bay, which coast is thus described: from Syedra a town of Pamphylia on the maritime coast are the following:

In Selinitis in rugged Cilicia

Iotape	64		36	45
Selinus	64	20	36	45
Antiochia near the mountains	64	40	36	50
Nephelis	64	50	36	35
In Cetidis				
Anemurium	65	10	36	50
mouth of the Orymagdus river	65	20	36	50
Arsinoe	65	30	36	50
Celenderis	65	45	36	50
Aphrodisias	66		36	50
Sarpedon promontory	66	10	36	45
mouth of the Calycadnus river	66	20	36	50
Zephyrium promontory	66	20	36	40
In the Cilicia lowlands				
Corycus	66	30	36	50
Sebaste	66	45	36	45
mouth of the Lamus river	67		36	45
Pompeiopolis or Soli	67	15	36	40
Zephyrium	67	10	36	20
mouth of the Cydnus river	67	45	36	40
river sources	66		38	30
mouth of the Sarus river	68		36	30
mouth of the Pyramus river	68	15	36	30
river sources	68	30	38	
Mallus	68	30	36	30
Serretillis	68	45	36	30
Aegae	69		36	30
Issus	69	20	36	25

The interior towns in Cilicia and in rugged Selinitis are

Caystros	64	45	37	10
Domitiopolis	65	25	37	5
Philadelphia	66		37	25
Seleucia	66	10	36	50
Dioscaesarea	66	10	37	10
In Cetidis				
Olbasa	64	30	37	30
In Lalassidis				
Ninica	65	30	37	30
In Characena				
Flaviopolis	66	20	37	30
In Lamotidis				
Lamus	67		37	
In Lacanitidis				
Irenopolis	67	50	37	20

In Bryelica

Augusta	68	30	37	30

Interior towns of the Cilician lowlands

Tarsus	67	40	36	50
Adana	68	15	36	45
Caesarea	68	30	37	
Mopsuestia	68	50	36	45
Castabala	69		37	
Nicopolis	69	30	37	15
Epiphania	69	30	36	40
Amanicae port	69	30	36	20

CHAPTER VIII

Location of Asiatic Sarmatia
(Second map of Asia)

ASIATIC Sarmatia is terminated on the north by unknown land; on the west by European Sarmatia from the sources of the Tanais river along the Tanais to its outlet in the Maeotis lake, and by the eastern part of this lake from the mouth of the Tanais river to the Cimmerius Bosphorus, along which part are the following:

From the mouth of the Tanais river

Paniardis	67	30	53	30
mouth of the Marubius river	68		53	
Patarue	68		52	30
mouth of the greater Rhombites river	68	30	52	
mouth of the Theophanius river	68	30	51	40
Azara town	68	30	51	20
mouth of the lesser Rhombites river	69		50	30
Azarabitis Taenia	68		50	
Tyrambae	69	40	49	50
mouth of the Anticites river	70		49	20
Gerusa town	70		49	
mouth of the Psathis river	69	30	48	45
Mateta	69		48	30
mouth of the Vardanes river	68		48	20
Cimmerium promontory	66	30	48	30
Apaturos	66	20	48	15
Achilleum at the mouth of the Bosporus	64	30	48	30

and in the Cimmerian Bosporus

Phanagoria	64	30	47	50
Corocondame	64	15	47	30

It is terminated on the south by a part of the Pontus Euxine thence as far as the Coras

river and the line limiting Colchis, Iberia and Albania, thence extending to the Hyrcanium or the Caspian sea; a description of this boundary is the following: after Corocondame on the Pontus

Hermonassa	65		47	30
Sindice harbor	65	30	47	50
Sinda village	66		48	
Bata harbor	66	30	47	40
Bata village	66	20	47	30
mouth of the Psychrus river	66	40	47	30
Achaia village	67		47	30
Cercetidis bay	67	30	47	20
Tazos town	68		47	30
Toreticum promontory	68		47	
Ampsalis town	68	30	47	15
mouth of the Burcas river	69		47	15
Oenanthia	69	40	47	15
mouth of the Thessyris river	69	40	47	
Carterontichos	70		46	50
mouth of the Corax river	70	30	47	
the terminus on the side of Colchis is in	75		47	

thence it extends along the border of Iberia in which are the Sarmatian

passes	77	47

then along Albania to the terminus on the Hyrcanium sea at the mouth of the Soanas

river	86	47

On the east it is terminated by a part of the Hyrcanium sea beginning at the point next to the mouth of the Soanas river, the location of which has been indicated.

mouth of the Alontas river	86	30	47	40
mouth of the Udon river	87		48	20
mouth of the Rha river	87	30	48	50

and partly by Scythia along the Rha river to the bend which is in

	85	54

then along the meridian leading into the unknown country.

There is another turning of the Rha river which is near the bend of the Tanais river in the locality

	74	56

above which two rivers unite coming from the Hyperborean mountains, the position of which junction is in

	79	58 30

the source of that river which is from the west is in

	70	61

the source of that which is from the east is in

	90	61

Of the mountains running through Sarmatia, among those which are named, are the famous Hippici, the Cerauni, the Corax, and those running along Colchis and Iberia which are called the Caucasus; and a branch of these also runs toward the Hyrcanium sea, the name of which is also Caucasus.

The extreme parts of the Hippici mountains are in

	74		54	
and	81		52	
of the Cerauni	82	30	49	30
and	84		52	
of the Corax	69		48	
and	75		48	
and of the Caucasus	75		47	
and	85		48	

which are near

Alexandri Colomnae	80	51	30
Sarmatian pass	81	48	30
Albanian pass	80	47	

Its cattle feed in the Sarmatian meadow lands in the region near the unknown land of Hyperborean Sarmatia; and below these are the *Basilici Sarmatians*; and the *Modoca* race; and the *Hippophagi Sarmatians*; and below these are the *Zacatae Sarmatians*, the *Suardeni* and the *Asaei*; then next to the northern bend of the Tanais river are the *Perierbidi*, a great race near the southern race of the *Iaxamatae*.

The towns on the Tanais are

Hexapolis	72	55	40
Navaris	70	55	
Tanais	67	54	20

Below the *Suardeni* are the *Chaenides*, and toward the east from the Rha river are the *Phthirophagi*, the *Materi* and the land of the *Nesioti*; then below *Iaxamatas* are the *Siraceni* and between the Maentim swamp and the Hippici mountains next to the *Siraceni* are the *Psessi*; then the *Thatemeotae*, below whom are the *Tyrambae*; then the *Aspurgiani*, and near the Corax mountains are the *Arichi* and the *Zinchi*; and above the Corax mountains are the *Conapseni*, the *Metibi*, and the *Agoritae*.

Between the Rha river and the Hippici mountains is the Mithridatis region; below which are *Melanchlani*, then the *Amazones*; and between the Hippici mountains and the Cerauni mountains are the *Suani* and the *Sacani*; moreover between the Cerauni mountains and the Rha river are the *Orinei*, the *Vali*, and the *Serbi*; between the Caucasus mountains and the Cerauni

mountains are the *Tusci*, and the *Diduri*; and near the Caspian sea are the *Udae*, the *Alontae*, the *Isondae*, and the *Gerri*; below the mountain ridge are the *Bosporani*, and on both sides of the *Bosporani* are the *Cimmeri*; on the sea coast of the Pontus are the *Achaei*, the *Cercitae*, the *Heniochi*, and the *Suanocolchi*; then above Albania the *Senaraei*.

The towns and villages on the lesser Rhombitus river are

Axaraba	70		50	30
on the Psathis river				
Auchis	70	40	49	40
on the Vardanus river				
Scopelus	68		48	
Suruba	72		48	20
Corusia	73	40	48	30
Ebriapa	75	20	48	30
Seraca	77		48	40
on the Burcas river				
Cucunda	70		47	45
on the Thessyris river				
Batrache	71		47	30
and on the Corax river				
Naana	73	30	47	15
Towns in the highest mountains				
Abunis	73		48	
Nasunia	74		48	
Halmia	75		48	

CHAPTER IX

Location of Colchis
(Third map of Asia)

COLCHIS is terminated on the north by a part of Sarmatia as we have said; on the west by a part of the Pontus Euxine which extends from the Corax river to the bend, where the Phasis empties into the sea, which part is thus described:

Dioscurias	71	10	46	45
mouth of the Hippus river	71		46	30
mouth of the Cyaneus river	71	30	46	10
Neapolis	71	30	46	15
mouth of the Cyaneus river	71	30	46	10
Siganeum	71	30	45	45
Aea town	72		45	30
mouth of the Chariustus river	72		45	15
mouth of the Phasis river	72	30	45	
Phasis town	72	30	44	45

It is bounded on the south by the Pontus, thence extending along Cappadocia to the

line we have mentioned; thence by a part of Armenia Major along that boundary to the terminus which is located in 74   47 on the eastern border is Iberia along the line as far as the Caucasus   75   47

The *Lazi* occupy the maritime coast of Colchis; the bordering region the *Manrali* inhabit, and the races which are in the Ecritica section.

In the interior region the towns and villages are

Mechlessus	74	30	46	45
Madia	74	15	46	15
Sarace	73		45	
Surium	73	20	44	40
Zadris	74		44	40

CHAPTER X

Location of Iberia
(Third map of Asia)

IBERIA is bounded on the north by the part of Sarmatia which we have mentioned; on the west by Colchis along that line to which we have referred; on the south by a part of Armenia Major, which extends from the terminus in the confines of Colchis to a terminus the location of which is in   77   47

The following are the towns and villages in this country:

Lubium village	75	40	46	50
Aginna	75		46	30
Vasaeda	76		46	20
Varica	75	20	46	
Sura	75		45	20
Artanissa	75	40	46	
Mestleta	74	40	45	
Zalissa	76		44	40
Harmastica	75		44	30

CHAPTER XI

Location of Albania
(Third map of Asia)

THE Albanian border on the north extends along the part of Sarmatia which we have described; on the west it is bounded by Iberia along the line designated; on the south by a part of Armenia Major which extends from the terminus near the border of Iberia to the Hyrcanium sea where the Cyrus river empties into it, which is in   79 40   44 30 on the east by the Hyrcanium sea extend-

ing to the Soana river, which coast is thus described: next to the mouth of the Soana

river which is in	86	47	
Telaeba city	85	46	40
mouth of the Gerrhus river	84 30	46	30
Gelda town	83	46	30
mouth of the Casius river	82 30	46	
Albana town	81 40	45	50
mouth of the Albanus river	80 30	45	30
Gaetara town	79 30	45	

after which is the mouth of the Cyrus

river	79 40	44	30

Between Iberia and the Albanus river, which, flowing from the Caucasus, empties into the Cyrus running along entire Iberia and Albania and separating Armenia from both, are the towns and villages,

Tagada	77 30	46	50
Bacchia	77	46	30
Sanua	77 40	46	40
Deglane	77 20	45	45
Niga	77 20	45	15

Moreover between that river (Cyrus) and the Albanus river which flows from the Caucasus are

Mosega	79	47	
Samunis	79	46	40
Iobula	78	46	20
Iuna	79	46	
Embolaeum	78 30	45	40
Adiabla	79	45	30
Ablana	78	45	15
Mamechia	79 45	45	40
Osica	77 30	44	45
Sioda	78 15	44	40
Baruca	79 20	44	40

The location of the Albanian passes, as we have said is in 80 47

Between the Albanus river and the Casius river are

Chabala	80	47	
Chobota	80 30	46	45
Boziata	80	46	20
Misia	81	46	20
Chadacha	81	46	
Alamus	82	46	15

between the Casius river and the Gerrhus river are

Thiauna	84 15	46	40
Thabilaca	82 45	46	50

between the Gerrhus river and the Soana river is

Thilbis	84 15	46	50

There are two marshy islands near Albania, the middle of which is in 80 30 45

CHAPTER XII

Location of Armenia Major
(Third map of Asia)

ARMENIA is terminated on the north by a part of Colchis, by Iberia, and Albania on the line which we have indicated as running along the Cyrus river; on the west by Cappadocia along the accessible part of the Euphrates and the part of Pontus Cappadocia which extends as far as the Colchis border after passing through the Mosechius mountains; on the east by a part of the Hyrcanium sea from the mouth of the Cyrus river to the terminus the location of which is in 79 45 43 20 and by Media on the line leading to the Caspius mountains and along these mountains, the termini of which are located in 79 42 30 and 80 30 40 on the south it is terminated by Mesopotamia along the line of the Taurus mountains which begins at the Euphrates river, the location of which is 71 30 38 and extends to the Tigris river in 75 30 38 30 then by Assyria on a line extending along the Niphates mountains, that line which we have said continues in a direct line as far as the indicated terminus of the Caspius mountains.

The noted mountains of Armenia are the Moschici extending along that part of Pontus Cappadocia, which is above them, and the Paryardes mountains, the terminal positions of which are 75 43 20 and 77 42 and the Udacespes mountains the central part of which is in 80 30 40 and a part of the Antitaurus mountains located on this side of the Euphrates, the middle of which is 72 41 40 and that which is called the Abas mountains the middle part of which is in 77 41 10 and the Gordyaei mountains, the middle of which is located in 75 39 40

The rivers which flow through this land are the Araxes river, the mouth of which is

in the Hyrcanium sea in the
location   79 45   43 50
the sources of which moreover are
in   76 30   42 30
increasing toward the east as far as the Caspius mountains, then turning toward the north, one part empties into the Hyrcanium sea, another joins with the Cyrus
in   78 30   44 30
and a part of the Euphrates river from that turning, which is from the east, as we have said, to the sources which are
in   75 40   42 40

And there is another noted river which empties into the Euphrates river, the terminus of which, where it joins with the Euphrates is   71 30   40 30
and the terminus near the source
is   77   41
then that part of the Tigris river which is within the region of Armenia from the entrance on the south border to the sources of the river, the location of which is
in   74 40   39 40
forming there the lake which is called Thospitis. There are other lakes, one of which is called Lychnitis, the middle of which is in   78   43 15
and the Arsesa lake the middle of which
is   78 30   40 45

In the region of Armenia which is included between the Euphrates river, the Cyrus and the Araxes, is Cotarzena which is near the Moschici mountains above that which is called Bochae near the Cyrus river, and Tobarena and Totene near the Araxes river and Colthene, and Soducene which are below this; then along the Paryardes mountains is Siracene and Sacapene; the towns in this section are

Sala	73	20	44	20
Ascura	74		44	10
Baraza	75	20	44	10
Lala	76	10	44	
Santuta	77	20	44	20
Santaphara	78		44	20
Toga	78	50	43	20
Vathura	73		43	
Azata	73	45	43	15
Cholua	74		43	10
Sedala	74	40	43	45
Surta	74	30	43	40
Tastina	74	40	43	
Cozala	75	20	43	30
Cotomana	75	15	43	40
Batinna	76	10	43	40
Dizaca	76	50	43	10
Ptusa	77		43	45
Glisma	78	20	43	40
Choluata	78	45	43	40
Sacalbina	79	10	43	15
Arsarata	79	30	43	15

along the Euphrates river

Bressus	72		42	15
Elegia	73	20	42	45
Chasira	74		42	40
Chorsa	74	40	42	50
Thalina	75	20	42	45
Harmaviria	76	40	42	45
Artaxata	78		42	40
Naxuana	78	50	42	45

In the section which is below this up to that river which flows into the Euphrates in the northern country are the regions, commencing in the west, Basilisene, Bolbene and Arsesa, below these Acilisene and Astaunitis and Sophene near the same bend of the river. The towns in this section are

Athua	71	30	42	30
Tinissa	73	30	42	30
Zoriga	71	30	42	
Sana	73	30	42	
Brizaca	74	50	42	30
Daranissa	76		42	20
Zogocara	77	15	42	20
Cubina	78	30	42	20
Codana	71	30	41	40
Cachura	72		41	20
Cholua	73	30	41	
Sogocara	74		41	
Phausya	74	15	41	45
Phandalia	74	50	41	30
Zaruana	75	40	41	45
Citamum	76		41	30
Anarium	76	50	41	30
Sigua	77		41	
Terua	78		41	50
Zurzua	78	30	41	40
Matustana	78		41	40
Astacana	78		41	
Tarina	72	20	41	
Balisbiga	73	40	40	40
Babila	74	20	40	45
Sagauana	75	15	40	45
Azara	76	10	40	50

In the remaining section located toward the south between the Euphrates and the sources of the Tigris, but below this is Anzi-

tene, and Thospitis region; then Coriaea; and the towns in this section are

Elegerda	72	15	40	15
Mazara	71	20	39	50
Anzeta	72		39	30
Soita	72	50	39	30
Belcania	73	30	39	20
Seltia	74		40	
Thospia	74	20	39	50
Colchis	75	30	39	
Siauana	71	30	38	20
Arsamosata	73		38	20
Corrha	74	30	38	40

Moreover toward the east from the sources of the Tigris river is Bagranandene, and Gordyene which is below this, from which to the east is Cotaea and below this Mardi. The towns which are in these parts are

Tasca	75	30	40	10
Phora	76		40	10
Maepa	76	10	40	40
Buana	76	45	40	
Cholimma	77	45	40	40
Terebia	77	40	40	55
Daudyana	77	40	40	20
Caputa	79	20	40	30
Artemita	78	40	40	20
Thelbalane	76	15	39	50
Siae	75	45	39	40
Pherendis	74	40	39	20
Tagranocerta	76	45	39	40
Sardeva	75	50	39	10
Colsa	78		39	50
Tigranoama	79	45	40	
Artagigarta	75	20	38	45

CHAPTER XIII

Location of Cyprus island
(Fourth map of Asia)

CYPRUS, is surrounded on all sides by the sea, on the west alone by the Pamphylium sea, which side is thus described:

Acamas promontory	64	10	35	30
Paphus Nova (new)	64	20	35	10
Zephyrium promontory	64	10	35	5
Paphus Vetus (ancient)	64	30	35	
Drepanum promontory	64	30	34	45

On the south by the Egyptian sea and the Syriacum sea, which side is thus described: after the Drepanum promontory

Phrurium promontory	64	45	34	50
Curium town	65		35	
mouth of the Lycus river	65	20	35	5
Curias promontory	65	30	34	45
Amathus	65	45	35	
mouth of the Tetius river	66	10	35	
Citium town	66	15	35	
Dades promontory	66	30	35	
Throni town and promontory	66	45	35	

On the east alone by the Syriacum sea, which coast is thus described: after the Thronos promontory

Pedalium promontory	67		35	10
mouth of the Pediaeus river	66	50	35	20
Salamis	66	40	35	20
Elaea promontory	67		35	40
Clides promontory	67	30	35	50

On the north by the Cilicius strait, which side is thus described:

Carpasia	66	50	35	50
Achaeorum Acte	66	40	35	50
Aphrodisium	66	30	35	40
Macaria	66		35	45
Cerynia	65	40	35	45
mouth of the Lapethus river	65	30	35	50
Lapethus town	65	20	35	50
Crommyon promontory	65	10	36	10
Soli	65		36	
Callinusa promontory	64	40	35	45
Arsinoe	64	40	35	35

In the eastern part of the island is Salaminia, in the western Paphia; in those parts which are between these in the south are Amathusia and the Olympus mountains; in the north Lapethia.

The towns in the interior are

Chytrus	66	10	35	35
Tremithus	66	25	35	25
Tamassus	66	40	35	25

The islands near this are called the Clides, the middle part of which is

in	67	35	35	45

and the middle of the Carpasian islands

is	67	5	35	45

CHAPTER XIV

Location of Syria
(Fourth map of Asia)

SYRIA is terminated on the north by Cilicia and the part of Cappadocia along that line which we have indicated running through the Amanus mountains;

on the west by the Syriacum sea, which side, in the following order, is thus described, after Issus and Cilicia Harbor:

Syria

Alexandria near Issus	69	30	36	10
Myriandrus	69	30	35	50
Rhosus	69	20	35	40
Rhosicus rocks	69		35	40
Seleucia Pieria	68	35	35	15
mouth of the Orontes river	68	30	35	30
river sources	70		33	20
Posidium	68	30	35	10
Heraclea	68	30	35	10
Laodicea	68	30	35	5
Gabala	68	20	34	55
Paltus	68	20	35	45
Balanea	68	20	34	35

Phoenices

mouth of Eleutherus river	68		34	25
Simyra	67	50	34	20
Orthosia	67	40	34	20
Tripolis	67	30	34	20
Theuprosopon promontory	67	20	34	20
Botrys	67	30	34	5
Byblus	67	40	33	55
mouth of the Adonis river	67	40	33	45
Berytus	67	30	33	40
mouth of the Leonis river	67	30	33	35
Sidon	67	10	33	30
Tyrus	67		33	20
Ecdippa	67	10	33	15
Ptolemais	66	50	33	
Sycaminon	66	50	32	55
Carmelus mountains	66	25	32	55
Dora	66	30	32	40
mouth of the Chorseas river	66	20	32	35

On the south moreover the border line of Judaea extends to the eastward, then to southward in the locality 67 10 32 20 and terminating in 68 31 and a part of Arabia Petraea along the line which, as we have said, leads to the terminus at Arabia Deserta the position of which is 70 30 31 50

On the east the border is terminated by the line which extends along Arabia Deserta to the Euphrates river near Thapsacus which position is in 73 20 35 5 thence along the Euphrates river near Mesopotamia, to the terminus on this river, which is on the border of Cappadocia and in the locality 71 20 38

The important mountains in Syria are the Pieria the central part of which is in 69 40 35 40 and the Casius mountains, the central part of which is in 68 45 34 45 and the Libanus mountains, the terminal positions of which are in 68 45 34 and 70 33 15 and the Antilibanus mountains, the limits of which are in 68 33 20 and 69 40 32 30 and near Arabia Deserta are the Alsadamus mountains, the middle part of which is in 71 33

Near Judaea moreover are the Hippus mountains, the middle of which is in 68 10 32

The river which flows through this land, is that near which is Palmyra, the terminals of which are in 71 15 34 and 71 40 33 40 then the river Chrysorrhoas by name which flows by Damascus, the terminal positions of which are in 69 15 34 and 69 45 32 and part of the Jordan river which is near Lake Gennesaret, the middle position of which is 67 20 32 20 then the river which is called Singas, flowing down from the Pieria mountains on the north then turning to the east, in the position 71 37 30 it joins the Euphrates river in the location 72 37 20

The towns in the Syrian interior beginning on the north, are

In Commagene

Areca	70	50	37	40
Antiochia near the Taurus mountains	70	15	37	20
Singa	71		37	30
Germanicia	70		37	
Catamana	70	40	37	
Doliche	70	40	36	40
Deba	70	20	36	30
Chaonia	70	30	36	20

and near the Euphrates river

Cholmadara	71	15	37	50
Samosata Legio (xvi) Flavia	71	30	37	35

The towns in Pieria are

Pinara	69	50	36	30
Pagrae	70		36	5
and the Syrian pass	69	40	36	15

The towns in Cyrrhestica are

Ariseria	71		37	
Rhegia	71	15	36	50
Ruba	71	20	36	40
Heraclea	71		36	30
Niara	70	50	36	10
Hierapolis	71	15	30	15
Cyrrhus	70	10	36	
Beroea	70	30	36	
Batna	70	50	36	
Paphara	71	30	36	

The towns on the Euphrates are

Urima	71	45	37	30
Arudis	71	55	37	15
Zeugma	72		37	
Europus	72		36	50
Caecilia	71	55	36	40
Bethammaria	71	50	36	30
Gerrhe	71	50	36	5
Arimara	72	10	36	
Eragiza	71	50	36	

The towns in Seleucis are

Gephyra	69	30	35	30
Gindarus	70		35	40
Imma	69	50	35	25

The towns in Casiotis are

Antiochia on the Orontes river	69		35	30
Daphne	69		35	25
Bacatailli	69		35	
Lydia	69	30	35	
Seleucia near Belum	69	30	34	45
Larissa	69	40	34	35
Epiphanea	69	35	34	25
Raphaneae, Third Legion	69	15	34	15
Antaradus	68	15	34	15
Marathus	68	40	34	25
Mariame	69	20	34	
Mamuga	69	20	33	45

The towns in Chalybonitis are

Thema	71	30	35	30
Acoraba	71	15	35	15
Derrhima	72		35	
Chalybon	71	20	35	
Spelunca	71	40	35	15

and on the Euphrates river

Barbarissus	71	55	35	45
Athis	72		35	30

The towns in Chalcidica are

Chalcis	70	30	35	40
Asaphidama	70	30	34	50
Tolmidessa	70	25	34	30
Maronia	71	10	34	30
Coara	70	50	34	10

The towns in Apamene are

Nazama	70	30	34	5

and toward the east from the Orontes river

Thelmenissus	69	40	35	
Apamea	70		34	45
Emisa	69	40	34	

Towns in Laodicene

Scabiosa Laodicea	69	40	33	45
Paradisus	69	45	33	35
Iabruda	70		33	30

The inland towns in Phoenicia are

Arca	68		34	
Palaeobyblus	67	45	34	
Gabala	67	15	33	
Caesarea Panias	67	40	33	

The towns in Coelesyria and Decapolis are

Heliopolis	68	40	33	40
Abila which is called Lysinia	68	45	33	20
Saana	69	20	33	25
Ina	68	30	33	
Damascus	69		33	
Samulis	67	30	32	30
Abida	68	15	32	45
Hippus	68		32	30
Capitolias	68	45	32	30
Gadara	68		32	10
Adra	68	40	32	10
Scythopolis	67	40	31	55
Gerasa	68	15	31	45
Pella	67	40	31	40
Dium	67	50	31	50
Gadora	67	45	31	30
Philadelphia	68		31	20
Canatha	68	50	31	45

The towns in Palmurene are

Rhesapha	72	15	34	45
Cholle	71	45	34	30
Oriza	72	15	34	30
Putea	71	20	34	30
Adada	71	20	34	15
Palmyra	71	30	34	
Adacha	72		34	
Danaba	70	50	33	50
Goaria	70	30	33	30
Aueria	71	30	33	40
Casama	70	40	33	20
Odmana	70	10	33	10
Atera	71	10	33	15

The towns near the Euphrates are

Alalis	72	20	35	15
Sura	72	40	35	20
Alamatha	73		35	5

In the Bathanaea region from which toward the east is the Saccaea region, and below the Alsadamus mountains are the *Trachonitae Arabes*

Gerrha	70		32	50
Elera	70		32	40
Nelaxa	70	10	32	30
Adrama	69	10	31	30

Islands near Syria

Aradus	68		34	30
Tyrus near the continent	67		33	20

CHAPTER XV

Location of Palestina or Judaea (Fourth map of Asia)

THE border of Palestina or Judaea on the north and the east is Syria along the line referred to above; on the south it is bordered by Arabia Petraea along a line drawn from the eastern terminus in the confines of Syria to the terminus in the confines of Egypt, the location of which terminus is 64 15 30 40 on the west by that part of Egypt which has been referred to, and continues on to the sea, and along that sea to the border of Syria, which coast is thus described:

After the mouth of the Chorseas river

Caesarea Stratonis	60	15	32	30
Apollonia	66		32	15
Iope	65	40	32	5
Iamnitarum harbor	65	30	32	
Azotus	65	15	31	55
Ascalon	65		31	40
Anthedon	64	50	31	40
Gazaeorum harbor	65	45	31	30

Part of the Jordan river flows through Judaea toward the Dead sea, the middle position of which is in 66 50 31 10

The interior towns are

In Galilaea

Sapphuri	66	40	32	25
Caparcotni	66	50	32	5
Iulias	67	5	32	15
Tiberias	67	15	32	5

In Samaria

Neapolis	66	50	31	50
Thena	67	5	31	45

In Judaea toward the west of the river Jordan

Raphia	65		31	10
Gaza	65	25	31	45
Iamnia	65	40	32	

Lydda	66		32	
Antipatris	66	20	32	
Drusias	66	30	31	55
Sebaste	66	40	32	10
Baetogabri	65	30	31	30
Sebus	65	40	31	25
Emmaus	65	45	31	50
Guphna	66	10	31	45
Archelais	66	30	31	45
Phaselis	66	55	31	35
Hiericus	66	45	31	25

Hierosolyma which now is called

Aelia Capitolia	66		31	40
Thamna	66	15	31	30
Engadda	66	30	31	15
Bedoro	66	30	31	
Thamaro	66	20	30	50

Toward the Orontes from the Jordan river

Cosmus	67	15	31	35
Livias	67	10	31	25
Callirrhoe	67	5	31	10
Gazorus	67	30	31	15
Epicaerus	67		31	

In Idumaea all of which is west of the Jordan river

Berzaba	64	50	31	15
Caparorsa	65	30	31	15
Gemmaruris	65	50	31	10
Elusa	65	10	30	50
Mapsis	65	40	30	50

CHAPTER XVI

Location of Arabia Petraea (Fourth map of Asia)

ARABIA Petraea is terminated on the west by that part of Egypt to which we have referred; on the north by Palestina or Judaea and the part of Syria along the line which we have indicated as its southern border; on the south by the bend of the Arabian bay and by the Heroopolites bay to the terminus as indicated on the confines of Egypt near the Pharan promontory, which is located in 65 28 30 and by the bay, which is the Elanite, to its turn which is in 66 29 the position of the village Pharan is 65 28 40 The village Elana, which is located in the angle of a bay of this name, has this position 65 50 29 15 on the east its boundary is the line leading

to the eastern terminus of Syria, as we have indicated, and very near Arabia Felix, to the part of this line which is in 70   30 30 along the Arabia Deserta and the remaining part of the line.

The mountains in this land called Melanes (Niger) extend from that angle of the bay which is near Pharan, toward Judaea.

From these mountains toward the west along Egypt is Saracene; below this Munychiatis; below which on the bay is the Pharanita region; near the mountains of Arabia Felix are the *Raitheni*.

The towns and villages in the interior are

Eboda	65	15	30	30
Maliattha	65	45	30	30
Calguia	66	20	30	30
Lysa	65	50	30	15
Gubba	65	50	30	
Gypsaria	65	40	29	45
Gerasa	65	30	29	30
Petra	66	45	30	20
Characmoba	66	10	30	
Auara	66	10	29	40
Zanaatha	66	45	29	50
Adru	67		29	55
Zoara	67	20	30	30
Thoana	67	30	30	30
Necla	67	30	30	15
Cletharrho	67	50	30	20
Moca	67	50	30	10
Esbuta	68	30	31	
Ziza	68	45	31	
Maguza	68		30	45
Medaba	68	30	30	45
Lydia	69		30	40
Rabathmoba	68	30	30	30
Anitha	68	40	30	15
Surattha	69	15	31	10
Bostra legion III Cyreniac	69	45	31	30
Mesada	69	20	30	30
Adra	69	40	30	40
Corace	68		30	5

CHAPTER XVII

Location of Mesopotamia
(Fourth map of Asia)

MESOPOTAMIA is terminated on the north by the part of Armenia Major which we have described; on the west by the part of the Euphrates river which, as we have stated, runs along the Syrian border; on the east by that part of the Tigris river,

which is near Assyria, from the confines of Armenia to the Hercules Altars, which location is in 80   34 20

On the south by the remaining part of the Euphrates river, along Arabia Deserta to the terminus, which position is 76 15 33 20 and along Babylonia to its junction with the Tigris near that point which we call the Altars; the position of this junction is 80   34 20

There are mountains in Mesopotamia renowned by name as the Masius mountains the central part of which is in 74   37 20 the Singaras mountains the central position of which is in 76 40 36 15

Moreover the rivers flowing through this land from the mountains which we have named, is that which is called the Chaboras the sources of which are in 74   37 15 it joins with the Euphrates river in 74   35 10 and that which is called the Saocoras river the sources of which are in 75   37 30 it joins with the Euphrates river in 75 45 33 55

Anthemusia is the part of this region near Armenia, below which is the Calchitis region; below this the Gauzanitis and near the Tigris river is Acabene; below Gauzanitis region is the Ingene region and nearer the Euphrates is Ancobaritis.

The towns and villages in Mesopotamia near the Euphrates are

Porsica	72		37	30
Aniana	72	20	36	40
Baisampse	72	20	36	15
Sarnuca	72	10	35	50
Bersiba	72	20	35	50
Maubae	72	50	35	20
Nicephorium	73	5	35	20
Maguda	73	15	35	10
Chabora	74		35	10
Thelda	74	15	34	45
Apphadana	74	30	34	35
Banace	74	45	34	25
Zitha	75	10	34	20
Bethauna	76		34	15
Rescipha	76		34	
Agamana	76	30	33	30
Eudrapa	77	10	33	40
Addaea	77	15	34	
Pacoria	77	20	34	45

Tiridata	77	30	35	20
Naarda	77	40	35	30
Sipphara	78	15	35	40

The position of the Euphrates where it divides into that which flows through Babylonia, and that which flows through Seleucia called the Regius river is

in	79		35	40
Seleucia town	79	20	35	40

On the banks of the Tigris river there are the following towns:

Dorbeta	76		38	
Sapphe	76		37	40
Deba	76		37	20
Singara	76		37	
Betoun	77		36	45
Lambana	77	50	36	30
Birtha	78	45	36	20
Carthara	79		36	15
Manchane	79	10	36	15

and below Seleucia

Scaphe	79	45	34	30
Apamea	79	50	34	20

below which is the junction of the Regius river and the Tigris

In the interior are the following towns:

Bithias	72	20	37	40
Edessa	72	30	37	30
Ombraea	73		37	10
Ammaea	73	20	37	50
Suma	73	30	37	40
Rhisina	73	30	37	30
Olibera	73	30	37	
Sarrara	74		38	15
Sacane	74	20	37	45
Arxama	74	40	37	15
Gizama	74	20	37	15
Sinna	74	15	37	30
Mambuta	74	45	37	25
Nisibis	75	10	37	30
Bithiga	75	10	37	45
Baxala	75	30	37	
Auladis	73		36	40
Ballatha	73	45	36	40
Carrae	73	15	36	10
Tirittha	73	50	36	15
Thengubis	74	40	36	30
Orthaga	74	40	36	
Eleia	75	40	36	45
Zama	75	30	36	20
Sinna	76	20	36	40
Gorbatha	77		36	15
Dabausa	76		36	
Bariana	77	40	36	

Acraba	73	10	35	50
Apphadana	74		35	30
Rhesaena	74	40	35	40
Peliala	75	45	35	50
Aluanis	74	15	35	20
Bimatra	76	15	35	20
Daremma	76	20	35	

CHAPTER XVIII

*Location of the Arabia Deserta
(Fourth map of Asia)*

ARABIA Deserta is terminated on the north by that part of Mesopotamia which borders on the Euphrates river as we have noted; on the west by a part of Syria and of Arabia Petraea; on the east by Babylonia separated by those mountains which begin at the terminus as we have indicated, near the Euphrates river extending to the interior bend of the Persian gulf near the bay, the location of which terminus is

in	79		30	10

and that part of the Persian gulf to a terminus, the location of which

is	79		29	

on the south moreover by Arabia Felix terminating in the confines of Arabia Petraea which we have indicated as being near the Persian gulf.

The *Cauchabeni* inhabit the parts of Arabia Deserta which are near the Euphrates river, the *Batanaei* the parts near Syria, the *Agubeni* the parts which are near Arabia Felix, next to these are the *Rhaabeni*, and the *Orcheni* on the shore of the Persian gulf; the *Aesitae* inhabit the parts near Babylonia and the parts which are below the *Cauchabeni*, and above the *Rhaabeni* the *Masani* (inhabit); in the interior moreover are the *Agraei* near the *Batanaei*, and the *Marteni* near Babylonia.

The towns and villages in this land and in that near the Euphrates river are

Thapsacus	73	30	35	5
Birtha	73	40	35	
Gadirtha	73	50	34	45
Auzara	74	5	34	30
Audattha	74	15	34	20
Addara	74	20	34	10
Balagaea	75		34	
Pharga	75	40	34	
Colarina	75	30	33	40
Belgynaea	76		33	30

In the parts near the Persian gulf are the towns

Ammaea	79	30	10
Idicara	79	29	30
Iucara	79	29	15

The inland towns are

Barathena	73 20	33	
Save	73	33	
Choce	72 30	32	30
Gauara	73 40	32	40
Aurana	73 15	32	20
Rhegana	75 40	33	20
Alata	72 30	32	
Erupa	72 30	31	15
Themme	75	31	40
Luma	75 40	31	
Thauba	72 45	30	30
Sevia	73 30	30	30
Dapha	74 15	30	30
Sora	75	30	20
Odagana	76 15	30	40
Tedium	77	30	30
Zagmais	76 30	30	10
Arrade	71 30	30	15
Obaera	71	30	45
Artemita	72 15	30	10
Banatha	73 15	29	40
Dumaetha	75	29	40
Alata	75 40	29	30
Bere	76 40	29	30
Calathua	77 30	29	30
Salma	78 20	29	30

CHAPTER XIX

Location of Babylonia
(Fourth map of Asia)

BABYLONIA is terminated on the north by Mesopotamia along the parts of the Euphrates river we have described; on the west by Arabia Deserta, next to which are the mountains which we have described; on the east by Susiana along the remaining parts of the Tigris river as far as its eastern mouth which opens into the Persian gulf in 80 30 31 on the south by a part of the Persian gulf as far as the terminus located on the border of the Arabia Deserta.

The river flowing through this land, is a large river, and running through Babylonia, is called the Macarsares; it unites with the Euphrates in 78 20 35 40 flowing into Babylonia in 79 34 20 these rivers form the arm of the lake and the swamp, the middle part of which is in 78 30 32 30

Moreover the region adjoining the Euphrates is called the Auranitis region, and that adjoining Arabia Deserta is called Chaldaea; surrounding the marshes is Amardocaea; below which are the habitations of those who are called the *Strophades*.

The towns and villages in Babylonia on the Tigris river to the sea below the city Apameam are

Bible	79 45	34	
Didigua	79 30	33	40
Punda	79 40	33	
Batracharta	79 40	32	40
Thalatha	80	32	10
Altha	79 30	31	15

Between the mouths of the Tigris river, that is, that which is toward the east in 80 30 31 and that to the west 79 30 30 15 Teredon 80 31 10

In the region near the Euphrates river

Idicara	77	33	20
Duraba	77 40	34	
Thaccona	77 45	34	30
Thelbencane	78 30	35	30

On the river flowing through Babylonia

Babylon	79	35	

On the Macarsares river

Volgaesia	78 20	34	30
Barsita	78 45	34	20

Below these near the swamps and Arabia Deserta

Beona	79	32	40
Chuduca	78	33	20
Chumana	79	33	10
Caesa	76 40	32	50
Birande	77 30	32	30
Orchoe	78 30	32	40
Bethana	79	32	55
Thelme	76 40	32	
Sorthida	77	32	30
Iamba	78	31	20
Rhagia	78 40	31	20
Chiriphe	79 15	31	10
Rhatta	79 15	30	50

END OF BOOK FIVE

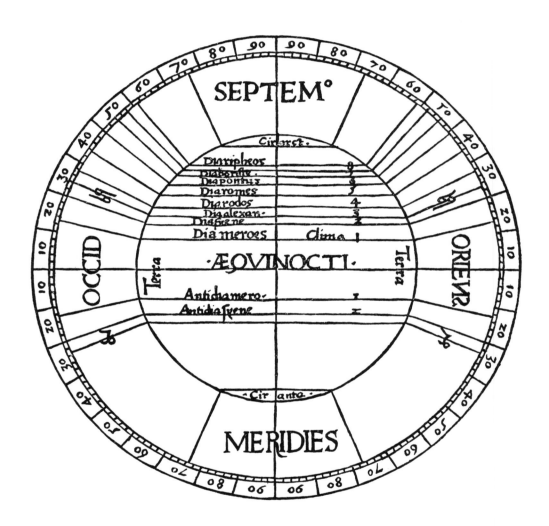

BOOK SIX

The following descriptions are contained in Book Six:

Description of the regions in Asia Major.

CHAPTER I

Location of Assyria
(Fifth map of Asia)

ASSYRIA is terminated on the north by the part of Armenia Major, as we have said, next to the Naphates mountains; on the west alone by Mesopotamia along the designated part of the Tigris river; on the south by Susiana to the boundary which runs along the Tigris river to the terminus, the location of which is in 84 36 on the east by the part of Media extending along the boundary joining those two termini, which we have named, along which boundary are the Choathras mountains, the terminal locations of which

are	80	39	30
and	83	38	

The part of this land which is near Armenia is called Arrapachitis; that which is near Susiana is called Sittacena; between these the *Garamaei* dwell; near these between Arrapachitis and the *Garamaei* is Adiadena; that which is between the *Garamaei* and Sittacena is called Apollonitas, and the race of the *Sambatae* is above this; above Adiabena is located Calacena and above the *Garamaei* is the Arbelitis region.

Rivers flowing through this land empty into the Tigris river, as the Lycus, the sources of which rivers are

in	78	39	
the Lycus unites with the Tigris			
in	79	36	20
and the Gorgos river, the sources of which			
are in	83	38	
unites with the Tigris in	80	35	40

The towns and villages of Assyria and in that part near the Tigris are

Marde	76		38	15
Savara	76		37	15
Bessara	77		37	20
Belciana	77	30	37	
Ninus	78		36	40
Sacada	78	30	36	30
Oroba	79	20	36	20
Thelde	80		36	
Ctesiphon	80		35	
in the remaining interior region				
Birthaba	77	40	38	40
Dartha	78	30	38	45
Zigira	79	40	38	45
Darna	80	30	39	30
Obana	81		39	
Thesara	81	15	38	20
Corcura	78	20	38	10
Oroba	79	20	38	10
Degia	80	45	38	10
Comopolis	81	30	38	10
Dosa	79		37	45
Gaugamela	79	30	37	15
Sarbina	79		37	
Arbela	80		37	15
Gomara	81	20	37	30
Phusiana	82	10	37	40
Isone	82	30	37	30

Sura	83		36	40
Chatracharta	80	30	36	10
Appolonia	81	30	36	30
Thebura	83	20	36	45
Arrapa	82		36	30
Cinna	83	20	36	10
Artemita	81	15	36	
Sittace	82		35	30

CHAPTER II

Location of Media
(Fifth map of Asia)

MEDIA is terminated on the north by a part of the Hyrcanium sea, which is thus described: after the terminus indicated on the border of Armenia are

Sanina	80		43	
mouth of the Cambysis river	81		42	45
river sources	80		41	
Taxina	81	40	42	30
Sabaea Altars	82	30	42	30
mouth of the Cyrus river	84		42	15
river sources	82		39	30
Cadusiorum fortification	84	40	42	
Cyropolis	85	30	41	30
mouth of the Amardus river	86	30	41	30
river sources	85		38	30

these rivers flow through a lake which is called Margiana located in the

interior	82	30	39	20
Amana	87	30	40	40
Acola	88	15	40	15
mouth of the Stratonis river	90	20	40	
river sources	88		38	30
Mandagarsis	92		40	
mouth of the Charinda river	93		40	30

the terminus located on the confines of Hyrcania is in 94   40 30 on the west the border is Armenia Major and Assyria along their eastern confines as we have indicated; on the south the border is Persia to the line beginning at the terminus near Assyria and Susiana thence leading from that position to that which is located in   94   34 30 This border is the western part of the Parchoathras mountains; on the east is Hyrcania and Parthia to the southern line, joining the indicated termini, which runs

along Hyrcania and Parthia, the position is in   94   39 The most important mountains of Media are the Zagros, the middle part of which is in   85   38 the Orontes, the middle part of which is in   88 30 38 the Iasonius, the middle part of which is in   90 30 36 and the western part of the Coroni, the western terminus of which is in   92   38 The *Caspi* dwell in the western part near Armenia, below whom is Margiana extending along the entire side of Assyria; near the sea moreover are the *Cadusi*, the *Geli*, and the *Dribyces*, next to whom, extending into the interior, are the *Amariacae* and the *Mardi*. The *Carduchi* inhabit the regions which are near the land of the *Cadusi*; the *Marundae* to Lake Margiana; then the *Margasi* who are below the *Geli*; after these is Propatena extending as far as Amariaca; and then the *Sagarti* toward the east of the Zagros mountains, after which is the Choromithrena region which extends even to Parthia; on the north of which is Helymais, from which to the source of the Charindas river are the regions the *Tapuri* inhabit; moreover toward the south from Choromithrena is Sidica, Sigrianica and Rhagiana, and from these below the Iasonius mountains is the region of the *Vadassi* and the *Dariti*; the Syromedia region runs along the entire boundary of Persia.

Moreover the Zagri pass is located in   84 30 37 and the Caspian Gates in 94   37 The towns and villages in the interior of Media are

Scabina	79	30	42	
Gabale	80		42	
Uca	80	40	42	30
Varna	81		42	
Candys	83	30	42	
Gabris	80	20	41	15
Sazoa	80	50	41	10
Tonzarma	81	30	41	30
Azaga	81	15	41	10
Morunda	82	20	41	10
Tigrana	82	40	41	30
Pharambara	84	10	41	20
Tachasara	84	20	41	
Zalace	86	15	41	

Aluaca	80	40	40	30	Dottha	88	35	25
Gauzania	82		40	40	Geresa	89 40		35	20
Phazaba	82	30	40	10	Rapsa	90 10		35	40
Pharaspa	85	30	40	30	Andriaca	91		35	10
Curna	86	15	40	30	Cluaca	92 40		35	10
Phanaspa	86	30	40		Argarausdaca	93 20		35	20
Gabris	87	40	40	20	Canatha	93 30		35	45
Nande	81	40	39	40	Aradriphe	93 20		34	45
Zazaca	83	40	39	30
Saraca	85	15	39	20
Mandagara	87	45	39	30
Aganzana	89		39	30
Galla	90	10	39	15
Oracana	91		39	30
Alicadra	93		39	
Phanaca	93	20	39	30
Nazada	83		38	10
Arsisaca	85		38	40
Alinza or Horosa	84		38	
Alisdaca	86	40	38	45
Dariausa	87	30	38	30
Sincar	88		38	30
Batina	89		38	40
Vesaspa	89	40	38	40
Niguza	90	15	38	
Sanais	92		38	20
Razunda	93	20	38	40
Veneca	93	20	38	15
Bithia	85	30	37	40
Alinza	86	10	37	45
Zaranis	86		37	
Gabena	87		37	30
Larasa	87	10	37	10
Ecbatana	88		37	45
Choastra	89		37	40
Niphavanda	88	50	37	10
Guriauna	91		37	20
Choana	92		37	15
Trauaxa	93		37	40
Auradis	93	40	37	15
Thebarga	84	15	36	40
Carine	85	10	36	20
Caberasa	86		36	30
Parachana	87	40	36	
Arsacia	88		36	30
Gauna	88	45	36	30
Heraclea	89		36	40
Zania	90	15	36	50
Aruzis	91		36	20
Zarama	92	20	36	30
Tautice	93	20	36	15
Europus	93	40	36	40
Abacaena	93		36	
Cigbina	87		35	30

CHAPTER III

Location of Susiana
(Fifth map of Asia)

SUSIANA is bounded on the north by that side of Assyria, the termini of which boundary we have indicated above; on the west by Babylonia along the designated part of the Tigris river to its termination on the sea coast; on the east by Persia along the boundary from the indicated terminus in the confines of Assyria and Media to the mouth of the Orontes river emptying into the Persian gulf, that is, from the Tigris to the mouth of the Orontes river, the location of which is 86 30 30 30 this coast is thus described:

after the other mouth of the Tigris river which is toward the east through which it flows into the sea 80 30 31
Charax Pasini 80 40 31
mouth of the Mosaeus river 82 30 40
river sources 82 30 33
Pelodes (Cenosus) bay 83 31
mouth of the Eulaeus river 84 30 30 40

The sources of the river which are in Susiana are in 83 35

The sources of the river in Media are in 86 38
Vadum arenosus 84 30 30 30
mouth of the Oroatis river 86 30 30 30
river sources 88 30 34 40

The *Elymaei* dwell on the maritime coast of Susiana, the *Cossaei* in the country on the border of Assyria; the region which is near the Tigris bank is called Melitene, that which is next to Persia (is called) Cabandene, that above Characena (is called) Characene; above the *Elymaei* is Cissia, above this Chaltapitis, between which and Cissia is the Decra country.

There are towns and villages in Susiana, and on the banks of the Tigris river next to the Herculis Altar, the locations of which are 80 34 5

Agra	80 30	33	45
Aracca	80 10	32	40
Asia	80 10	31	40

The towns in the interior are

Palinza	83 45	35	30
Sacrone	82 45	35	
Bergan	84 15	34	45
Susa	84	34	15
Saura	85	34	
Dera	81 30	33	40
Agarra	83 40	33	20
Abina	85 10	33	10
Tariana	82	32	30
Sele	84	32	30
Graan	82	31	30
Anuchta	83 30	31	40
Urzan	84 40	31	40

The island adjacent to Susiana is

Taxiana	84	29	20

CHAPTER IV

Location of Persia
(Fifth map of Asia)

ON the north the border of Persia is Media along the line running through the Parchoathras mountains; on the west is Susiana, the eastern line of which territory we have indicated; on the east it is bordered by Carmania to the southern line near the terminus in the border of Media and Parthia running to the mouth of the Bagradus river in the Persian gulf in 94 29 15 on the south by the Persian gulf from the mouth of the Oroatis river to the mouth of the Bagradas river, which coast is described as follows: next to the mouth of the Oroatis river

Taoce promontory	87 30	30	10
mouth of the Rhogomanis river	88 30	30	
river sources	92	35	
Chersonesus promontory	89 40	29	30
Ionaca town	90	29	45
mouth of the Brisoana river	92	29	40
river sources	93	34	30
Ausinza	93	29	20
mouth of the Bagradas river	94	29	15
river sources	94	35	15

The region of Persia which is near Media is called Paraetacene, from which toward the south are the *Mesabatae* and the *Rapsi*,

below whom is Misdia, and as far as the sea Mardycena and Taocena, and the *Hippophagi* and *Suzaei*; also below Mardycena are the *Megores*, above the *Suzaei* moreover the *Gabaei*.

The towns and villages in the interior of Persia are

Ozoa	85 45	35	20
Tanagra	86	34	30
Marrasium	92 30	34	30
Aspadana	86	33	50
Axima	87 45	33	50
Poryospana	89	33	50
Persepolis	90 15	33	20
Niserge	91	34	
Sicta	91 30	34	
Arbua	92 15	33	
Cotamba	93 30	33	40
Poticara	87 15	32	15
Ardea	88	32	30
Cauphiaca	89	32	30
Batthina	90	32	20
Cinna	92 20	32	20
Paradona	93 50	32	15
Taepa	87	31	45
Tragonice	87 40	31	40
Maetona	89 10	31	45
Chorodna	90	31	15
Corra	91 20	31	40
Gabra	92 15	31	30
Orobatis town	87	30	50
Taocae	89	30	20
Parta	90	30	20
Mammida	91	30	20
Usia	91 40	30	
Pasarracha	93	30	30
Gabe	93 40	30	10

Islands adjacent to Persia

Tabiana	87	29	15
Sophtha	88	29	20
Alexandria or Aracia	90	29	

CHAPTER V

Location of Parthia
(Fifth map of Asia)

PARTHIA is bordered on the west by a part of Media, as we have set forth; on the north by the line extending along the Hyrcanian region and through the Coronus mountains to the terminal position in the same, the location of which is in 101 39 on the east by the boundary line of Aria from

the terminus, which we have mentioned, leading through the Masdoranus mountains to the end in 102 30 33 20 on the south by the border line of the Carmania Deserta, which runs through the Parchoathras mountains.

The part of Parthia which joins Hyrcinia is called Comisena, below which is Parthyena; next is Chorana and Partauticena, after this is Tabicena near Carmania, then Sobide.

The towns and villages of Parthia are the following:

Ambrodax	94	30	38	20
Oeminia	95		38	40
Caripraca	97	15	38	40
Rhoara	78	30	38	20
Suphtha	100		38	30
Araciana	94	15	38	
Dordomana	94	15	37	40
Hecatompylon regia	96		37	50
Sindaga	96	10	37	
Parbara	98	50	37	30
Mysia	100	30	37	30
Charax	94	15	36	40
Apamia	94	15	36	
Semina	96		36	40
Marriche	98		36	40
Tastache	99		36	20
Armiana	101	20	36	10
Choana	95	15	35	30
Pasacartia	94	15	35	15
Rhuda	95		35	
Simpsimida	96	30	35	40
Artacana	96		34	30
Appha	98	30	35	20
Rhagaea	98	20	34	20

CHAPTER VI

Location of Carmania Deserta
(Fifth map of Asia)

THE Carmanian desert is bordered on the west by that part of Persia which is terminated by the Bagradas river thence to the terminus in the Parcoathras mountains the location of which is in 94 31 on the north by Parthia the border of which runs through the Parcoathras mountains; on the east by a part of Aria along the line which we have indicated, to the terminus which is located in 104 28 50 on the south by the border line of Carmania

Pars uniting the indicated termini. The regions of the *Isatichae* and *Chuthi* are used as pasture lands in the southern parts; in the interior are the *Gadanopydres*; the region in the north and the east is called Modomastica.

CHAPTER VII

Location of Arabia Felix
(Sixth map of Asia)

ARABIA Felix is terminated on the north by the designated border of Arabia Petraea and of Arabia Deserta; on the northeast by a part of the Persian gulf; on the west by the Arabian gulf; on the south by the Red sea; on the east by that part of the Persian gulf and the sea, which extends from the entrance to this gulf as far as the Syagros promontory.

The maritime coast of this region is thus described: from the terminus of the Arabian gulf near the Elanite bay:

The Arabian gulf

Omne	66	20	28	50
Modiana	66	40	27	45
Hippos mountains	66	30	27	20
Hippos village	67		26	40
Phoenicum village	67	20	26	20
Raunathi village	67	15	25	40
Chersonesus promontory	67		25	40
Iambia village	68		24	

The *Thamyditae* inhabit the upper shore of this gulf, and then the *Sideni*; then the *Darrae*; next to these the *Banubari*; then the *Arsae*.

Cinaedocolpite region

Copar village	68	30	23	15
Arga village	69		22	40
Zabram region	69	20	22	
Centos village	69	20	21	30
Thebe town	69	40	21	
mouth of Betius river	69	30	20	40
river sources	76		24	30
Cassanita region				
Badeo regia	70		20	15
Amba town	70	40	19	30
Mamala village	71	45	18	10
Adedi village	72	15	17	10
Elesara region				
Pudni town	72	30	16	30
Eli village	73	30	16	30
Napegus village	73	30	15	
Sacatia town	74	15	14	30

Muza market town	74 30	14	
Sosippi port	74 45	13	
Pseudocelis	75	12	30
Ocelis market town	75	12	
Palindromus promontory	74 30	11 40	
on the strait entering the Red sea			
Posidium promontory	75	11 30	
Sanina town	75 30	11 45	
Cabubathra mountains	76 15	11 15	
Homerita region			
Modocae town	77	11 45	
Mardacha town	78	11 45	
Lees village	78 40	11 30	
Ammonium promontory	79 20	11 10	
Arabia market town	80	11 30	
Agmanispha village	80 40	11 45	
Niger mountains	81 30	11 45	
Atramita region			
Abisama town	82	11 45	
Magnum coast (littus)	82 30	11 30	
Mada village	83	11 30	
Eristha town	83 30	11 45	
Parvum coast (littus)	83 40	11 30	
Cana market town and			
promontory	84	11 30	
Trulla harbor	84	12 40	
Maethath village	84 20	13	
Prionotus mountains	84 40	13	
mouth of the Prionis river	85	13 30	
river sources	82	17 30	
Embolium village	85 30	13 20	
Pretos harbor	86 20	13 45	
Thialemath village	87	14	
Mosoha harbor	88 30	14	
Syagros promontory	90	14	
Sachalitarum in Sachalite bay			
Metacum village	88	16	
Ausara village	87 20	16 45	
Anga village	87 30	17 30	
Astoa village	88 30	18 30	
Neogilla naval station	89	19	
mouth of the Hormanus			
river	89 30	20 30	
Didyma mountains	90 15	19 20	
Coseude town	91	20	
Oracle of Diana	91 40	20	
Abissa town	92 20	20 15	
Corodamum promontory	93	20 15	
At the entrance to the Persian gulf			
Cryptus harbor	92 40	21 30	
Melanes mountains which are called Asa-			
bon, the middle part of which is located near			
the sea	93	22	
Asabon promontory	92 30	23 30	

Persian gulf

In the widely extended bay of the *Ichthy-ophagi* near which toward the interior, are the *Macae*; then the towns of the *Anaritae*

Rhegama town	88	23 10	
Sacrum Sun promontory	87 20	23 30	
mouth of the Laris river	86 30	23 30	
river sources	81	18	
Capsina town	86	23 10	
Cauana town	85	23	
then of the *Egei*			
Sarcoa town	84 15	23	
Carada town	83 40	23 30	
Atta village	82	23 15	
then of the *Gerraei*			
Magindanata town	81	23 20	
Gerra town	80	23 20	
Bilbana town	80	24 10	
then of the *Thaemi*			
Ithar town	80	25	
Magorum bay	80	25 20	
Istriana town	80	25 40	
then of the *Laenitae*			
Mallada town	80 10	26 10	
Chersonesus promontory	80 20	26 30	
Leanites bay	79 15	27	
Itamos harbor	79 40	27 40	
Adari town	79 15	27 40	
then of the *Abucei*			
Sacer bay	78 15	28 15	
Coromanis town	79	28 45	

next the terminus on the confines of the desert and the Mesanites

bay	79	30 10

The noted mountains of this land are those which we have mentioned toward the interior which are called the Zames, the middle part of which is located

in	76	25	
the Marithi mountains	80	21 10	
the Climax mountains	76 30	16	

near which mountains is the fountain of the

Stygian waters	78	15

other mountains wanting names

above Cinaedocolpitae	71	25
above Cassanitae	73	20

below the Marithos moun-

tains	84 30	17 40

and above the Asabon moun-

tains	88	22 30

The *Scenitae* dwell in the interior near that part toward the north which is entirely mountainous; above are the *Oaditae*; toward the south from these are the *Saraceni*

and the *Thamydeni;* then around the Zames mountains and toward the west from this are the *Apataei* and the *Atritae,* and near these the *Mesamanes* and the *Udeni;* toward the east are the *Laeeni,* the *Asapeni* and the *Iolysitae;* to the south are the *Catanitae,* then the *Thanuitae;* from these toward the west the *Manitae,* above whom are the *Alapeni,* and near Cinaedopolita the *Malichae.* And below the *Manitae* is the Smyrnofera interior region; then the *Minaei,* a numerous race, below whom are the *Doreni* and the *Mocritae;* then the *Sabaei* and the *Anchitae* above the Climax mountains; around the Marithos mountains are the *Malangitae* to the north, and the *Dachareni,* the *Zeiritae,* then to the south the *Bliulaei* and the *Omamitae,* from whom to the river source are the *Cottabani* as far as the Asabon mountains, below whom is the Libanotofora region; then near the Sachalita region are the *Iobaritae;* below the *Gerraei* are the *Alumaeotae,* then the *Sophanitae* and the *Cithibanitae,* and extending as far as Climax mountains the *Arabanitae;* below all these the *Chatramonitae* from the Climax mountains even to Sachalitas; toward the south from the Climax are the *Masonitae;* then the *Asaritae,* and near Homerita the *Sappharitae* and the *Ratheni,* above whom are the *Maphoritae,* thence to the beginning near the *Chatramonitae* is the Smyrnofera exterior region; near Syagrum as far as the sea are the *Ascitae.*

The towns and villages which are in Arabia Felix in the interior are the following:

Aramava	67	30	29	10
Ostama	69	30	29	
Thapava	71	40	29	
Macna	67		28	45
Angala	68	15	28	45
Madiama	68		28	15
Achrona	70		28	15
Obraca	71	30	28	20
Rhadi village	73	30	28	30
Pharatha	73	40	28	40
Satula	77	30	28	10
Laba	68	10	27	40
Thaema	71		27	
Gea town	71	15	27	20
Aina	75	40	27	20
Lugana	76	30	27	15
Gaesa	78	40	27	15
Soaca	68		26	15
Egra	70	30	26	
Salma	74	30	26	
Arra village	75	40	26	10
Digema	77		26	30
Saptha	78	15	26	20
Phigea	79		26	
Badais	68	30	25	30
Ausara	71		25	30
Iabri	74	30	25	
Alata	77	20	25	30
Mochura	69	40	24	30
Thumna	71	10	24	50
Alvara	71		24	15
Phalbinum	73	15	24	
Salma	73	20	24	20
Gorda	76	10	24	30
Marata	79	20	24	20
Ibirtha	79	40	24	40
Lathrippa	71	40	23	20
Carna	73	30	23	15
Biavanna	76	30	23	
Goeratha	77	40	23	
Catara	79	30	23	20
Baeba	71	30	22	30
Macoraba	73	20	22	
Sata	81	10	22	20
Masthala	81	45	22	30
Domana	82	20	22	30
Atia	85		22	15
Ravana regia	87		22	
Chabuata	89	15	22	
Thumata	74	20	21	20
Olaphia	77	40	21	45
Inapha	79	10	21	40
Tiagar	85		21	20
Aspa	91		21	
Agdamum	73	30	20	20
Carman regia	75	15	20	15
Irala	80	20	20	15
Maocosmus metropolis	81	15	20	40
Labris	82		20	15
Lattha	83	20	20	15
Accipitrum village	84	30	20	30
Albana	71	30	19	15
Chargatha	73	10	19	15
Laththa	75	20	19	20
Omanum market town	87	40	19	45
Marasdu	74	30	18	30
Mara metropolis	76		18	40
Amara	78	30	18	40
Nagara metropolis	81	45	18	40
Iula	85	20	18	15
Magulaba	75	30	17	

Sileum	76 40	17	
Mariama	78 10	17 10	
Thumna	79	17 15	
Vodona	80	17 20	
Marimatha	85 10	17 40	
Saba	73 40	16 55	
Menambis	75 45	16 30	
Thauba	78 40	16 10	
Saudatha metropolis	77	16 30	
Madasara	81 45	16 20	
Gorda	82 30	16	
Thabane	85 40	16 20	
Miba	74 20	15 20	
Source of Stygia water	78	15	
Draga	79 10	15 15	
Sarvon	80 40	15 15	
Maepha metropolis	83 15	15	
Saraca	75 30	14 30	
Sapphar metropolis	78	14	
Ara regia	80 30	14 30	
Rhaeda	83 40	14 10	
Baenun	84 30	14 15	
Thuris	75 15	13	
Lachchera	77 30	13 20	
Hyaela	79	13 50	
Maccala	81	13 45	
Sachla	82 40	13 20	
Sava regia	76	12	
Deva	77 40	12 45	
Sochchor	78 30	12 40	
Bana	80 20	12 40	
Dela	82	12 40	
Coa	83 30	12 30	

Islands adjacent to this region and those which are in the Arabian gulf are

Aeni	65 45	27 20	
Timagenis	66	25 45	
Zygena	66 15	24 20	
Daemonum	66 45	23 15	
Polybii	67 40	27 40	
Accipitrum	69 30	19	
Socratis	70	16 40	
Cardamine	71	16	
Are	71 30	15 20	
Combusta	70 30	14 30	
Malicha II	71 40	14	
Adani duae	72 30	12 30	

in the Red sea

Agathoclis II	81 20	10	
Cocconati III the middle of which	83	9	
town of Dioscordi island	86 40	9 30	
terminus of the western island	85	10 30	

Trete	86 30	12	

and near Sachalites bay, the Zenobi VII islands the middle of which

is	91	16 30	
Organa	92	19	

Sarapidis, in which is a temple in the Persian

gulf	94	17 30	
Apphana island	81 20	28 40	
Ichara	82	25	
Tharo	85 15	24 45	
Tylus	90	24 40	
Arathos	91 40	24 40	

CHAPTER VIII

Location of Carmania
(Sixth map of Asia)

CARMANIA is terminated on the north by the line which we have referred to as extending along the side of Carmania Deserta: on the east by Gedrosia along the Persian mountains, and running through these to the southern boundary as far as the confines of the desert located near the Indian sea, which terminus is

in   104   20

on the west by a part of Persia to the terminus on the border of Carmania Deserta, at the mouth of the Bagradas river, and where it is called the Carmanicus bay, a description of the coast of which is the following:

After the mouth of the Bagradas river

mouth of the Daris river	95 15	28 40	
mouth of the Cathrapius river	95 30	27 40	
mouth of the Corius river	96	26	
mouth of the Achindanus river	96 40	26	
mouth of the Andanis river	96	25	
mouth of the Saganus river	95 40	24 30	
Armuca	94 30	23 30	
Armozon promontory	94	23 40	
Carpella promontory	94	22 10	

on the south by that part of the Indian sea which extends to the indicated terminus; of this part the following is a description:

From the Carpella promontory in the Paragonicus bay

Canthatis town	96	22 30	
Agris	96 30	23	
Commana	97 30	23	
Rhogana	98 15	22 30	

mouth of the Salaris river	98	10	22	40
Masin	99		22	40
Samydaca	99	10	22	40
mouth of the Samydaches river	100	30	22	20
river sources	104	30	25	
Tesa	101	10	22	
mouth of the Caudriacis river	101	15	21	40
Bagia promontory	101		21	
Cuiza harbor	101	15	20	40
Alambater promontory	101		20	

Thus far the bay is called Paragonicus; after this are

Deranoebila	101	30	20	10
Cophanta harbor	101	30	20	
mouth of the Zoromba river	102	30	20	
Badara	103		20	10
Musarna	103	15	20	10

next after this terminus, as we have said, is the Indian sea 104 20

Mountains are in this land near those which we have said are next to Gedrosia, which are called Semiramidis or Strongylus, so called from the round figure, the middle part of which is in 94 30 23

Others are an equal distance from Persia from which the rivers run westward as the Samydaches, the middle of which is in 99 26

The *Camelobosci*, who are also called *Sozotae* inhabit parts of this land near the desert; below these is Rhudiana and Agdenitis extending to the sea; then Paraepaphitis, below which are the *Arae* and the *Caradrae* races; then Cabadena and Canthonice, and along the sea the *Pasargadae* and the *Chelonophagi*.

The towns and villages that are known in the interior of Carmania are

Portospania	96		28	45
Carmana metropolis	100		29	
Thaspis	98		27	40
Nipista	97	30	26	
Chodda	101	30	25	
Taruana	96		24	30
Alexandria	99		24	20
Sabis	97	30	24	10
Throasca	99	40	23	40
Ora	103	20	23	40
Cophanta	102	15	23	

The islands adjacent to Carmania and those which are in the Persian gulf

Sagdana in which is

Cinnabar	94		27	15
Vorochtha	94	20	25	30

in the Indian ocean

Polla	98		19
Carminna	102		18
Liba island	104		19

CHAPTER IX

Location of Hyrcania
(Seventh map of Asia)

HYRCANIA is terminated on the north by that part of the Hyrcanium sea which extends from a terminus in the confines of Media to the mouth of the Oxus river located in 100 43

in which region are

Saramanne town	94	15	40	30
mouth of the Maxera river	97	20	41	30
river sources	98		38	40
Socana town	97	20	42	
mouth of the Oxus river	100		43	6

On the west by a part of Media, as we have stated, which extends as far as the Cronus mountains, the middle of which is in 94 39

On the south by Parthia along the border running through the Cronus mountains, as we have noted; on the east by the line running through the Cronus mountains, as the designated terminus.

The *Maxerae* and the *Astaveni* pasture their flocks in Hyrcania, being located near the maritime coast; below the *Maxerae* are the *Chrindi*; next to these is the region of Arsitis along the Cronus mountains, and below the *Astaveni* is Siracene.

The interior towns are

Barange	99		42	
Adrapsa	98	30	41	30
Casape	95	30	40	20
Abarbena	97	30	40	10
Sarba	98		40	30
Sinica	100		40	30
Amarusa	95		40	
Hyrcania metropolis	98	30	40	
Sace	94	15	39	30
Asmurna	98	15	39	30
Maesoca	98	30	39	30

and the island in this region near the shore is Talca 95 43 5

CHAPTER X

*Location of Margiana
(Seventh map of Asia)*

ON the west Margiana is bounded by Hyrcania along the side to which we have referred; on the north, by a part of Scythia which is near the mouth of the Oxus river and along the section of this river on the confines of Bactria, the location of which is in 103 44 on the south by a part of Aria along the line marking the confines of Hyrcania and Parthia, through the Sariphos mountains to the terminus which is located in 109 39 on the east by the Bactrian mountains in which are the indicated termini.

An excellent river flows through this land which is known as the Margus, the sources of which are located in 105 20 39 and its junction with the Oxus 102 40 43 30

The *Derbiccae* dwell in this region near the Oxus river, and below these are the *Massagetae*, next to these are the *Parni* and the *Dahae*; below whom is a desert land, and from this toward the east are the *Tapuri*.

Its towns are

Ariaca	103	43	10
Sena	102 30	42	20
Aratha	103 30	42	30
Argadina	101 20	41	40
Iasonium	103 30	41	30

near which another river flows into the Margus coming from the Sariphis mountains, the sources of which are

in	103	39	
Rhea	102	40	30
Antiochia Margiana	106	40	40
Guriana	104	40	10
Nigaea	105 15	39	10

CHAPTER XI

*Location of Bactriana
(Seventh map of Asia)*

ON the west Bactriana is bounded by Margiana; on the north and also on the east by Sogdiana and a part of the Oxus river; on the south by the part of Aria which

extends from the terminus in the confines of Margiana to the terminus in 111 30 39 and along the parallel of Paropanisadus an equal distance through the mountains to the sources of the Oxus which are located in 119 30 39

Rivers flow through Bactria which rivers empty into the Oxus, and the Oxus river, the sources of which are in 110 39 the Dargamanis, the sources of which are in 116 30 36 40 the Zariaspes the sources of which are in 113 39 the Artamis the sources of which are in 114 39 the Dargoedus the sources of which are in 116 39 it flows into the Oxus in 116 30 44 the others are the Artamis and the Zariaspes which, after uniting their waters in 113 40 they flow into the Oxus in 112 30 44 the Dargamanis moreover after uniting with the rivers in the location 109 40 10 flows into the Oxus 109 44 20

The *Salaterae* and the *Zariaspae* inhabit northern Bactria along the Oxus river; toward the south below the *Salaterae* are the *Chomari*; below whom are the *Comi*, then the *Acinacae*, then the *Tambyzi*; below Zariaspa are the *Tochari* a great race; below these are the *Marycaei*, the *Scordae* and the *Varni*, and below these are the *Sabadi*; and next below *Sabadi* are the *Orsipi* and the *Amarispi*.

The Bactrian towns in that part near the Oxus are

Charracharta	110	44	10
Zarispa	115	44	
Choana	117	42	
Suragana	117 30	40	30
Phratrua	119	39	20

near the other rivers

Alicodra	107 30	43	30
Chomara	106 30	42	30
Curiandra	109 30	12	10
Cavaris	111 20	43	
Astacana	112	43	20
Evusmi regia	108 20	41	10
Menapia	113	41	20
Eucratidia	115	42	

Bactra regia	116		41	
Estobara	109 30		39 40	
Maracanda	112		39 15	
Maracodra	115 40		39 40	

CHAPTER XII

Location of Sogdiana
(Seventh map of Asia)

THE boundary of Sogdiana on the west is a part of Scythia near the section of the Oxus river which runs along the confines of Bactria and Margiana, then through the Oxius mountains near the Jaxartes river in 110 49 on the north by a part of Scythia along the Jaxartes river where it bends near the terminus which is in 120 48 30 on the east alone by the Sacara region along the Jaxartes river where it bends from the sources in 125 43 and along a direct line to the terminus which is located in 125 38 30 on the south and the west by Bactriana along the Oxus, which section we have noted, and near the Caucasus mountains which are called the mountains of India, to the line which connects the indicated terminus and the sources of the Oxus river 119 30 39

The mountains between the rivers of Sogdiana have their termini in 111 47 and 122 46 30 one of its rivers flows from the Oxia lake, the middle of which is located in 111 45 and there are other rivers flowing from these mountains called the Comedarum from which the Jaxartes flows, and into which river they empty; another is called the Dymus, the sources of which are in 124 43 where it joins with the Jaxartes 123 47 another of these rivers is called the Bascatis, the sources of which are in 123 43 and where it unites with the Jaxartes 121 47 30

In parts of the region near the Oxius mountains the *Pasicae* dwell, near the section of Jaxartes on the north dwell the *Iati* and the *Tachori*, below whom are the *Au-*

gali; then next to the Sogdios mountains are the *Oxydrancae*, the *Drybactae* and the *Candari*, and below the mountains are the *Mardyeni*; and near the Oxius are the *Oxiani* and the *Chorasmi*; in the parts which are near these toward the east dwell the *Drepsiani* bordering both of the rivers; and near these but more toward the source are the *Aristenses* near the Jaxartes, the *Cirrodaces* near the Oxus; and between the Caucasus mountains and Imaus mountains the region is called Vandabanda.

The mountain towns of Sogdiana near the banks of the Jaxartes are

Cyrescha	125	46 20	
and near the Oxus			
Oxiana	117 30	44 40	
Maruca	117 15	43 40	
Cholbisina	117 40	41	
between the rivers and more remote			
Trybactra	112 15	45 30	
Alexandria Oxiana	113	44 40	
Indicomordana	115	44 40	
Drepsa metropolis	120	45	
Alexandria ultima	122	41	

CHAPTER XIII

Location of Sacara
(Seventh map of Asia)

THE boundary of Sacara on the west is Sogdiana on the side of which as we have before mentioned, is this country's eastern boundary. The northern boundary looks toward Scythia, the boundary line running along the bend of the Jaxartes river extends to a terminus in 130 49 on the east moreover it is bounded by Scythia along the line running through the Ascatancas mountains to the Imaus mountains 140 43 extending through the Imaus mountains northward, terminating in 145 35 on the south Sacara is bounded by the Imaus mountains along the line uniting the mentioned termini.

The mountains in Sacara, as we have said, are the Comedarum, which extend along Sogdiana 125 43 near the pass of the Comedarum 130 39 here is the Stone Tower in 135 43

Nomads occupy the land of Sacara; but the towns are without caves or forests. Those who are near the Jaxartes are the *Caratae* and the *Comari;* those along the mountain region are the *Comediae,* and the *Massagetae,* who are along the Ascatanca mountains; next, between these are the *Grynaei,* the *Scythae* and the *Toornae,* below whom near the Imaus mountains are the *Byltae.*

CHAPTER XIV

Location of Scythia within the
Imaus mountains
(Seventh map of Asia)

SCYTHIA within the Imaus mountains is terminated on the west by the side of Asiatic Sarmatia, as we have said; on the north by Terra Incognita (unknown land); on the east alone by the Imaus mountains running toward the north along the meridian line which, as we have stated, extends to the Terra Incognita; on the south by eastern Sogdiana and Margiana and along their indicated boundary to the mouth of the Oxus river which flows into the Hyrcanium sea, and by a part of the Hyrcanium sea as far as the Rha river, a description of the coast of which is the following:

Next to the mouth of the Rha river

mouth of the Rhymmus river	91	48	15
mouth of the Daix river	94	48	15
mouth of the Jaxartes river	97	48	
mouth of the Istaus river	100	47	20
mouth of the Polytimetus river	103	45	30
Aspabota town	102	44	

Next to this the mouth of the Oxus

river	100	43

The important mountains of Scythia which are between the Imaus and the eastern parts of the northern mountains are called the Alani, the termini of which are

in	105	59	30
and	118	59	30

Rhymmici mountains the termini of which

are in	90	54	
and	99	57	10

from which the Rhymmus and other rivers flow into the Rha river, and some into the Daix river; Norossus mountains, the termini of which are in 97 53

and	106	52	30

Aspasio mountains, the extreme parts of

which are located in	111	55	30
and	117	52	30

from these also a number of rivers empty into the Iaxartis

Tapuri mountains, the terminal positions

of which are in	120	56
and	125	49

from which also a number of rivers flow into the Iaxartes.

Next to these mountains are those which are in the Imaus region, also the Syebi mountains, the terminal locations of which

are in	121	58
and	132	62

mountains which are called the Anaraei, the termini of which are in 130 56

and	137	50

After this is a bend of the Imaus mountains toward the north. Those who inhabit Scythia toward the north along the Terra Incognita are called *Alani-Scythae,Suobeni,* and *Alanorsi.* The part which is below these is held by the *Satiani,* the *Massaei,* and the *Syebi.* Near the Imaus mountains are the *Tectosaces.* Near the eastern sources of the Rha river are the *Rhobosci;* below these are the *Asmani,* and next the *Paniardi;* below whom along the river is the Canodipsa region; below this are the *Coraxi,* then the *Orgasi,* next to this along the coast the *Erymmi,* from which region toward the east are the *Asiotae,* next the *Aorsi,* then the *Iaxartae,* a great race having the same name as the river and extending as far as the bend of Tapuros mountains. Below the *Setiani* are the *Mologeni;* below these, up to the Rhymmicos mountains, are the *Samnitae;* below the *Massaei* and the Alani mountains are the *Zaratae* and the *Sasones,* and more to the east are the *Tybiacae.* Next below the *Zaratae* are the *Tabieni* and the *Iastae;* then the *Machetegi* near the mountains; below these are the *Norosbenses* and the *Norossi,* and below these the *Cachagae Scythae* along the Iaxartes; to the west of the Aspasiis mountains are the *Aspasii Scythae* or *Aspasii;* and to eastward are the *Galactophagi;* and eastward from the Tapuris mountains and the *Scymbi Scythae* are the *Tapurei.* The *Ascotancae* are between the Anariae mountains and the mountains having the same name, also the *Scythae.* The *Anaraei* are be-

low the *Alanorsis*. The *Ascotancae* are near the Tapuris mountains and inhabit the region up to the Imaus mountains. Between the Oxus mountains and the region which is near the mouth of the Iaxartes and along the coast which lies between two rivers dwell the *Ariacae;* below them are the *Namastae;* next are the *Sagaraucae* and near the river Oxus are the Rhibii, in which region is the city

Dauaba	104	45

CHAPTER XV

Location of Scythia beyond the
Imaus mountains
(Eighth map of Asia)

SCYTHIA beyond the Imaus mountains is terminated on the west by Scythia within the mountains and next to Sacae, the mountain range separating it running northward; on the north is unknown land; on the east it is bounded by Serica along a direct line which terminates in 150   63
and 160   35
on the south by the part of India beyond the Ganges river as far as the line which unites the designated termini; a part of the western section of the Auzaciis mountains is in Scythia, the terminus of which is
in 149   49
and a part of the Casii mountains, as they are called, the terminus of which is
in 152   41
and an equal part of the western section of the Emodus mountains, the terminus of which is in 153   36

In the Auzaciis mountains is the source of the Oechardis river which is located
in 153   51

The *Scythian Abii* inhabit the northern parts of this Scythia, and below these are the *Scythian Hippophagi;* next to these is the Auzacitis region; below this is the region which they call Casia, and below this are the *Scythian Chatae;* then the Achassa region and below this next to the Emodus mountains the *Scythian Chauranaei.*

The towns in this region are

Auzacia	144	49	40
Issedon Scythia	150	48	30
Chaurana	150	37	15
Sotta	145	35	20

CHAPTER XVI

Location of Serica
(Eighth map of Asia)

SERICA is terminated on the west by Scythia beyond the Imaus mountains along the line which we have mentioned; on the north is unknown land to that parallel which extends through Thule; which unknown land extends to the meridian line, the termini of which are located
in 180   63
and 180   35
on the south by the remaining part of India beyond the Ganges and along that parallel line to the terminus, the location of which is in 173   35
and beyond Sinis leading direct along that line to the terminus which is near the unknown land we have mentioned.

The mountains running into Serica, and which are called Annibi, terminate
in 153   60
and 171   56
the eastern part of Auzacis mountains the terminus of which is located
in 165   54
and the mountains of Asmiraei which are located in 167   47 30
and 174   47 30
the eastern part of Casius, the terminus of which is in 162   44
the Thagurus mountains, the central part of which is located in 170   43
the Emodi, the eastern part of which is called Serici, the terminus of which is
in 165   36
and that which is called the Ottorocoras, the termini of which are located
in 169   36
and 176   39

Two rivers flow through the greater part of Serica: the Oechardes, a source of which in the Auzaciis mountains has been described, and another in the Asmiraeis mountains in 174   47 30
one from the Casius mountains flows into it in 160   49 30
the source of which in these mountains is in 161   44 15
and the river Bautisus, as it is called, the source of which is in the Casius mountains, in 160   43

another which rises in the
Ottorocoras 176 39
one from the Emodus which flows into
this 168 39
the source of which in these mountains
is 160 37

In the northern parts of Serica the races of the *Anthropophagi* pasture their flocks, below whom the race of the *Annibi* reside in the mountains of this name; between these and the *Auzacios* is the *Sizyges* race, below whom are the *Damnae*; then the *Pialae* on the Oechardes river, and below this the *Oechardae* of this same name. Toward the east from the *Annibi* are the *Garinaei* and the *Rhabbanae*, and below these the Asmiraea region above the mountains of this name; below these mountains of Casius the great race of the *Issedones* dwell, and near the beginning of these mountains are the *Throani*; below these toward the east are the *Thaguri*, near the mountains of this name; below the *Issedones* are the *Aspacarae*, and below these the *Batae*, and further southward, next to the Emodi and Serici mountains are the *Ottorocorae*.

These are the important towns of Serica

Damna	156		51	40
Piale	160		49	40
Asmiraea	170		48	20
Throana	174	40	47	40
Issedon Serica	162		45	
Aspacarea	162	30	41	40
Drosache	167	40	42	30
Palliana	162	30	41	
Thogara	171	20	39	40
Abragana	163	30	39	30
Daxata	174		39	40
Orosana	162		37	30
Ottorocora	165		37	15
Solana	169		37	30
Sera metropolis	177	15	38	35

CHAPTER XVII

Location of Aria
(Ninth map of Asia)

ARIA is terminated on the north by Margiana and by a part of Bactriana, the south boundary of which we have mentioned; on the west by Parthia and Carmania Deserta along the eastern lines of these as we have also mentioned; on the south by Drangiana along the line which be-

ginning at this terminus near Carmania, as we have indicated, turns toward the north running thence through the Bagous mountains to the point where it turns toward the terminus, the location of which is
in 111 30 34
this mountains bends into that direction
in 105 32
on the east the boundaries of Aria are Paropanisades along the meridian line which joins the mentioned termini in the western part of Paropanisades. The position of Paropanisades is defined by the three points
on the south 111 36
on the north 111 30 39
on the farthest east 119 30 39

An important river flows through this land which is called the Arius, the sources of which are in the Paropanisus mountains
in 111 38 15
and in the Sariphos 103 38 40
at the terminus it flows into a lake which is formed by it; this lake is called
Aria 108 40 36

The *Nisaei* and the *Astabeni* inhabit the northern parts of Aria; the *Masdorani* are near Parthia and the Carmanian desert; the *Cesirotae* are near Drangiana, and next to Paropanisades are the *Parutae*, below whom are the *Obares*, and the parts which lie between these the *Drachamae* inhabit, below whom are the *Etymandri*, then the *Borgi*, and below these is the Scorpiofera region.

The towns and villages in Aria are these

Dista	102	30	38	45
Namaris	105	40	38	50
Tava	109		38	45
Augara	102		38	
Bitaxa	103	40	38	
Sarmagana	105	20	38	10
Siphara	107	15	38	15
Rhaugara	109	30	38	10
Zamuchana	102		37	
Ambrodax	103	30	37	50
Bogadia	104	15	37	40
Varpna	105	30	37	
Godana	110	30	37	30
Phorava	110		37	
Chatrischa	103		36	20
Chaurina	104	20	36	20
Orthiana	105	15	36	20
Tauciana	106	10	36	
Astanda	107	40	36	

Articaudna	109 20	36	10
Alexandria in Aria	110	36	
Babarsana	103 20	35	20
Capotana	104 30	35	30
Aria town	105	35	
Casta	107 20	35	20
Sotira	108 40	35	10
Orbitane	109 20	35	30
Nisibis	111	35	20
Paracanaca	105 30	34	20
Sariga	106 40	34	40
Darcama	111	34	40
Cotaca	107 30	33	40
Tribazina	106	33	
Astasana	108	33	
Zimyra	109 30	34	

Parsia	113 30	35	
Locharna	118	35	
Daroacana	118 45	34	45
Cabura or Ortospana	118	34	
Tarbacana	114 20	33	40
Bagarda	116 40	33	40
Arguda	118 45	33	30

CHAPTER XVIII

Location of Paropanisades
(Ninth map of Asia)

PAROPANISADES is bounded on the west by the eastern side of Aria as we have indicated above; on the north by the part of Bactria which we have mentioned; on the east by the part of India joining the meridian line, which extends from the sources of the Oxus river through the Caucasus mountains to the terminus, the location of which is in   119   32 40 on the south moreover it is terminated by the northern border of Arachosia along the line which runs through the Parvetis mountains.

Rivers flow from this land; one the Gardamanis into Bactria, the sources of which are indicated above; another joins with the Coa river in the Goryaea region, the sources of which are in   115   34 30

The *Bolitae* inhabit the northern parts of this land, the *Aristophyli* the west, and below these are the *Parsii*, in the south the *Parsietae*, in the east the *Ambatae*.

The towns and villages in Paropanisades are

Parsiana	118 30	38	45
Barzaura	114	37	30
Artoarta	116 30	37	30
Baborana	118	37	20
Catisa	118 40	37	30
Niphanda	119	37	
Drastoca	116 30	36	30
Gazaca	118 30	36	15
Naulibis	117	35	30

CHAPTER XIX

Location of Drangiana
(Ninth map of Asia)

THE border of Drangiana on the west and also on the north is Aria along the line which we have said passes through Bagous mountains; on the east the boundary is the meridian line of Arachosia to the terminus which is in the confines of Aria and Paropanisades running in a straight line, the position of which is in   111 30 28 on the south it is bounded by the part of Gedrosia along the line which connects the termini in the Baetius mountains.

The river which flows through this land empties into the Arbis, the sources of which are located in   109   32 30

The *Darandae* inhabit the part near Aria; next are the *Batri* near Arachosia; the region which lies between is called *Tatacena*.

The towns and villages said to be in Drangiana are

Prophthasia	110	32	20
Ruda	106 30	31	30
Inna	109	31	30
Aricada	110 20	31	20
Asta	107 30	30	40
Xarxiare	106 20	29	15
Nostana	108	29	40
Pharazana	110	30	
Bigis	111	29	20
Ariaspa	108 40	28	40
Arana	111	28	15

CHAPTER XX

Location of Arachosia
(Ninth map of Asia)

ARACHOSIA is bordered on the west by Drangiana; on the north by that side of Paropanisades which we have mentioned; on the east by a part of India along the meridian line, the terminus of which is

on the confines of Paropanisades, thence to a terminus which is located

in   119   28

on the south it is terminated by the part of Gedrosia along the line which connects the mentioned limits through the Betius mountains.

The river which flows from this land emptying into the Indus river has its source

in   114   32 30

and joins it in   122 30   27 30

in which locality it empties into a lake which it forms, and which lake is called the

Arachotus   115   29 40

The parts of the land which are called the northern the *Pargietae* inhabit, those below them are the *Sydri*, and next to these are the *Roplutae* and the *Eoritae*.

The towns and villages of Arachosia they say are

Azola	114	15	32	15
Phoclis	118	15	32	10
Alexandria	114		31	
Rhizana	115		31	10
Arbaca	118	20	31	20
Sigara	113	15	30	
Choaspa	115	15	30	10
Arachotos	118		30	20
Asiaca	112	20	29	20
Gammaca	116	20	29	20
Maliana	118		29	20
Dammana	113		28	40

CHAPTER XXI

Location of Gedrosia
(Ninth map of Asia)

GEDROSIA is terminated on the west by Carmania along the meridian, leading as we have stated above, as far as the sea coast; on the north by Drangiana and Arachosia as mentioned; on the east by the part of India next to the Indus river along the line leading from the terminus in the confines of Arachosia to the terminus which

is located on the shore of the

sea   109   20

on the south by that part of the Indian sea, which is described in the following manner: after the terminus located in the confines of Carmania

mouth of the Arbis river	105		20	15
river sources	110		27	30

where the river rising in Drangiana flows

into it	107	40	25	
Rhagiava town	106		20	
Mulierum harbor	107		20	15
Coeamba	108		20	
Rhizana	108	40	20	15

after which is the indicated terminus near the sea.

The mountains which extend through Gedrosia are called the Arbiti, the termini

of which are   107   22

and   113   26 30

from which rivers flow into the Indus, the source of one of which is

in   111   25 30

in like manner one flowing from the Baetis mountains runs through Gedrosia

On the maritime shores of the land are the *Arbitari* villages; in the direction toward Carmania dwell the *Parsirae*; near Arachosia the *Musarnaei*; all of the intermediate region is called Paradene and below this Parisine; after this near the Indus dwell the *Rhamnae*.

The towns and villages of Gedrosia are

Cuni	110		27	
Badara	113		27	
Musarna	115		27	30
Cottobara	108		25	30
Soxistra	112	30	25	45
Oscana	115		26	
Parsis metropolis	106	30	23	30
Omiza	110		23	30
Arbis town	105	20	20	30

Islands adjacent to Gedrosia

Asthea	105		18
Codane	107	30	17

END OF BOOK SIX

BOOK SEVEN

❧

CHAPTER I

Location of India this side the Ganges (Tenth map of Asia)

INDIA this side the Ganges is bounded on the west by Paropanisades, Arachosia, and Gedrosia along their eastern side; on the north by the Imaus mountains near Sogdiana and Sacae; on the east by the Ganges river; on the south and west by a part of the Indian ocean, the shore of which is thus described:

On the bay which is called Canthicolpus

Syrastrena region

Canthinaustathmus station	109	45	20	

Western mouth of the Indus river which is called

Sagapa	110	20	19	50
the second mouth is called				
Sinthum	110	40	19	50
the third is called				
Aureum	111	20	19	50
the fourth is called				
Cariphi	111	40	19	50
the fifth is called				
Sapara	112	30	20	15
the sixth is called				
Sabalassa	113		20	15
the seventh is called				
Lonibare	113	20	20	15

Bardaxima city	113	40	20	40
Syrastra village	114		19	30
Monoglossum emporium	114	10	18	40
Larica region				
mouth of the Mophidis river	114		18	20
Pacidara village	113	45	17	50
mouth of the Namadus river	112		17	45
Baleon promontory	111		17	30

On Barigazenus bay

Camanes	112		17	
Nusaripa	112	30	16	30
Pulipula	112	30	16	20
Ariaca region				
Suppara	112	30	15	50
mouth of the Gaoris river	112	15	15	10
Dunga	111	30	15	
mouth of the Byda river	111	30	15	
Symilla emporium and promontory	110		14	45
Balepatna	111		14	20
Hippocura	111	45	14	10
Viripyra				
Mandagora	113		14	10
Byzantium	113	40	14	40
Chersonesus	114	30	14	30
mouth of the Nanagunna river	114	30	13	45
Harmagara	115		14	20
Nitra emporium	115	30	14	40
Lymirica region				
Tindis city	116		14	30
Bramagara	116	45	14	20
Calecarte promontory	116	40	14	
Muziris emporium	117		14	
mouth of the Pseudostomus river	117	20	14	
Podoperura	117	40	14	15
Semna	118		14	20
Cerevra	118	40	14	20
Bacare	119	30	14	30
mouth of the Baris river	120		14	20
Aii region				
Melcynda	120	20	14	20
Elancor emporium	120	40	14	
Cottiara metropolis	121		14	30

Bambala	121 20	14	
Commaria promontory	121 45	13 30	

On the bay of Colchicus in which are pigeons
    Carei region

Sosicuri	122	14 30	
Colchi emporium	123	15	
mouth of the Solenis river	124	14 45	

On the Argaricus bay
Cory promontory also called Calligicum on the Argaricus bay in the Pandiones

region	125 40	13 20	
Argari city	125 15	14 20	
Salur emporium	125 20	15 10	

    Batii region

Nigamma metropolis	126	16	
Thelchyr	127	16 10	
Curula city	128	16	

In that which is called Paralia or the coast of Soretarum

Chaberis city	128 20	15 45	
mouth of the Chaberus river	129	15 20	
Sobura emporium	130	14 30	

    Aruarni region

Poduca emporium	130 15	14 45	
Melanga emporium	131	14 20	
mouth of Tyna river	131 40	12 45	
Cottis	132 20	12 30	
Maliarpha emporium	133 10	12	

    Mesoli region

mouth of the Maesolus river	134	11 30	
Contacossyla emporium	134 30	11 30	
Coddura	135	11 20	
Alosygni emporium	135 40	11 10	

port whence those set sail who navigate the

bay	136 20	11	

On the Gangeticus bay

Palura city	136 40	11 30	
Nanigaena	136 20	12	
Caticardama	136 20	12 50	
Cannagara	136 30	13 30	
mouth of the Manda river	137	14	
Cottobara	137 15	14 40	
Sippara	137 50	15 30	
mouth of the Tyndis river	138 30	16	
Mapura	139	16 30	
Minagara	140	17 15	
mouth of the Dosaron river	141	17 40	
Cocala	142	18	

mouth of the Adamas river	142 50	18	
Cosamba	143 30	18 15	

Western mouth of the Ganges river which is called

Cambysum	144 30	18 15	
Palura city	145	18 30	

second mouth which is called

Magnum	145 40	18 30	

third mouth which is called

Camberycum	146 30	18 40	
Tilogrammum city	147	18 30	

fourth mouth which is called

Pseudostomum	147 50	18 30	

fifth mouth which is called

Antibola	148 30	18 15	

Important mountains in the accessible parts of India; Apocopis mountains, which are called the Vengeance of the

Gods	116	23	
and	124	26	

Sardonix mountains, in which is stone of this name, the middle of which is

in	117 30	21	

Vindius mountains, which are

in	127	27	
and	135	27	

Bettigo mountains, the limits of which are

in	123	21	
and	130	20	

Adisathrus mountains, the middle of which

is in	132	23	

Uxentus mountains, the limits of which are

in	136	22	
and	143	24	

Orudii mountains, the limits of which are

in	138	18	
and	133	16	

The rivers in India flowing from the Imaus mountains are the following:

Coa river sources	120	37	
Suastus river sources	122 30	36	
Indus river sources	125	37	
Sidaspus river sources	127 30	35	
Sandabalis river sources	129	36	
Adris river sources	130 30	37	

the turning of the Coa river near Paropani-

sades	121 30	33	

the junction of the Coa and the Suatus

rivers	122 30	31 40	

the junction of the Coa and the Indus

rivers	124 30	31	

the junction of the Sidaspus and the Sandabalis rivers 126 40 32 40
the junction of the Sidaspus and the Zuadris rivers 126 30 31 30
junction of the Zuadris and the Bibassis rivers 131 34
the junction of the Bibassis and the Zaradrus rivers 126 30 15
the junction of the Zaradrus and the Indus rivers 124 30
the bending of the Indus near the Vindius mountains 122 29 30
the bending of the Indus near Arachosia 122 30 27 30
various river sources in 111 25 30
various river sources in 127 27
a source of the Indus in the Arbetis mountains 117 25
bending of the Indus near the mouth of the Sagapa river 113 40 23 15
branching into the Sagapa and the Sinthum rivers 111 21 30
branching of the Indus into the Aureum river 112 30 22
into the Sapara and Cariphi rivers 113 30 22 20
into the Cariphi near the mouth of the Sabalassa river 113 21 20
branching from the Cariphi river into the Lonebare river 113 20 21 40

A list of the rivers which flow into the Ganges
Diamona river sources 134 30 36
sources of the Ganges river 136 37
sources of the Sarabis river 140 36
union of the Diamona and the Ganges 136 34
union of the Sarabis and the Ganges 136 30 32 30
Flowing into the Ganges from the Vindius mountains
Soas river 136 20 31 30
river sources 131 28
deflection of the Ganges near the Uxentus mountains 142 28
source of its branch from the Uxentus 137 23
branching of the Ganges into the Cambusum mouth 146 22
branching from the Cambusum into the Magnum mouth 145 20
branching from the Magnum to the Camberichum mouth 145 30 19 30
branching of the Ganges into the Pseudostomum 146 30 20
branching of the Ganges into the Antibola mouth 146 30 21
and of other rivers there are
Namadus river, sources of which are in the Vindius mountains 127 26 30
bend of this river near Siripalla 116 30 22
near this it unites with the Mophidis river 115 18 30
sources of the Nanaguna river in the Vindius mountains 122 26 30
where it divides into the Gaoris and the Bynda 114 16
sources of the Pseudostomus river in the Bittigo mountains 123 21
bend of the river 124 18
sources of the Chaberus river in the Adisathrus mountains 132 22
sources of the Tyna river in the Orudi mountains 133 17
sources of the Maesolus river in the same mountains 134 30 17 30
sources of the Manda river in the same mountains 136 30 16 30
sources of the Tyndis in the Uxentus mountains 137 22 30
sources of the Dosaronus river in the same mountains 140 24
sources of the Adamas river in the same mountains 142 24

A list of the provinces and towns which are in this region is the following: below the sources of the Coa river is Lambata, and its mountains extend as far as the mountains of Comedorum. Below the sources of the Suastus river is Sustena. Below the sources of the Indus are the *Duradrae* and their mountains above. Below the sources of the Bidaspus, of the Sandabalis and of the Adris, is the Caspiria region. Below the Bibasis sources, and those of the Zaradrus, is the Diamona region, and below the sources of the Ganges is Cylindrina, and below Lambata and Suastena is Goryaea.

The cities are
Carnasa 120 34 15
Barborana 120 15 33 40
Gorya 122 34 15

Nagara, which also is called

Dionysopolis	121	30	32	30
Drastoca	120	30	32	30

Between the Suastus and the Indus rivers is the Gandarae region, and the cities are

Poclais	123		33	
Naulibi	124	20	33	20

Between the Indus and the Bidaspus rivers, next to the Indus, is the Varsa region, and the cities are

Ithagurus	125	40	33	20
Taxiala	125		33	15

Along the Bidaspus river is the Pandouorum region, in which are the following cities:

Labaca	127	30	34	15

Sagala, which is also called

Euthymedia	126	40	32	
Bucephala	125	30	30	20
Iomusa	124	15	30	

And those who are toward the east as far as the Vindius mountains are the *Caspiraei*, and among them are the following cities:

Salagisa	129	30	31	30
Astrassus	131	15	31	15
Labocla	128		33	20
Batanagra	130		33	20
Arispara	130		32	50
Amacatis	128	15	32	20
Ostabalassara	129		32	
Caspira	127		31	15
Pasicana	128	30	31	15
Daedala	128		30	30
Ardona	126	15	30	10
Indabara	127	15	30	
Liganira	125	30	29	
Chonnamagara	129		29	20
Gagasmira	126	40	27	30
Hararassa metropolis	123		26	
Modura or Deorum	125		27	10
Connbanda	124		26	

Farther to eastward are the *Gymnosophistae*, and near these along the Ganges but more to southward are the *Daetychae*, among whom are the following cities:

Conta	133	30	34	20
Margara	135		34	
Batancaesara	132	40	33	20

and east of the river

Passala	137		34	15
Orza	136		33	20

Below these are the *Manichae*, among whom are the cities

Persacra	134		32	44
Sannaba	135		32	30

and east of the river

Toana	136	30	32	

Below this is Prasiaca and the following cities:

Sambalaca	132	15	31	50
Adisdara	136		31	30
Canagora	135		30	40
Cindia	137		30	30
Sagala	139		30	20

and east of the river

Aninacha	137	20	31	50
Coanca	138	40	31	30

Below this are the *Saudrabati*, and the following cities:

Empelathra	130		30	
Nadubanthagar	138	40	29	
Tamasis	133		30	20
Curaporina	130		29	

Moreover the region which is next to the western part of India, is called Indoscythia.

A part of this region around the river mouths is Patalena, above which is Abiria. That which is about the mouth of the Indus and the Canthicolpus bay is called Syrastrena.

The cities of Indoscythia which are remote from the river are the following:

Artoarta	121	30	31	15
Andrapana	124	15	30	40
Sabana	122	10	30	40
Banagara	122	15	30	20
Codrana	121	15	29	40

and along the river

Embolima	124		31	
Pentagramma	124		30	20
Asigramma	123		29	30
Tiausa	121	40	28	50
Aristobathra	120		27	30
Azica	119	15	27	
Pardabathra	117		25	30
Pisca	116	30	25	
Pasipeda	114	30	24	
Susicana	112		22	20
Bonis	111		21	30
Colaca	110	30	20	40

In the island formed by this river are the cities

Pantala	112	50	21	
Barbaria	113	15	22	30

On the east side of the river more remote from it are the following cities:

Xodraca	116		24	
Sarbana	116		22	50
Auxoamis	115	30	22	20
Ausinda	114	15	22	
Orbadarum	115		22	
Theophila	114	15	21	10
Astacapra	114	40	20	15

Near this river are the following cities:

Panassa	122	30	29	
Budaea	121	15	28	15
Naagramma	120		27	
Camigara	119		26	20
Binagara	118		25	20
Parabali	116	30	24	30
Sydrus	114		23	30
Epitausa	113	45	22	30
Xoana	113	30	21	30

The Larica region of Indoscythia is located eastward from the swamp near the sea, in which on the west of the Namadus river is the interior city

Barygaza emporium	113	15	17	20

on the east side of the river

Agrinagara	118	15	22	30
Siripalla	116	30	21	30
Bamogura	116		20	45
Sazantium	115	30	20	30
Xerogeri	116	20	19	50
Ozena-Regia Tiastani	117		20	
Minagara	115	15	19	30
Tiatura	115	50	18	50
Nasica	114		17	

There dwell above these in Pulinde the *Agriphogi*, and above these the *Chatriaei*, among whom on the west and the east of the Indus river are the following cities:

Nigranigramma	124		28	15
Antachara	122		27	
Sudassana	123		26	50
Syrnisica	121		26	30
Patistama	121		25	
Tisapatinga	123		24	20

Moreover between the Sardonix mountains and the *Bettigi* dwell the *Tabasi*, a race of philosophers (wise men) and above these extending as far as the Vindius mountains are the *Parapiotae*, who are nomads; east of the river, are the following cities:

Cognabanda	120	15	23	
Ozoabis	120	30	23	40
Ostha	122	30	23	40

Cosa, in which are diamonds

	121	20	22	30

Near the Nanaguna river are the *Phyllitae* and the *Bettigi*, between whom are the *Gondali* who are next to the *Phyllitae* and the river. The *Ambastae* are next to the *Bettigi* and the mountains of that name; and their cities are

Agara	129	20	25
Adisathra	128	30	24 30
Soara	124	20	24
Nindosora	125		23
Anara	122	30	22

Between the *Bettigi* and the Adisathrus mountains are the *Sorae-Nomades*, and their cities are

Sangamarta	123		21
Sora-Arcati. Regia	130		20 15

On the eastern side of the Vindius mountains are the *Biolingae*; among these are the cities

Stagabaza	133		28 30
Bardaotis	137	30	28 30

Below these dwell the *Porvari*, among whom are these cities

Bridama	134	30	27 30
Tholobana	136	20	27
Malaeta	133	30	25 50

Below these, extending as far as the Uxentus mountains, are the *Adisathri*; among whom are the cities

Maliba	140		27
Aspathis	138	30	25 40
Panassa	137	40	24 30
Sageda metropolis	133		23 30
Balantipyrgum	136	30	23 30

More to eastward extending as far as the Ganges are the *Mandalae*; among these is the city

Asthagura	142		25

Along the river are the cities

Sambalaca	141		29 30
Sigalla	142		28
Palibothra regia	143		27
Tamalites	144	30	26 30
Oreophanta	146		24 30

Likewise below the Bettigus mountains are the *Brachmani-Magi* (wise men) up to the *Bati*, among whom is the city

Brachma	128	19

and below the Adisathro mountains as far as the Orundus mountains dwell the *Badiamae*, among whom is the city

Tathilba	134	18	50

and below the Uxentus mountains dwell the *Dryllophyllitae*, whose cities are

Sibrium	139	22	20
Opotura	137 30	21	40
Ozoana	138 15	20	30

More to eastward as far as the Ganges are the *Cocconagae*, whose cities are

Dosara	142 30	22	30

and in the east near the river

Cartinaga	146	23	
Cartasyna	145 30	21	40

Above the *Mesoli* are the *Salaceni* along the Orundus mountains, among whom are the following cities:

Benagurum	140	20	15
Castra	138	19	30
Magaris	137 30	18	20

Near the Ganges river are the *Sabarae* in whose region diamonds are found, whose cities are

Tasopium	140 30	22	
Caricardama	141	20	15

In the entire region about the mouth of the Ganges are the *Gangaridae*, whose city is

Gange regia	146	19	15

The cities and villages which are in the interior region of Ariaca and west of the Byda river are

Manippala	119 30	20	45
Sarisabis	119	20	
Tagara	118	19	
Betana regia	117	18	10
Deopolli	115 40	17	50
Gamaliba	115 15	17	20
Menogara	114	16	20

Between the Byda river and the Pseudostomus are

Nagaruraris	120	20	15
Tabasa	121 30	21	40
Lida	120 40	20	50
Tiripangalida	121 15	19	40
Hippocuri regia	119 45	19	10
Subuttum	120 15	19	10
Siramalaga	119 20	18	30
Calligeris	118	18	
Modogulla	119	18	
Petirgala	117 45	17	15
Banavasi	116	16	45

Moreover the interior cities of Viripyra are the following:

Olochoera	114	15	
Musopalle metropolis	115 30	15	45

In the western part of Limyrica interior on the Pseudostomus river are the cities

Naruila	117 45	15	50
Cuba	117	15	
Pallura	117 15	14	40

Between the Pseudostomus and the Baris rivers are the following cities:

Pasaga	124 20	21	50
Mastanur	121 30	18	40
Curellur	119	17	30
Punnata in which is beryl	120 40	17	30
Haloa	120 40	17	
Carura regia Cerobrothi	119	16	20
Arembur	121	16	20
Berderis	119	15	50
Pantipolis	118	15	20
Adarima	119 30	15	20
Coreur	120	15	

In the interior of Aii

Morunda	121 20	14	40

In the interior of Carei

Mendela	123	17	20
Selur	121 45	16	30
Tittua	122	15	40
Matitur	123	15	45

In the interior of Pandiones

Taenur	124 45	18	40
Perincari	123 20	18	
Corindiur	125	17	40
Tangala	123 30	16	45
Modura regia	125	16	
Acur	124 45	15	20

In the interior of Bati

Calindoca	127 40	17	30
Bata	126 30	17	
Tallara	128	16	45

Cities in the interior of Paralia-Soretarum are

Caliur	129	17	40
Tenagora	132	17	
Icur	129	16	40
Orthura regia	130	16	20
Bera	130 20	16	15
Abur	129	16	
Carmara	130 20	15	40
Magur	130	15	15

Cities in the interior of Arvarni are

Cerauga	133	16	15
Phrurium	132	15	
Cariga	132 40	15	
Poleur	131 30	14	40
Picendaca	131 30	14	
Iatur	132 30	14	
Scopolura	130 15	15	36

Icarta	133	30	13	40
Malanga regia	133		13	
Candipatna	133	30	12	20

In the interior of Mesoli

Calliga	138		17	
Bardamana	136	15	15	15
Coruncala	135		17	
Pharytra	134	40	13	20
Pitynda metropolis	135	30	12	30

Islands adjacent to the accessible parts of India in the Canthicolpus bay are

Baraca	111		18	

On the coast as far as the Colchicus bay

Milizigeris	110		12	30
Heptanesia island	113		13	
Tricadiba	113	30	11	
Peprina	115		12	40
Trinesia island	116	20	12	
Leuca	118		12	
Nanigeris	122		12	

In the Argaricus bay

Cory island	126	30	13	

CHAPTER II

*Location of India beyond the Ganges
(Eleventh map of Asia)*

INDIA beyond the Ganges is terminated on the west by the Ganges river; on the north by the accessible parts of Scythia and Serica; on the east by the Sinae region along the meridian line running from the border of Serica as far as the bay called the Great bay; on the south by the Indian sea and a part of the Parassadis sea which extends from the Menuthiadae island as far as the opposite shore of the Great bay; the coast of this part is described as follows:

In the Gangeticus bay, after the mouth of the Ganges is Antibolum, called the city of the gods

Pentapolis	150		18	
mouth of the Catabeda river	151	20	17	
Baracura emporium	152	30	16	
mouth of the Tocosanna river	153		14	30

In the Argentea region

Samba city	153	30	13	45
mouth of the Sadus river	153	30	12	30
Sada city	154	20	11	20
Barabonna emporium	155	30	10	40

mouth of the Temala river	157	30	9	
promontory next to this	157	20	8	

On the Subaricus bay of the *Besyngiti Anthropophagi*

Sabara city	159		8	30
Bsyga emporium	162	20	8	26
mouth of the Besynga river	162		9	
Berobae city	162	30	6	
promontory next to this	159		4	20

In the Golden Chersonesus

Tacola emporium	160	15	4	15
promontory next to this	158	40	2	40
mouth of Chrysoana river	159		1	
Sabana emporium	160	south	3	
mouth of Palanda river	161	south	2	
Maleicolon promontory	163	south	2	
mouth of Attaba river	164	south	1	
Calipolis	164	20	equator	
Perimula	163	15	2	40
Perimulicus bay	162	30	4	15

In the region of Lestorum

Samarada	163		4	50
Paprasa	165		4	50
mouth of Sobanus river	165	40	4	45
river sources	162	30	13	
Thipinobosti emporium	166	20	4	45
Acadra	167		4	50
Zabe city	168	20	4	45

On the Great bay next to the beginning of the Great promontory

tory	169		4	15
Thagora	168		6	
Balonga metropolis	167	30	7	
Throana	167		8	30
mouth of Daona river	167		10	
river sources	153		27	
Cortatha metropolis	167		12	
Sinda city	167	15	13	40
Paprasa	167	30	14	30
mouth of Dorius river	168		15	30
river sources	163		27	
Aganagara	169		16	40
mouth of Serus river	171	30	17	20
river sources	170		32	
other sources	173		30	
river junction	171		27	

limits of the Great bay toward

Sinae	173		17	20

The mountains in this part are called Bepyrrus, the limits of which

are	148		34	
and	154		26	

Maeandrus, the limits of which
are 152 24
and 160 16
Damasi, the limits of which
are 162 23
and 166 33
Semanthini, western part, the limits of
which are 170 33
and 180 26

Two rivers from the Bepyrrus mountains empty into the Ganges; one of these which comes from the north has its sources
in 148 33
the junction with the Ganges is
in 140 15 30 20
the sources of the river next to this are
in 152 27

From the Maeandrus mountains, which are near the Ganges, there are many rivers as far as the Besynga. The Serus river flows from the Semanthini mountains, having two sources; the one farthest west is
in 170 30 32
the one further east is in 173 30 30
they unite in about 171 27

From the Damasi mountains flow the Dorius and the Daona rivers. The Daona comes from as far away as the Bepyrrus mountains and the Dorius from the location 164 30 28
the Daona flows from the Damasi mountains
in 162 20 30
and from the Bepyrrus in 152 30 27 30
and these branches unite
in 160 20 19
the source of the Sobanus is
in 163 30 13
that which flows into the Golden Chersonesus branching in the center of the peninsula is without name, from which however one branch flowing eastward is the Attaba
from about 161 30 3
another, the Chrysoana, from
about 161 20
the other is the Palanda

The *Gangani* occupy that part along the eastern side of the Ganges throughout its entire course, but especially in the north, through whose territory the Sarabis river flows.
Among them are these cities
Sapolus 139 35
Storna 138 40 34 40

Heorta 138 30 34
Rhappha 137 40 33 40
Below these are the *Marundae* extending as far as the *Gangaridae*, among whom are the following cities on the east of the Ganges:
Boraeta 142 20 29
Corygaza 143 30 27 15
Condota 145 26 30
Celydna 146 30 25 30
Aganagora 146 30 22 30
Talarga 146 40 21 40
Between the Imaus and the Bepyrrus mountains are the *Tacoraei* extending northward; below these are the *Corancali*, and next the *Passalae*. Next to these above the Maeandrus mountains are the *Tiledae* who are also called *Besadae* as they are short, stooping, ignorant, uncultivated, with broad foreheads, and of white color. Moreover above Cirradia is the region in which they are said to produce the best cinnamon; those who dwell near the Maeandrus mountains are the *Tamere Anthropophagi*. Above the Argentia Regio, in which there is said to be much well-guarded metal, is a region near the *Besyngiti*, where there is very much gold. Those who inhabit this region are likewise white, short, with flat noses.

Between the Bepyrrus mountains and the Damasi mountains, extending northward, dwell the *Aminachae*. Below these are the *Indaprathae*; next are the *Iberingae*; next the *Dabasae*, and the *Nangalothae* as far as the Maeandrus mountains which is an unprotected country. Between the Damasi mountains and their terminus which is toward Sinae but in the north, dwell the *Cacobae*; and below these are the *Basanarae*; then the Chalcitis region in which there is much metal. Below this as far as the Great bay (Magnus Sinus) are the *Cudutae* and the *Barrae*; next to these are the *Sindi*; next are the *Daonae* along the river of this name. After these are the mountains along the *Lestori* region or the habitat of tigers and elephants. Here is the region of lions and robbers and wild men who live in caves, having skins like the Hippopotamus, who are able to hurl darts with ease.

The cities and villages of this interior region are all renowned. After those along the Ganges, are the following:
Selampura 148 30 33 20

Canogiza	143		32	
Cassida	146		31	30
Eldana	152		31	
Asanamara	155		31	
Archinara	163		31	
Urathene	170		31	20
Suanagura	145	30	29	30
Sagoda	155	20	29	20
Anthina	162		29	
Salatha	165	40	28	20
Rhandamartotza	172		28	
in which is Nardus				
Athenagurum	146	20	27	
Maniaena	147	15	24	40
Tosale metropolis	150		23	20
Alosanga	152		24	15
Cimara	170		23	15
Parisara	149		22	15
Pandassa	165		21	20
Sipiberis	170		21	15
Triglyphon regia	154		18	

In this region are said to be bearded fowl, ravens, and white parrots

Lariagara	162	30	18	15
Rhingiberi	166		18	
Agimoetha	170	40	14	40
Tomara	172		18	
Daona	165		15	45
Mareura metropolis	158		12	30
Lasyppa	161		12	30
Barevaora	164		12	50

In the Golden Chersonesus

Balonca	162		4	40
Coconnagara	160		2	
Tharra	162	south 1	40	
Palanda	161	south 1	30	

Island said to be near the accessible part of India

Bazacata	149 30	9	40

Here are many shellfish, and the inhabitants of the island are said at all times to go without clothing. They are called *Agmatae*. There are three Sindae islands of the *Anthropophagi*, the middle of which is 152 south 8 40
Bonae Fortunae 145 equator
Brussae, five islands, the middle of which is in 152 40 south 5 20

In this the *Anthropophagi* are said to be natives. Likewise there are three other islands of the *Anthropophagi* which are called the Sabadicae the middle of which is in 160 south 8 30

Labadius or Barley island is said to be a most fruitful one, and to produce much gold.

This has a metropolis on the north side toward the west called Argentea, which is in 167 south 8 30
the eastern end of the island is in 169 south 8
the Satyrorum islands are three in number, the middle of which is in 171 south 2 30

Those who inhabit these are said to have tails such as they picture satyrs having.

There are said to be other islands here adjoining, ten in number, called Maniolae, from which they say that boats, in which there are nails, are kept away, lest at any time the magnetic stone which is found near these islands should draw them to destruction. For this reason they say that these boats are drawn up on the shore and that they are strengthened with beams of wood. They also say that these islands are occupied by cannibals called *Manioli*. There are means of approach from these islands to the mainland.

CHAPTER III

Location of Sinae
(Eleventh map of Asia)

SINAE is terminated on the north by the accessible part of Serica; on the east by the meridian marking the unknown land; on the west by India beyond the Ganges along the indicated boundary as far as the Great bay (Sinus Magnus), and from the Great bay and the parts adjacent to the land of wild beasts, and by that part of Sinae which the *Aethiopes Ichthyophagi* inhabit next to that we have described.

From the boundary limit on the bay near India, as noted

mouth of the Aspithara river	175	16	
river sources flowing from the eastern regions; out of the Semanthini mountains	180	26	
Brama city	176 40	12	30
mouth of the Ambastus river	177	10	
river sources	179	15	
Rhabana city	177	8	30
mouth of the Saenus river	176 20	6	30

Notium promontory	175		4	
Recess of Indian sea	176		2	
Satyrorum promontory	175		equator	
Sinarus bay	178	south	2	20

Here dwell the *Aethiopes Ichthyophagi.*

mouth of the Cutiaris river	177	south		7

near which the *Seniamni*

dwell	179	south	
river sources	180	south	2
Cattigara Sina, roadstead	177	south 8	30

The *Semanthini* occupy the region farthest north, and above them are mountains of the same name. Below them and the mountains are the *Acadrae*, and next are the *Spiorae;* next are the *Ambastae* on the Great bay (Magnus Sinus), and bordering them are the *Ichthyophagi* on Sinae bay.

The cities of Interior Sinae have the following names:

Acathara	178	20	21	15
Aspithra	175	30	16	15
Coccoranagara	179	south	2	
Sarata	180	south	4	
Thyne metropolis	180	south	3	

They are said to have walled towns, but none deservedly renowned. It is surrounded toward the east from Cattigara by unknown land, and bordered by the Prasus sea as far as the Prasum promontory, from which, as is said, begins the bay of the encircling ocean connecting the land from the Rhaptum promontory and the southern parts of Azan on the northeast coast of Africa.

CHAPTER IV

*Location of the island of Taprobana
(Twelfth map of Asia)*

CORY, a promontory of India is opposite the promontory of the Island of Taprobana, which formerly was called the Island of Symondi, now by the natives Salica. Those who inhabit it, in the common language, are called *Salae;* all of the women are covered with hair.

Among these rice, honey, ginger, beryl, amethyst, also gold, silver, and other metals are found. It produces elephants and tigers. Its promontory, which is said to be opposite Cory has the location 126   12 30 and is called Boreum.

Its high surrounding coast is thus described: after the promontory of Boreum, which has been mentioned as located

in	126		12	30
Galiba extrema	124		11	20
Margana city	123	30	10	20
Iogana city	123	20	8	50
Anarismundi promontory	122		7	45
mouth of Soana river	123	20	6	
river sources	124	30	3	
Sindocanda city	122		5	
Priapidis harbor	122		3	40
Anubingara	121		2	40
Prasodis bay	121		2	
Jovis extrema, or promontory	120	30	1	
Nubartha city	121	4	equator	
mouth of Azanus river	123	20	1	so.
Hodoca city	123		2	so.
river sources	126	north	1	
Ornion or Avium promontory	125	south	2	30
Dagana city, sacred to Luna	126	south	2	
Corcobara	127	40 so.	2	20
Dyonisi, or city of Bacchus	130	south	1	30
Cetaeum promontory	132	south	2	20
mouth of Baracus river	131	30	1	
river sources	128		2	
Bocana city	131		1	20
Mordulae harbor	131		1	20
Abaraththa city	131		3	15
Solis harbor	130		4	
Great coast (Magnum littus)				
Procuri city	130	15	4	40
Rhizala harbor	130	40	6	10
Oxia promontory	130		7	30
mouth of Gangis river	129		7	20
river sources	127		7	15
Spatana harbor	129		8	
Nagadina city	129		8	30
Pati bay	128	30	9	
Anubingara city	128	40	9	40
Modurgi emporium	128		11	20
mouth of Phasis river	127		12	20
river sources	126		8	
Talacori emporium	126	20	11	40
after this is the northern promontory	126		12	30

The most important mountains in the island are called the Galibi, from which flow the Phasis and the Gangis, and from the mountains which are called Malaea flow

the Soana, the Azanus, and the Baracus rivers. Below these mountains near the sea is the feeding ground of the elephant; in the north of the island are the *Galybi* and the *Mudunti*, below whom are *Anurogram-mi* and the *Soani*. Below the *Nanagadibi* are the *Semni*, and below these are the *San-docandae* toward the west; then near the feeding ground are the *Bumasani*. The *Tarachi* are toward the east, below whom are the *Bocani*, the *Morduli*, and more toward the south are the *Rhogandani*, and the *Nanigiri*. The interior cities of the island are

Anvrogrammum regia	124	10	8	40
Magrammum metropolis	127		7	20
Adisamum	129		5	
Poduca	124		3	40
Ulispada	126	20 north	40	
Nacaduma	128	30 equator		

There are many islands around Taprobana, which are said to number one thousand three hundred and seventy-eight, but the names of those which have been handed down are

Vangana	120	15	11	20
Canathara	121	40	11	15
Orneos	119		8	30
Egidion	119		8	30
Harmacha	116	15		15
Ammina	117		4	30
Carcus	118	south	40	
Philicus	116	30 so.	2	40
Irena	120	south	2	30
Calandadrus	121	south	5	30
Arana	125	south	5	30
Bassa	126	south	6	30
Balaca	129	south	5	30
Alaba	131	south	4	
Cumara	133	south	1	40
Zaba	135	equator		
Nagadiba	135	north	8	30
Zibala	135	north	4	15
Susuara	130	north	11	15

The description of the inhabited earth has been made thus part by part, according to provinces and satrapies. But since in the beginning of the work we have shown in what form the known parts of the world could be marked out on a sphere, and on a plane in such manner as to be most truthful and with relative dimensions such as are to be found on a solid sphere; it is fitting to add to the exposition of the whole

inhabited earth an epilogue for the demonstration of those things which have been expounded in general; this now will be appropriately done.

CHAPTER V

A descriptive summary of the map of the inhabited earth

WE have divided the inhabited regions into three large divisions as seemed proper to the ancient writers who examined these areas, and have left us their conclusions in their commentaries, as we ourselves desire to do, partly from what we have seen and partly from the traditions of others. We have set ourselves to depict such a map of the whole inhabited earth presenting nothing untried concerning those things which in part are useful and can well fill the mind by giving it something which is historical, arousing and exciting it to exercise its powers.

That part of the earth which is inhabited by us is bounded on the east by the unknown land which borders on the eastern races of Greater Asia, namely the *Sinae* and the *Seres*, and on the south by the likewise unknown land which encloses the Indian sea and which encompasses Ethiopia south of Libya, the country called Agisymba, and on the west by the unknown land encircling the Ethiopian gulf of Libya and by the Western ocean bordering on the westernmost parts of Africa and Europe, and on the north by the continuous ocean called the Ducalydonian and Sarmatian which encompasses the British islands and the northernmost parts of Europe, and by the unknown land bordering on the northernmost parts of Greater Asia, that is to say on Sarmatia and Scythia and Serica. The water moreover is much greater in extent than is the land.

Our sea (Mediterranean) has many bays which open into it — the Adriatic, the Aegean, the Propontis, the Euxine, and the Sea of Maeotis — and it flows into the ocean through but one outlet, the Straits of Hercules resembling an isthmus, for these narrow inlets of the sea have the shape of a chersonesus. The Hyrcanium sea, called also the Caspian, is surrounded on all sides

by land and has the shape of an island; and we may say the same of the Indian sea, for with its gulfs, the Arabian, the Persian, the Gangetic, and that which is called the Great gulf, it is entirely shut in, like the Caspian, by land on all sides. Wherefore the entire earth consists of three continents, Asia, Africa, and Europe. Asia is joined to Africa by the part of Arabia enclosed by our sea and the Gulf of Arabia, and by the unknown land which is washed by the Indian sea, and is joined to Europe by the land which lies between the Sea (swamp) of Maeotis and the Sarmatic sea in which is the basin of the river Tanis.

Africa is separated from Europe by the Atlantic Straits of Hercules, touching Europe nowhere by itself but only through Asia since the latter is coterminous with both the other continents along their eastern borders.

Of these three parts of the world Asia is the largest, Africa is next in size and Europe is the smallest. Of the seas surrounded by land, as has been said before, the first in size is the Indian sea, the second is our sea, the third is the Hyrcanium or Caspian. Of the most notable gulfs the first and largest is the Gangetic, the second is the Persian gulf, the third is that one which is called the Great gulf, the fourth is the Arabian, the fifth the Ethiopian, the sixth the Pontic, the seventh is the Aegean sea, the eighth is the Maeotis, the ninth the Adriatic sea, the tenth the Propontis.

Of the most noted islands the first is Taprobana, the second the island of Albion, one of the British islands, the third is the Golden Chersonesus, the fourth is Hibernia one of the British islands, the fifth is the Peloponesus, the sixth is Sicily, the seventh Sardinia, the eighth Corsica also called Cyrnos; the ninth Crete, the tenth Cyprus.

The southern boundary of the inhabited earth is defined by the parallel which is south of the equator sixteen degrees and twenty-five minutes of such degrees as are those of which the great circle has three hundred and sixty, and the parallel through Meroe is precisely the same number of degrees north of the equator. The most northern parallel is sixty-three degrees north of the equator and is called the parallel passing through the island of Thule. Where-

fore the breadth of the entire earth, which as yet is known to us is seventy-nine degrees and twenty-five minutes, or approximately eighty degrees or 40,000 stadia, inasmuch as one degree measures 500 stadia, as has been found by careful measurement, and the circuit of the whole earth is 180,000 stadia.

The extreme eastern region of the world known to us is defined by the meridian passing through the metropolis of Sinae, which meridian is distant from that drawn through Alexandria measured to eastward on the equator, one hundred and nineteen and one-half degrees, that is, about eight hours.

The extreme western limit is defined by the meridian drawn through the Fortunate Isles which is distant from the meridian of Alexandria sixty and one-half degrees or four equatorial hours, and distant from the semicircle which is farthest east one hundred and eighty degrees or twelve equatorial hours. Therefore the known length of the earth, measured along the equator, is ninety thousand stadia, but measured along the most southern parallel is approximately eighty-six thousand three hundred and fifty stadia, and measured along the most northern parallel it is forty thousand eight hundred and fifty-four stadia; and again, along the parallel of Rhodes, upon which measurements are usually made, and which is thirty-six degrees distant from the equator, approximately seventy-two thousand stadia; and along the parallel through Syene, which is twenty-three degrees and fifty minutes from the equator, being in about the middle of the world's breadth, is eighty-two thousand three hundred and thirty-six stadia. These calculations are made according to the proportion of the aforesaid parallels to the equator. The length therefore of the inhabited earth is greater than its breadth, in the northernmost climates by approximately one-fifth of the breadth, and in the climate of the parallel of Rhodes by about one-sixth more, and of that under the parallel of Syene by an amount equal to that along the parallel of Rhodes, and in the southernmost climates about the same, and along the equator by as much and in addition one-fourth.

The length of the longest day or night on the southernmost parallel is thirteen equa-

torial hours; on that through Meroe is twelve hours; on that through Syene thirteen and one-half hours; and on that through Rhodes fourteen and one-half hours; and on the northernmost, passing through Thule, it is twenty hours, and furthermore the extreme differences in latitude are eight equatorial hours.

CHAPTER VI

Description of the Armillary Sphere with a representation of the inhabited earth

IN what we have stated above concerning the relative location of different places on the earth we have made use of equal measurements. It will not be out of place to add to this an explanation of the way in which our earth can be depicted on a plane surrounded by an armillary sphere. Several have attempted to give this demonstration but have ended with this most absurd statement: "Let those represent the earth as a sphere who understand the earth's interior."

Let it now be our plan to delineate on a plane an armillary sphere enclosing a part of the earth, with the assumption that the point of view is such that we look directly at the intersection of the meridian passing through the signs of the tropics and cutting in half the length of the inhabited earth and the parallel drawn through Syene which cuts in half the breadth of the inhabited earth.

Let the calculations of the size of the armillary sphere, of the earth, and the distance of the point of view be such, that in the interval between the circle of the equator and that along the circle of the summer solstice the whole known part of the earth shall appear with the more southerly semicircle constructed to appear through the middle of the circle upon the earth, in order that there may not be by this any obscuration of the inhabited earth placed in the northern hemisphere. Following this plan it is clear that the aforesaid meridians will present the appearance of one straight line following the same axis, and further for like reason as the parallel through Syene will appear perpendicular to that line it will make all others appear to be drawn in the form of curves to these

straight lines, namely, the meridian which cuts both poles and the parallel which is drawn through Syene, and let these lines be more curved than others which are more distant from the straight lines, which is an obvious adjustment.

An easy method whereby we can give a representation, to the eye, as nearly as possible, will be as follows:

Let the meridian which crosses the equator on the sphere be marked A B C D, and passing through the center E the diameter

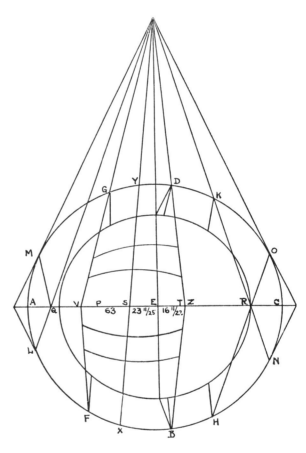

A E C. Let A be the arctic pole, and let C be the antarctic pole. Let us then take B F and D G, and B H and D K on the circumference covering the distance that the tropics are from the equator; also A L and A M, N C and C O at distances of the arctic and antarctic poles; and let us divide the summer solstice A E at P. Since then the parallel passing through Syene should fall between E and P, and the ratio of the parallel through Syene to the equator is that of about four to five, let the length of E P which divides E P A be about four to

fifteen (i. e. 24° to 90°), thus E A will be four thirds (the length) of the line passing through the center of the earth.

Let us also take E Q of three parts of the same length as each of the four parts of E A, and with the center E and the radius E Q there is drawn the circle Q R which extends around the earth in the same plane. Then making use of a straight line equal in length to E Q and dividing it into ninety equal parts, or one quadrant, E P is given sixty-three such parts, E S sixteen and five-twelfths, and E T sixty-three of the same parts.

Produce X S Y to intersect the perpendicular, namely that along the parallel of Syene, T will thus be the point through which is drawn the parallel cutting the southern limit of the inhabited earth, or that opposite the parallel through Meroe, and V is similarly the point through which is drawn the parallel limiting the arctic boundary passing through Thule.

Then take another point more to the south than T as Z, and let Z and D be joined, and let S Y and Z D be produced to meet at W. If then we regard these circles as in the plane through the signs of the tropics and the poles, and through the axis of the eye (the lines) produced from W to A C through M, G, D, K and O make thereon sections of five parallels to Z through which is drawn the equator D A. Those parallels which join W to D, B, F, H, and G, make at A C the sections through which are drawn the terminal parts of the earth on the same parallels. Likewise also in drawing the parallels to be described on the earth, taking upon Q R the individual distances from the equator, as Z and T, the sections of the semi-circle Q V R made by these straight lines joined from W, and opposed to these sections points at corresponding distances, we will have the sections, as seen by the eye, of five parallels to W, through which is drawn the equator D. The lines from W to D, B, F, H, and G make portions such as A T B and C T B the same as A E of the aforesaid parallels. Taking from these the intervals of the several meridians on either side of A V, and on the line X Y, and in the proper ratio on three parallels, we draw through the corresponding three points the portions of the neighboring meridians, as

also those terminating longitude E Y, F G, and P G.

The number of lines to be drawn on the map will be determined by the amount of the descriptive material to be inserted. Care must be taken in the planning of the circles that each be graded through the four assumed points, and care taken in the picture that it does not end too sharply in the section of the circle's termination and that it produces no extraordinary appearance. Also the circle must be adapted to its contents, although the names of cities may be inserted outside the circle of the map itself (that is, in the margin) by surrounding in that case the defective appearance of the map with an outer circle which agrees with the true circle itself.

Care must be taken that the lines through the poles are circles with suitable differences of width and color. Moreover the portions which are placed outside the earth should have fainter color than the portions which are offered to our view, and because they are more remote than the parts to which they are joined, let them be shown in their true likeness in circles and spaces of their own.

In addition, as to the circles of the signs, let them fall on the earth along the more southern semicircles and through the winter solstice, and let us give them in places here and there their proper denominations. On the circles of the earth itself let us write their distance or degree numbers, and the hour numbers of that location. Let us place around the outside circle the names of the winds likewise, just as on the circular sphere at the adjacent five parallels and the poles.

CHAPTER VII

Epilogue to the foregoing

IT seems fitting to insert an epilogue after the foregoing. Our representation of an armillary sphere (with the earth placed in the same) will be understood if the eye is fixed on a locality in relation to which the meridian circle (as commonly divided) passes between the points that mark the tropics and becomes a straight line, which straight line as a circle divides into two equal parts, as noted, the longitude of the inhabited earth.

Moreover the parallel which we draw through Syene is a circle which has a latitude almost equal to that given to the earth itself. Let the ratio of the size be so arranged, that is, of the sphere and the earth and the perspective itself, that in the space which lies between the circle of the equinoctial line and the circle of the summer solstice, the entire inhabited earth may be shown to us. (See title-page illustration.)

Let the more southern semicircle be drawn on the earth through the middle circle of the signs; let there be no northern addition to our habitable earth which extends to the hemisphere of the arctic. Wherefore the said meridian lines, drawn around the axis of one straight line, will give us a fanciful representation, as though the eye were surveying a plane surface, and the parallel which is drawn through Syene will seem for the same reason to be a straight line. The rest of the true circles, drawn through the cities, will appear as straight lines. Let the meridians be adjusted to that which passes through Syene, and let the parallels be the more carefully adjusted which are the more distant from it on both sides, in order that the arctic circle may curve more toward the north than the summer solstice, and the winter solstice curve more than the equator because it is bent more to the south, and the antarctic circle curve more than the winter solstice.

The known part of the earth is so situated that it is nowhere entirely walled around by the ocean, except only in case of the land of Raptis, which belongs in part to Africa and in part to Europe, according to the testimony of the ancients.

END OF BOOK SEVEN

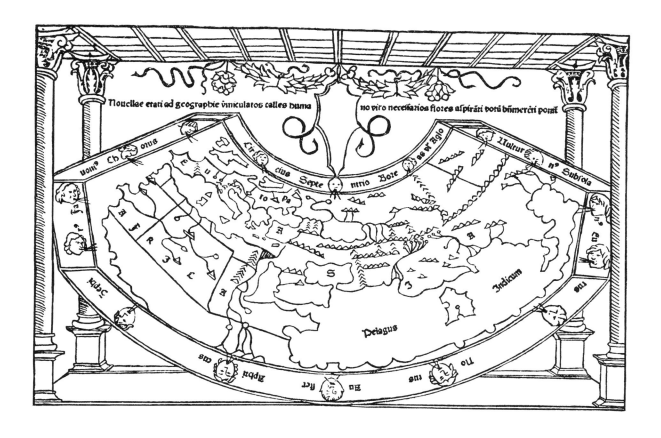

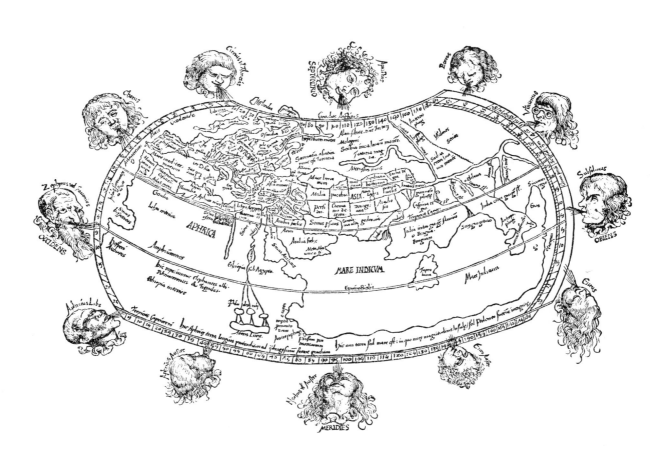

BOOK EIGHT

CHAPTER I

What presuppositions are necessary in making a division of our habitable earth in the maps

WHAT is the part of the diligent and assiduous traveler in the field of geographical investigations; what is the part of a reasonable consideration of the subject matter of geography with which we are familiar and which is within our province rather than that of the former; all this we have sufficiently explained, in my opinion.

As the practice of our predecessors advises us, we should here repeat, by means of an epilogue, through what places each parallel or meridian is drawn, lest we should become subject to ridicule in setting down our places in haphazard manner, not locating them correctly on a given circle nor properly placing them between the adjacent parallels in the manner in which a representation of the whole habitable earth should be set out before the eyes in one complete map.

It remains for us to show how we set down all places, so that when we divide one map into several maps, we may be able accurately to locate all of the well-known places through the employment of easily understood and exact measurements.

As it is necessary therefore, in a single map of the entire habitable earth — since there must be kept a proper proportion in the location of the sites of the different parts of the earth which we set down — to contract some parts on account of the crowding of others, and to expand yet other places on account of the lack of knowledge of certain others, that which many do without sufficient reason — lest they should appear to depart from traditional accounts — who in their maps consequently are led to make many errors in the measurements and representations of regions, or who give the greatest part of their map to Europe in latitude and longitude because the sites and places to be inserted therein are more numerous. They leave very little space for Asia in longitude, and for Africa little space in latitude, on account of an erroneous consideration of the relative size of the countries, and therefore misplace the Indian sea to the north of Taprobana, and in the same map give intimation of an empty space toward the east, and have nothing to describe toward the north, and extend the western ocean to the eastern shore.

Then, too, their map is often drawn out of proportion in a southerly direction, in connecting the vast extent of Africa with India making them a continuous whole; this, however, they may have done to make room for the numerous places to be located on the western coast.

Some surround the earth on all sides with an ocean, imbued with such an opinion, making a fallacious description, and an unfinished and foolish picture.

We can avoid this common error by dividing our map in such manner that the regions which are the more crowded with places are shown alone, or in a map with other regions in which there is greater distance between the circles; then the countries with fewer inhabitants and containing fewer sites in one map will be included in spaces of lesser size between the circles than when represented on a single map.

All maps need not measure the same distances between the circles, but in each map the same proportion however must be kept throughout, as for example, when we describe the head alone we speak in terms of the head, or when we speak of the hand alone we speak in terms of the hand, and we do not figure equally for the head and the hand unless we are drawing a figure of the whole man in one image. And so it does not matter whether we sometimes increase the size of the whole or sometimes lessen it; likewise it matters not in the special part which we can increase, or lessen, for instance, if there should be numerous localities in certain parts in which there are to be many entries. Again it will not be far from the truth if instead of circles we draw straight lines as we have shown at the beginning of this work.

Moreover in the separate maps we shall show the meridians themselves not inclined and curved but at an equal distance one from another, and since the termini of the circles of latitude and of longitude of the habitable earth, when calculated over great distances do not make any remarkable excesses, so neither is there any great difference in any of our maps. When we divide our map according to the proportion of the several parallels to the greatest circles, we say it ought to be done by comparing distances and we do not seek out every distance on the map but that which is from one extreme locality to another extreme.

CHAPTER II

What adaptation on each map is necessary

SUCH things therefore being presupposed, let us begin the task of a division such as the following:

We will make ten maps for Europe; we will make four maps for Africa; for Asia we will make twelve maps to include the whole, and we will state to which continent each map belongs, and how many and how great are the regions or provinces in each, and we will further explain what ratio the parallel which passes through the middle of the region has to the meridian, stating also what is the circumference of the entire map, and giving throughout each region the assumed elevation (latitude and longitude) of the chief cities, and the greatest length of a day in each of them.

We shall take the measure of distances in longitude without traveling to each mentioned locality, but from the meridian of Alexandria, either at sunrise or sunset, and from the number of equinoctial hours between the places. Besides this we shall find in which of the constellations of the celestial circle is the longitude of the places, and in which of the constellations the sun is once or twice directly overhead, and the constellation's position with regard to the tropics themselves. We shall learn in addition what stars each may have overhead, if by observation the latitude should appear at the same equinoctial point, that is if the latitude were always measured on the same parallel.

We have shown in a mathematical work that the sphere of the fixed stars revolves as the revolution of the earth and of the equinoctial signs, not around the equinoctial poles, but around the pole of the circle through the middle of the zodiac, erratically, so to speak. The same stars are not at all times directly overhead in the same place, but of necessity are more northward at one time than at another, and others are more southward.

But it might be considered useless to add such an epilogue, since it is according to law in the celestial sphere, following this hypothesis in stated durations of time, that we fix the site of a place on a circle which extends from pole to pole, counting the whole distance on one meridian, and noting that the same is as many degrees from the equator as the parallel of the place to be determined is distant.

And this it also will be easy to perceive at both poles although the location of no place is determined by the constellations of the fixed stars whether many or few.

These things being settled beforehand we can now attend to that which remains.

The following are the known provinces and prefectures as listed in Ptolemy's ten maps for Europe, four for Africa, and twelve for Asia.

To the reproduction of the twenty-seven maps from the Ebner manuscript, including his world map, have here been added two maps which appear in printed editions of Ptolemy's Geography published after the discovery of America — the Ruysch world map from the 1508 edition, and the Lorenz Fries world map from the 1522 edition.

WORLD MAP

EUROPE

FIRST MAP

Britannia island Hibernia
Britannia island Albion
Thule island

SECOND MAP

Hispania Baetica
Hispania Lusitania
Hispania Tarraconensis

THIRD MAP

Gallia Aquitania
Gallia Lugdunensis
Gallia Belgica
Celtogalatia Narbonensis

FOURTH MAP

Greater Germania

FIFTH MAP

Rhetia and Vindelicia
Noricum
Pannonia Upper
Pannonia Lower
Illyria
Liburnia
Dalmatia

SIXTH MAP

Italia
Cyenos island (Corsica)

SEVENTH MAP

Sardinia island
Sicily island

EIGHTH MAP

Sarmatia in Europe
Tauric peninsula

NINTH MAP

Iazyges Metanastae
Dacia
Mysia Upper
Mysia Lower
Thracia
Chersonesus (peninsula)

TENTH MAP

Macedonia
Epirus

EUROPE, TENTH MAP, *cont'd*

Achaia
Peloponnesus
Crete island
Eubea island

AFRICA

FIRST MAP

Mauritania Tingitana
Mauritania Caesariensis

SECOND MAP

Africa
Numidia

THIRD MAP

Cyrenaica
Marmarica
Libya
Egypt
Thebes

FOURTH MAP

Libya Interior
Ethiopia below Egypt
Ethiopia and all south

ASIA

FIRST MAP

Pontus
Bithynia, Phrygia, Lycia
Pamphylia, Pisidia
Galatia, Paphlagonia,
  Isauria
Cappadocia
Armenia Lesser
Cilicia

SECOND MAP

Sarmatia Asiatica

THIRD MAP

Colchia
Ileria
Albania
Armenia Greater

FOURTH MAP

Cyprus island
Syria
Phoenicia

ASIA, FOURTH MAP, *cont'd*

Judea Palestina
Arabia Petraea
Arabia Deserta
Mesopotamia
Babylonia

FIFTH MAP

Assyria
Susiana
Media
Persis
Parthia
Carmania Deserta
Hyrcania

SIXTH MAP

Arabia Felix
Carmania

SEVENTH MAP

Margiana
Bactriana
Sogdiana
Sacae
Scythia this side the Imaus
  mountains

EIGHTH MAP

Scythia beyond the Imaus
  mountains
Serica

NINTH MAP

Aria
Paropanisadae
Drangiana
Arachosia
Gedrosia

TENTH MAP

India along the Ganges

ELEVENTH MAP

India beyond the Ganges
Sinae Region

TWELFTH MAP

Taprobana

RUYSCH WORLD MAP

LORENZ FRIES WORLD MAP

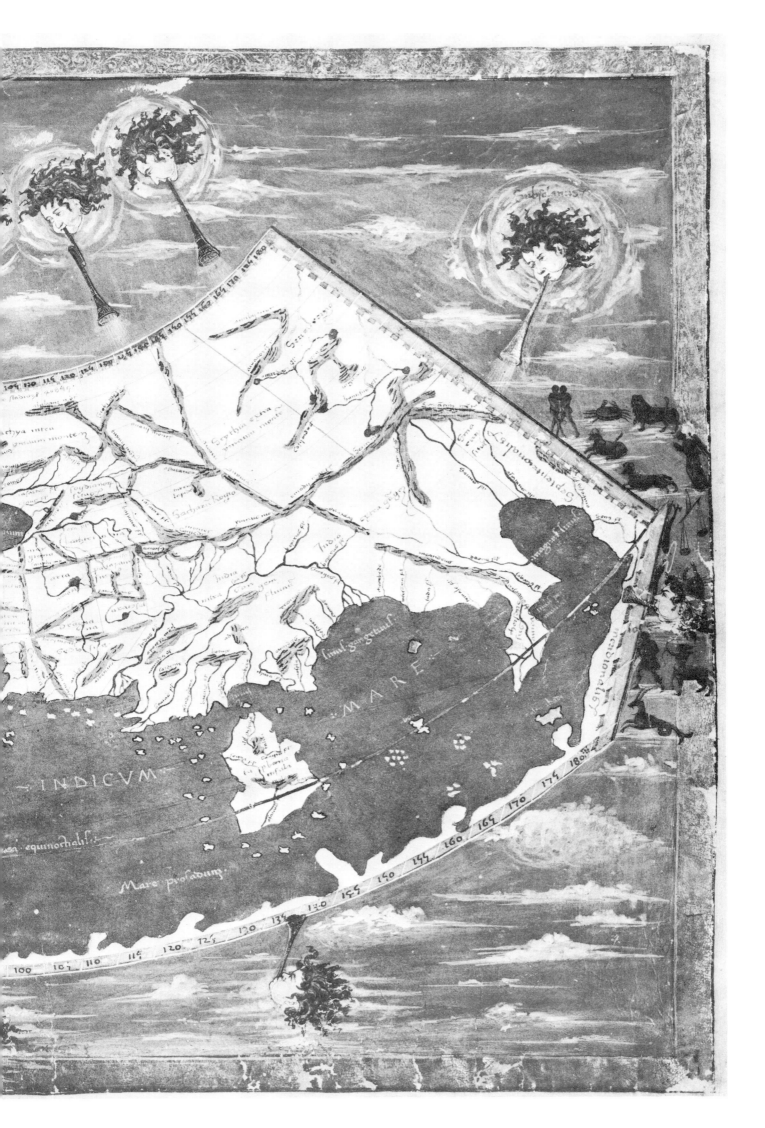

Expositio omnium summaru[m] quib[us] continentur in europa tabule decem p[ro]uinc[i]e a uiginti quatuor

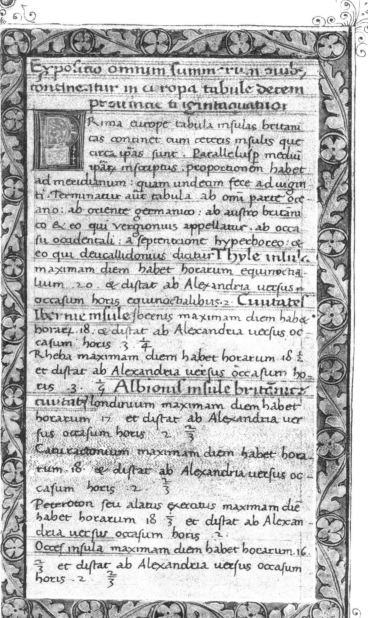

Rima europe tabula insulas britani
cas continet cum ceteris insulis que
circa ip[s]as sunt. Parallelusp[er] medii
ip[s]aru[m] inscriptus proportionem habet
ad meridianum: quam undecim fere ad uigin
ti. Terminatur aut tabula ab om[n]i parte oceano: ab oriente germanico: ab austro britani
co & eo qui vergionus appellatur. ab occasu occidentali: a septentrione hyperboreo: &
eo qui deucallidonius dicitur Thyle insula
maximam diem habet horarum equinochia-
lium 20. & distat ab Alexandria uersus
occasum horis equinochalibus 2. Ciuitates
Ibernie insule Iberms maximam diem habet
horaru 18. & distat ab Alexandria uersus occasum horis 3. $\frac{1}{4}$
Rheba maximam diem habet horarum 18 $\frac{1}{2}$
et distat ab Alexandria uersus occasum horis 3. $\frac{1}{4}$ Albionis insule brit[ann]icę
ciuitat[es] londinium maximam diem habet
horarum 17 et distat ab Alexandria uersus occasum horis 2. $\frac{2}{3}$
Cantiactonium maximam diem habet horarum 18. & distat ab Alexandria uersus occasum horis 2. $\frac{2}{3}$
Peteroton seu alatus exercatus maximam die[m]
habet horarum 18 $\frac{2}{3}$ et distat ab Alexandria uersus occasum horis 2.
Occes insula maximam diem habet horarum 16.
$\frac{2}{3}$ et distat ab Alexandria uersus occasum
horis 2. $\frac{2}{3}$

Vnus gradus longitudinis
in hoc palello p thylen
habet miliaria 28 3/8 stadia uero
228.

Differentia partis superioris
ad inferiorem tabule in
stadys quidem 2340 In
miliaribus autem 240.
Ergo it

miliaria

miliaria 36 1/2

Vnus g̃ longitud̃ co̅ti
net stadia 317 et
miliaria 38.

OCEANVS IPERBOREVS

OCEANVS OCCIDENTALIS

IBER
NIA
BRIT
ANNIA
IISV
LA

hiberni

OC IBERNICVS

mona
insula

OC VERGINVS

Coznavi

BRI

TAN NI

aquicalide

Belge

CA

damones

OC BRITANNICVS

22 23 24 25 26 27 28 29 30 31 Thile insla

OCEANVS · DVECALLEDONIVS

OCEANVS · GERHANICVS

Magne Germanie pars

Gallie Belgice pars

22 23 24 25 26 27 28 29 30 31 32 33

Vigesimus pmus Paralellus
Differt ab equinoctiali horis octo.
habens maximu diem horar · 20 ·

Vigesimus paralellus
Differt ab equinoctiali horis X
habens die maximu horu · 19 ·

Denmuisionus paralellus
Differt ab eqnoctiali hö · 6 ·
et habet maximu diem hör · 18 ·

18 · paralellus
Differt ab equinoctiali
hö · 4 ½ · habens diem
maiorem horar · 18 ½ ·

17 · paralellus
differt ab eqnoctiali
horis · 4 · habens diem
maxim horar · 18 ·

16 · paralello
Differt ab eqnoctiali
horis · 3 ½ · habes
maxim diem hör
ibi et medie

Secunda europe tabula continet
ſpaniam totam in tribus proui
cijs partitam cum inſulis ſibi ad
iacentibus . Parallelus p eius me
dium ductus proporaonem habet ad me
ridianum : quam tres ad quatuo fere.
Circumſcribitur autem tabula ab oriente
montibus pyreneis : A meridie balearico
&ſberico mari freto q̃ herculeo : ac par
te exterioris pelagi : ab occaſu occeano oc
cidentali ab arcto occeano centaurico.

Luſitanie Nocba ceſarea maximam diẽ
habet horarum 14 $\frac{1}{2}$ $\frac{1}{3}$ $\frac{1}{12}$ & diſtat ab
Alexandria uerſus occaſum horis 3 $\frac{1}{2}$.
Auguſta emerita maximam diem habet
horarum 14 $\frac{1}{4}$ $\frac{1}{3}$ & diſtat ab alexandria ũ
ſus occaſum horis . 3 $\frac{1}{2}$ Betice cuulni
Corduba maximam diem habet horarum
14 $\frac{2}{3}$ & diſtat ab Alexandria uerſus oc
caſum horis . 3 . $\frac{1}{3}$ $\frac{1}{14}$ Hiſpanie tar
raconenſis. Aſturica auguſta maxima
diem habet horarum 14 $\frac{1}{2}$ $\frac{1}{12}$ & diſtat
ab Alexandria uerſus occaſum horis . 3 $\frac{1}{3}$ $\frac{1}{14}$
Noua carthago maximam diem habet
horarum 14 $\frac{2}{3}$ & diſtat ab Alexandria
uerſus occaſum horis . 3 . $\frac{1}{6}$
Tarracon maximam diem habet horarum
14 fere & diſtat ab Alexandria uerſus
occaſum 2 $\frac{1}{2}$ $\frac{1}{3}$ $\frac{1}{12}$
Cluma maximam diem habet horarum
14 $\frac{1}{8}$ et diſtat ab Alexandria uerſus
occaſum horis . 3 $\frac{1}{4}$
Ceſarea auguſta maximam diem habet
horarum 14 $\frac{1}{12}$ & diſtat ab Alexandria ũ
ſus occaſum . 3 . $\frac{1}{14}$
Gadira inſula maximam diem habet hora
rum 14 $\frac{1}{2}$ & diſtat ab Alexandria uerſus
occaſum horis . 3 . $\frac{2}{3}$

Vnuf g longitz ualet mlia 42

miliaria 44 ⅓.

miliaria 47.

miliaria 40.

OCEANVS

OC OCCIDENTALIS

HIS

PA

N

TAR PELLA

LVSITA NiA

Carpit

HISPA NIA

NE

HISP AllA BE

CA A

MARE IBERIC

fretum herculeum

EXTERIVS MARE

Mauritani

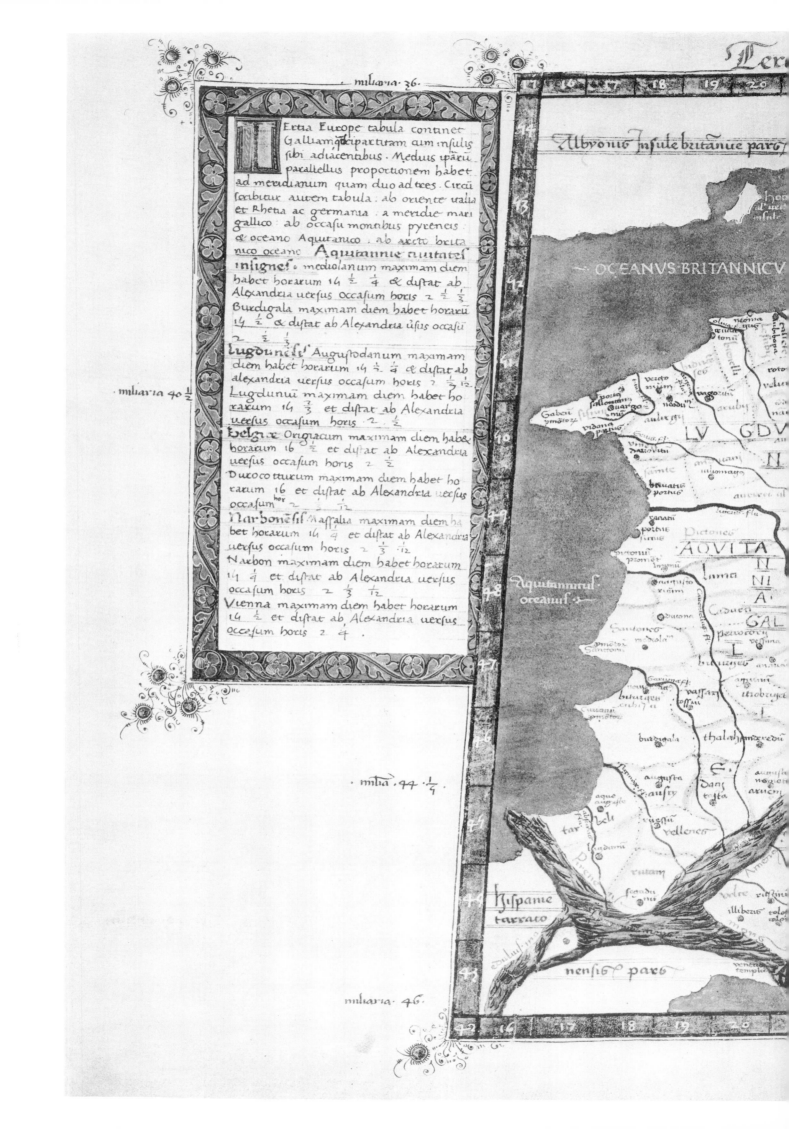

miliaria· 36·

Tertia Europe tabula continet
Galliam quadripartitam cum insulis
sibi adiacentibus. Medius ipsarum
parallellus proportionem habet
ad meridianum quam duo ad tres. Circum
scribitur autem tabula: ab oriente italia
et Rhetia ac germania: a meridie mari
gallico: ab occasu montibus pyreneis:
& oceano Aquitanico: ab arcto brita
nico oceano **Aquitannie ciuitates
insignes**. mediolanum maximam diem
habet horarum 14 $\frac{1}{2}$ $\frac{1}{4}$ & distat ab
Alexandria uersus occasum horis 2 $\frac{1}{2}$ $\frac{1}{3}$
Burdigala maximam diem habet horarum
14 $\frac{1}{2}$ & distat ab Alexandria uersus occasum
2 $\frac{1}{2}$ $\frac{1}{3}$
Lugdunensis Augustodanum maximam
diem habet horarum 14 $\frac{1}{2}$ $\frac{1}{4}$ & distat ab
alexandria uersus occasum horis 2 $\frac{1}{3}$ $\frac{1}{12}$
Lugdunum maximam diem habet ho
rarum 14 $\frac{2}{3}$ et distat ab Alexandria
uersus occasum horis ·2· $\frac{1}{2}$
Belgice Origiacum maximam diem habet
horarum 16 $\frac{1}{2}$ et distat ab Alexandria
uersus occasum horis 2 $\frac{1}{2}$
Durocotturum maximam diem habet ho
rarum 16 et distat ab Alexandria uersus
occasum hor 2 $\frac{1}{3}$ $\frac{1}{12}$
Narbonensis Massalia maximam diem ha
bet horarum 14 $\frac{1}{4}$ et distat ab Alexandria
uersus occasum horis 2 $\frac{1}{3}$ $\frac{1}{12}$
Narbon maximam diem habet horarum
14 $\frac{1}{4}$ et distat ab Alexandria uersus
occasum horis 2 $\frac{1}{3}$ $\frac{1}{12}$
Vienna maximam diem habet horarum
14 $\frac{1}{2}$ et distat ab Alexandria uersus
occasum horis 2 $\frac{1}{4}$.

miliaria 40 $\frac{1}{2}$

milia· 44 $\frac{1}{4}$·

miliaria· 46·

23 24 25 26 27 28 29

Germaniu

Gesouani
Inu pro
nouale
mozini
tatnaia
atuacui
tongri

ambiany
samarobnga

castellu
monappy

BELGI   CA
cesiomaquo
belluary   crusy
metaui

GAL
L
I
E

Inferior

baru

vgteia
luppia

aquenio
nensis

Bithau

vbanerti
rotomaguo

traiane
motoh
aniy

romandiffi
augusta
romandiffa

vessones

tribey
augusta
tibrora

neomagi
rufiniana
nemen

Reny
diuscor
tu gru

vangy

berbeto
magus
augetora
aim
bento
magus

augusta
vessonu
leuta
tecia
pazisy

LIE

augusto
bora
teurisy

mediomatrecto

treiboy elrebu

augutaru
rauzice
augusta
raureia

medule

nonk

dinoduru

nasice

tullai

Ican

mely
latni
tabulliz

andima
tunum
longontes

olona
gue

visonnu

gamadu
ru
cluem
fou
tibery

Enoy
cenc
lugduni
metropo

radiary

feguany

diatouru

anar flu

equesbis

anaui

feirati
teemenes lanis
neomagu

viena allobuges
Sucuro flu

votam
pation

feni noza
nis
memmy

druta

Sony

vaena
rolola
ateon rolola

caiffion
arauson

Canary

BONENSIS

R
auenion
rolola

trauison
glanu
falce

maffilia
greca

elucion
GALLIE

albanjusta

venary

anan a

Oucontii

GALLICVM

23 24 25 26 27 28

Sextuisdecimus paralellus

Differt ab equinoctiali horis 9 habens maximu
diem horaru 19

Sextusdermus Paralellus

Differt ab equinoctiali horis 8 1/2 Et habet
maximu diem horaru 16 et medie

14 paralellus per borischenen

Differt ab equinoctiali horis 9 habens
maximu diem horaru 16

Clima Septimu

14 paralellus per Vontum

Differt ab equinoctiali horis 3 1/2
habens maximu diem horis 14 et medie

Clima sextum

13 paralellus per lifontiu

Differt ab equinoctiali horis 3 1/2
habens maximu diem horaru 14 et quite

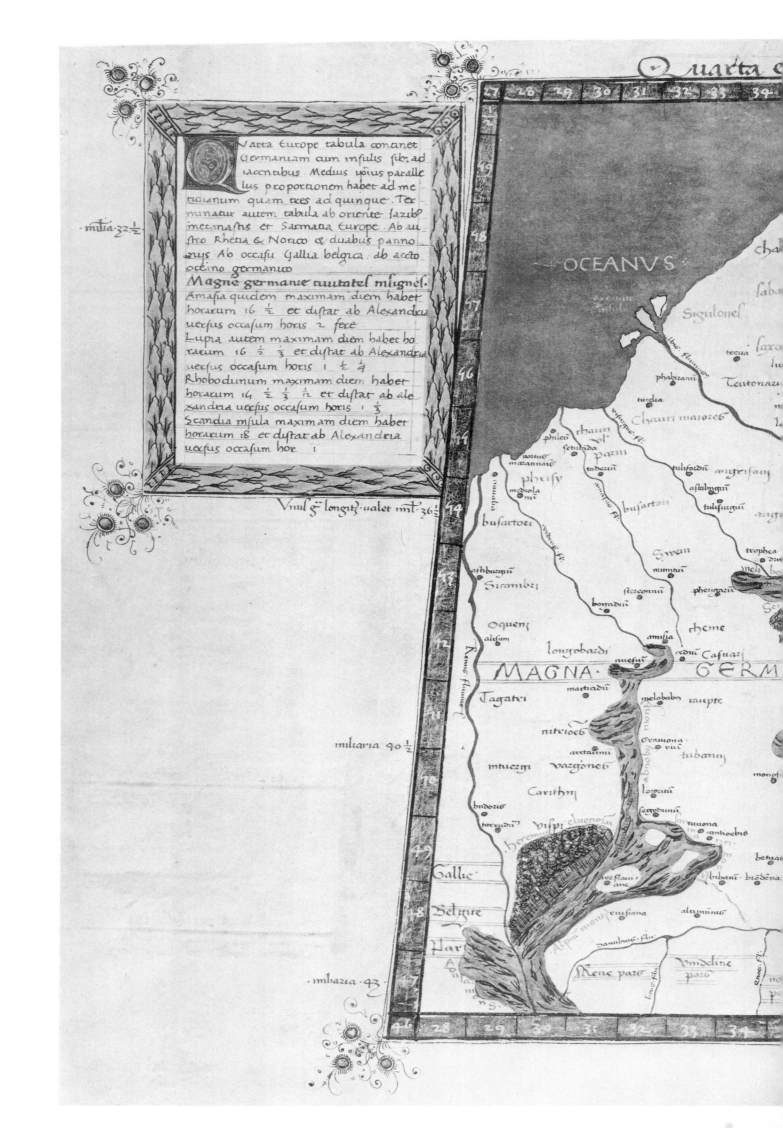

Varta Europe tabula continet
Germaniam cum insulis sibi ad
iacentibus. Medius ipsius paralle
lus proportionem habet ad me
ridianum quam tres ad quinque. Ter
minatur autem tabula ab oriente sazib
metanastis et Sarmatia europe. Ab au
stro Rhetia & Norico & duabus panno
nijs. Ab occasu Gallia belgica. ab arcto
oceano germanico

Magne germanie ciuitates insignes.
Amasia quidem maximam diem habet
horarum 16 ½ et distat ab Alexandria
uersus occasum horis 2 fere
Lupia autem maximam diem habet ho
rarum 16 ½ ⅓ et distat ab Alexandria
uersus occasum horis 1 ½ ¼
Rhobodunum maximam diem habet
horarum 14 ½ ⅓ ½ et distat ab ale
xandria uersus occasum horis 1 ⅓
Scandia insula maximam diem habet
horarum 18 et distat ab Alexandria
uersus occasum hor. 1

Vnul gⁱ longitꝫ ualet mt 36⅔

miliaria 90 ½

· milia · 32 ½

OCEANVS

chal

saba

Sigulonei

saxo

tecua

lu

phabiranii   Teutonau

turdia

Chauri maiores

philei chauci
        ol
        secunda   pazin
uothic
mazannaii   tudezin   tulisordin angrisacy

phisy   astalingu
     mediola   busartoii   tulisurginu
     mi
busartoii   angi

ashburgiu   Suen   trophea
Sirambri   muniun   di
              stercontau   pheugaru mel bo
              bouadii
Oquenz   theine
  alisum   amisia
           longobardi   redni Casuari
MAGNA · nnesui   GERM
  Tagatri   machadii   melobabi raupte

           nitioes
                        cramona
        arctalini   rui   tubana;
intuezin varzones

       Carithni   losunii
 bndius   sergdnnin
  targndii vispi cluenorum   tuuona
                              cantioebis
                         ane
Gallie .heremudii   betuau
                ane flauiane

Setpire   altimuio
                     eusiana
Hart   Alpes montes
         Rene paro   Vindine danubius flu
· milia · 43   paro

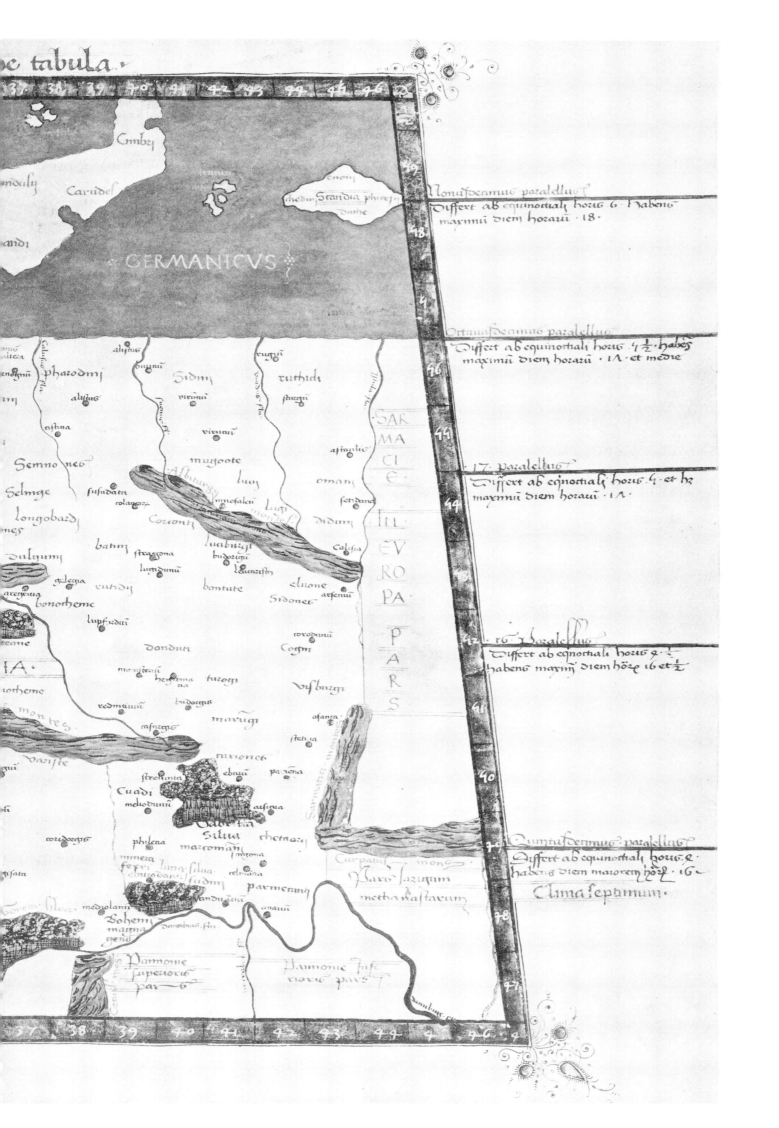

37. 38. 39. 40. 41. 42. 43. 44. 45. 46.

Cimbri

andali

Caruder

andi

GERMANICVS

enom
hedim Scandia phirefni
Daithe

Nonusdecimus paralellus
Differt ab equinoctiali horus 6. Habens
maximu diem horaru . 18.

49

48

4

Octauusdecimus paralellus
Differt ab equinoctiali horus 4 ½. habes
maximu diem horaru . 1A . et medie

pharodmi

Sidmi

ruthidi

Semno neb

murgoote

SAR
MA
CI
E.

17. paralellus
Differt ab equinoctiali horus 4 . et ht
maximu diem horaru . 1A.

Selinge

longobard

Coronti

luaburgi

IVE
VR
O
PA

 barim

Dulgumi

bonotheme

lupfriddii

eluone
Sidones
arsenui

Dandtri
Corim

16. paralellus
Differt ab equinoctiali horus 9 . ½
habens maximi diem höre 16 et ½

PA
R
S

turonice

Cuadi
medioduni

Visburgi

Silua
marcomani

Carpanis mons

Quintusdecimus paralellus
Differt ab equinoctiali horus 9.
habens diem maiorem höre 16.

Bohemi

Pamonie
fuperioris
pars.

Pamonie Infe
rioris pars

Marus Iazugum
metha nastarum

Clima feptimum.

47

38

37

37. 38. 39. 40. 41. 43. 43. 44. 9. 46.

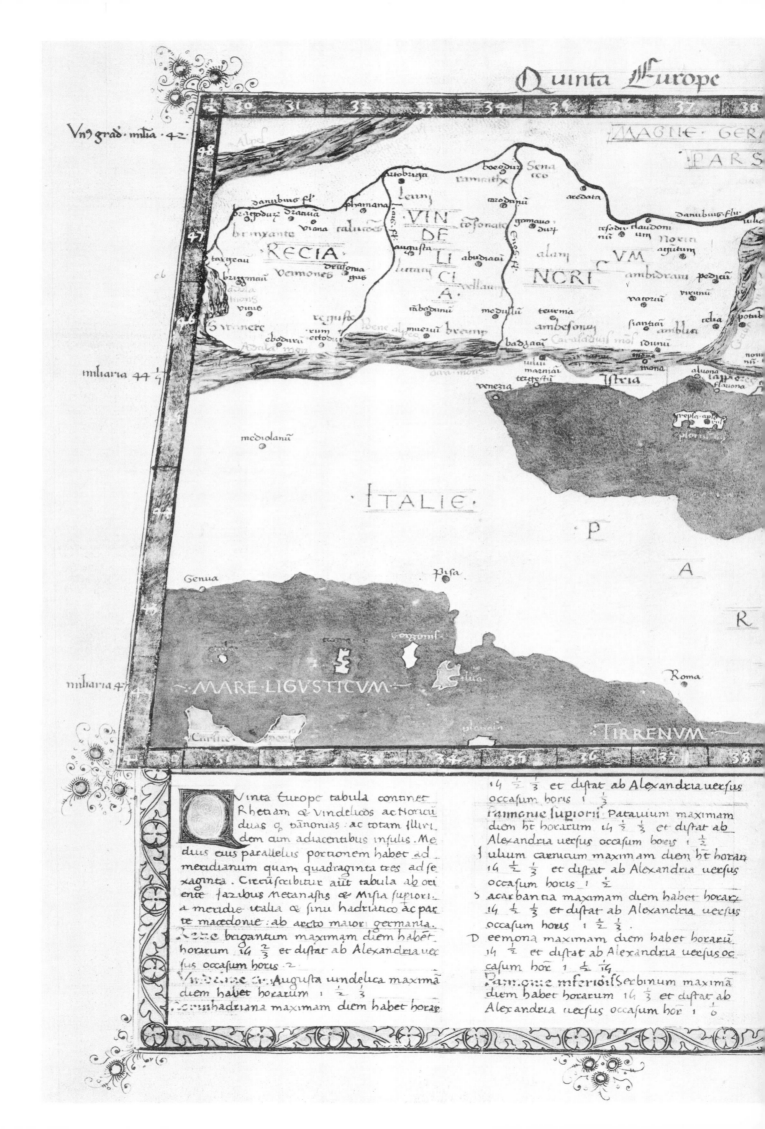

Quinta Europe

Vn⁹ grad· milia ·42·
miliaria 44 ½
miliaria 47
MAGNE· GER
PARS
danubius fl'
danubius flu
RECIA
VIN
DE
LI
CI
A
NORI
CUM
Istria
venezia
mediolanũ
·ITALIE·
P
A
R
Genua
Pisa
Roma
MARE·LIGVSTICVM
TIRRENVM

Quinta europe tabula continet Rhetiam et vindelicos ac Noricũ duas q3 pãnonias : ac totam Illiridem cum adiacentibus insulis. Medius eius parallelus portionem habet ad meridianum quam quadraginta tres ad sexaginta. Circũscribitur aũt tabula ab oriente Iazibus Metanastis et Misia supiori. a meridie italia et sinu hadriatico ac parte macedonie : ab arcto maiori germania.

Retie brigantum maximam diem habēt horarum 14 $\frac{2}{3}$ et distat ab Alexandria uersus occasum horis 2

Vindelicie ciu. Augusta uindelica maximã diem habet horarum 1 $\frac{1}{2}$ $\frac{1}{3}$

Norici hadriana maximam diem habet horarum 14 $\frac{1}{2}$ $\frac{1}{3}$ et distat ab Alexandria uersus occasum horis 1 $\frac{1}{3}$

Pannonie supioris Patauium maximam diem hꞇ horarum 14 $\frac{1}{2}$ $\frac{1}{3}$ et distat ab Alexandria uersus occasum horis 1 $\frac{1}{2}$

Iulium carnicum maximam diem hꞇ horarum 14 $\frac{1}{2}$ $\frac{1}{3}$ et distat ab Alexandria uersus occasum horis 1 $\frac{1}{2}$

Sacarbantia maximam diem habet horarum 14 $\frac{1}{2}$ $\frac{1}{3}$ et distat ab Alexandria uersus occasum horis 1 $\frac{1}{2}$ $\frac{1}{3}$.

Deemona maximam diem habet horarũ 14 $\frac{1}{2}$ et distat ab Alexandria uersus occasum hor 1 $\frac{1}{2}$ $\frac{1}{14}$

Pannonie inferioris Serbinum maximã diem habet horarum 14 $\frac{1}{3}$ et distat ab Alexandria uersus occasum hor 1 $\frac{1}{6}$

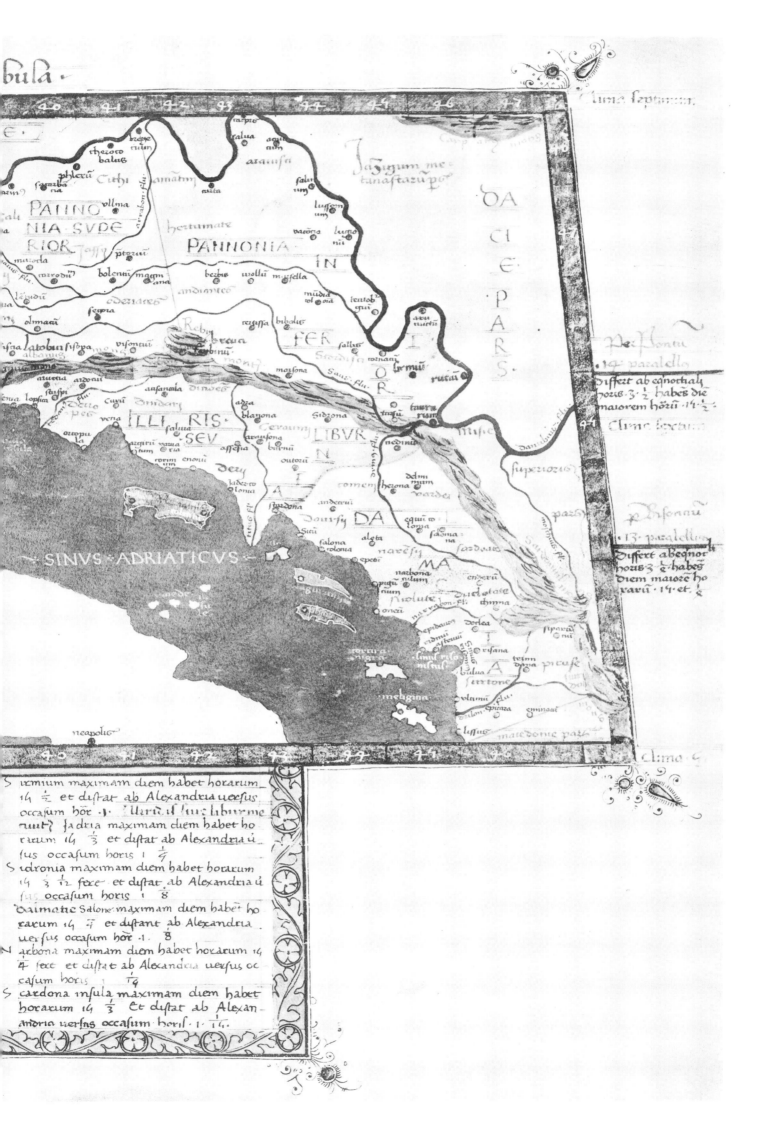

SINVS · ADRIATICVS

Sirmium maximam diem habet horarum
14 ½ et distat ab Alexandria uersus
occasum hor. 1. Illiru. il. sur. libur me
ruit ? Iadria maximam diem habet ho
rarum 14 ⅓ et distat ab Alexandria u
sus occasum horis 1 ¼

Sidronia maximam diem habet horarum
14 ⅓ ½ fere et distat ab Alexandria u
sus occasum horis 1 ⅛

Dalmatie Salone maximam diem habet ho
rarum 14 ⅔ et distant ab Alexandria
uersus occasum hor. 1. ⅛

Narbona maximam diem habet horarum 14
¼ fere et distat ab Alexandria uersus oc
casum horis 1/4

Sardona insula maximam diem habet
horarum 14 ⅓ Et distat ab Alexan_
andria uersus occasum horis 1 · 1/4

MARE · LIGVSTICVM

MARE

MARE SARDOVM

SARDINIE
INSVLE PARS

Vnal̄ g̃ · longit̄ · ualet
miliaria 44

miliaria 47

milia · 49

Sexta Europe tabula Italiam continet
et Cyrnum insulam cum ceteris sibi
adiacentibus insulis. Parallellus ipsius
medius proportionem habet ad meri
dianum quam tria ad quatuor. Circũscribitur
autem tabula ab oriente hadriatico sinu &
mari Ionio a meridie ligustico pelago atq tyr
reno & parte hadriatici: ab occasu alpium
montibus atq Gallia A septentrione Rhetia &
Norico & parte hadriatici sinus

Italie ciuitates insignes hee sunt.

Vrbs Roma regia maximam diem habet horarum
14 $\frac{1}{12}$ et distat ab Alexandria uersus occasum
horis 1 $\frac{1}{2}$ $\frac{1}{8}$

Nicea Massaliensium maximam diem habet horarum
14 $\frac{1}{4}$ et distat ab alexandria uersus occasum hor
2 $\frac{1}{8}$

Tarracine maximã diem habet horarum 14 $\frac{1}{4}$
& distat ab alexãdria uersus occasũ hor 1 $\frac{1}{2}$

Neapolis maximam diem habet horarum 14 $\frac{1}{2}$ $\frac{1}{3}$ &
& distat ab alexandria uersus occasum hor 1 $\frac{1}{3}$

Brendesium maximam diem habet horarum 14
$\frac{1}{2}$ $\frac{1}{3}$ et distat ab Alexandria uersus occasũ hor 1 $\frac{1}{3}$

Ancon maximam diem habet horarum 14 $\frac{1}{3}$ et di
stat ab alexandria uersus occasũ hor 1 $\frac{1}{2}$ $\frac{1}{4}$

Rauenna maximã diem habet horarũ 14 $\frac{1}{3}$ $\frac{1}{12}$
fere et distat ab Alexandria uersus occasum
hor 1 $\frac{2}{3}$

Aculia maximam diem habet horarum 14 $\frac{1}{2}$
& distat ab alexandria uersus occasũ hor 1 $\frac{1}{2}$ $\frac{1}{4}$

Beneuentus maximam diem habet horarum
14 $\frac{1}{12}$ fere & distat ab Alexandria uersus oc
casum hor 1 $\frac{1}{4}$

Capua maximam diem habet horarum 14 $\frac{1}{12}$
et distat ab alexandria uersus occasũ hor 1 $\frac{1}{3}$

[illegible] Alercia maximam diem habet horarum
14 $\frac{1}{2}$ $\frac{1}{3}$ $\frac{1}{12}$ et distat ab alexandria uersus
occasum horis 2 fere

Mariana maximam diem habet horarum 14
fere & distat ab Alexandria uersus occasum
horis 2 fere.

Septima Europe tabula continet Sardiniam & Siciliam insulas. Parallelus ipsius medius proportionem habet
ad meridianum quam quatuor ad
quinque. Circunscribitur autem tabula ab oriente
parte pelago: ab ortu hadriaco a meridie
Aphricano: ab occasu Sardoo: a septentrione ligustico.

Sardinie insule ciuitates insignes

Sulacos maximam diem habet horarum 14 $\frac{1}{2}$ $\frac{1}{12}$
& distat ab alexandria uersus occasum horis 1
$\frac{1}{2}$ $\frac{1}{3}$ $\frac{1}{14}$

Caralis maximam diem habet horarum 14 $\frac{1}{2}$
& distat ab alexandria uersus occasu hore 1 $\frac{1}{2}$ $\frac{1}{3}$

Turris bissonis maximam diem habet horarum
14 $\frac{1}{2}$ & distat ab alexandria uersus occasum horis 2 fere.

Guculus noua maximam diem habet horaru
14 $\frac{1}{2}$ $\frac{1}{8}$ et distat ab alexandria uersus occasum horis 1 $\frac{1}{2}$ $\frac{1}{3}$ $\frac{1}{8}$

Sicilie insule insignium ciuitatum

Lilybeum maximam diem habet horarum 14
$\frac{1}{2}$ et distat ab alexandria uersus occasum
horis 1 $\frac{1}{2}$ $\frac{1}{3}$ $\frac{1}{8}$

Syracuse maximam diem habent horarum 14
$\frac{1}{2}$ $\frac{1}{8}$ & distat ab alexandria uersus occasum
horis 1 $\frac{1}{3}$ $\frac{1}{14}$

Mesena maxima diem habet horar 14 $\frac{1}{2}$ $\frac{1}{4}$ et
distat ab alexandria uersus occasum hor 1 $\frac{1}{3}$ $\frac{1}{8}$

Segesta maximam diem habet horarum 14 $\frac{1}{4}$ et
quid parum & distat ab Alexandria uersus
occasum horis 1 $\frac{1}{2}$ $\frac{1}{14}$

Catana maximam diem habet horar 14 $\frac{2}{3}$ &
distat ab alexandria uersus occasu hore 1 $\frac{1}{3}$ $\frac{1}{14}$

Septima Europe

TIRRENVM PELAGVS

PARS ITALIE

ispomast\
simul

11 Paralellus\
Differt ab equinoctial\
horis 2 ½ ⅛ habet\
die maximū die hora\
rum 14 ½ ¼

Regnū

SI\
CILIA

messeny

Cath nati

Orbite

ADRIATICV

INSVLA

Seggestani\
Siram

Per Rodum

10 paralellus\
Differt ab eqnoth\
horis 2 ½ habet\
die maiorē horaz\
14 et medie vnā

Clima quartum

AFFRICVM

Ctaua europe tabula continet Sarma
tiam que in ea est et tauricam chersone
sum . parallelus ipius medius propor
tionem habet ad meridianum quam un
decim ad uiginti Terminatur aut tabula ab ortu
solis bofphoro Cimerico & Meoti palude ac Tanai
fluuio iuxta Sarmatiam Asie A meridie pontico
mari & parte Mysie inferioris et Dacia ac Iazib
Metanastis : ab occasu montibus Sarmaticis appel
latis ac germania & vistula fluuio : a septentrio
ne uenedico sinu & Sarmatico oceano ac terra
incognita . Sarmatie in europa ciuitates .

Tamyraca maximam diem habet horarum 16 & distat
ab alexandria uersus occasu horis 1 $\frac{1}{14}$

Naubarum maximam diem habet horarum 16 $\frac{1}{3}$ et
distat ab alexandria uersus occasu hor 1 $\frac{1}{8}$

Olbia que et Borysthenes maximam diem habet ho
rarum 16 $\frac{1}{2}$ & distat ab alexandria uersus occasum
horis 1 $\frac{1}{4}$

Thaurice chersonesi Theodosia maximam diem ha
bet horarum 14 $\frac{2}{3}$ et distat ab alexandria
uersus occasum horis 1 $\frac{1}{4}$.

Unus gradus longitudinis.
in hac latitudine regionis. continet
stadia. 227. que faciut milia 28½ fere.
Est ergo spaciu totius tabule 7008 stadiorum
que faciut miliaria. 876.

63

62

61

60

Milia 32½

Differentia ptis superioris ad
inferiorem tabule in stadijs
quidem 3480. in miliarib
uero. 435.

OCEANVS · SARMATICVS ·

Samaia insula

46

Githones   phiun
Venedia   mo
                n

Magne   Sulones

Germanie   phrugudiones

Pars   auarini   Gilliones

              ombrones   Cistobori

              anartophearti tranomotani

              burgiones

              arsiete

Milia 40½   poengite   Sabori

Milia 36½

SARMA

Bodini

Geuini

Carie

EV

R

amazo

bousthenes: fluuis

leuci mons   mons.   amodou
                     palus

Penius   Carpiam

peumi   basterne

azagai

amado

leinu   sarg

barsaui

mes

me

PE

briesi Carpatus mons

Carmatum montes

Carpatus mons

depidam uilbata
              herathun
atreodu metonu

thunis
ordes

auia

twas. fl.

Iasigum meta
nastaus pc

Panno
nie In
feriorus
pars

DACIE · PARS ·

misie Inferioris
pars

osha Istru. flu

Spacium totius tabule in
miliarib quid 1311. In sta
dijs uero. 10488.

Milia 43

45   7   46   46   47   48   49   40   41   42   43   44   44   46

Sarmatum montes

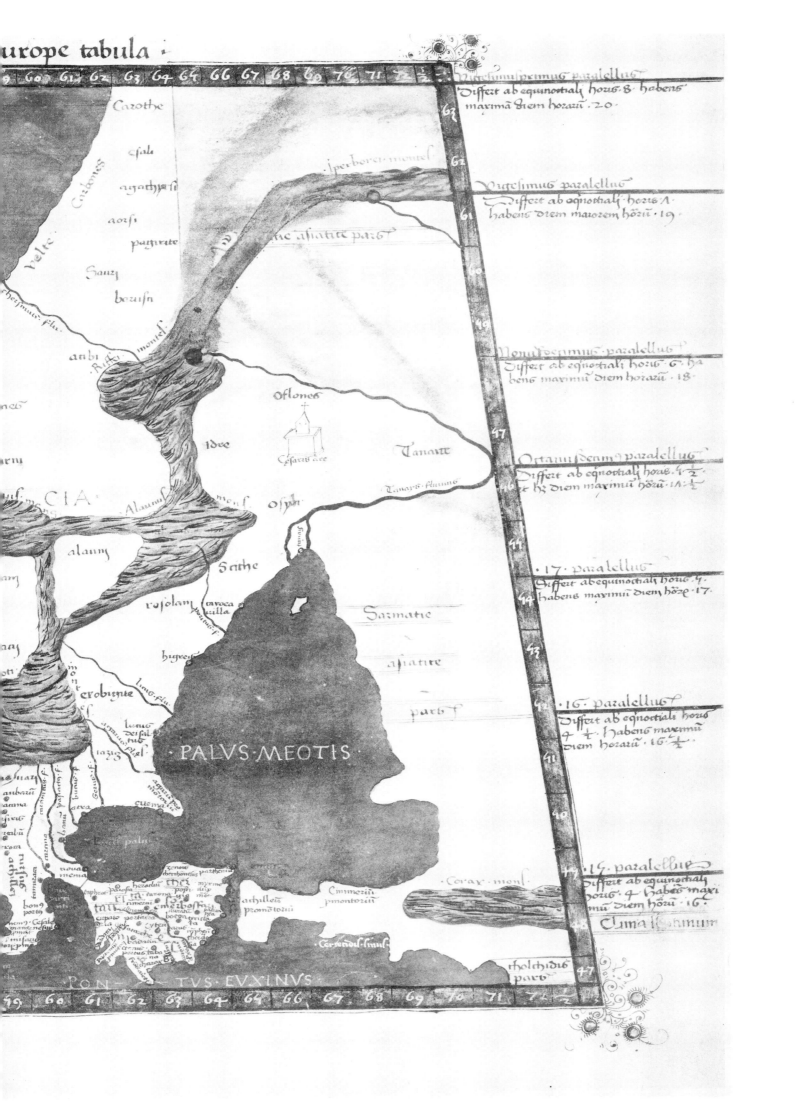

59 60 61 62 63 64 64 66 67 68 69 76 71 72 ½

Cazothe

csali

agathyrsi

aorsi

paginate

Sauri

bouisn

othesmutes flu.

anbi

Ristei

montes

CIA.

Alanus

mont.

alanus

Scithe

rosolani

turca

partus f.

nei

higrei

crobiente

linus flu.

mont

tazig

lenus

dei sal

tus

plagi

novaa

rmatu

anbaru

varua

alex

nusiacu

archilleii

bong

potin

mons Cesale

nphon

nisiach

mph

Iperborei montes

ne asiatice pars

Oftones

Cesarii acc

Idee

Osph

Tanaite

Tanayis flauius

Sarmatie

asiatice

pars f

PALVS MEOTIS

tenue dei sal palu

hezadu

parofia

turca raiona

tapheas

nephii

archileii promtoru

Cimmerii pmontoriu

Corax mons.

Terendis sinus.

tholchidis pars 47

63

62

61

60

49

48

47

46

45

44

43

42

41

40

47

47

Maximus primus paralellus
Differt ab equinoctiali horis 8 habens
maximā diem horarū 20.

Vigesimus paralellus
Differt ab equinoctiali horis 1
habens diem maiorem hōrū 19.

Nonusdecimus paralellus
Differt ab equinoctiali horis 6 ha
bens maximū diem horarū 18.

Octauus decim paralellus
Differt ab equinoctiali horis 4 ½
et hz diem maximū hōrū 14 ½

17 paralellus
Differt ab equinoctiali horis 4
habens maximū diem hōre 17.

16 paralellus
Differt ab equinoctiali horis
4 ¼ habens maximū
diem horarū 16 ½

15 paralellus
Differt ab equinoctiali
horis 4 habens maxi
mū diem hōru 16.
Clima septimū

Nona Europe tabula continet Iazyges me-
tanastas. Daciam utranq Mysiam Thra-
ciam & chersonesum. Parallelus ipsius medius proportionem habet ad meridianum.
quam quadraginta tres ad sexaginta. Terminatur aut
tabula ab ortu pontico mari: et thracio bosphoro.
atq propontide & helesponto. Ab austro egeo pelago ac macedonia: ab occasu panonia inferiori ac
dalmacia: ab arcto Sarmatia Europe

Iazigum. Bormanum maximam diem habet horar
16 et distat ab alexandria uersus occasu hor 1 $\frac{1}{12}$

Indacia Saline maximam diem habem habent hor
14 $\frac{1}{2}$ $\frac{1}{3}$ et distant ab Alexandria uersus occasum horis 1 $\frac{2}{3}$ aut 1 $\frac{1}{4}$ $\frac{1}{14}$.

Zarmisegethusa regia maximam diem habet horarum
14 $\frac{1}{2}$ et distat ab alexandria uersus occasum n
horis 1 $\frac{1}{2}$ $\frac{1}{3}$

Misie superioris Rhetaria maximam diem habet
horarum 14 $\frac{1}{4}$ et distat ab alexandria uersus
occasum horis 1 $\frac{1}{2}$ $\frac{1}{4}$

Scupi maximam diem habet horarum 14 $\frac{1}{2}$ et distat ab alexandria uersus occasum horis 1 $\frac{1}{2}$ $\frac{1}{4}$

Misie inferioris Odyssus maximam diem habet
horarum 14 $\frac{1}{2}$ et distat ab alexandria uersus
occasum horis 1 $\frac{1}{4}$

Ocesus maximam diem habet horarum 14 $\frac{1}{4}$ $\frac{1}{8}$
et distat ab alexandria uersus occasu horis 1 $\frac{1}{12}$

Tratie Enos maximam diem habet horarum
14 $\frac{1}{2}$ et distat ab alexandria uersus occasum
horis 1 $\frac{1}{3}$ $\frac{1}{8}$

Apollonia maximam diem habet horarum 14 $\frac{1}{2}$ $\frac{1}{12}$
et distat ab alexandria uersus occasu hor 1 $\frac{1}{3}$

Byzantium maximam diem habet horarum 14 $\frac{1}{4}$
& distat ab Alexandria uersus occasum hor 1 $\frac{1}{4}$

Perinthos maximam diem habet horarum 14 $\frac{1}{6}$ &
distat ab alexandria uersus occasum hor 1 $\frac{1}{3}$

Nicopolis maximam diem habet horarum 14 $\frac{1}{6}$ et
distat ab alexandria uersus occasum hor 1 $\frac{1}{2}$ 14

Lysimachia maximam diem habet horarum 14 $\frac{1}{12}$
& distat ab alexandria uersus occasum horis
1 $\frac{1}{2}$ $\frac{1}{14}$.

Proconesus maximam diem habet horarum 14 $\frac{1}{8}$
& distat ab Alexandria uersus occasum horis 1
$\frac{1}{3}$ fere.

Cherionesi. hecleus maximam diem habet horar
14 $\frac{1}{8}$ et distat ab alexandria uersus occasum horis 1 $\frac{1}{3}$

Sestos maximam diem habet horar 14 $\frac{1}{8}$ & distat
ab alexandria uersus occasum hor 1 $\frac{1}{3}$.

Miliaria 41 ½

milia 47 ¼

Miliaria 47

oscenum
gormanu
abrieta
praca
trissu
Candanu

·I AZIGES·
METANASTE·

pessu

partiscum

·PAN
NONIE·
INFERIORIS
·PARS·

Danubius fl.

sauus fl.

Rebrynion tee

ILLIRIDIS·

ET·

DALMACIE·

·P
A
R
S·

Tagurium
pharie
narrabon fl

Simul
Rulo
mlus.

ionium mare·

SINVS ADRIATICVS

Denuie fl.

Derion fl.

zividana

biepin

zinobara

lusio
Zarmizegethusa
regia

alboensy
nbysa

Signidocyu

MI
SI
A·

tritorne siy

SVPE

Orchea

Duensu

tumaci

narrabon fl

Drinus fl.

Stauaus mons.

Erigon fl.

DACIA

burideensy

Zeugma

diezna

R

R

I

Viminaciu legior
tanasu

eteta

dortini

vendenis

nessu

Dardania

Arrhiba

MACE
DONIE·

Axius fl.

Saldensy

Rhetaria
mysor
mysi

 vlpianu
saup

pysanio

mo ni

Orbeul

Steimonu fl.

P

A

R

S·

haliacmon fl.

sondana
napoca
vlpianu
patruissa
saline
macod

smidana Rhatarensy zirid
apuli

zermize

ague

tivisai

acmonia

argid

arcina

phirates

Gagili

Rabolius flu

S

Decima europe tabula continet macedoniam & epyrum & Achaiam & peloponesum et cretam insulam & euboeam cum insulis adiacentibus. parallelus ipsius medius proportionem habet ad meridianum quam septem ad nouem. Terminatur aut tabula ab oriente Egeo pelago Myrtoo q. & carpathio. ab austro hadriatico. ab arcto Dalmatia & Mysia superiori ac Tehacia

Macedonie insignium ciuitatum in ea.

Dirachium maximam diem habet horarum 14 & distat ab alexandria uersus occasum hor 1

Thessalonica maximam diem habet horarū $14\ \frac{1}{2}\ \frac{1}{3}\ \frac{1}{12}$ & distat ab alexandria uersus occasum hor $\frac{2}{3}$

Amphipolis maximam diem habet horarum $14\ \frac{1}{12}$ & distat ab alexandria uersus occasū hor $1\ \frac{2}{3}$

Heraclea maximam diem habet horarum 14 & distat ab alexandria uersus occasum hor $1\ \frac{1}{2}\ \frac{1}{3}$

Pella maximam diem habet horarum $14\ \frac{1}{2}\ \frac{1}{3}\ \frac{1}{12}$ fere & distat ab alexandria uersus occasū hor $1\ \frac{1}{2}\ \frac{1}{4}$ fere

Larissa pelasgiensium maximam diem ht hor $14\ \frac{1}{2}\ \frac{1}{3}$ & distat ab alexandria uersus occasum horis $1\ \frac{2}{3}$

Casandria maximam diem habet horaꝝ $14\ \frac{1}{2}\ \frac{1}{3}$ et distat ab alexandria uersus occasū hor $1\ \frac{1}{2}\ \frac{1}{12}$

Lemnos insula maximam diem habet horarum 14 et distat ab alexandria uersus occasū horis $1\ \frac{1}{2}$

Epiri. Nicopolis maximam diem habet horaꝝ $14\ \frac{2}{3}$ & distat ab alexādria uersus occaum hor $1\ \frac{1}{2}\ \frac{1}{3}$ fere

Ambracia maximam diem habet horarum $14\ \frac{1}{2}\ \frac{1}{4}$ et distat ab alexandria uersus occaum hor $1\ \frac{1}{2}\ \frac{1}{3}$ fere.

Corcyre insule ciuitas Corcyra maximam diem habet horarum $14\ \frac{2}{3}$ et distat ab alexandria uersus occasum horis $1\ \frac{1}{2}\ \frac{1}{3}$

Achaye thebe boetie maximā diem hnt horaꝝ $14\ \frac{2}{3}$ & distant ab alexandria uersus occasū hor $\frac{1}{2}$

Megara maximam diem habet horaꝝ $14\ \frac{1}{2}\ \frac{1}{3}$ et distat ab alexandria uersus occasum hor $1\ \frac{1}{2}\ \frac{1}{30}$

Athene maximam diem habet horarum $14\ \frac{1}{2}\ \frac{1}{8}$ et distant ab alexandria uersus occasum horis $1\ \frac{1}{2}$

Peloponesi ciuit. Mesena maximā die ht horaꝝ $14\ \frac{1}{3}\ \frac{1}{12}$ & distat ab alexandria uersus occasum hor $1\ \frac{1}{2}\ \frac{1}{14}$

Corinthus maximam diem habet horarum $14\ \frac{1}{2}\ \frac{1}{12}$ et distat ab alexandria uersus occasū hor $1\ \frac{1}{2}\ \frac{1}{8}$

Tegea maximam diem habet horarum $14\ \frac{1}{2}$ & distat ab alexandria uersus occasum $1\ \frac{1}{2}\ \frac{1}{4}$

Argos maximam diem habet horarum $14\ \frac{1}{2}$ & distat ab alexandria uersus occasum horis $1\ \frac{1}{2}\ \frac{1}{8}$

Lacedemon maximam diem habet horarum $14\ \frac{1}{3}\ \frac{1}{12}$ & distat ab alexandria uersus occasum hor $1\ \frac{2}{3}$

Euboee insule Chalcis maximam diem habet horaꝝ $14\ \frac{2}{3}$ & distat ab alexandria uersus occaum hor $1\ \frac{1}{2}$

Carystus maximam diem habet horaꝝ $14\ \frac{2}{3}$ et distat ab alexandria uersus occasum hor $1\ \frac{1}{3}\ \frac{1}{30}$

Crete insule ciuitates. Gortina maximū diē habet horaꝝ $14\ \frac{1}{3}$ et distat ab alexandria uersus occasum horis $1\ \frac{1}{3}\ \frac{1}{14}$

Cnossos maximam diem habet horarū $14\ \frac{1}{3}$ et distat ab alexandria uersus occasum hor $1\ \frac{1}{3}$.

Finis tabularum europe decem.

Vnuf graduf longi tenet
miliaria · 8 · 46 ·

Milia · 48 ·

Miliaria · 50 ·

Dalmatie et
Illiridis pars

Simul riso
msinus.

Ionium mare

Elymioti

MACE

DONIA

MARE · ADRIATICVZ

∴ Affrice tabule quatuor quaru pima

Prima libie tabula continet ambas mauri
tanias tinganicam et cesariensem. Paralle
lus ipius medius proportionem habet ad
meridianum quam decedecim ad quindea
terminatur aut tabula ab ortu aphrica A meridie
interiore lybia iuxta getuliam. Ab occasu ociden
tali oceano. Ab arcto freto herculeo et sberico ac
Sardoo pelago Mauritanie tinginire ciuit

Tingis maximam diem habet horarum 14 $\frac{1}{2}$ et di
stat ab Alexandria versus occasu hor 3 $\frac{1}{2}$ $\frac{1}{12}$

Lyx maximam diem habet horarum 14 $\frac{1}{2}$ et distat ab
Alexandria versus occasum horis 3 $\frac{1}{2}$

Volbilis maximam diem habet horarum 14 $\frac{1}{2}$ et distat
ab alexandria versus occasum horis 3 $\frac{1}{2}$

Cesariensis. Cartina maximam diem habet horaru
4 $\frac{1}{4}$ et distat ab alexandria versus occasu hor 3

Iol cesarea maximam diem habet horaru 14 $\frac{1}{4}$ et di
stat ab alexandria versus occasum hor 2 $\frac{1}{2}$ $\frac{1}{3}$ $\frac{1}{14}$

Salde maximam diem habet horarum 14 $\frac{1}{6}$ et distat
ab Alexandria versus occasum hor 1 $\frac{1}{2}$ $\frac{1}{14}$

h oppidum maximam diem habet horarum 14 $\frac{1}{2}$
et distat ab Alexandria versus occasum hor 2 $\frac{1}{3}$ $\frac{1}{14}$

Zuchabari maximam diem habet horar 14 $\frac{1}{4}$ et
distat ab alexandria versus occasum horis 2 $\frac{1}{2}$ $\frac{1}{3}$ $\frac{1}{14}$

Busuptis maximam diem ht horar 14 $\frac{1}{8}$ et distat
ab alexandria versus occasu hor 2 $\frac{1}{3}$ $\frac{1}{14}$

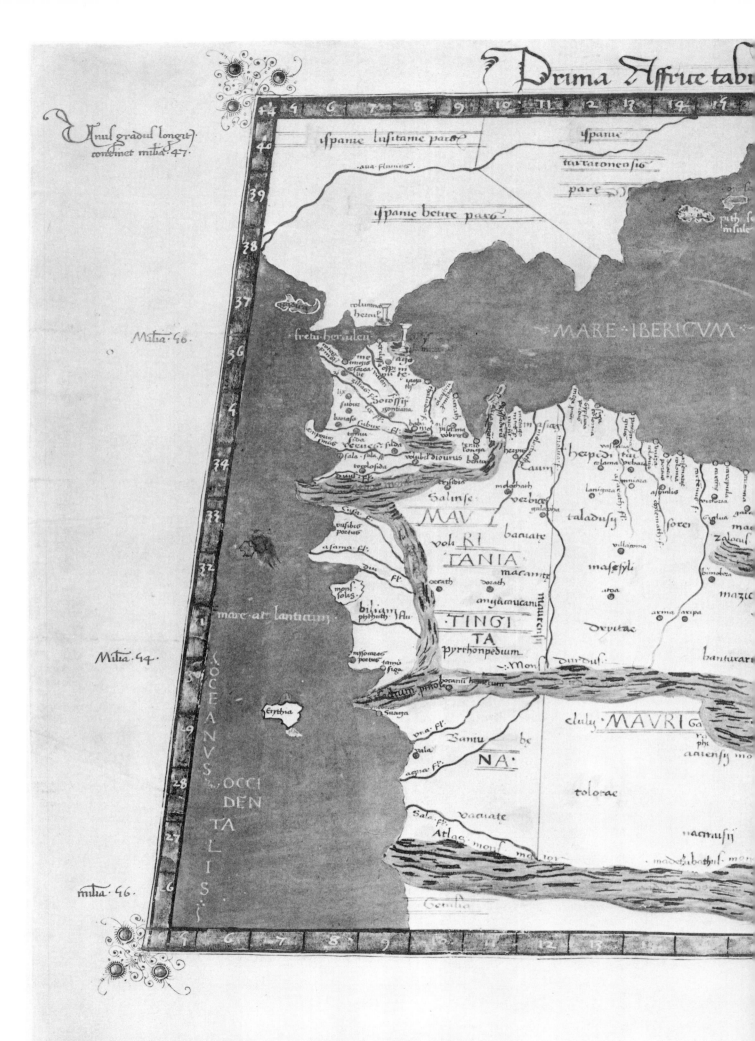

Unul gradul longit)
condinet milia·47·

14 4 6 7 8 9 10 11 12 13 14 15

40   ispanie lusitanie pars   ispanie

                                    tarraronensis

39   aua flumus·   pars

38   ispanie betire pars·

37   columna
      hezal'

Milia·46·   MARE·IBERICVM

36   fretu herculen

       lix
       subur
       banasa cibus

        enporus
       tomus
34   sala· sala· ft·
       roglosida

       Cusa·   Salinse
33   vusbus
       poztus   MAV
       asama· ft·   vol RI

32   monf·   TANIA   baniate
       solas·
                                            macant
                                              ocrath   vorath

       bilian   anjumucani
       phthuth · f Au·
Milia·44·   TINGI
                                         TA
       mysomeas   pyrrhonpedium
       poztus   ·:·Monf· durduf·
       tamis
       siga

31   Adrum pmof·

30   Erythia   vra· ft·
                                    Bantu   be
29   vula·
                                    agna· ft·   NA·
28   OCCI
       DEN   tolorae
27   TA
       LIS·   Sala· ft·   vacuate
26   Atlac· monf·   me   ior
milia·46·

                                    Gentia

4 5 6 7 8 9 10 11 12 13

       mare·at lanticum

OCEANVS

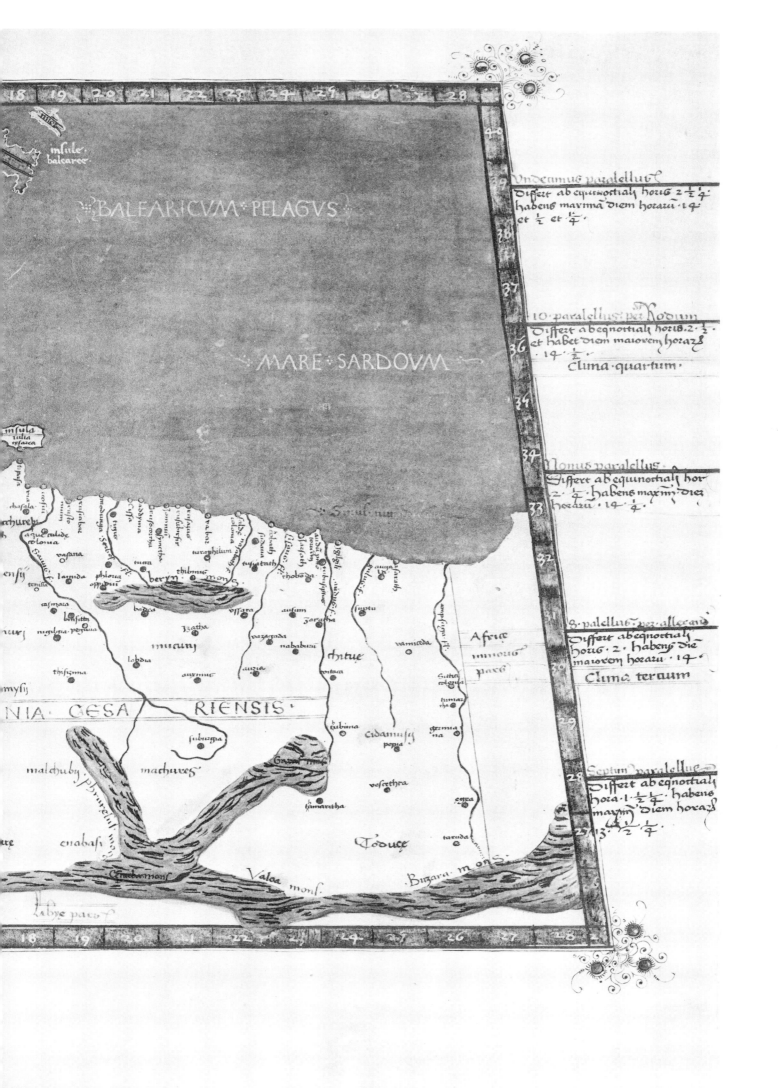

18 19 20 21 22 23 24 6 7 28

insule balearee

*BALEARICVM*PELAGVS*

*MARE*SARDOVM*

insula iulia refaica

Sinul nur

Africe inucius pacs

NIA CESA RIENSIS

40

39 Vndeamus paralellus
Differt ab equinoctiali horis 2 ½ ¼
habens maxima diem horaru 14
et ½ et ¼

38

37

10 paralellus per Rodum
36 Differt a beqnoctiali horis 2 ½
et habet diem maiorem horaz
14 ½
Clima quartum

35

34 Nonus paralellus
Differt ab equinoctiali hor
2 ¼ habens maxim diez
33 horaru 14 ¼

32

31 8 palellus per alleran
Differt abeqnoctiali
30 horis 2 habens die
maiorem horaru 14
Clima tertium

29

28 Septim paralellus
Differt ab eqnoctiali
27 hora 1 ½ ¼ habens
maxim diem horaz
26 25 13 ½ ¼

18 19 20 1 22 23 24 25 26 27 28

Ecunda aphrice tabula continet Aphri
cam & insulas que circa ipam sunt. Parallelus ipius medius proporcionem habe
ad meridianum quam tredecim ad quindecim. Terminatur aut tabula ab oriente Cyrenaica. a meridie interiori libya iuxta getuliam
et eremum. ab occasu mauritania cesariensin
Ab arcto pelago Aphro.

Affrice minorii insignes ciuitates :·

Thabraca maximam diem habet horarum 14 $\frac{1}{6}$ et
distat ab alexandria uersus occasum hor 2 fere
Tycha maximam diem habet horar 14 $\frac{1}{4}$ et distat
ab alexandria uersus occasum hor 1 $\frac{1}{2}$ $\frac{1}{3}$
Chatago maximam diem habet horarum 14 $\frac{1}{4}$ et
distat ab alexandria uersus occasum hor 1 $\frac{1}{2}$ $\frac{1}{3}$
Adrumentum maximam diem habet horaru 14 $\frac{1}{4}$
et distat ab alexandria uersus occasum hor 1 $\frac{1}{2}$ $\frac{1}{12}$
Magna leptis maximam diem habet hor 14 $\frac{1}{8}$ et di
stat ab alexandria uersus occasum hor 1 $\frac{1}{9}$
Curteulia maximam diem habet horor 14 $\frac{1}{12}$ et di
stat ab alexandria uersus occasum hor 2 $\frac{1}{4}$
Succa Venneria maximam diem habet horar 14 et
qd parte et distat ab alexandria uersus occasum hor. 2
Bullaria maxima diem ht horar 14 $\frac{1}{12}$ & distat ab
alexandria uersus occasum hor. 2.
Vtina maximam diem habet horar 14 $\frac{1}{12}$ et distat
ab alexandria uersus occasum hor 1 $\frac{1}{2}$ $\frac{1}{4}$
Thisbros insula maximam diem habet horar 14 $\frac{1}{8}$ et distat
ab alexandria uersus occasum hor 1 $\frac{1}{2}$
Menix insula maximam diem ht horar 14 $\frac{1}{12}$ et distat ab
alexandria uersus occasum hor 1 $\frac{1}{3}$ $\frac{1}{16}$
Cossera insula maximam diem habet horar 14 $\frac{1}{3}$ & distat
ab alexandria uersus occasum horis 1 $\frac{1}{6}$
Meleta insula maximam diem habet horarum 14 $\frac{1}{3}$
et distat ab alexandria uersus occasu hor 1 $\frac{1}{3}$ $\frac{1}{8}$

TIRRENVM

Onul ꝗ̄ cōtinet milia 48·

Miliaria· 40

MARE· SARDOVM

SARDINIA INSVLA

M A R E A

Milia 44

Milia 46

Calata

simul achites

Cirtesi Vzicath

Cirta iulia

Genabatte

laceo

mireu

apari

misulami

nattabute

azama
Nisibes

FIVMI oprij
nulaia simithi DIA

gausaphna

thieba
thinudeo mit

lambesa

Auduf
mon
fuf

thubatis

Saburbures

hAhardi

Sittaphius campus

bagrada flu

thubursica

naran

voibi thebesta

AFFRI CA·

miedy

sigauen ria

assuius

amedara

musuni Cirna

thanureda

gaza

vazia

cerophei
ague
nfide

zizura
thafa thinaba
mista mamp

motutury

LIBYAE IN· TERIORIS PARS.

TERCIA Aphrice tabula continet Cyre-
naicam et egyptum cum adiacentibus
insulis. Parallelus ipsius medius propor
tionem habet ad meridianum quam qn
quaginta tres ad sexaginta. Terminatur aut tabu
la ab ortu iudea et arabia petrea ac arabico sinu
Ab austro interiori desecta libia et ethyopia que
sub egypto est. ab occasu aphrica et magna syrte
et parte interioris libye. Ab arcto libyco et egyptio
pelago Cirenaice regionis ciuitates insignes.
Beronice que et Esperides maximam diem habet ho
rarum 14 $\frac{1}{12}$ et distat ab alexandria uersus occasum
horis 1 $\frac{1}{2}$ $\frac{1}{3}$ $\frac{1}{14}$
Ptolemais maximam diem habet horarū 4 $\frac{1}{12}$ et distat
ab alexandria uersus occasum horis 1 $\frac{1}{2}$ $\frac{1}{3}$ $\frac{1}{4}$
Apollonia maximam diem habet horarum 14 $\frac{1}{8}$ et
distat ab alexandria uersus occasum hor 1 $\frac{2}{3}$
Cyrene maximam diem habet horarum 14 $\frac{1}{12}$ et distat
ab alexandria uersus occasum hor 1 $\frac{2}{3}$
M[illegible]rmarice chersonesus maximam diem habet horarum
14 $\frac{1}{8}$ et distat ab alexādria uersus occasum horis 1 $\frac{1}{2}$ $\frac{1}{19}$
[illegible]bia Paretonium maximā diem ht hor 14 $\frac{1}{12}$ et distat
ab alexandria uersus occasum horis 1 $\frac{1}{4}$
Alexandria maximam diem ht hor 14 $\frac{1}{12}$ et distat a
meridiano fortunatarum insularum ab ortu solis horis. 4.
Pelusium maximam diem ht horarum 14 $\frac{1}{12}$ et distat
ab alexandria uersus ortū horis 1 $\frac{1}{9}$
Memphis maximā diem ht horarum 13 $\frac{1}{2}$ $\frac{1}{4}$ $\frac{1}{9}$ et distat
ab alexandria uersus ortum 1 $\frac{1}{8}$
[illegible] ptolemais maximam diem ht horarum 13
$\frac{2}{3}$ et distat ab alexandria uersus ortū hor 1 $\frac{1}{8}$
Magna diopolis maximam diem habet horarum 13 $\frac{1}{2}$
$\frac{1}{8}$ et distat ab alexandria uersus ortū 1 $\frac{1}{8}$
Syene maximam diem ht horarum 13 $\frac{1}{2}$ et distat ab
alexandria uersus ortum hor 1 $\frac{1}{8}$
Hic sol semel in āno fit supra uerticē capitis quādo
in estiuo est tropico
Ammon maximam diem ht horarum 13 $\frac{1}{2}$ $\frac{1}{3}$ et distat ab
alexandria uersus ortum hor 1 $\frac{1}{3}$
Magna Oasis maximam diem habet horarum 13 $\frac{2}{3}$ et distat ab alexandria uersus ortū hor 1 $\frac{1}{19}$
Mysormus maximam diem habet horarum 13 $\frac{1}{2}$ $\frac{1}{4}$ et
distat ab alexandria uersus ortū hor 1 $\frac{1}{4}$
Berenice maximam diem habet horarum 13 $\frac{1}{2}$ et distat ab alexandria uersus ortum horis 1 $\frac{1}{4}$
Hic sol semel fit in anno supra uerticem quando
est in tropico estiuo.

PVNICVM · · · LIBICVM · MARE

LIBYE · CHERSIS

CYRENES

MARMARICA · LIBY

LIBYAE · INTERIORIS · PARS

Vnu̅ g̅ fornet miliaria 42

Milia 44

Vnu̅ graduſ continet miliaria · 44 ¼ ·

hora hesperidu̅

lora ferax plena phylli

al magna hueu̅ſq̅

herculis turris

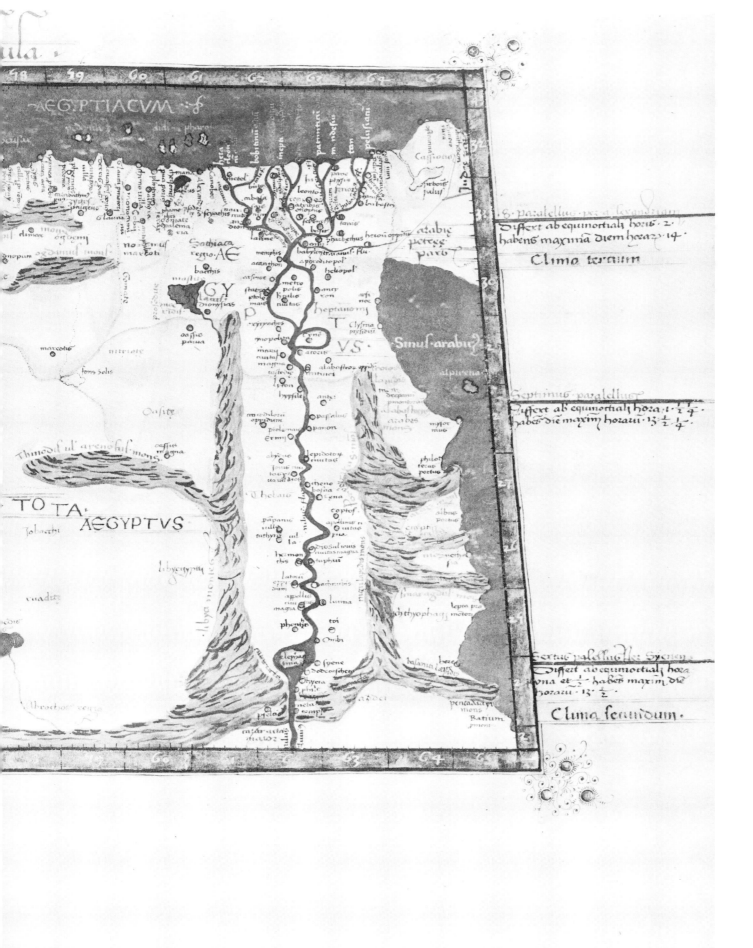

Left column

Quarta et ultima aphrice tabula continet
interiorem libyam & ethyopiam que sub
egypto est & que est interius cum insulis
ei adiacentibus. Parallelus ipsius medius
proportionem habet ad meridianum eandem fere.
Terminatur aut tabula ab ortu sinu arabico & mari
rubro ac sinu barbarico & parte indici pelagi. a me
ridie terra incognita & oceano occidentali. A septen
trione utraq Mauritania & aphrica ac cyrenaica e
gypto q

Civitatum insignium secundum interiore libiam

Autole maximam diem habet horar $13\frac{1}{2}$ & distat ab
alexandria uersus occasum horis $2\frac{2}{3}$

Hec sol semel in anno fit supra uerticem capitis in tro
pico estiuo

Tarzita maximam diem habet horar $12\frac{1}{2}\frac{1}{3}\frac{1}{12}$ et di
stat ab Alexandria uersus occasum horis $3\frac{1}{3}$

Huc sol bis in anno fit supra uerticem capitis quando di
stat a tropico estiuo ex utraq parte gradib' $48\frac{2}{3}$

Thamondocana maximam diem habet horar 13 et di
stat ab alexandria uersus occasum horis $2\frac{1}{2}$

Sumit aut bis in anno solem supra uerticem quado
distat a tropico estiuo ex utraq parte gradibus 43

Gira maximam diem habet horarum $13\frac{1}{12}$ & distat
ab alexandria uersus occasum horis $1\frac{1}{3}\frac{1}{8}$

Habet aut solem bis in anno supra uerticem quando
distat a tropico estiuo ex utraq parte gradibus 43

Garame maximam diem habet horar 13 et distat ab
alexandria uersus occasum horis $1\frac{1}{6}$

Huc sol bis in anno fit supra uerticem cum distat a
tropico estiuo ex utraq parte gradibus 24

Ethiopie sub egypto insignium ciuitatum

Nupata maximam diem habet horarum $13\frac{1}{4}$ et distat
ab alexandria uersus ortum horis $1\frac{1}{6}$

Huc sol fit supra uerticem bis in anno cum distat a tropi
co estiuo ex utraq parte gradibus $31\frac{1}{6}$

Mecoe maximam diem habet horar 13 et distat ab Ale
xandria uersus ortum horis $1\frac{1}{14}$

In ea sol bis in anno fit supra uerticem quado distat a
tropico estiuo ex utraq parte gradibus 44

Ptolemais ferar maximam diem habet horarum 13 &
& distat ab alexandria uersus ortum $1\frac{1}{3}\frac{1}{14}$

In ea sol bis in anno fit supra uerticem cum distat a
tropico estiuo ab utraq parte gradibus 44

Adulis maximam diem habet horarum $12\frac{2}{3}$ et distat
ab alexandria uersus ortum horis $1\frac{1}{3}\frac{1}{8}$

Huc sol bis in anno fit supra uerticem cum distat a tropico
estiuo ab utraq parte gradib' 62.

Dera maximam diem habet horar $12\frac{2}{3}$ et distat ab
alexandria uersus ortum horis 1

Sumit autem solem bis in anno supra uerticem cum
distat a tropico estiuo ex utraq parte gradib' $63\frac{1}{2}\frac{1}{4}$

Right column

Mosylum maximam diem habet horarum $12\frac{1}{2}$ et distat ab alexandria uersus ortum
horis $1\frac{1}{3}$ fere

In bis sol bis in anno fit supra uerticem cum
distat a tropico estiuo ab utraq parte
gradibus gradibus $68\frac{1}{2}\frac{1}{4}$

Aromata maximam diem habet horarum
$13\frac{1}{3}\frac{1}{8}$ & distant ab alexandria uersus
ortum horis $1\frac{1}{2}$

In his bis in anno sol fit supra uerticem
quando distat a tropico estiuo ab utraq
parte gradibus .76

Finis tabularum Affrice quatuor.

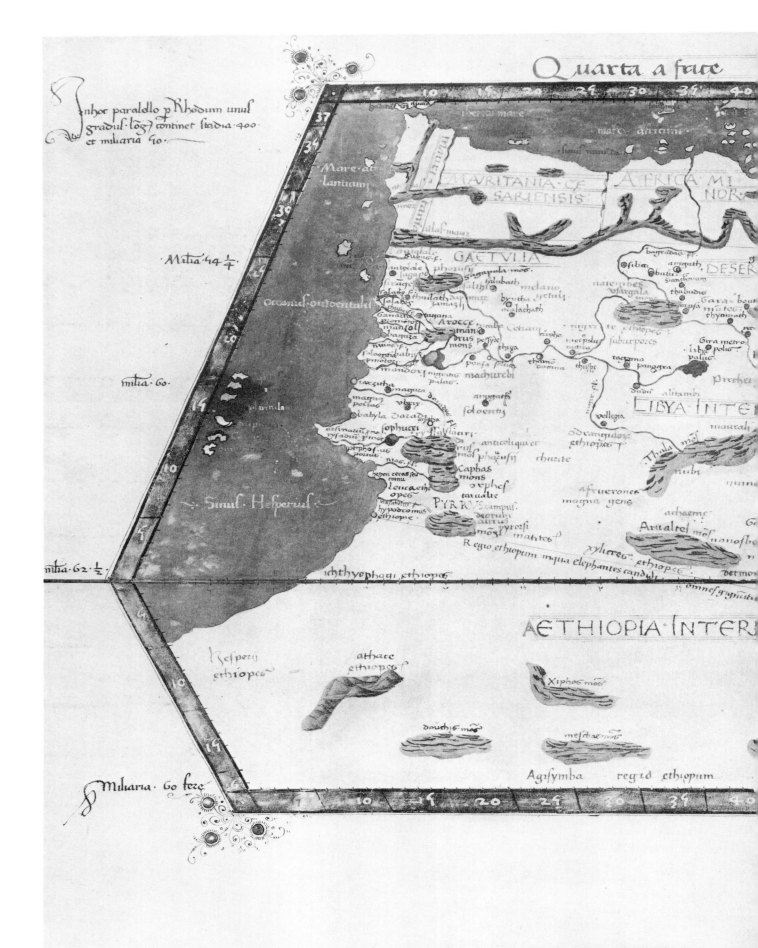

In hoc paralello p Rhodum unus
gradus log^9 continet stadia 400
et miliaria 90.

Mare at
lantinum

Mitia 44 ¼

Occeanuf occidentalif

mitia 60

Sinuf Hesperiuf

mitia 62 ½

Miliaria 60 fere

MAVRITANIA CE
SARIENSIS

AFRICA MI
NOR

GAETVLIA

DESER

Arocce

LIBYA INTE

Sophucei

PYRRVS campus

Regio ethiopum inqua elephantes candid

ichthyophagi ethiopes

AETHIOPIA INTER

Hespery
ethiopes

athace
ethiopes

Xiphos mos

douchis mos

meschae mos

Agisymba regio ethiopum

bula

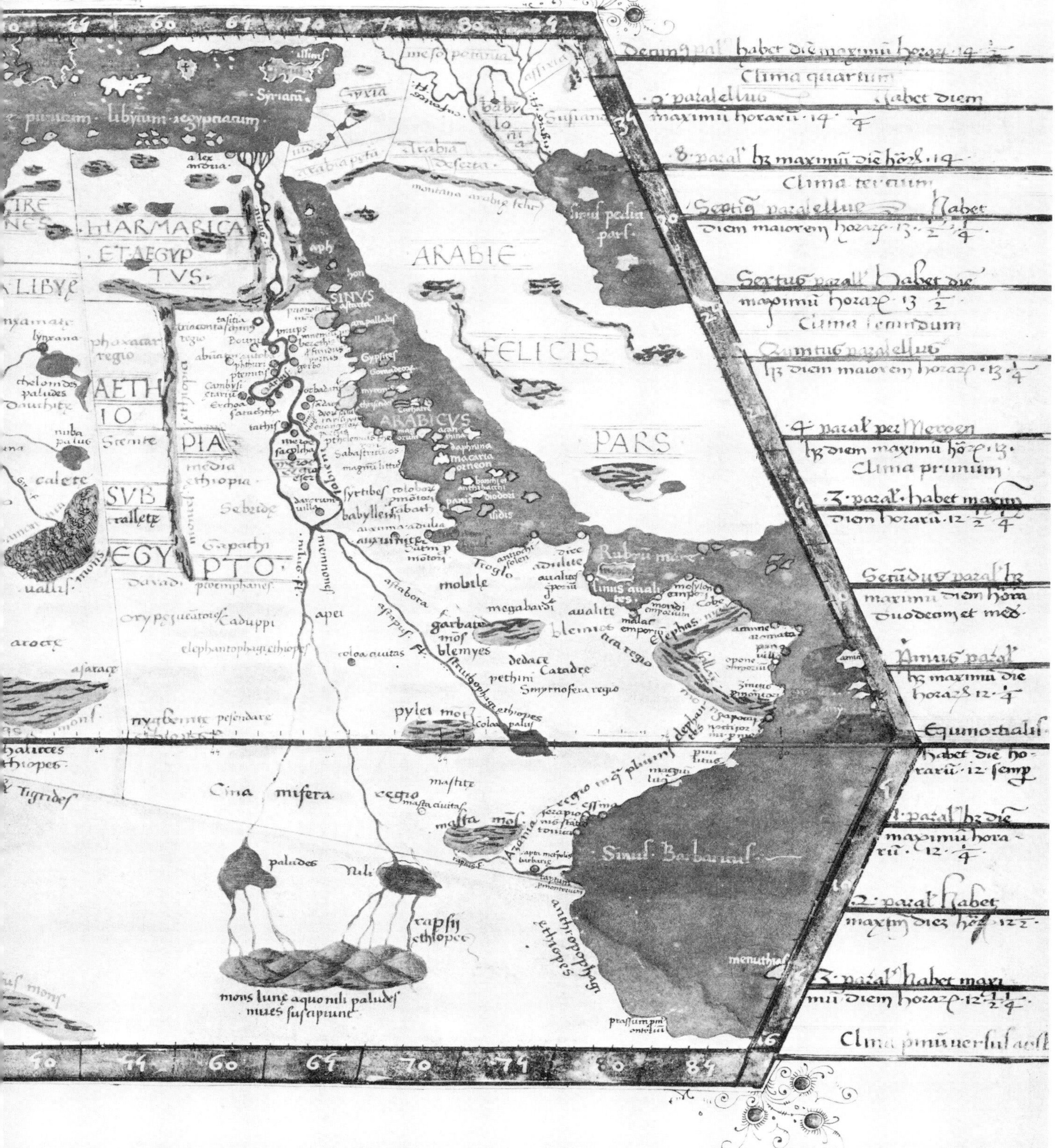

MARMARICA ET AEGYPTVS

LIBYE

AETHIOPIA

SVB trallele

EGYPTO

ARABIE FELICIS

PARS

ARABICVS

Rubrū mare

Sinus Barbaricus

mons lune aquo nili paludes mues fufcapiunt

Cira mifera regio

Syriani

Arabia Deferta

Clima quartum

Clima tertium

Clima fecundum

Clima primum

Equinoctialis

Asie maioris tabule duodecim. Quarū prima

PRima Asie tabula continet pontum & bithyniam & regionem que proprie Asia dicitur: ac Liciam & Gallaciam ac Pamphyliam & Cappadociam armeniam minorem & Ciliciam. Parallelus ipsius medius proportionem habet ad meridianū quam tria ad quatuor. Circūscribitur autem tabula ab ortu quidem armenia maiori & parte Syrie. Ab austro Carpathio liciano & Pamphylio mari angustys q Cilicie & sinu Issico. Ab occasu thracio bosphoro & propontide ac helesponto & egeo pelago ac Icario & Mirtoo. Ab arcto mari pontico.

Ponti et Bithynie ciuitates insignes.

Chalcedon maximam diem habet horar. 14 1/4 et distat ab Alexandria uersus occasum 1 1/4.

Nicomedia maximam diem habet horar. 14 1/6 & distat ab alexandria uersus occasum 1 1/6

Apamia maximam diem habet horar. 14 1/8 et distat ab alexandria uersus occasum hor̄ 1 1/6

Heraclea ponti maximam diem habet horarum 14 1/3 & distat ab alexandria uersus occasum horis 1 1/10

Nicea maximam diem habet horar. 14 1/8 & distat ab alexandriam uersus occasum horis 1 1/7

In Asia proprie dicta ciuitates insignes.

Cyzicus maximam diem habet horar. 14 1/12 et distat ab alexandria uersus occasum horis 1 1/3

Pergamus maximam diem habet horar. 14 1/2 1/4 1/8 et distat ab alexandria uersus occasum horis 1 1/4

Smyrna maximam diem habet horar. 14 1/2 1/4 et distat ab alexandria uersus occasum horis 1 1/8

Ephesus maximam diem habet horarum 14 2/3 et distat ab Alexandria uersus occasum horis 1 1/6

Miletus maximam diem habet horarum 14 1/2 1/12 et distat ab alexandria uersus occasum horis 1 1/6

Cnidos maximam diem habet horar. 14 1/2 et distat ab alexandria uersus occasum horis 1 1/4

Sardis maximam diem habet horarum 14 1/2 1/4 et distat ab alexandria uersus occasum horis 1 1/8

Magnesia maximam diem habet horarum 14 2/3 et distat ab alexandria uersus occasum horis 1 1/8

Apamia maximam diem habet horar. 14 1/2 1/4 et distat ab alexandria uersus occasum horis fere nihil.

Cibera maximam diem habet horar. 14 1/2 1/4 et distat ab alexandria nihil

Mithylene maximam diem habet horarum 14 1/2 1/4 et distat ab alexandria uersus occasum hor̄ 1 1/4

Rhodos maximam diem habet horar. 14 1/2 et distat ab alexandria uersus occasum hor̄ 1 1/8

Licie pattara maximam diem habet horar. 14 1/2 & sb eodem alexandrie meridiano sita est

Chios maximam diem habet horar. 14 1/2 1/4 & quid parum & distat ab alexandria ūsus ortū hor̄ 1 1/4

Andriaca maximam diem habet horar. 14 1/2 & quid parum & distatat ab alexandria ūsus ortū parū quid.

Mira maximam diem habet horarum 14 1/2 1/12 et distat ab alexādria uersus ortū hor̄ qd par.

Galatie Sinope maximā diem habet horar. horis 13 1/3 et distat ab alexandria uersus ortum horis 1/4

Amisos maximam diem habet horarum 14 1/4 & distat ab alexādria ūsus occās hor̄ 1 1/3

Angyra maximam diem ħt hor̄ 14 1/8 et distat ab alexandria uersus ortū horis 1 1/6

Germa maximam diem habet horar. 14 1/8 et distat ab alexandria uersus ortū par. qd

Pessenuus maximam diem habet horarum 14 1/12 et distat ab alexandria uersus ortū parum quid

pamfilie Sida maximā diē ħt hor̄ 14 1/2 & qd par. et distat ab alexādria ūsus ortū hor̄ 1 1/4

Perga max maximam diem ħt horar. 14 1/2 1/12 & distat ab alexandria uersus ortū hor̄ 1 1/8

Aspendus maximam diem ħt horar. 14 1/2 1/12 et distat ab alexandria q̄tum perga

Termissus maximā diem ħt hor̄ 14 1/2 1/8 et distat ab alexādria ūsus ortū q̄tū pga & aspēdus

Capadocie trapezos maximā diem habet horar. 14 1/4 et distat ab alexandria uersus ortum horis 1 2/3

Comana pontica maximā diem ħt horarum 14 1/12 et distat ab alexandria uersus ortū 1 1/3

Maza que et cesarea maximam diem habet horar. 14 1/2 1/3 et distat ab alexandria uersus ortum hor̄ 1 1/14

Comana cappadocie maximā diem ħt horar. 14 1/2 1/4 fere & distat ab alexandria uersus ortum hor̄ 1 1/2

Militina maximam diem habet horarum 14 1/2 1/3 et distat ab alexandria uersus ortū horis 1 1/2 1/4

Armenie mi. nicopolis. maximā diem ħt horar. 14 1/8 et distat ab alexandria uersus ortū horis 1 1/2 1/14

Satala maximam diem ħt horar. 14 1/8 et distat ab alexandria uersus ortū hor̄ 1 1/2 1/8

Cilicie Selinuns maximā diem habet horarum 14 1/2 1/12 et distat ab alexandria uersus ortum horis 1 1/4

Pompeiopolis maximam diem habet horarū 14 1/2 1/12 & distat ab alexandria uersus ortum 1 1/2 fere

Malos maximam diem habet horar. 14 1/2 1/14 et distat ab alexandria uersus ortum horis 1 1/2

Tarsos maximam diem ħt horar. 14 1/2 1/12 et distat ab alexandria uersus ortum horis 1 1/2

MARE · PONTICVM · SIVE

MYSIAE INFERIORIS PARS.

THRACIAE · PARS ·

Miliaria 43 fere

Propontidis

CHERSO NESI · PARS ·

Mitia · 47

ASIA

PROPRIE

MARE · EGEVM

PARS EVBOEAE

Miliaria 90

PON

TVS · ET

BITHY NIA

IONIA

CARIA

myrtoum mare

Carpathus

CRETAE INSVLAE

Eundam Asie tabula continet Sarmatiam ip=
sius. Parallelus ipius medius proportionem
habet ad meridianum quam septem ad duo=
deam. Terminatur aut tabula ab ortu Scy
thia intra smaum montem & parte Caspij maris. Ab
austro Albania & Iberia & dholdride & parte Eu
xini ponti. Ab occasu ammerio bosphoro & palude
meotide atq Sarmatia Europe. Ab areto terra inco
gnita Sarmatie asiatice ciuitate. insignes

Hermonasa maximam diem ht horar. 14 ½ ⅓ et distat
ab alexandria uersus ortum hor 1 ⅓ fere

Oenanthia maximam diem ht horar. 14 ½ ⅓ fere et
distat ab alexandria uersus ortum hor 1 ⅓ fere

Tyramba maximam diem ht horar. 16 ⅓ et distat ab
alexandria uersus ortum horis 1 ⅓ fere

Tanais maximam diem habet horar. 17 ⅙ et distat
ab alexandria uersus ortum hor 1 ⅓ ¹⁄₁₀

Naubaris maximam diem ht horar. 17 ¼ et distat ab
alexandria uersus ortum horis 1 ⅔

Vnus gr̃ad̃ lõg̃ in hor loco cõtinet stadia .227.
et milia .28 .½ .quasi. Est ergo longitudo
totius palelli p̃ thiler 40400 stadiorũ
que faciũt miliaria .4062 .½

oceani
sarmatiæ
pars

hyperborei sarmatæ

Montes

Basilia
seu regis sarm

SARMATIAE

Çacatĩ

Suardeni

Periexbidu
numerosũ
genus

Ripheu montes

Alani Alanii

Caesaris Aræ

Miliaria 32 ½

EVROPAE

Alan
nus
mons

P

tanais flu

cropol

nauaris

Jaxarnatæ

SARMATIA

Pfeffy

A

alopesa

R

pamardiu

marubiius flu

themeote

S

patarua

rombitus magnus flu

theophanius flu

tyramb

PALVDES MEOTIDES

azara

rombitus pang flu

azaraba

arichi

arabinf
tenia

treamba

auchia

Aticius fl

Miliaria 40 ½

Gorua

Pfebis fl

Conapsem

juruba

bosf palus

bospho

achilleum
tram
phana
genas

synda

quilla

sen cuu
promuneu
apasturgus scopelus

hcf horus

napeta

vardanus fr corax mõt

bataria achei

TAVRICA·
CHERSONE
SVS

sh

coros
oana

physa
chea

tge

lsyl
salter secunda

nika

barrace

thia

in terris thessiris suanolstij

corax flu

COLCHIN

PONTI · EVXINI · PARS

milia 43 fere

PARS

| 77 | 78 | 79 | 80 | 81 | 82 | 83 | 84 | 85 | 86 | 87 | 88 |

Vigesimusprim9 paralellus Ver Tyle
Differt ab equinoctiali horis·8· habet maxim̄
diem horarū· 20·

·· Hyperborei

Hyppophagi sarmate

modoq̄ yontes

Vicesimus paralellus
Differt ab equinoctiali horis·Λ·habet
maxim̄ diem horarū·19·

Ase

SCY

THI

AE·

P
A
R
S·

Nonusdecimus paralellus
Differt ab equinoctiali horis·6·habet
18 maxim̄ diem horarū·18·

trophagi

materi

Rha·flauius·

Octausdecimus paralellus
Differt abequinoctiali horis·4·½·
habet maxim̄ diem horaz·1Λ·½·

SIATICA·

mithridatis regio

Hyppici

melanchlani

montes Serinitis

Sapothreni

Septimusdecim9 paralellus·
Differt ab equinoctiali horis·4·habet
maxim̄ diem horarū·17·

Amaçones

Orinei

furani

Columne Alexandri

Sacani

vali

Serbi

vde

Rha fluuius·

Sextusdecim9 paralellus
Differt ab equinoctiali horis·4·½·
habet maxim̄ diem horaz·16·½·

Tusri

Zinchi

Porte sarmatice

Ordar

vdon·flu·

olonde

Camasus mons

aleus·flu·

isonde

Gerri

Soana·flu·

Quintusdecim9 paralellus
Differt ab equinoctiali horis·4·
habet maxim̄ diem hōz·16·

Clima septimum

Sanara Canalis

mon S

Iberie pars

portę albanię

ALBANIE PARS·

Hyrcani maris·ps·

| 76 | 77 | 78 | 79 | 80 | 81 | 82 | 83 | 84 | 85 | 86 | 87 | 88 |

Ercia Asie tabula continet Cholchidem ↄ
Iberiam Albaniam ↄ maiorem Armeniam
Parallelus ipius medius proportionem habet
ad meridianum quam undecim ad quinde
cim. Terminatur tabula ab ortu parte Caspij maris
ↄ medorum. Ab austro assyria ↄ Mesopotamia ab
occasu cappadocia ↄ parte Euxini ponti. Ab arcto
Sarmatia asiatica Colchidis insignes ciuitates.

Dioscurias maximam diem habet horarum 14 $\frac{1}{2}$ $\frac{1}{4}$ et
distat ab alexandria uersus ortū horis 1 $\frac{1}{2}$ $\frac{1}{3}$

Iberie. Artanissa maximam diem ht horar 14 $\frac{2}{3}$ ↄ
distat ab alexandria uersus ortū horis 1 $\frac{1}{30}$

Armattica maximam diem habet horar 14 $\frac{1}{2}$ fere et
distat ab alexandria uersus ortū hor 1

Albanie Getara maximam diem habet horar 14 $\frac{1}{2}$
ↄ distat ab alexandria uersus ortū hor 1 $\frac{1}{4}$

Albana maximam diem habet horarū 14 $\frac{2}{3}$ et distat
ab alexandria uersus ortū horis 1 $\frac{1}{3}$ $\frac{1}{10}$

Armenie maior⟩ Artaxata maximam diem habet
horarum 14 $\frac{1}{6}$ et distat ab alexandria uersus or
tum horis 1 $\frac{1}{6}$

Armauria maximā diem habet horar 14 $\frac{1}{4}$ fere et
distat ab alexandria uersus ortū hor 1 $\frac{1}{10}$

Thospia maximā diem habet horarū 14 $\frac{1}{2}$ $\frac{1}{4}$ $\frac{1}{8}$ et di
stat ab alexandria uersus ortum horis 1 fere

Accenita maximam diem habet horarum 14 $\frac{1}{2}$ $\frac{1}{3}$
$\frac{1}{12}$ ↄ distat ab alexandria uersus ortū hor 1 $\frac{1}{4}$

Miliaria 43 fere

mitia. 44 ⅓

mitia 47·

SARMATIA

rorax fla.

maurali

Caucasus

drosai ria.

lubui villa

COL

hipus f.

iagoda sarma

Cyaneus. fla.

CHIS.

mori lessica

aizama

bucchia

iobula

siganeam

Ercchia Regio

mgdia

ocsaeda

ALB

neapolis

IBERIA

maxen aera missa

Acapolis

detglana

fale

Chariustus f.

saua

nina

abliana

favan

mesthen

favan

phasis fl.

suun

Zabus

PONTI EVXINI

armac tia

zalissa

Ossica

lisoda

PARS

mosthini mons

Toscena

santura

Torgna

sala

afsica

baraza

Sathaphara

Lala

azam

sedala

cotomana

Girarena

pitia

glsim

facta

cozala

bacinna

ARME

cozala

AR

lychmita palus

NIE

togia

Paryardes

cizam

arsa valac

choua

mons

Sacapena regio

artesata

varu tha

tasena

Thalina

ano niousa

araxes flu

bochae

chorsa

Euphrates fl.

HI

elena

chasua

bizaca

Zorscara

NO

Attua

bresus

tinissa

Basilissena regio

Kobordena regio

daranussa

arsea

RI

zorura

S.

anti taurus mons

sana

ME

phausia

Zorua na

texra

rosana

phanda lia

utamum

anavium

mani tana

3i

cuchura

NIA.

MA

Astaunttis regio

Acilisena regio

P

Sophena

tarma

Colua

sogeon ca

Anhtaurus mons

sigua Anul mo

asin tsa

Anntaurus mos

babila

tovebia

A

babila

halif bufa

sagauana

azora

Cholina

Bayraudauena palu

R

lorreda

I

mepa

daudi ani

lidacres mons

S

Anzitena regio

tasia

ploza

Goidena regio

buana

O

felta

masara

thossua

thelba lana

Tigranocerta

colsa

anzeta

soita

belonna

Gordyei montes

3ie

Mardi

Thospitis regio

thospitis palus

Pheron suo

Gordyei

mons.

R.

tigris fl.

sadeua

colchis

Niphates

torra

Artasigarta

Taurus mons

Corica regio

arsamo sata

mesopo tamie

As

siouana

pars

30 81 82 83 84 86 87

PARS

AE

Soana fl.

thabilaca thilbis teleta
Gerrusfl:

thiauna

Gelda

Alba
me por
te

Taurusul mons

Cerus fl: alamus

boziata misia

I A chadacha

albanus f. alba
na

mamechia

Fla del
nsule

~ HYRCANI ·SIVE·CASPII·MARIS·PARS ~

re pal· p Pontum

Differt ab equinocti
ali hoies· 3· ½· habes
Diem maximu hoeaꝝ
9· 14· ½

Clima sextum

13· pal· p Byzantiu·

Differt ab equinor
tiali hoes· 3· ¼
hmo die minorem
hoeaꝝ· 14· ¼

MEDIAE · PARS ·

12· pal· p Hellel
pontu habens
maximu diem
hoeaꝝ· 14·

Cuma quintu

E PARS

12· paralellus·

39· Differt ab eq
noctiali hoes
½· ¼· hmo
maxmu die
14· ½· ¼·

0 81 82 83 84 85 86 87

Quarta Asie tabula continet cyprum & Syriam & Iudeam & utranq arabiam petreā & desertam ac Mesopotamiam & Babiloniam. Parallelus ipsīus medius proportionem habet ad meridianum quam quinq ad sex. Terminatur aūt tabula ab ortu Assyria & susiana & parte sinus psici a meridie parte ipsīus psici sinus & felici Arabia: & interiore parte sinus arabici. Ab occasu part egypti & egyptio Syriaco: & pamphylio mari: ac Issico sinu & cilicia. Ab arcto augustus cilicie & parte cappadocie & maioris armenie. **Cipri insule ciuitates**

Paphos maximā diem habet horar 14 $\frac{1}{3}$ $\frac{1}{12}$ et distat ab alexandria uersus ortū horis 1 $\frac{1}{4}$

Amathusa maximam diem habet horarum 14 $\frac{1}{3}$ $\frac{1}{12}$ fere & distat ab alexandria uersus ortum horis 1 $\frac{1}{3}$ $\frac{1}{14}$

Salamis maximam diem habet horar 14 $\frac{1}{2}$ fere et distat ab alexandria uersus ortum horis 1 $\frac{1}{3}$ $\frac{1}{8}$

Syrie Laodicia maximā diem hēt horar 14 $\frac{1}{3}$ $\frac{1}{12}$ et distat ab alexandria uersus ortum horis 1 $\frac{1}{2}$ $\frac{1}{14}$

Hyerapolis maximam diem habet horarum 14 $\frac{1}{2}$ et distat ab alexandria uersus ortū hōr 1 $\frac{1}{2}$ $\frac{1}{4}$

Antiochia maximam diem habet horarū 14 $\frac{1}{2}$ fere et distat ab alexandria uersus ortum horis 1 $\frac{1}{2}$ $\frac{1}{12}$

Apamia maximam diem habet horar 14 $\frac{1}{3}$ $\frac{1}{12}$ fere et distat ab alexandria uersus ortū horis 1 $\frac{2}{3}$

Palmira maximam diem habet horarum 14 $\frac{1}{3}$ fere & distat ab alexandria uersus ortum horis 1 $\frac{1}{2}$ $\frac{1}{4}$

Heliopolis maximam diem habet horarum 14 $\frac{1}{4}$ & qd & distat ab alexandria uersus ortum horis 1 $\frac{1}{2}$ $\frac{1}{14}$

Cesarea maximam diem habet horar 14 $\frac{1}{4}$ fere & distat ab alexandria uersus ortū horis 1 $\frac{1}{2}$

Damascus maximam diem habet horar 14 $\frac{1}{4}$ fere et distat ab alexandria uersus ortum horis 1 $\frac{1}{2}$ $\frac{1}{12}$

Palestine iudee ciui Cesarea stratonis maximam diem habet horarum 14 $\frac{1}{6}$ et distat ab alexandria uersus ortum horis 1 $\frac{1}{3}$ $\frac{1}{14}$

Ascalon maximam diem habet horar 14 $\frac{1}{8}$ & distat ab alexandria uersus ortum horis 1 $\frac{1}{3}$

Hierusalem maximam diem habet horarum 14 $\frac{1}{8}$ fere & distat ab alexandria uersus ortum horis 1 $\frac{1}{3}$ $\frac{1}{14}$

Arabia petrea Petra maximam diem habet horar 14 et distat ab alexandria uersus ortū horis 1 $\frac{1}{3}$ $\frac{1}{10}$

Medana maximam diem habet horar 14 et distat ab alexandria uersus ortum horis 1 $\frac{1}{2}$ $\frac{1}{14}$

Bostra maximam diem habet horar 14 $\frac{1}{12}$ et distat ab alexandria uersus ortū horis 1 $\frac{2}{3}$ fere

Mesopotamie Edessa maximam diem habet horarū 14 $\frac{1}{2}$ $\frac{1}{8}$ et distat ab alexandria uersus ortū horis 1 $\frac{1}{2}$ $\frac{1}{3}$

Nisibis maximam diem habet horarum 14 $\frac{1}{2}$ $\frac{1}{8}$ et distat ab alexandria uersus ortū horis 1

Nicephorium maximam diē hēt horar 13 $\frac{1}{3}$ $\frac{1}{12}$ et qd et distat ab alexandria uersus ortum horis 1 $\frac{1}{2}$ $\frac{1}{3}$

Labbana maximam diem habet horar 14 $\frac{1}{2}$ et quid & distat ab alexandria uersus ortū hōr 1 $\frac{1}{6}$

Seleucia maximam diem habet horarum 14 $\frac{1}{2}$ fere & distat ab alexandria uersus ortū hōr 1 $\frac{1}{2}$ $\frac{1}{4}$

Babilonie Babilon maximam diem habet horarum 14 $\frac{1}{3}$ $\frac{1}{12}$ et distat ab alexandria uersus ortū horis 1 $\frac{1}{4}$

Barseta maximam diem hēt horarū 14 $\frac{1}{3}$ et distat ab alexandria uersus ortum horis 1 $\frac{1}{4}$ fere

Orchoa maximam diem hēt horar 14 $\frac{1}{6}$ et qd et distat ab alexandria uersus ortū hōr 1 $\frac{1}{7}$

Teredon maximam diem habet horar 14 $\frac{1}{12}$ fere et distat ab alexandria uersus ortū horis 1 $\frac{1}{3}$

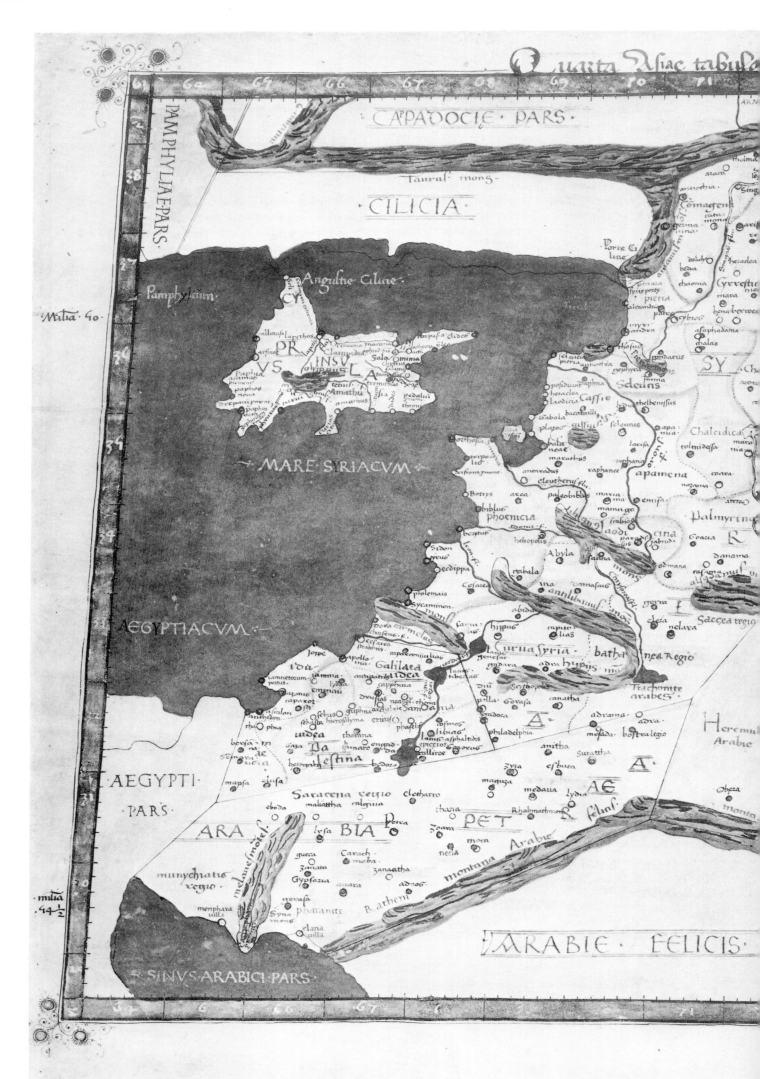

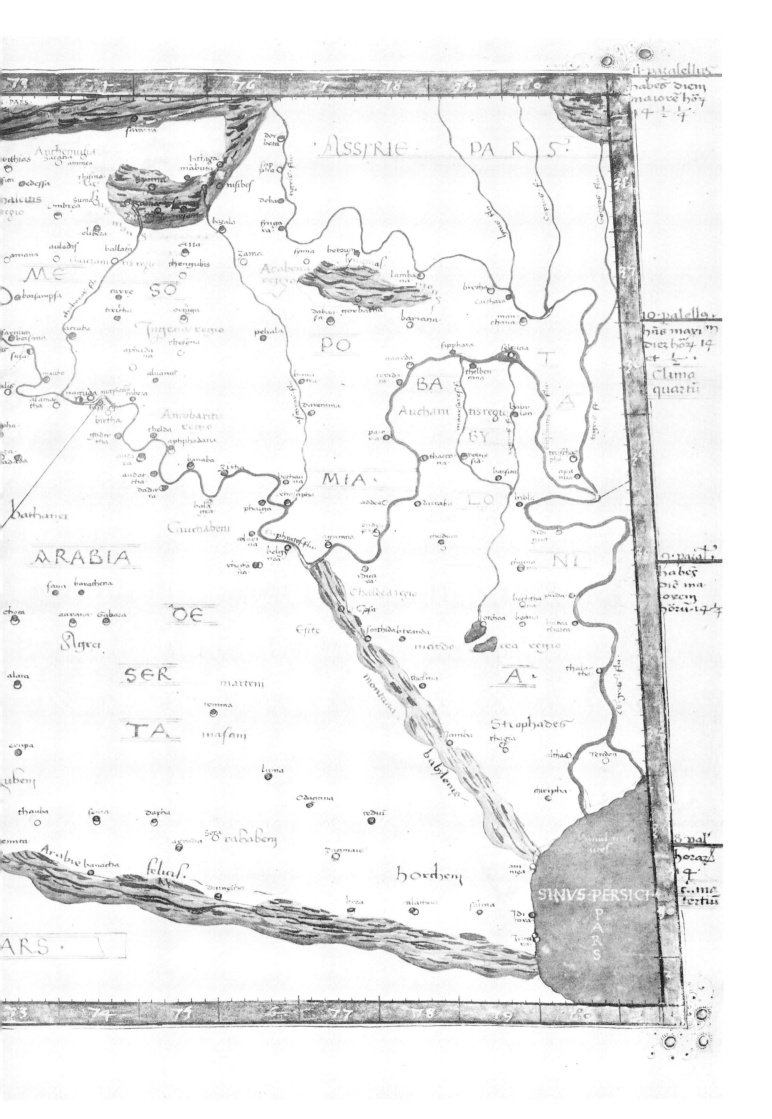

Vinta Asie tabula continet Assyriam Su-
sianam medos. persidem parthiam et carmaniam desertam; atq; hircaniam; Parallelus ipius medi'
proportionem habet ad meridianum quam
quatuor ad quinq. Terminatur autem tabula ab
ortu Aria. ab austro Carmania & sinu psico. ab
occasu Babylonia ac Mesopotamia & parte maioris armenie. ab arcto hircani maris parte. & regione hyrcanie

Assirie insignium ciuitatum

Ninos maximam diem habet horas 14 $\frac{2}{3}$ $\frac{1}{12}$ et distat
ab alexandria uersus ortum horis 1 $\frac{1}{4}$

Arabia maximam diem habet horarum 14 $\frac{1}{2}$ $\frac{1}{8}$ et distat ab alexandria uersus ortu horis 1 $\frac{1}{3}$

Ctesiphon maximam diem habet horas 14 $\frac{2}{3}$ $\frac{1}{12}$ fere
et distat ab alexandria uersus ortu horis 1 $\frac{1}{3}$

Suliane. eiusde noi$\bar{s}$ susa maximam diem habet
horarum 14 $\frac{2}{3}$ et distat ab alexandria uersus
ortum horis 1 $\frac{1}{2}$ $\frac{1}{12}$

Tariana maximam diem habet horarum 14 $\frac{1}{6}$ et
distat ab alexandria uersus ortum 1 $\frac{1}{2}$ fere

Medie Gyropolis maximam diem habet horarum

14 & distat ab alexandria uersus ortu horis 1 $\frac{2}{3}$

Achatana maximam diem habet horas 14 $\frac{2}{3}$ et distat
ab alexandria uersus ortu horis 1 $\frac{2}{3}$

Resacia maximam diem habet horarum 14 $\frac{1}{2}$ $\frac{1}{12}$ et distat
ab alexandria uersus ortum horis 1 $\frac{1}{2}$ $\frac{1}{3}$

Europus maximam diem habet horarum 14 $\frac{1}{2}$ $\frac{1}{12}$ et
distat ab alexandria uersus ortum horis 2 $\frac{1}{4}$

In perside Axima maximam diem habet horarum
14 $\frac{2}{3}$ et distat ab alexandria uersus ortum horis 2 $\frac{1}{19}$

Arassium maximam diem habet horarum 14 et distat
ab alexandria uersus ortu horis 2 fere

Parthie hecatompolis maximam diem habet horarum 14 $\frac{2}{3}$ et distat ab alexandria uersus ortum
horis 2 $\frac{1}{3}$ $\frac{1}{19}$

Ambrode maximam diem habet horarum 14 $\frac{1}{2}$ $\frac{1}{4}$ et
distat ab alexandria uersus ortum horis 2 $\frac{1}{3}$ fere

Artacana maximam diem habet horarum 14 $\frac{1}{4}$ $\frac{1}{8}$ et
distat ab alexandria uersus ortum horis 2 $\frac{1}{3}$ $\frac{1}{19}$

Hircanie insignium ciuitatum

Hircania ciuitas maximam diem habet horaru 14
$\frac{1}{2}$ $\frac{1}{3}$ $\frac{1}{12}$. Et distat ab alexandria uersus ortu h$\bar{r}$ 2 $\frac{1}{2}$

Amarusa maximu die habet hor 14 $\frac{1}{2}$ $\frac{1}{4}$ $\frac{1}{8}$. Et distat
ab alexandria uersus ortum horis 2 $\frac{1}{2}$ $\frac{1}{19}$. :—

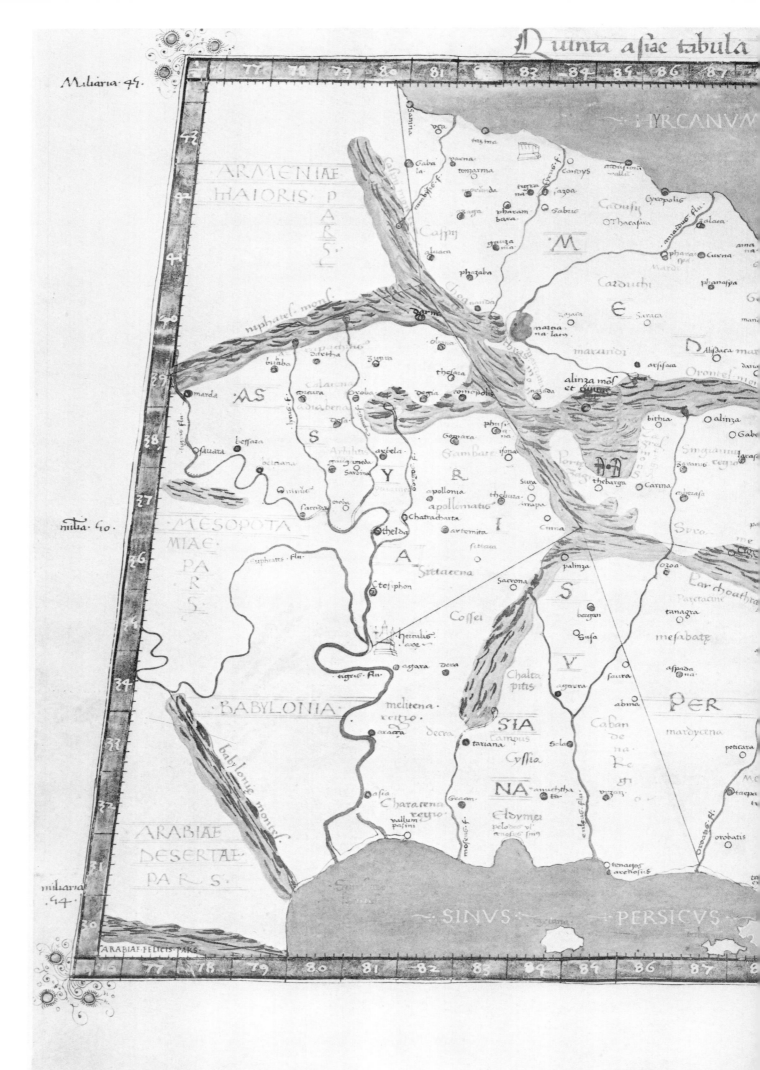

Miliaria·45·

HYRCANVM

ARMENIAE
MAIORIS· P
ARS·

Caspij

niphatel· mons·

AS
S
Y
R
I
A

MESOPOTA
MIAE·
PARS·

Euphrates· flu·

Sittacena

Ctesiphon

Cosser

BABYLONIA
regio·

babylonie· montes·

ARABIAE
DESERTAE
PARS·

miliaria
·44·

ARABIAE·FELICIS·PARS·

SINVS   PERSICVS

nutia·40·

Caduſij

Carduchi

maxandi

alinza· mons·
et· ciuitas·

Oronteſ· mons·

Singianiru
regio·

Carina

Susa

SIA
campus
Cyssia

NA

Elymei

Caban
de
na
Re
gi

PER

mardycena

Chalta
pitis

SVSO

tigris· flu·

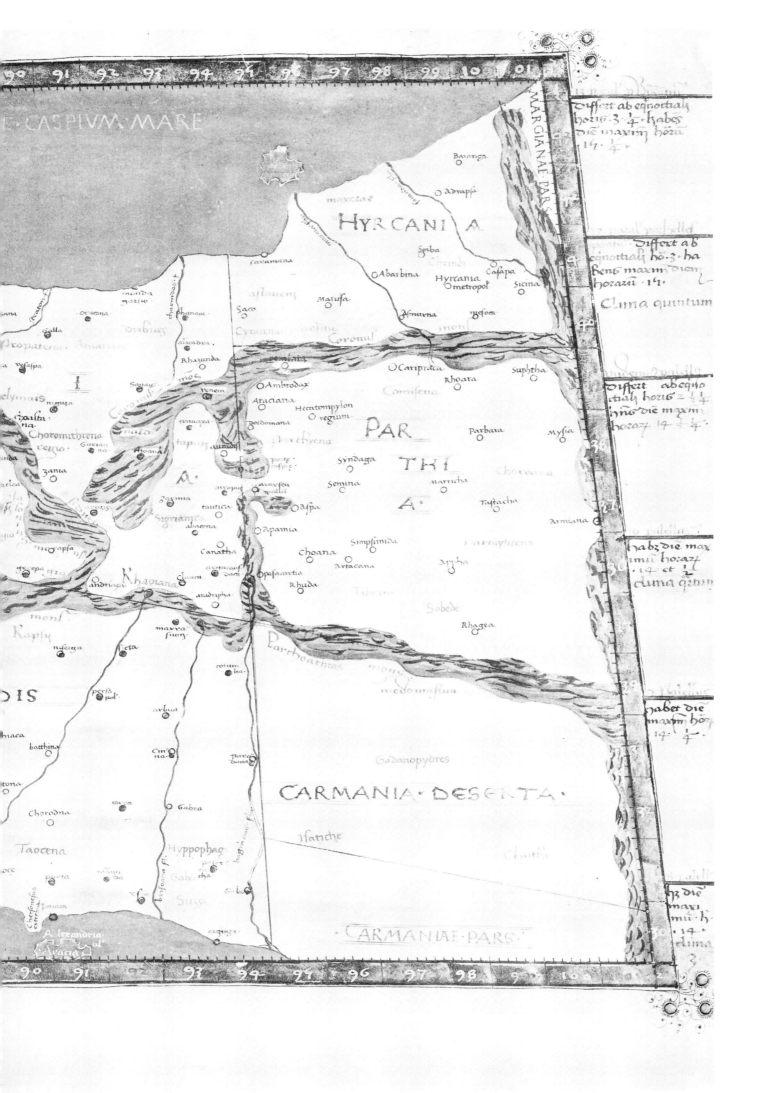

Sexta Asie tabula continet Arabiam felicem atq Carmaniam cum adiacentib insulis. Parallelus ipius medius proportionem habet ad meridianum quam undecim ad duodecim. Terminatur autem tabula ab ortu Gedrosia & indico pelago. Ab austro ipo indico pelago & mari rubro Ab occasu sinu arabico Ab arcto utraq arabia petrea et deserta ac sinu pico & Carmania deserta

Arabie felicis insignium civitatum.

Badeo maximam diem habet horar 13 1/4 et distat ab alexandria versus ortum horis 1 1/3

Hic aut sol bis in anno fit supra verticem distas ab utraq parte estivi tropici gradibus 30

Pudnos maximam diem habet horarum 13 et distat ab alexandria versus ortu hor 1 1/2 1/3

Hic q sol bis in anno fit supra verticem distans a tropico estivo ab utraq parte gradib 44 1/3

Muza maximam diem habet horar 12 1/2 1/3 et distat ab alexandria versus ortum T fere

Hic sol bis in anno fit supra verticem distans a tropico estuo ab utraq parte gradibus 44 1/3

Ocelis maximam diem habet horarum 14 1/3 1/4 fere & distat ab alexandria versus ortu hor T

Hic sol bis in anno fit supra verticem distans a tropico estuo ab utraq parte gradibus 61 1/4

Arabia emporium maximam diem habet horar 12 2/3 & distat ab alexandria versus ortum horis 1 1/3

Hic sol bis in ano fit supra verticem cum distat a tropico estuo ab utraq parte gradib 62 1/3

Cana maximam diem habet horarum 12 1/2 1/4 et distat ab alexandria versus ortum horis 1 1/2 1/12

Hic sol bis in anno fit supra verticem distans a tropico estuo ab utraq parte gradibus 4 1/3

Mara maximam diem habet horar 13 1/8 & distat ab alexandria versus ortum horis 1 1/14

Hic sol bis in anno fit supra verticem distans a tropico estuo ab utraq parte gradib 32

Merambis maximam diem habet horar 13 et distat ab alexandria versus ortum hor 1 1/20

Hic sol bis in anno fit supra verticem distant a tropico estuo ab utraq parte gradibus 44

Sabbada maximam diem habet horar 13 et distat ab alexandria versus ortum horis 1 1/8

Hic sol bis in anno fit supra verticem distans a tropico estuo ab utraq parte gradib 44

Saba maximam diem habet horarum 12 1/2 1/4 30 et distat ab alexandria versus ortum hor 1 1/14

Hic sol bis in anno fit supra verticem distans a tropico ab utraq parte gradibus 18

Saphar maximam diem habet horaru 12 1/2 1/4 1/8 et distat ab alexadria versus ortu hor 1 1/2 1/3 1/30

Hic sol bis in anno fit supra verticem distans a tropico estuo ab utraq parte gradib 62 1/2

Dioschori insula maximam diem habet horar 12 2/3 & distat ab alexandria versus ortu hor 1 2/3

Hic sol bis in ano fit supra verticem distans a tropico estuo ab utraq parte gradib 61 1/2

Sarapidis insula maximam diem ht horaru 13 1/12 fere et distat ab alexandria versus ortu hor 2 1/4 1/60

Hic sol bis in anno fit supra verticem distans a tropico estuo ab utraq parte gradibus 41

Insignium Carmanie civitatum :-

Carmania regia maxima diem ht horaru 13 1/2 1/4 1/8 & distat ab alexandria versus ortu hor 2 2/3

Armuza maximam diem habet horarum 13 1/2 fere et distat ab alexandria versus ortum hor 2 1/4 1/20

Hic q sol bis in anno fit supra verticem distans a tropico estuo ab utraq parte gradib T

Carmina insula maximam diem habet horar 13 1/8 fere et distat ab alexandria versus ortu hor 2 1/2 1/4 1/20

Hic q sol bis in anno fit supra verticem distans a tropico estuo ab utraq parte gradib 40 fere.

Vnus g̃ longitus̃ totinet
miliaria 44 fere.

In hor circulo tantei unus g̃
longits̃ totinet miliaria 47.

miliaria 60

miliaria 61 fere

SINVS ARABICVS

AETHIOPIE SVB EGYPTO PARS

MARE RVBRVM

ARAB

IA

FE

LIX

PERSIDIS PARS

Carmaniae deferte po

Cameloboſci vł Sozote

rhudiana

Dara

poſo
ſpania
aydem

Sagdana

rathrappis f.

Corius f.

C
A
R
M
A
N
I
A

Carmana
metro
pol.

Gedro
ſis
paro

S · PERSICVS

orathos

tylus
Aɪ
tos

andanis f.

ſuʒanuſ ſabiſ

rhodda

ichthyophaɡi

aſabo

ſpaſargade

alexā
dria
nmeta

Caradre
Throaſca
Cauthonite

ora

corpella
pmont

rhoɡana

ſamydaca

tophana

melum marie
appa eg̃. cryptus
Diane
portus

coſcu

Sinus paragonicus

thelono
pha
teſa

Reg

Simul ſachalites
in quo colymbiſis pinci
ſup utribus na
uigauit

Polla

Zenobu
inſula

motha

Carmn
inſul

ſapphar
metropol
moſcha ſyagro
portus pmont

MARE INDICVM

Octauus paral' per alexandriam
Differt ab equinoctiali horis · 2
habes maxim diem horaɜ · 14 ·

Clima tertium

Septimus paralellus
Differt ab equinoctiali 1 $\frac{1}{2}$ $\frac{1}{4}$
habes maiorem diem horu 13 $\frac{1}{2}$ $\frac{1}{4}$

Sextus pal' per Syenen
Differt ab equinoctiali hora 1 $\frac{1}{2}$
habes diem maxim die horaɜ
13 $\frac{1}{2}$ Clima ſecundum

Quintus paralellus
Differt ab equinoctiali hora
1 $\frac{1}{4}$ Habens maxim diem
horaɜ 13 $\frac{1}{4}$

4 paral' ulterion
Differt ab equi 9 hora 1
habens maxim die ho
ru tredecim
Primum dime

Tertius paralellus
Differt ab equnoc 9 ho
$\frac{1}{2}$ $\frac{1}{4}$ Habes maxi
diem horaru 12 $\frac{1}{2}$ $\frac{1}{4}$

S Eptima Asie tabula continet hyrcaniam Mar
gianam . Bactrianam . Sogdianos . Sacas &
Scythiam intra imaum montem . Parallelus
ipsius medius proportionem habet ad me
ridianum quam duo ad tria . Terminatur aũt aũt
tabula ab ortu scythia que intra imaum montem est
Ab austro monte imao qui supra indos est . qui intra
et extra Gangem sunt . Preterea paropanisadibus
& Aria ac parthia & parte hyrcani maris . ab occasu parte medorum & hyrcani pelagi & Sarmatia asiatica : ab arcto terra incognita . Insigniorum
hyrcanie ciuitatum eiusdem nominis cum regione
H yrcania ciuitas maximam diem habet horarum 14
$\frac{1}{2}$ $\frac{1}{3}$ $\frac{1}{12}$ & distat ab alexãdria uẽsus ortũ hõr 2 $\frac{1}{2}$ $\frac{1}{14}$
A marusa maximam diem habet horar⁊ 14 $\frac{1}{2}$ $\frac{1}{4}$ $\frac{1}{8}$ et
distat ab alexandria uersus ortum hõr 2 $\frac{1}{2}$ $\frac{1}{14}$

Margiane ciuitatum insignium :—

A ntiochia maximam diem habet horar⁊ 14 fere et di-
stat ab alexandria uersus ortum hõr 1 $\frac{1}{14}$
N igea maximam diem habet horar⁊ 14 $\frac{1}{9}$ et distat ab
alexandria uersus ortũ hõr 3
Bactriane Characharta maximã diẽ hт hõr 14 $\frac{1}{3}$ $\frac{1}{12}$
et distat ab alexandria uersus ortum hõr 3 $\frac{1}{3}$
Z arispa maximam diem hт hõr 14 $\frac{1}{4}$ $\frac{1}{8}$ et distat
ab alexandria uersus ortum hõr 3 $\frac{2}{3}$
B actra maximam diem hт horarum 14 & distat ab
Alexandria uersus ortum hõr 3 $\frac{1}{3}$ $\frac{1}{14}$
M aracanda maximam diem habet horarũ 14 $\frac{1}{2}$ $\frac{1}{3}$
& distat ab alexandria uersus ortũ hõr 3 $\frac{1}{3}$ fere
Sogdiane . Oxiana maximam diem habet hora-
rum 14 $\frac{1}{2}$ fere et distat ab alexandria uersus
ortum horis 3 $\frac{1}{2}$ $\frac{1}{3}$ fere .
M aruca maximam diem habet horarum $\frac{1}{3}$ fere et di-
stat ab alexandria uersus ortum horis 3 $\frac{1}{2}$ $\frac{1}{3}$ fere
D repsa maximam diem habet horarũ 14 $\frac{1}{2}$ & distat
ab alexandria uersus ortũ hõr 4
V ltima Alexandria maximã diem hт horar⁊ 14 & distat
ab alexandria uersus ortum hõr 4 $\frac{1}{8}$
Scithie que intra imaum est montem ciuit[illegible]
A spabota maximam diem hт horar⁊ 14 $\frac{1}{2}$ $\frac{1}{8}$ et distat ab alexandria uẽsus ortũ hõr 2 $\frac{1}{2}$ $\frac{1}{3}$ fere
D anaba maximam diem hт horar⁊ 14 $\frac{1}{2}$ et distat
ab alexandria uersus ortum horis 2 $\frac{1}{2}$ $\frac{1}{3}$ $\frac{1}{14}$

Vnus gradus longitud in har
poli eleuatione continet mili
aria 28½ fere.
Est ergo spaniu longitudinil huis
tabule in hoc loco miliariū 1842.

mitia 32 ½

Differentia ptis superioris
ad inferiorem tabule
. 1408. miliariū

mitia 40 ½

miliaria 44 ¾

Hyperborei montes

alamforthe   Suobem

Rhoboſci   Schani   maſſei   Alan

asmani   nologeni   Zacate   Sa

SARMA
TIAE scha ſi   Samnitr   Zacate   Ja
ASIA
TICE   Pamazdj

P   Tybiare   Jabion
A   Canodipſac   SCYTHIA · IN
R   regio   Rhymmici montes   machetegi   Jaſie
S   norosſuſ mon
        Coraxi   aſpifi
                              Oxiaſi   norosbeſ   noroſſi   Sachag ſcythe
        Erymmi   rhymmus flu   aorſi   Jaxarte   mag
                              aſtore   Daix flu
                                    ariace   Jaxartis · flu
ceram   iſtauſ f
caucaſus   edon f   Namaſte   SOC
ALBANIAE PARS   Heladeſ   trybacti
                          inſule   oxiſsu   orea
                                                                              lauu
~MARE · HYRCANVM · SIVE · CASPIVM~   alpanoi   alicodra   charracharta
                                              bolgar   chomari   Salatere
                                                    M   azatha   chomara   BAC
                                          AR   argadina aſonium   nigza   TRIA   aſtaraua
                              HYRCANIA   A   rhea   anthochia   euuſim Acinaces
                                          NA parni   Guri margiana   regia
                                          parni   anam   tapuri   tambyr
MEDIAE   ci tapuri   maracana Da
PARS   ſtoboia
ASSY   Sariphi   montes   pa
RIAE   PARTHIAE   ARIE PARS   PA
PARS   PARS   NIS
ſuſiane
pars   perſidis pars

Vnus gradus longitudinis in hoc palello
rhodienſi continet mitia. 40. Est ergo
spaniu totius tabule in har pte 3240 miliariū

129　　130　　135　　140　　145

SCYTHIE EXTRA IMAVM MONTEM PARS

Differt ab equinoctiali horis 8 habens diem maximū horarū 20·

Differt ab equinoctiali horis 7 habens maximū diem horarū ·19·

Differt ab equinoctiali horis 6 habet maximū diem horarū ·18·

Differt ab equinoctiali horis 4½ habet maximū diem horarū ·17·½·

Differt ab equinoctiali horis 4 habens maximū diem horarū ·17·

Differt ab equinoctiali horis 4·½ habet maximū diem horarū ·16·½·

Differt ab equinoctiali horis 4 habens maximū diem horarū ·16·
Clima septimum·

Differt ab equinoctiali horis 3·¼ habet maximū diem horarū 14½· Clima sextum

Differt ab equinoctiali horis ·½ habet maximū diem horarū ·14·¼·

habens maximū diem horarū ·14·
clima quintum·

habens maximū diem horarū 14·¼·

habens diem maximū horarū 14·½
Clima·4·

Scymbi

Sydri montes

Torrfacis

IMAVM MONTEM·

Labium montes

Auxatij montes

ascatace

Alaxamūs mons

SACARVM·

REGIO

GI

massagetæ

oppidū siue pecsidiū eorū qui apud seras profosluntur

Toornæ

Imaus mons

Sacarū regio nomadū est oppida ēm non habent Nemora aut et speluncas habitant·

Bylte

Imaus mons

INDI　　AE· PARS

129　　130　　　　140　　145

Ctaua Asie tabula continet Scytham que
citra smaum est & Seras. Parallelus ipsius,
medius proportionem habet ad meridianum
quam duo ad tria. Circuscribitur autem tabula ab arcto & oriente terra incognita. Ab austro sinis
& parte indie. Ab occasu Sacis & Scythia que intra
montem smaum est

Scithie intra smaum montem ciuitates

Issidon scythia maximam diem habet horarum 16 et distat
ab alexandria uersus ortum horis 6.

Auzacia maximam diem habet horar 16 $\frac{1}{4}$ fere et distat
ab alexandria uersus ortu hor 9 $\frac{1}{3}$ $\frac{1}{10}$

Que apud seras sunt ciuitates insignres

Issidon serica maximam diem habet horar 14 $\frac{1}{2}$ et distat
ab alexandria uersus ortum horis 6 $\frac{1}{2}$ $\frac{1}{3}$ fere

Drosica maximam diem habet horar 14 $\frac{1}{6}$ et distat ab alexandria uersus ortu hor 7 $\frac{1}{6}$ fere

Ottorocora maximam diem habet horarum 14 $\frac{2}{3}$ fere
et distat ab alexandria uersus ortum horis 7 $\frac{1}{2}$
$\frac{1}{3}$ aut 8 integris

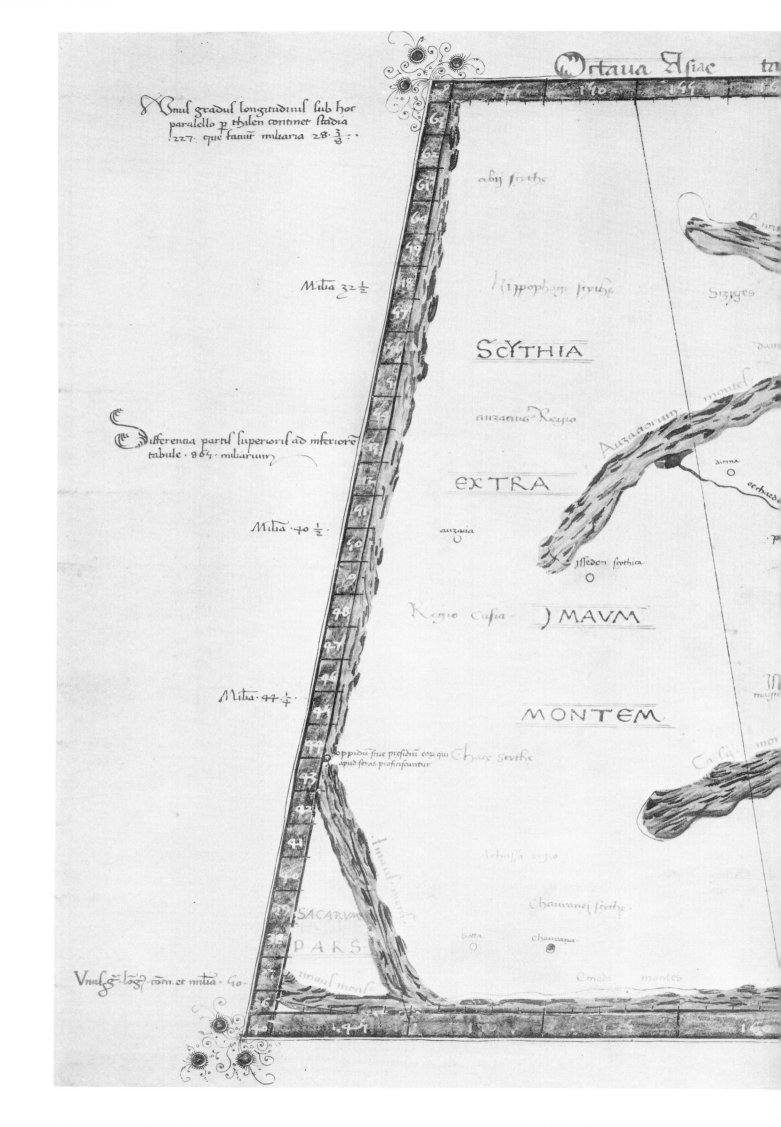

Unus gradus longitudinis sub hoc
paralello p̃ thilen continet stadia
227 que faciunt miliaria 28 3/8

Milia 32 1/2

Differentia partis superioris ad inferiore
tabule 864 miliarium

Milia 40 1/2

Milia 44 1/4

oppidum siue presidii eor qui
apud seras proficiscuntur

Unus g̃ log̃ cõtm et milia 40

aborii scithe

hippophagi scithe

SCYTHIA

auzacius Regio

EXTRA

auzacia

Issedon scythia

Regio Cassia)MAVM

MONTEM

Chate scithe

Achassa regio

Chauranei scithe

Scitta   Chaurana

Cmedi   montes

SACARVM

PARS

la ·

Antropophagi

ERICA

Garine

Annibi

rhabbana

R E

Asmirea Regio

G

oechardes.fl.

asmirea

Asmirei montes

throana

throana

1

apurare Lacurul mons

cafpana

drosacha

liana

Bate

abragana

thogara

daxata

battifug flauiuß

battifus.fl.

ofana

battifus.fl.

Seca metropolis

folana

Ottorocorra mon

Ottororra

ottorocore

Sinæ montes

Viresimusprimus paralellus p Thyle
magis appinquus arcto. differt ab equinoctiali horis 8·
habens diem maxim horaru 20.—

Viresimus paralellus
Differt ab equinoctiali horis 7. Habes maxim diem
horaru 19.

Nonusdecimus paralellus
Differt ab equinoctiali horis 6. Habens diem
maxim horaru ·18·

Octauusdecimus paralellus
Differt ab equinoctiali horis 4 ½ habens
diem maxim horaru ·17· ½·

Septimusdecimus paralellus
Differt ab equinoctiali horis 4 habens
diem maxim horaru ·17·

Sextusdecimus paralellus
Differt ab equinoctiali horis 4 ½· habens
maxim diem horaru ·16· ½·

Quintusdecimus palella p Boryfthenem
Differt ab equinoctiali horis 4 huo
maxim diem horaru ·16·

Clima·septimum

Quartusdecimus p Pontu
Differt ab equinoctiali horis 3 ½
habens maxim diem horaru 14 ½

Clima sextum

Tertiusdecima palella p Byzantiu
Differt ab equinoctiali horis hö 3 ¼
habens maxim diem höru ·14· ¼

12 paralellus p Hellespontu
Differt ab equinoctiali hö 3·
huo maxim die horaru ·14·

Clima quintum

Undecimus paralellus
Differt ab equinoctiali horis
2 ½ ¼· habens maxim
diem horaru 14 ½ ¼·

10 palella p Rodu
Differt ab equinoctiali
horis 2 ½· huo diem
maxim horaru 14 ½·

Clima Quartum

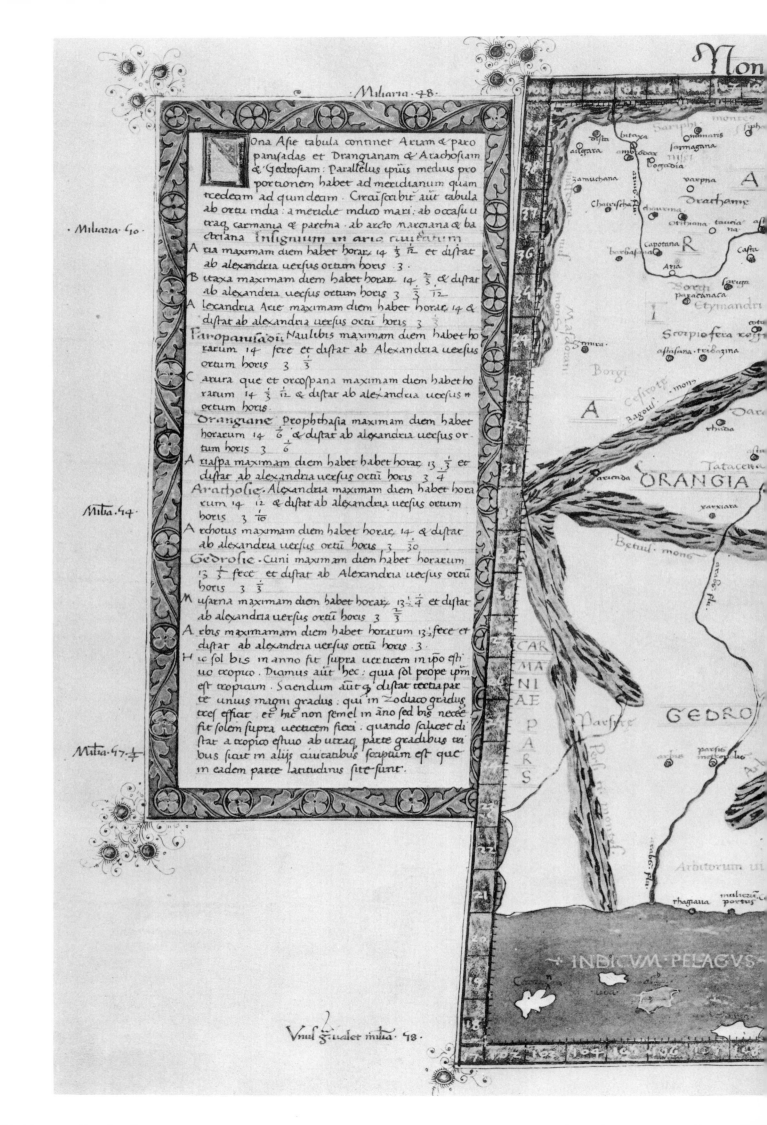

Miliaria 48

Miliaria 40

Nona Asie tabula continet Ariam & paro
panisadas et Drangianam & Arachosiam
& Gedrosiam: Parallelus ipsius medius pro
portionem habet ad meridianum quam
tredecim ad quindecim. Circūscribitur aūt tabula
ab ortu india: a meridie indico mari: ab occasu u
traq carmania & parthia. ab arcto margiana & ba
ctriana Insignium in ario ciuitatum

A ria maximam diem habet horarum 14 $\frac{1}{3}$ $\frac{1}{12}$ et distat
ab alexandria uersus ortum horis 3.

B itaxa maximam diem habet horarum 14 $\frac{2}{3}$ & distat
ab alexandria uersus ortum horis 3 $\frac{1}{3}$ $\frac{1}{12}$

A lexandria Arie maximam diem habet horarum 14 &
distat ab alexandria uersus ortū horis 3 $\frac{1}{3}$

Paropanisadori Naulibis maximam diem habet ho
rarum 14 fere et distat ab Alexandria uersus
ortum horis 3 $\frac{1}{3}$

C arura que et orcospana maximam diem habet ho
rarum 14 $\frac{1}{3}$ $\frac{1}{12}$ & distat ab alexandria uersus
ortum horis.

Drangiane Prophthasia maximam diem habet
horarum 14 $\frac{1}{6}$ & distat ab alexandria uersus or
tum horis 3 $\frac{1}{6}$

A riaspa maximam diem habet habet horarum 13 $\frac{1}{3}$ et
distat ab alexandria uersus ortū horis 3 $\frac{1}{4}$

Milia 44

Arachosie. Alexandria maximam diem habet hora
rum 14 $\frac{1}{12}$ & distat ab alexandria uersus ortum
horis 3 $\frac{1}{10}$

A rchotus maximam diem habet horarum 14 & distat
ab alexandria uersus ortū horis 3 $\frac{1}{30}$

Gedrosie. Cuni maximam diem habet horarum
13 $\frac{1}{3}$ fere et distat ab Alexandria uersus ortū
horis 3 $\frac{1}{3}$

M usarna maximam diem habet horarum 13 $\frac{1}{2}$ $\frac{1}{4}$ et distat
ab alexandria uersus ortū horis 3 $\frac{2}{3}$

A rbis maximamam diem habet horarum 13 $\frac{1}{2}$ fere et
distat ab alexandria uersus ortū horis 3.

H ic sol bis in anno fit supra uerticem in ipso esti
uo tropico. Dicimus aūt hec: quia sol prope ipm̄
est tropicum. Sciendum aūt q distat tertia par
te unius magni gradus: qui in Zodiaco gradus
tres efficit et hic non semel in āno sed bis necēe
fit solem supra uerticem fieri: quando scilicet di
stat a tropico estiuo ab utraq parte gradibus tri
bus sicut in aliis ciuitatibus scriptum est que
in eadem parte latitudinis site sunt.

Milia 47 $\frac{1}{4}$

Vnus g. ualet milia 48.

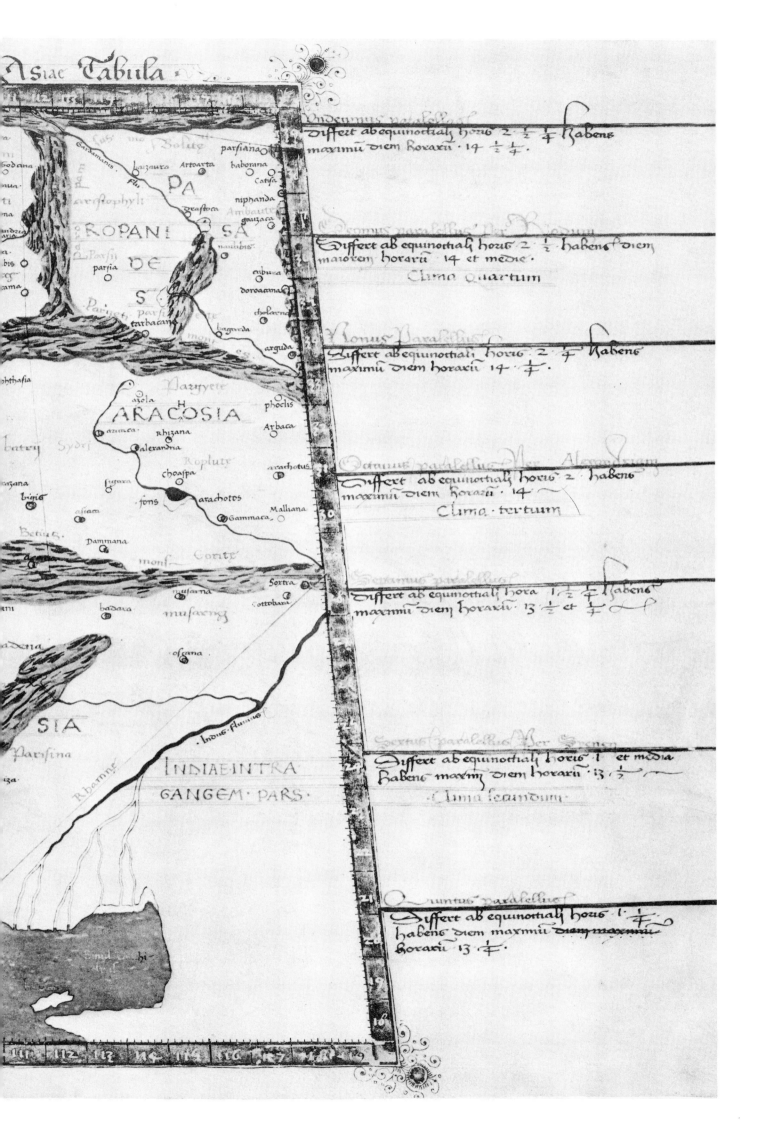

Asiae Tabula

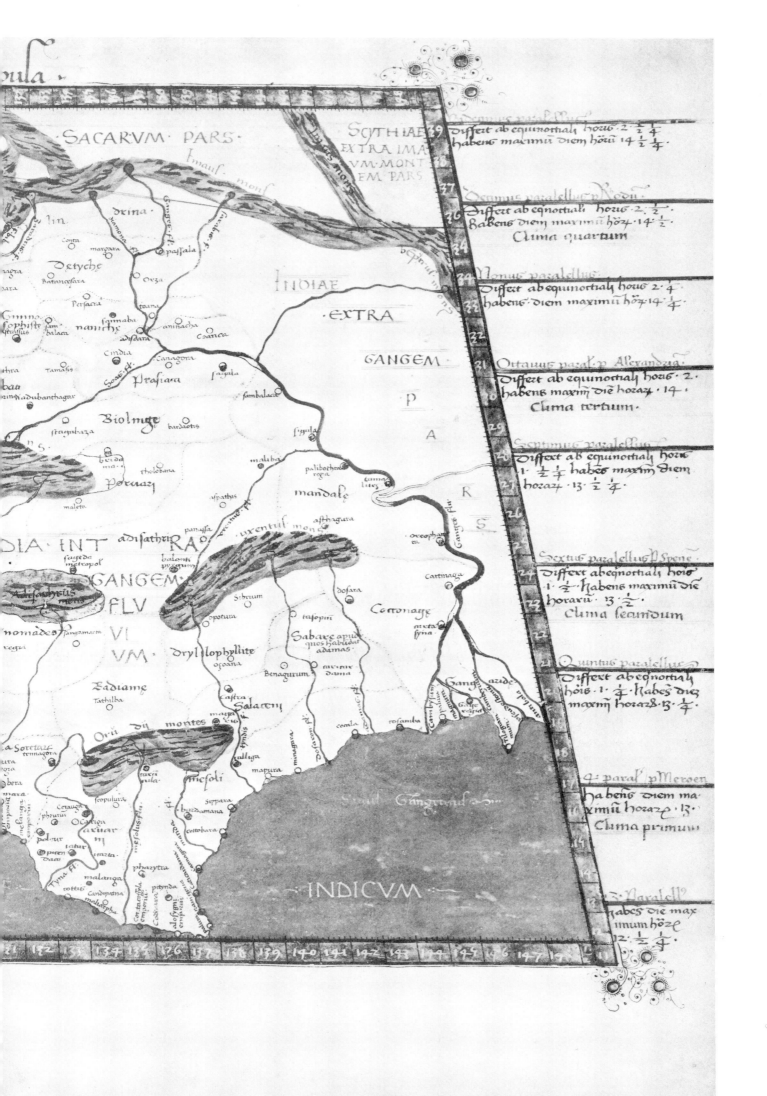

Decima Asie tabula continet indiam intra Gangem fluuium cum insulis sibi adiacentibus. Parallelus ipsius medius proportionem habet ad meridianū quam undecim ad duodecim. Circūscribitur autem tabula ab ortu India extra Gangem. Ab austro parte gangetica fluuij & indici pelagi. ab occasu Gedrosia & arachosia & paropanisadis: ab arcto parte Imai montis que sub Sogdianis & Sacis est

Indie intra Gangem ciuitates insignes

Symilla maximam diem habet horarū 12 $\frac{1}{2}$ $\frac{1}{3}$ $\frac{1}{12}$ fere et distat ab alexandria uersus ortū hor 3 $\frac{1}{3}$

Hic sol bis in anno fit supra uerticē quando distat a tropico estiuo ab utraq parte gradib' 41 $\frac{1}{3}$

Muzoris maximam diem ht horarū 12 $\frac{1}{2}$ $\frac{1}{3}$ et distat ab alexandria uersus ortū hor 3 $\frac{1}{3}$

Hic sol bis in anno fit supra uerticem quando distat a tropico estiuo ab utraq parte gradibus 44 $\frac{1}{2}$

Chaberis maximā diem ht horarū 12 $\frac{1}{2}$ $\frac{1}{3}$ $\frac{1}{12}$ aut 13 fere & distat ab alexandria ūsus ortū hor 4 $\frac{1}{12}$

Hic sol bis in anno fit supra uerticem cum distat a tropico estiuo ab utraq parte gdib' 47 $\frac{1}{2}$ $\frac{1}{12}$

Palura maximam diem ht horarū 12 $\frac{2}{3}$ $\frac{1}{40}$ et distat ab alexandria uersus ortum horis 4 $\frac{1}{9}$

Hic sol bis in anno fit supra uerticem cum distat a tropico estiuo ab utraq parte gradib' 7

Caspira maximam diem ht horarū 14 $\frac{1}{12}$ fere et distat ab alexandria uersus ortū hor 4 $\frac{1}{2}$ fere

Bucephala maximam diem ht horarū 11 $\frac{1}{4}$ fere et distat ab alexandria uersus ortū hor 4 $\frac{1}{3}$ $\frac{1}{30}$

Palimbothra maximam diem ht horarū 13 $\frac{1}{2}$ $\frac{1}{4}$ fere & distat ab alexandria uersus ortū hor 4 $\frac{1}{2}$ $\frac{1}{30}$

Patala maximam diem habet horarū 13 $\frac{1}{2}$ fere et distat ab alexandria uersus ortū horis 3 $\frac{1}{2}$

Hic sol bis in anno fit supra uerticem distās a tropico estiuo ab utraq parte gradib' 23 $\frac{1}{2}$ $\frac{1}{3}$

Barbara maximam diem habet horarū 13 $\frac{1}{3}$ $\frac{1}{12}$ et distat ab Alexandria uersus ortū horis 3 $\frac{1}{2}$ $\frac{1}{20}$

Hic sol bis in anno fit supra uerticem distans a tropico estiuo ab utraq parte gradib' 23 $\frac{1}{2}$ $\frac{1}{3}$

Barizaga maximam diem ht horarū $\frac{1}{3}$ $\frac{1}{12}$ et distat ab alexandria uersus ortū hor 3 $\frac{1}{20}$

Hic sol bis in anno fit supra uerticē distans a tropico estiuo ab utraq parte gradib' 41 $\frac{2}{3}$

Ozena maximam diem habet horarum 13 $\frac{1}{4}$ fere & distat ab alexandria uersus ortum horis 4

Hic sol bis in anno fit supra uerticem cum distat a tropico estiuo ab utraq parte gradib' 31

Bethana maximam diem habet horarū 13 $\frac{1}{8}$ fere et distat ab alexādria uersus ortū hor 3 $\frac{1}{3}$ fere

Hic sol bis in anno fit supra uerticem distans a tropico estiuo ab utraq parte gradib' 38 $\frac{1}{4}$

Hippotura maximam diem habet horarū 13 $\frac{1}{2}$ & distat ab alexandria uersus ortum horis 4

Hic sol bis in anno fit supra uerticem distans a tropico estiuo ab utraq parte gradibus 34 $\frac{1}{3}$

Carura maximam diem habet horarū 13 et distat ab alexandria uersus ortum horis 3 $\frac{1}{2}$ $\frac{1}{3}$

Hic sol bis in anno fit supra uerticem distans a tropico estiuo ab utraq parte gradibus 44 $\frac{1}{3}$

Modura maximam diem habet horarū 13 & distat ab alexandria uersus ortū horis 4 $\frac{1}{3}$

Hic sol bis in anno fit supra uerticem distās a tropico estiuo ab utraq parte gradibus gradibus 44

Orthura maximam diem habet horarū 13 & distat ab alexandria uersus ortum horis 4 $\frac{2}{3}$

Hic sol bis in anno fit supra uerticem distās a tropico estiuo ab utraq pte gdib' 46

Pityndra maximā diem habet horarum 12 $\frac{1}{2}$ $\frac{1}{4}$ & distat ab alexandria uersus ortum horis 4

Hic q sol bis in anno fit supra uerticē cum distat a tropico estiuo ab utraq parte gradibus. 60.

Ndecima Asie tabula continet indiam
extra Gangem & Sinas. Parallelus ipius
medius fere eandem habet proportionem
quam meridianus. Circuscribitur aut
tabula ab ortu terra incognita. Ab austro parte
Gangetici sinus & pelago indico & sinu magno &
terra & incognita. Ab occasu india intra Gange
Ab arcto parte Scythie atq Seris.

Indie extra gem fluuiu ciuit) insignes

Tacola maximam diem ht horaru 13 equinochalium
14 $\frac{1}{4}$ & distat ab alexandria uersus ortu hor. 6. $\frac{2}{3}$

Hic sol bis in anno fit supra uerticem distans a tropico
estiuo ab utraq parte gradib' 79 $\frac{1}{2}$

Zame maximam diem habet horaru 14 $\frac{1}{4}$ et distat
ab alexandria uersus ortu horis 7 $\frac{2}{3}$

Hic sol bis in anno fit supra uerticem distans a tropi
co estiuo ab utraq parte gradibus 78 $\frac{1}{2}$ $\frac{1}{4}$

Tosala maximam diem ht horarum 13 $\frac{1}{2}$ et distat
ab alexandria uersus ortu horis 6.

Hic sol semel in anno fit supra uerticem in tropi
co ipo estiuo

Soagina maximam diem ht horaru 13 $\frac{1}{4}$ et distat
ab alexandria uersus ortu horis 6 $\frac{1}{8}$

Hic sol bis in anno fit supra uertice distans a tropi
co estiuo ab utraq parte gradibus 19

Trilingum maximam diem habet horaru 13 et distat
ab alexandria uersus ortum horis 6 $\frac{1}{4}$.

Hic sol bis in anno fit supra uerticem distans a tro
pico estiuo ab utraq parte gradib' 39

Marcura maximam diem habet horariu 12 $\frac{1}{2}$ $\frac{1}{4}$
et distat ab alexandria uersus ortum hor 7 $\frac{1}{2}$ fere

Sinaru Aspithra maximam diem habet hor 13 $\frac{1}{8}$
& distat ab alexandria uersus ortu hor 7 $\frac{2}{3}$

Hic q sol bis in anno fit supra uerticem distans a
tropico estiuo ab utraq parte gradib' 44 $\frac{1}{2}$ $\frac{1}{4}$

Tine metropolis maxima diem habet horariu 13 $\frac{1}{8}$ et
distant ab alexandria uersus ortu horis 7 $\frac{2}{3}$

Hic q sol bis in anno fit supra uerticem distans a
tropico estiuo ab utraq parte gradib' 43 $\frac{1}{8}$

Cattigara statio maximam diem habent horarum
12 $\frac{1}{2}$ & distant ab alexandria uersus ortum
7 $\frac{1}{2}$ $\frac{1}{4}$ polo australi supra terram elato

Hic q sol bis in anno fit supra uerticem distans a
tropico estiuo ab utraq parte gradib' 68 $\frac{1}{2}$ $\frac{1}{4}$

Delta Abadei insula: ubi metropolis none argen
tea maximam diem ht hor 12 $\frac{1}{2}$ similiter au
strali polo supra terram elato & distant ab ale
xandria uersus ortum hor 7 $\frac{2}{3}$

Hic sol bis in anno fit supra uerticem distans a
tropico estiuo ab utraq parte gradib' 68 $\frac{1}{2}$ $\frac{1}{4}$

Vndeama afiae

SCYTHIAE EXTRA IMAVM MONTEM PA...

Vnus gradus longitudinis m hor paledo
rhodienli contmet miliaria · 40 · et
stadia · 400 ·

· miliaria · 44

Vnus gradus longitudinis m circulo Cancri siue
paledo p Sienen contmet stadia 467 que fa
cut miliaria · 57 · 1/4 ·

· miliaria · 60 ·

⋅ INDIAE INTRA GANGEM · PS

Gangaris

Storna

Theorta

Rhappha

Ganzane

Canogiza

taffida

borein
ma

orizenza   Athenagurum

condata

Celidna

maniena

cum
aganagura

Talarga

orientus mons

tateres felam
puza

Coramali

Suanagura

passale

INDIA

GAN

alasarga

tosale meltpol

pavisera metropolis
Cirradia iqua optimu
alabastrum sit

hic galli gallinaq barbati
esse dicut · et corui ac psitani
albi
pentapolis

Beppyrus

Oeldana

Sygola

Indaprathe

Tilede quid h
em anubati & cra
fronte latiori
no

tugma

Triglyphon
regia

⋅ Sinus gangeticus ⋅

Ycacata

⋅ INDICVM ⋅

M

Vnus gradus log? et latitud sub
equinoctiali contmet stadia · 500
que fanut miliaria · 62 · 1/2 ·

⋅ Equinoctialis Circulus ⋅

Hic lapis
gignitur her
culeus · obq?
hor nauigia
que clauos ferreos
hut detmentur · Haru
incole antropophagi sunt ·

Mamole
antido

Barule
miis antropop
incole est phebm

hic incole ar
pophagi s

Samba
Regni
argentea

Sadus fl
sada Ing
dim
krabenna
coni

aurea
regio

Tecolsine

haragura
emporiu

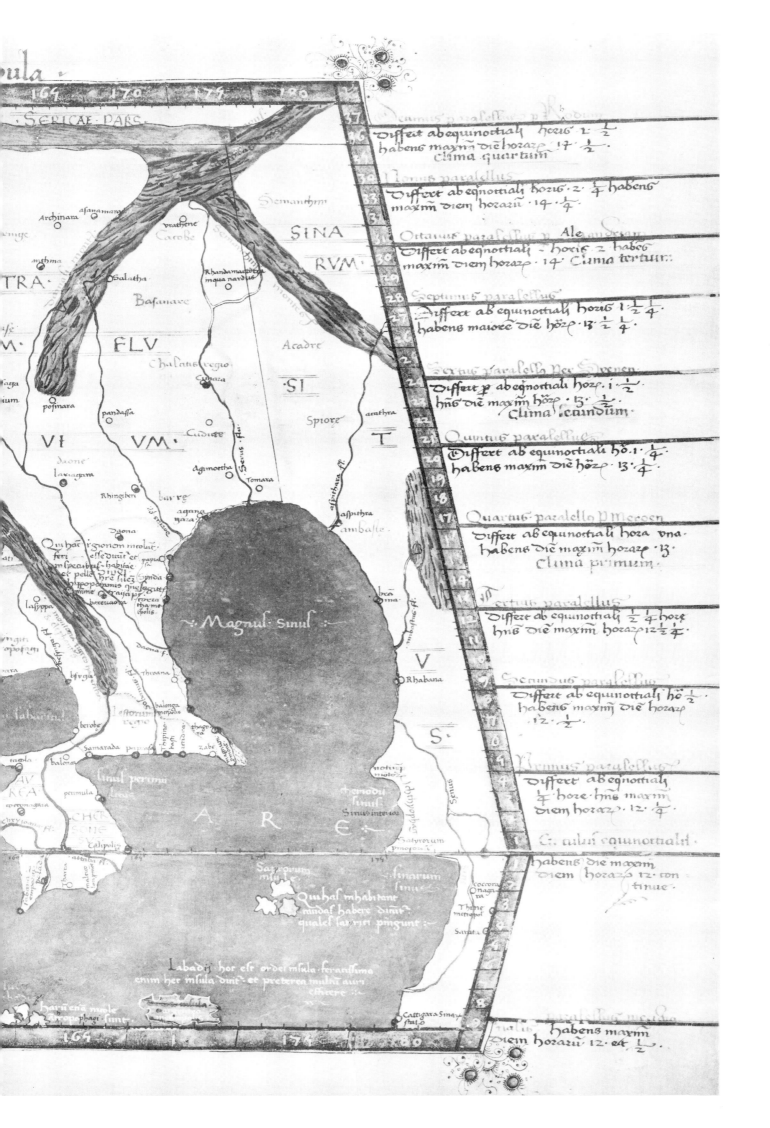

Duodecima. Asie tabula continet Taprobanem
insulam cum ceteris insulis adiacentibus. Parallelus ipsius medius proportionem habet ad
meridianum eandem. Circumscribitur autem
tabula ab omni parte indico pelago

Taprobane insule ciuitates insignes

Talacoris emporium maximam diem habet horarum e-
quinoctialium 11 ⅔ & distat ab alexandria uersus
ortum horis 4 ½ 1/14

A gadiba maximam diem habet horas 12 ½ & distat
ab alexandria uersus ortum horis 4 ½ 1/14

Hic q̄ sol bis in anno fit supra uerticem cum distat a
tropico estiuo ab utraq̄ parte gradibus 69 ½ ¼

Maugramum metropolis maximā diem habet horas
12 ½ 1/12 & distat ab alexandria uersus ortū hor. 4 ½ 3/12

Hic sol bis in ano fit supra uerticem cum distat a tropico estiuo ab utraq̄ parte gradibus 72 ½ ¼

~ finis tabularum Asie maiorū duoder. in ~

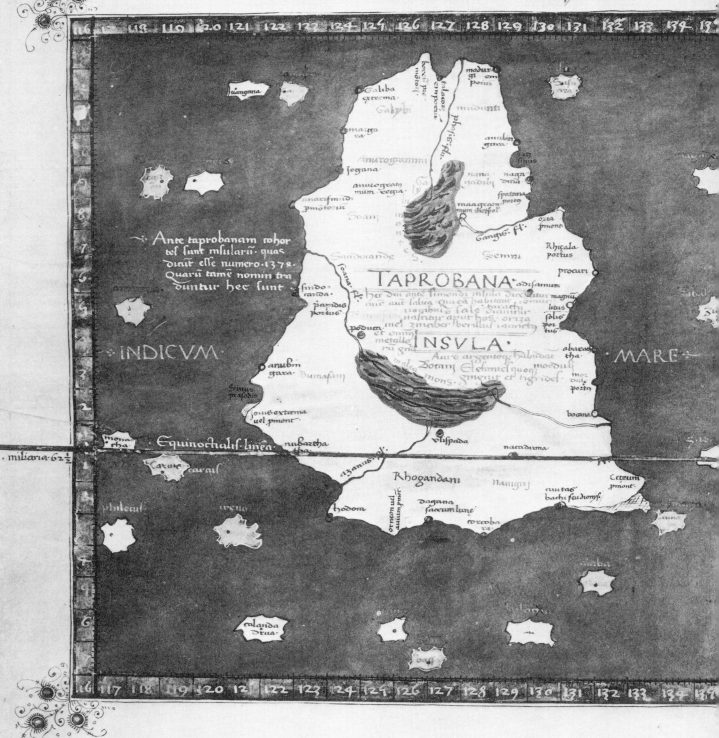

TAPROBANA·

INSVLA·

INDICVM

MARE·

Left margin	Europa	lat	long		Asia	lat	long	
	In sc̄o lo̅ — In europ trigĩta & quatuor				Que proprie Asia dr̄	48	68	
	Ibernia insula britanica	11	48½		Pheygia magna	60	38	
	Albion insula britanica	20	94		Lycia	60	37	
	Ispania betica	73	38 ⅓		Galatia	62	41	
	Ispania lusitanica	8	39½		Paphlagonia pisididia	62	43	
	Ispania tarraconensis	11	42		Pamphilia isauria	61	37	
	Gallia aquitanica	18	43½		Cappadocia	64	39	
	Gallia lugdonensis	23	48		Armenia minor	71	39	
	Gallia belgica	26	47		Cilicia	68	37	
	Gallia narbonensis	22	44½		Sarmatia asiatica	74	44	
	Germania magna	34	42		Colchis	73	44	
	Retia & vindelica	32½	26 ⅓		Iberia	74	44	
	Horicum	37	46		Albania	78	44	
	Pannonia supior	39½	47		Armenia maior	77	41	
	Illiris	41	44		Cyprus insula	66	34	
	Delmatia	44	42		Syria caua	71	36	
	In r̄co Italia	46⅔	41⅔		Syria phenicea	71	33	
	Cyrnos insula	30	40		Syria palestina iudea	67	31	
	Sardinia insula	31	38		Arabia petrea	68	31	
	Sicilia insula	39	36		Mesopotamia	73	37	
	Sarmatia in europa	47	40		Arabia deserta	79	32	
	Taurica chersonesus	62	48		Babylonia	78	32	
	Iaziges metanaste	43	48		Assyria	80	37	In Sexto
	Dacia	49	44		Susiana	84	34	
	Mysia supior	43	43		Media	83	39	
	Mysia inferior	46	44		Persis	90	32	
	Thracia	43	44		Parthia	96	37	
	Chersonesus	44	41		Carmania deserta	96	32	
	Macedonia	40	41		Carmania altera	99	24	
	Epirus	44	38		Arabia felix	86	22	
	Achaia	40	37		hyrcania	94	40	
	Euboea insula	42	37		Margiana	103	40	
	Peloponesus	41	36		Bactriana	116	41	
	Creta insula	44	34		Sogdiana	113	44	
	In Aphrica prouincie seu Satrapie duodecim				Saces	130	43	
	In Quarto Mauritania	8	33		Scythia intra imaü montem	120	46	
	Mauritania cesariensis	18	32		Scythia extra imaü montem	140	48	
	Numidia	30½	30		Serica	162	44	
	Aphrica	36	31		Aria	104	37	
	Cyrenaica que & pentapolis	40	28		Paropanisade	117	34	
	Marmarica	42	28		Drangiana	108	29	
	Libya	47	29		Arachosia	114	30	
	Egyptus inferior	61	30		Gedrosia	114	29	
	Egyptus thebais	62	24		India intra gangem	132	27	In septimo.
	Libya aphricae	18	22		India extra gangem	132	27	
	Ethyopia supra egyptum	62	12		Sinarum regio	172	16	
	Ethyopia omnibus his australior	40			Taprobane insula	124	3	
	australis	12						
	Asie magne prouincie quadragita & octo				Omnes prouincie nostre habitabiles sunt nonaginta & quatuor.			
	In qnto Pontus	43	48					
	Bythinia	48	38					

Left margin notes:

Parallelus ab equinoctiali ½ & ½ hore maxim hor̄ 12 ½ ½ .

[...]us Paralellus ab equinoctiali hō ½. die maxim hor̄ 12 ½ .

[...] Paralellus ab equinoctiali ¼ hore [...]iuim diez hor̄ 12 & ¼ .

[...]nottialis [...] die hor̄ 12 semper

[...]lus primus uersus austrũ ab equinoctiali hō ¼ hui maiorem horũ 12 ¼ .

Vot quot gentes subiacent zodiaco his sol fit supra verticem a borea
descendens ad austrum· Ascendens q̃ si-
militer· bis q̃ semel in anno· aliis bis·
Omnes autem qui sub zodiaco habitant
ab occasu ad ortum solis ethyopes sunt
pari modo coloribus nigri· & hi maxime
qui sub circulo equinoctiali sunt, abũ-
de nigri sunt· Qui aũt extra lineam
catheton zodiaci incolunt remissiores
colore sunt & in albedinem tendunt
secundum distantie rationem usq̃ ad Sar-
matas hyperboreos· Eadem est ratio ab
utraq̃ parte equinoctialis versus boreã
atq̃ austrum usq̃ ad utrosq̃ polos zo-
diaci·

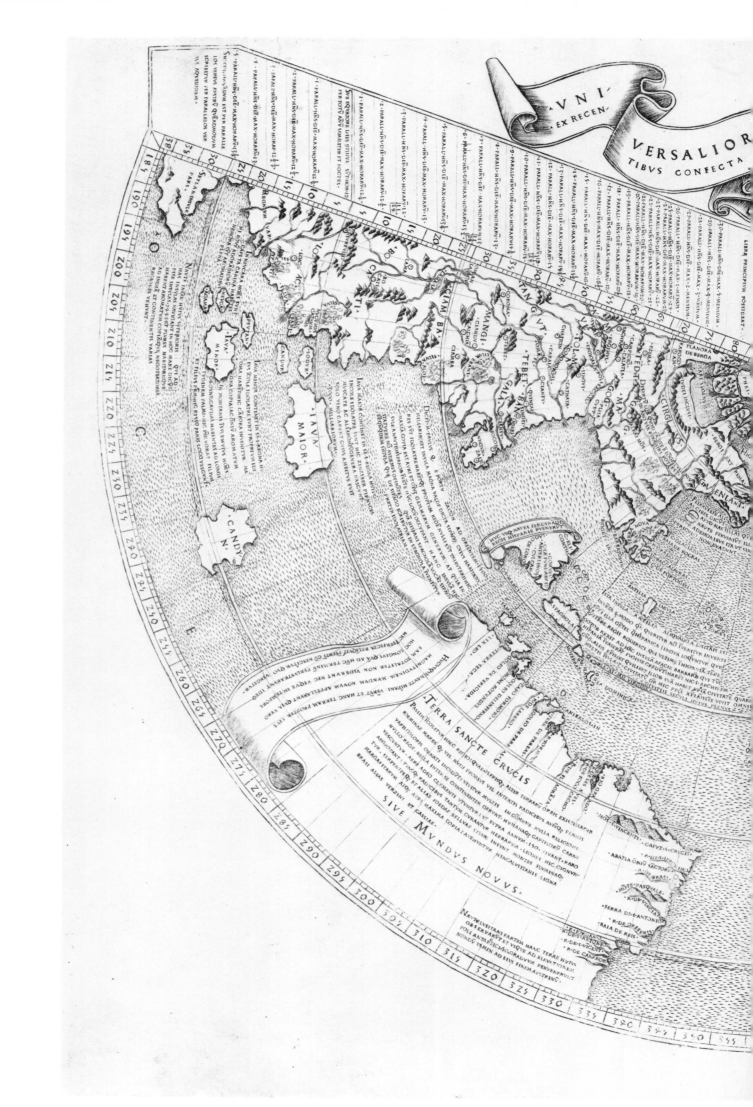

126.

TABVLA BVS.

OGNITI ORBIS OBSERVATIONI

QVARTVM CLIMA·
TERTIVM CLIMA·
CIRCVLVS CAPRICORNI·
SECVNDVM CLIM·
PRIMVM CLIMA·
CIRCVLVS ÆQVINOCTIALIS·
REGN
SECVNDVM CLIMA
PRIMVM CLIMA
CIRCVLVS CANCRI
TERTIVM CLIMA
QVARTVM CLIMA·
QVINTVM CLIMA·
SEXTVM CLIMA·
SEPTIMVM CLIMA·
CIRCVLVS ARTICVS·

PELAGVS·

AEQVINOCTIALIS·

INDICVM

CIRCVLVS·

CAPRICORNI·

AETHIOPIA · INTE-
RIOR·

AGISYMBA · REGIO·

LIBYA
INTERIOR·

DESERTA · LIBE·

AGISIMBVS · SINVS·

CIRCVLVS·

A

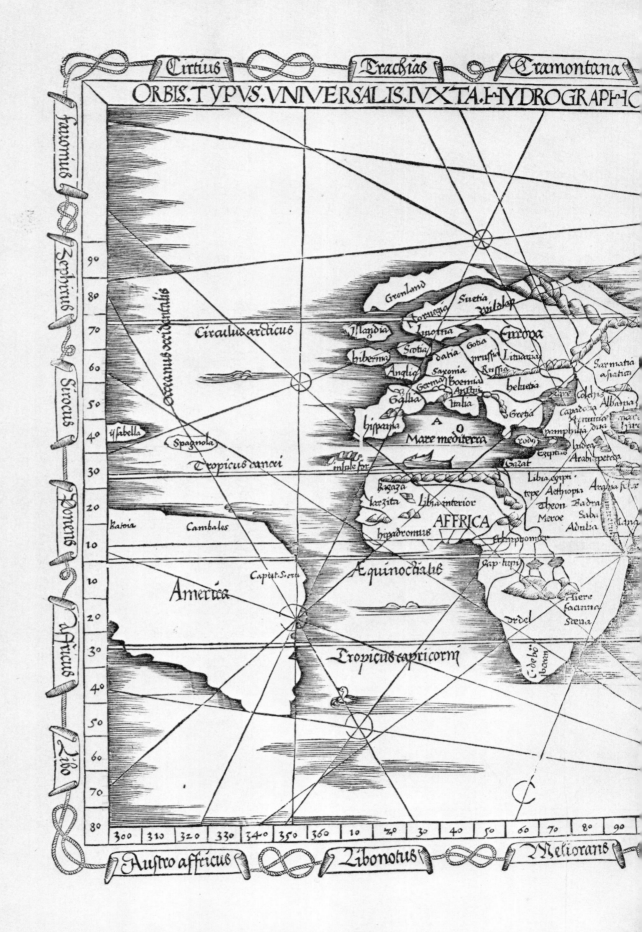

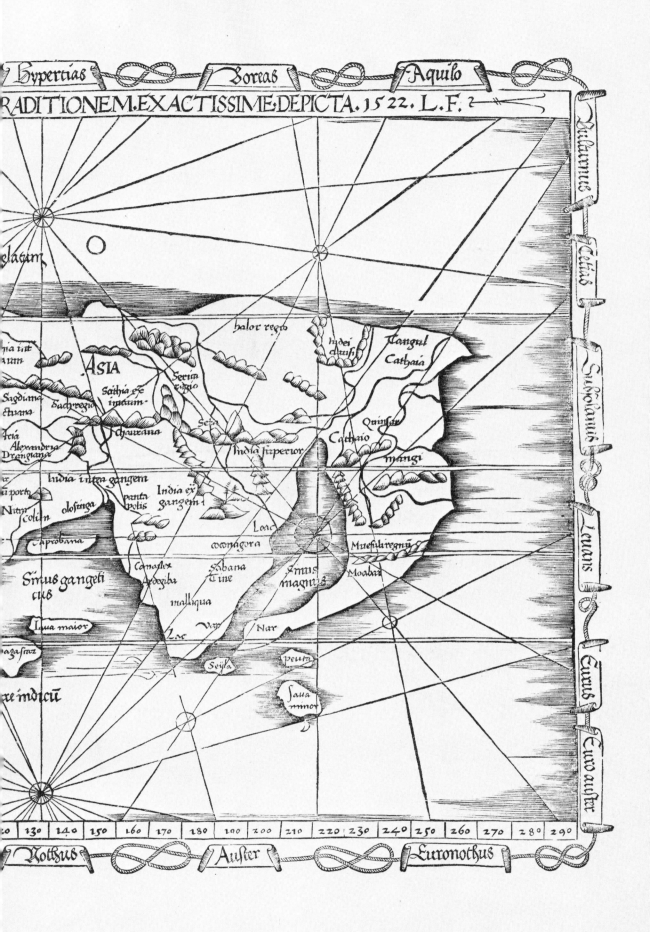

ASIA

halor regio

Indei clausi

Tangul
Cathaia

Seria regio

Scithia eꝝ imaum

Sachregio

Sagdiana

Chaurana

Seira

Quinsai

Aria
Alexandria
Drangiana

India superior

Cathaio

mangi

India intra gangem

India ex gangem

panta polis

Taprobana

Loac

coenagora

Muefuliregnū

Simus gangeticus

Conofler
Ardenba

Sabana
Tine

Simus magnus

Moabar

malliqua

Iaua maior

Lac   Vap   Nar

peuta

Seyla

Iaua minor

Sularnus

Tetias

Subſolanus

Leuans

Eurus

Eurauster

130 140 150 160 170 180 190 200 210 220 230 240 250 260 270 280 290